Piotr de Bończa Bukowski
Friedrich Schleiermacher's Pathways of Translation

Schleiermacher-Archiv

Herausgegeben von
Notger Slenczka
und
Andreas Arndt, Jörg Dierken,
Lutz Käppel, André Munzinger

Band 34

Piotr de Bończa Bukowski

Friedrich Schleiermacher's Pathways of Translation

―

Issues of Language and Communication

Translated from the Polish by Daniel J. Sax

DE GRUYTER

The author:
Piotr de Bończa Bukowski is a professor and the head of the Translation Working Group at the Institute of Germanic Studies, Jagiellonian University in Kraków. His main research interests concern the theory and history of translation, hermeneutics, and comparative literature. He is an Alexander von Humboldt Foundation fellowship holder.

The translation of this publication has been supported by a grant from the Priority Research Area "Heritage" under the Strategic Programme Excellence Initiative at Jagiellonian University.

ISBN 978-3-11-162088-6
e-ISBN (PDF) 978-3-11-074547-4
e-ISBN (EPUB) 978-3-11-074554-2
ISSN 1861-6038

Library of Congress Control Number: 2022944805

Bibliographic information published by the Deutsche Nationalbibliothek
The Deutsche Nationalbibliothek lists this publication in the Deutsche Nationalbibliografie; detailed bibliographic data are available on the internet at http://dnb.dnb.de.

© 2024 Walter de Gruyter GmbH, Berlin/Boston
This volume is text- and page-identical with the hardback published in 2023.
This title is an English translation of the Polish title *Friedricha Schleiermachera drogi przekładu* (Wydawnictwo Uniwersytetu Jagiellońskiego, Krakow 2020)

www.degruyter.com

Contents

Note from the translator on texts and citations —— 1

I Introduction —— 4
1   Seeking pathways of translation —— 4
2   Life and translation —— 7
3   Signposts to the pathways —— 13

II Lectures on Style: Rhetoric, Hermeneutics, and Issues of Translation —— 24
1   The significance of the young Schleiermacher's lectures *On Style* —— 24
2   Genesis, general shape, and distinctive qualities —— 25
3   Scientific contextualizations of the lectures *On Style*: hermeneutics, dialectics, dogmatics, and rhetoric —— 30
4   Style and communication: Analysis of the lectures from Schlobitten —— 35
5   Obstacles to communication: vagueness, ambiguity, and incomprehensibility —— 42
6   *Elocutio* and *translatio* – an attempt to summarize and contextualize —— 61
7   The further pathways of Schleiermacher's reflection: Rhetoric and style in the hermeneutic perspective —— 65

III Schleiermacher's and Schlegel's Contributions to the Theory of Translation —— 75
1   Assumptions and preliminary remarks —— 75
2   Schlegel's influence —— 76
3   Rediscovering translation: Schlegel, *Athenaeum*, and the framework of ideas —— 79
4   The "German Plato" project —— 89

IV The Dead Letter and Living Spirit of Mediation —— 100
1   Introduction: Schleiermacher's "ingenious" *Jugendwerk* —— 100
2   *Apology*: mediation and transfer —— 105
3   On the essence of religion: spirit and letter —— 119
4   The transmission of insight and the problem of understanding —— 130
5   The social element —— 134
6   On religions and the dynamics of the Christian faith —— 137
7   Concluding thoughts: how to express the inexpressible? —— 143

V Modelling Translation Criticism: Schlegel and Schleiermacher —— 153
1. Preliminary historical remarks on translation criticism —— 153
2. The poet of prose in translation: Friedrich Schlegel on Tieck's Cervantes —— 158
3. Schiller's "astonishing" Macbeth —— 165
4. Schleiermacher's analysis —— 172
5. Academic criticism of translation and hermeneutics —— 177

VI Philology and the Question of "the Original": Schleiermacher Translates Plato —— 180
1. The problem of the original – an introduction —— 180
2. Enlightenment, Romanticism, and the rediscovery of the original —— 186
3. Schleiermacher's Dialogues of Plato —— 190
4. Schleiermacher's *Phaedrus* – selected aspects of the translator's strategy —— 200

VII Conclusion: Translation and Dialectics —— 213
1. Rhetoric, hermeneutics, dialectics, and translation —— 213
2. Schleiermacher's dialectics in general —— 214
3. Lecture on translation at the Prussian Academy of Sciences —— 217
4. Translation in the domain of difference —— 221
5. Communication, understanding, and translation —— 226
6. Dialectics and the problem of translation —— 236

VIII Summary —— 239

Bibliography —— 242
1. Primary Sources —— 242
2. Secondary Sources —— 248

Index —— 268

Note from the translator on texts and citations

Friedrich Daniel Ernst Schleiermacher (1768–1834), one of the most prominent figures of German Romanticism, was a phenomenally productive and innovative intellectual who left behind a broad range of writings, stretching across quite a number of fields. However, citing these writings in English is not always straightforward. Many of them exist in more than one "original" version in German (sometimes in the form of unfinished or reconstructed drafts), and there may be multiple English translations for a given work, often based on different versions of the original. Moreover, some existing English translations are quite dated, others quite recent.

Throughout this book, English translations of all source texts in German (including the various works of Schleiermacher, but also cited works of other authors) and in other languages (French, Greek, Italian, Latin, Polish) have been drawn whenever possible and appropriate from existing English versions, naming the source and translator in a footnote or sometimes with an abbreviation inserted in the running text.

Schleiermacher's original texts in German are predominantly cited herein from the critical edition of his complete works (*Kritische Gesamtausgabe*), using the commonly accepted abbreviation "KGA," followed by the part, volume and page number (e.g.: KGA I/11, 67), inserted in the running text. An updated list of published volumes of the *Kritische Gesamtausgabe* (not only those cited herein) is given in the bibliography at the end of the book.

Schleiermacher's lecture on translation methods, *Ueber die verschiedenen Methoden des Uebersetzens* – which serves as a certain thread linking together the various chapters of this book – exists in English in several published versions. The one cited in this book is "On the Different Methods of Translating," trans. Douglas Robinson, in *Western Translation Theory: From Herodotus to Nietzsche*, ed. Douglas Robinson (Manchester: St. Jerome, 1997), 225–238. For this, the abbreviation "DR" (after the translator's initials) is adopted in running text, followed by the page number. It is worth noting, however, that at least three other versions exist: one by Susan Bernofsky,[1] another by André Lefevere,[2] and a (partial) translation by Waltraud Bartscht.[3] As is noted in the Introduction, this multiplicity of English versions is evidence of

---

[1] Friedrich Schleiermacher, "On the Different Methods of Translating," trans. Susan Bernofsky, in *The Translation Studies Reader*, ed. Laurence Venuti, 3rd edition (London: Routledge, 2012), 43–63.
[2] Friedrich Schleiermacher, "On the Different Methods of Translation," trans. André Lefevere, in *Translating Literature: The German Tradition from Luther to Rosenzweig* (Assen: Van Gorcum, 1977), 67–89, also published in *German Romantic Criticism*, ed. A. Leslie Wilson (New York: Continuum, 1982), 1–30.
[3] Friedrich Schleiermacher, "From *On the Different Methods of Translating*," trans. Waltraud Bartscht, in *Theories of Translation: An Anthology of Essays from Dryden to Derrida*, eds. Rainer Schulte, John Biguenet (Chicago: Chicago Univ. Press, 1992), 36–56.

the broad popularity this lecture has enjoyed in recent decades, with the burgeoning field of translation studies.

Also heavily cited herein are Schleiermacher's speeches on religion and his work on hermeneutics. Passages from *Ueber die Religion – Reden an die Gebildeten unter ihren Verächtern* are cited from the Cambridge edition *On Religion: Speeches to its Cultured Despisers*, trans. Richard Crouter (Cambridge: Cambridge Univ. Press, 1988), abbreviated in running text as "RC," which contains English translations of all four of the speeches (based on the first German edition of 1799). Another, quite dated English translation of all four speeches was produced by John Oman (based on the third German edition of 1821),[4] and an alternate translation of one of the speeches on religion (the second speech) was more recently published by Julia A. Lamm (based on the second German edition of 1806).[5]

As for *Hermeneutik*, the passages cited herein are cited predominantly from another Cambridge edition, namely *Hermeneutics and Criticism and Other Writings*, ed. Karl Ameriks and Desmond M. Clarke, trans. Andrew Bowie (Cambridge: Cambridge Univ. Press, 1998). This volume, for which the abbreviation "AB" is adopted in running text, includes contains English translations of two of the versions of Schleiermacher's hermeneutics (namely *Hermeneutics 1819*, based on the German edition edited by Manfred Frank,[6] and *General Hermeneutics 1809/1810*, based on a transcript recovered by Wolfgang Virmond[7]). Other English translations of versions of Schleiermacher's hermeneutics have been published by James Duke and Jack Forstman[8] (based on the German edition edited by Heinz Kimmerle),[9] by Timothy R. Clancy[10] (based on Kimmerle's edition and Virmond's reconstructions), and also a fragmentary translation by Jan Wojcik and Roland Haas.[11]

Reference has also been made to several other English editions of Schleiermacher's works, including the quite dated *Introductions to the Dialogues of Plato*, trans. William Dobson (Cambridge and London, 1836; reprint, New York: Arno Press,

---

[4] Friedrich Schleiermacher, *On Religion: Speeches to its Cultured Despisers*, trans. John Oman (London: Paul, Trench, Trubner & Co., 1893).
[5] Friedrich Schleiermacher, "The Second Speech," in idem. *Christmas Dialogue, The Second Speech, and Other Selections*, trans. Julia A. Lamm (Mahwah, NJ: Paulist Press, 2014), 101–151.
[6] Friedrich Schleiermacher, *Hermeneutik und Kritik*, ed. Manfred Frank (Frankfurt am Main: Suhrkamp, 1977).
[7] As described in: Wolfgang Virmond "Neue Textgrundlagen zu Schleiermachers früher Hermeneutik," in *Internationaler Schleiermacher Kongreß, Berlin, 1984*, ed. Kurt-Viktor Selge, vol. 1 (Berlin: De Gruyter, 1985), 576–590.
[8] Friedrich Schleiermacher, *Hermeneutics: The Handwritten Manuscripts*, trans. James Duke and Jack Forstman (Oxford: Oxford Univ. Press, 1978; Atlanta: Scholars Press, 1986)
[9] Friedrich Schleiermacher: *Hermeneutik*, ed. Heinz Kimmerle, 2nd ed. (Heidelberg: Heidelberger Akademie der Wissenschaften, 1974).
[10] Friedrich Schleiermacher, *Schleiermacher's Early Lectures on Hermeneutics: The 1805 "First Draft" and the 1809 "General Hermeneutics,"* trans. Timothy R. Clancy (Lewiston: Edwin Mellen, 2004).
[11] Friedrich Schleiermacher, "Outline of the 1819 Lectures," trans. Jan Wojcik and Roland Haas. *New Literary History* 10, no. 1, Literary Hermeneutics (Autumn, 1978): 1–16.

1973) and *Christmas Eve: A Dialogue on the Celebration of Christmas*, trans. W. Hastie (Edinburgh: T. & T. Clark, 1890), as well as the more recent *Dialectic, or the Art of Doing Philosophy, A Study Edition of the 1811 Notes*, trans. Terrence N. Tice (Atlanta: Scholars Press, 1996).[12]

Within each chapter of this book, the original title of each work in German is used at first mention, in conjunction with the chosen English title, which is then retained for subsequent mentions.

All passages cited from Schleiermacher's works in English, if not marked as coming from one of these previously published translations, have been newly translated directly from the KGA. These, as well as all other English translations from sources in German (and other languages) included herein, if not attributed to any other translator, represent the collaborative work of Daniel J. Sax and Piotr de Bończa Bukowski. Mostly we offer our own translations directly from sources when no English version of the given passage has yet been published, but occasionally we have found existing translations lacking or inappropriate for our purposes, and so offer our own rendition, and a few times we have justified in a footnote a correction we have made to an existing English translation.

As this introductory note serves to show, bringing this book to life in English has required considerable cooperative translational effort (indeed, *hermeneutical* effort) on the part of both the translator and author.

---

[12] Which is based on the first version of Schleiermacher's dialectics: *Dialektik (1811)*, ed. Andreas Arndt (Hamburg: Felix Meiner, 1986).

I Introduction

> Schleiermacher was a thinker in the beautiful Greek sense,
> a thinker who spoke only of what he knew
>
> Søren Kierkegaard[1]

1 Seeking pathways of translation

On 24 June 1813, at the Royal Academy of Sciences in Berlin, one of the most eminent theologians in the history of Protestantism and one of the greatest minds underpinning the intellectual prowess of the nineteenth-century Prussian state – Friedrich Daniel Ernst Schleiermacher (1768–1834) – delivered a lecture on the subject of translation and the methods of performing it. This lecture later appeared in print and would grow increasingly popular over time, to eventually, in the latter half of the twentieth century, became a canonical text in the field of translation studies – which it indeed remains today. However, as influential as the text of the lecture *Ueber die verschiedenen Methoden des Uebersetzens* (*On the Different Methods of Translating*)[2] has been, I strive to make clear in this book that it reflects just a small part of the myriad ways the notion of translation, or *transfer*, figures in the extensive work of this extraordinary intellectual (including his work on rhetorical stylistics, hermeneutics, religion, dialectics – to name just some of the relevant fields). As such, this single text, studied by itself, represents a mere fraction of Schleiermacher's multifaceted contributions to modern-day insight into the nature of translation. Moreover, I seek to show how the famous lecture *On the Different Methods of Translating* becomes fully understandable only in the light of other important texts by its author.

Schleiermacher opens the published version of the lecture with the claim: "Everywhere we look we meet up with the fact that utterances are rendered, in one form or another, from one language to another" (DR 225; KGA I/11, 67).[3] He then goes on to list the most important of forms of this: communication between geographically distant communities using different languages, the assimilation into one language of concepts from another, translation within the confines of a single lan-

---

[1] Søren Kierkegaard, *The Concept of Anxiety*, trans. Reidar Thomte (Princeton: Princeton Univ. Press, 1980), 20.
[2] Older German works, such as this one, are cited herein in their original orthography; in modern German orthography the title of the lecture, for instance, is *Über die verschiedenen Methoden des Übersetzens*.
[3] Friedrich D. E. Schleiermacher, "On the Different Methods of Translating," trans. Douglas Robinson, in *Western Translation Theory: From Herodotus to Nietzsche*, ed. Douglas Robinson (Manchester: St. Jerome, 1997), 225 (hereafter cited in text as "*DR*"); *Schleiermacher Kritische Gesamtausgabe* (hereafter cited in text as "*KGA*").

guage community, the use of different substandard and differentiated styles of linguistic expression, and lastly, also the translation of our very own words, which as time passes become alien and incomprehensible to us, and thus require a new act of transmuting thoughts into words. We are continually confronted with incomprehensibility and incommensurability, making mediation necessary – the essence of this mediation lies in *motion*, in the fundamental sense a "hermeneutic motion" (G. Steiner),[4] directed at explanation through the transformation of meanings.

By the time he gave this lecture in 1813, Friedrich Schleiermacher was already a member of the Royal Academy of Sciences in Berlin and had for years been a leading figure in European Romanticism. As such, he was certainly a scholar who knew enough about literature, philology, philosophy, theology, and also the art of translation to be able to claim, without a shadow of a doubt, that translation is an activity/ process that manifests itself "everywhere" (*überall*, KGA I/11, 67). This is because communication and transfer – processes that have the character of translation – are ubiquitous phenomena in the human world. They are related to Schleiermacher's key notion of mediation (*Vermittlung*), which also characterizes his "dialectical style of thinking" (H. Fischer),[5] prompting him to seek similarities between phenomena and relate them to one another within a systematic scientific framework. The "inclusiveness" of Schleiermacher's dialectics[6] is directly connected with a conviction that knowledge needs to seek confirmation in dialogue, in the mutual communication of standpoints, verifying the scope of their mutual translatability and working to reconcile them through conversation.[7]

The basic tool of human communication is language. Reflecting on the nature of language itself was a constant element of Schleiermacher's work, not only in the domain of science, but also in religion. Language was for him something as fascinating as it was mysterious – a key to understanding humanity, often resisting scientific understanding, not easy to grasp speculatively. The process of the schematization of our experience that is realized in language is thoroughly paradoxical: it combines universalism and relativity.[8]

In his notes for a set of lectures on pedagogy given in the winter semester 1813/ 1814, Schleiermacher remarks:

> With language man begins, for the first development of reason is revealed through it; and with language man ends, for the philosopher has completely fulfilled his vocation when he has fixed

---

[4] George Steiner, "The Hermeneutic Motion," in George Steiner, *After Babel: Aspects of Language and Translation* (Oxford: Oxford Univ. Press, 1975), 296–303.
[5] Hermann Fischer, *Friedrich Daniel Ernst Schleiermacher* (Munich: C.H. Beck, 2001), 13.
[6] Ibid.
[7] Cf. Grażyna Woroniecka, *Interakcja symboliczna a hermeneutyczna kategoria przed-rozumienia* [Symbolic Interaction and the Hermeneutic Category of Pre-Understanding] (Warsaw: Oficyna Naukowa, 2003), 54.
[8] Cf. Lawrence K. Schmidt, *Understanding Hermeneutics* (Stocksfield: Acumen Publishing, 2006), 21–24.

> his discoveries in language. In language, everyone sees only what he is capable of; everyone has enough and no one too much; there is therefore total freedom (KGA II/12, 296).

This is the freedom to be oneself, to express oneself, the basic principle of which is that of the *difference* (*Differenz*) revealed in and through language. Schleiermacher argues that it is thanks to such difference that we learn about ourselves and others, including about what is individual, particular (*eigentümlich*) in our common world. Without difference there can be no real communication or mediation (*Vermittlung*). The awareness of such difference, with the simultaneous conviction that we, human beings, are united by a common "principle of thought,"[9] is the driving force behind translational transfer, which is constitutive of our civilization. Such transfer reaches into the very depths of our minds, where thinking meets speaking and where the translation between what is internal and what is external takes place, so that impressions take on the form of concepts and become communicable.[10]

While exploring the world of communicative interactions and information transfers, Schleiermacher also investigated pathways to translation that lead via the terrain of various scholarly disciplines. In this book, I attempt to describe some of these pathways, analyzing the various texts and areas of scholarly reflection from which they emerged, linking together strands of thought and juxtaposing concepts. Moreover, I try to show how truly broad the space of Schleiermacher's intellectual work is, and to map out where the thoughts and motifs that have been adopted and popularized by contemporary translation studies are actually situated within that larger space. I seek to show how much we lose by decontextualizing and simplifying Schleiermacher's ideas on translation. I do not wish to claim that the image of Friedrich Schleiermacher as a translation theorist that has functioned for decades is a distorted one; rather, I will merely try to convince readers that this brilliant thinker and Romantic polymath (theologian, philologist, philosopher, pedagogue, psychologist, historian)[11] did not dogmatically compartmentalize problems and concepts but instead tried to link them together, to reveal their interconnectedness.[12] And, if Schleiermacher is held up today as a patron of the contemporary field of translation studies, it is above all because of his merits as a precursor of *interdisciplinary* research (combining perspectives focused on translation) or indeed even of *transdisciplinary* research (exploring the heuristic potential of the concept of translation as consisting in the transmission and transformation of information).

---

9 As Schleiermacher said in a lecture on psychology in the summer semester of 1830 (KGA II/13, 159).
10 Cf. lectures on psychology in the summer term of 1821 (KGA II/13, 965).
11 In the introduction of one interdisciplinary collective volume devoted to Schleiermacher, the editor calls him a "universal thinker" – Dietz Lange, ed. *Friedrich Schleiermacher 1768–1834: Theologe – Philosoph – Pädagoge* (Göttingen: Vandenhoeck & Ruprecht, 1985), 5.
12 On this method, cf. Wolfgang H. Pleger, *Schleiermachers Philosophie* (Berlin: Walter de Gruyter, 1988), 6.

Given the overwhelming breadth of Friedrich Schleiermacher's scholarly investigations and endeavors, the analysis proposed here is of necessity somewhat restricted in terms of scope. I have narrowed it down to just several of the fields in which Schleiermacher worked; some that I believe to be of particular importance, others that are less well known. My analysis will therefore embrace Schleiermacher's philology, criticism, hermeneutics, and dialectics, as well as his rhetoric and philosophy of religion. Other domains of his thought (above all, his Protestant theology, exegetics, socialization theory, and psychology) are left to be further incorporated in the future. It is indeed my intention to make the picture of Schleiermacher's pathways to translation presented herein more comprehensive and complete in the relatively near future by considering more of these other fields in the same vein as those that are considered in this book (perhaps, in so doing, altering some particular elements presented herein).

I realize that the endeavor of "co-thinking" together with Schleiermacher – a thinker on par with Schelling or even Hegel, a scholar of immense horizons and depth of reflection – is a challenge difficult to meet. A hermeneutical ambition to present a unifying understanding of Schleiermacher's writings in terms of the issues of transmission, transfer, and translation could ultimately fail as a research enterprise. Instead of such a risky grand synthesis, therefore, I have opted to pursue a more narrowly conceived analysis. The most important operations making up my framework are these: (1) close reading of the relevant Schleiermacher texts, (2) interpretation that seeks to contextualize those texts (focused on relations of metonymy and metaphor within the space of ideas) and (3) confrontational analysis within a single paradigm (in this case, Romantic translation theory and practice). If, by applying these methods, I succeed in convincingly presenting and problematizing the translation-studies (in the broad sense of the term) aspect of Schleiermacher's vast work, I will be fully satisfied.

2 Life and translation

It will be no exaggeration to say that translation, in its theoretical and practical dimensions, is something that accompanied Schleiermacher throughout his entire life.[13] He was constantly engaged in translation-related matters: as a translator, literary critic, philologist, philosopher, and theologian. In reading Schleiermacher's work, one can notice a certain continuum of development, as he built thoughts, views and creative practices on the basis of successively acquired knowledge (read-

---

13 An important context here is Schleiermacher's postulate of linking together theory and practice in science, above all in philosophy (cf. Pleger, *Schleiermachers Philosophie*, 3–11), but not exclusively so.

ings, projects, and academic collaborations) and accumulated experience (at actually producing his own translations).

Interestingly, we do know about a certain experience in Schleiermacher's life that might be regarded as formative in this respect. While emphasizing the scholar's excellent linguistic preparation, including his solid command of the most important ancient and modern languages,[14] Keith W. Clements draws attention to an interesting autobiographical passage about when Schleiermacher was learning Latin as a boy: "Here I saw nothing but darkness," Schleiermacher recalls, "for although I learnt to translate the words mechanically into my mother tongue, I could not penetrate into the sense, and my mother, who directed by German readings with much judgement, had taught me not to read without understanding."[15] Clements aptly comments: "Perhaps it was exactly those early problems with his Latin which prompted his lifelong interest in the nature of translation and interpretation," adding also that this passage explains the method of unhurried reading, oriented towards the synthesis of meaning ("slow reading"),[16] so important in the context of Schleiermacher's hermeneutics (and also his philology).

With the consent of his father (a reformed military chaplain[17]) Schleiermacher left the seminary at Barby in 1787 to study theology at the University of Halle, which he continued for four consecutive semesters.[18] However, he took a greater interest in philosophy and philology than in theology, under the influence of his professor Johann August Eberhard, a proponent of Christian Wolff's philosophy, an opponent of

---

14 Schleiermacher owed his competence in this field to the schooling of the Moravian Brethren (Herrnhut), with whom his family was strongly connected. It is known that he attended, among other schools, the "Pedagogium" in the town of Niska, where he had the opportunity to learn Latin, Greek, Hebrew, French, and English (*Einleitung der Bandherausgeber*, KGA IV/1, XVI). For a detailed discussion of Schleiermacher's Pietist education, cf. Andreas Arndt, *Die Reformation der Revolution – Friedrich Schleiermacher in seiner Zeit* (Berlin: Matthes & Seitz, 2019), 11–46.
15 Keith W. Clements, "Introduction," in *Friedrich Schleiermacher: Pioneer of Modern Theology*, ed. Keith W. Clements (London: Collins, 1987), 48–49. Clements' source is a short autobiography written by Schleiermacher for official purposes, included in the compilation *Aus Schleiermachers Leben – In Briefen*, vol. 1, 2nd ed. (Berlin: Georg Reimer, 1860), 4–5.
16 Clements, "Introduction," 49.
17 Friedrich was born into a family with strong pastoral traditions. His father Gottlieb Adolph Schleyermacher (known under this more archaic spelling of the surname) was a Reformed pastor, as the grandfather Daniel had also been. After the Seven Years' War, Gottlieb settled in Breslau (today Wrocław in Poland), where he married Elisabeth Maria Katharina Stubenrauch, daughter of Timotheus Christian, preacher at the Berlin cathedral. Her younger brother was Samuel Ernst Stubenrauch, later a preacher and professor of church history, with whom Friedrich felt particularly attached. Cf. Karol Karski, *Friedrich Daniel Ernst Schleiermacher – życie i dzieło* [Friedrich Daniel Ernst Schleiermacher: Life and Work], in *Europa – Slavia – Germania: Hermeneutyka pogranicza* [Europa – Slavia – Germania: Hermeneutics of the Borderland], ed. Maciej J. Dudziak (Gorzów Wielkopolski: Wydawnictwo Państwowej Wyższej Szkoły Zawodowej, 2010), 98, and Kurt Nowak, *Schleiermacher – Leben, Werk und Wirkung* (Göttingen: Vandenhoeck & Ruprecht, 2001), 19–24.
18 Fischer, *Friedrich Daniel Ernst Schleiermacher*, 22.

Kant, and an expert on Plato and Aristotle. Under Eberhard's guidance, Schleiermacher began working on commentaries to the eighth and ninth books of the *Nicomachean Ethics* and on their translation. He may have harbored a plan to publish an annotated German translation of the whole of this fundamental work.[19] In any case, it was certainly no coincidence that Schleiermacher first took an interest in the chapters on friendship, given that he was preoccupied with the question as to where the feelings that shape social relations and friendship come from (KGA I/1, 5).[20] In any event, in the summer of 1789 Schleiermacher completed the translation (KGA I/1, 45–80)[21] and began to solicit it for publication. Unfortunately, competing translations appeared rather quickly – in 1791, a critical edition of the entire *Ethics* translated and edited by Daniel Jenisch was published, conclusively thwarting the young theologian and translator's own publication plans.[22]

Kurt Nowak is undoubtedly right when he argues that this work on fragments of the *Nicomachean Ethics* prepared Schleiermacher for the great project of translating Plato's works into German, initiated not long thereafter.[23] It gave him valuable experience as a philologist, hermeneuticist, and translator, without which he probably would not have undertaken the risky enterprise that would be urged upon him by the typically over-ambitious Friedrich Schlegel. It should be remembered, however, that Schleiermacher studied Aristotle consistently from 1788 to 1807, including the *Ethics*, but also the treatises on *Metaphysics*, *Politics*, *On the Soul*, and *Physics*. His notes, commentaries, extracts, and translation of a short fragment from the *Metaphysics* bear testimony to this.

The text of Schleiermacher's translation of the two chapters of the *Nicomachean Ethics* is itself very interesting from the translation-studies perspective. In it, Schleiermacher seems to lean towards a domesticating strategy, clearly manifested on the stylistic level through his transformation of Aristotle's dry style, focused on concreteness, into the lengthy discourse of eighteenth-century German academic philosophy, imbued with the extended constructions of the period. This strategy was aptly noted by Dilthey, who nevertheless wrongly considered the translation a paraphrase – as it is in fact faithful in the functional sense.[24]

After passing his final theology exam in 1794, Schleiermacher embarked upon a career as a Protestant clergyman. He took on the duties of an assistant pastor to Johann Lorenz Schumann in Landsberg an der Warthe (today Gorzów Wielkopolski in Poland).[25] There, at the instigation of Friedrich Samuel Gottfried Sack (his scientific

---

19 Nowak, *Schleiermacher – Leben, Werk und Wirkung*, 36.
20 Cf. Arndt, *Die Reformation der Revolution*, 52–53.
21 Cf. the publishers' detailed commentary: KGA I/1, XXXVI–XL.
22 Nowak, *Schleiermacher – Leben, Werk und Wirkung*, 37.
23 Ibid.
24 Wilhelm Dilthey, *Leben Schleiermachers*, vol. 1: *Denkmale der inneren Entwicklung Schleiermachers, erläutert durch kritische Untersuchungen* (Berlin: Georg Reimer, 1870), 4.
25 Fischer, *Friedrich Daniel Ernst Schleiermacher*, 24.

mentor, supervisor, and later adversary), he began to translate the sermons of Hugh Blair (1718–1800), a Presbyterian preacher, expert in Shakespeare and classical rhetoric, and an outstanding representative of the Scottish Enlightenment.[26] In fact, Sack decided to use Schleiermacher's translations in the multi-volume German edition of Blair's *Sermons* that he was publishing and translating. As a result, they were partly included in volume four (1795) and made up the entirety of volume five (1802) of this edition.[27] This means, as Kurt Nowak aptly notes in the context of the fourth volume of the *Sermons*, that: "The first texts that the great theologian submitted for publication were thus translations from English."[28]

In the translator's preface to volume 5 (*Vorbericht des Uebersetzers*), Schleiermacher offers readers of his translation of Blair some very interesting insights that seem so far not to have caught the attention of translation-studies scholars. Among other things, he stresses the great importance of uniformity of style when translating a work which reflects an author's life-path. He also writes that he does not feel obliged to "replace" the author and to explain in separate notes the "system" that underlies his arguments. Finally, he points out the distance that separates him from the latter, emphasizing at the same time his respect for the Scottish author's "true and profound piety" (KGA IV/1, 407). This brief preface eloquently testifies to the fact that Schleiermacher was aware of how multifaceted an activity translation is: how many functions it performs and how many roles it projects for the translator.

Perhaps while still in Landsberg, he decided to translate the sermons of Joseph Fawcett (1758–1804), a London-based Presbyterian minister and respected speaker. Schleiermacher held him in even higher esteem than Blair, finding much homiletical inspiration in Fawcett.[29] Schleiermacher's two translated volumes of the English preacher's *Predigten* appeared in print in 1798, with an introduction by F.S.G. Sack.

After the death of Pastor Schumann, Schleiermacher left Landsberg and accepted the position of preacher at the Charité hospital in Berlin. The year 1796 thus ushered in a new Berlin phase in his life, which soon yielded new interests and friendships. Above all, this pupil of the Moravian Brethren became acquainted with the local circle of early Romantics (*Frühromantiker*), centered around Friedrich Schlegel, and with Henrietta Herz, the wife of Marcus Herz, a physician, writer, and favorite student of Kant's.[30] Henrietta and Friedrich's friendship bore fruit in a lively and sincere correspondence, which today serves as an invaluable source of knowledge about

---

[26] Cf. ibid., 25, and KGA IV/1, XVIII.
[27] On the details of this: KGA IV/1, XXXII–XL. ibid., 25, and KGA IV/1, XVIII.
[28] Nowak, *Schleiermacher – Leben, Werk und Wirkung*, 73.
[29] Cf. Christoph Meier-Dörken, *Die Theologie der frühen Predigten Schleiermachers* (Berlin: Walter de Gruyter, 1988), 46 ff. (on Blair, cf. 34–45). On Schleiermacher's editorial decisions, cf. KGA IV/2 XVI-XIX.
[30] Friedrich Wilhelm Kantzenbach, *Friedrich Daniel Ernst Schleiermacher in Selbstzeugnissen und Dokumenten* (Reinbek bei Hamburg: Rowohlt, 1967), 41.

Schleiermacher's ongoing activities, feelings, and views, as well as on their mutual projects.³¹

One of these was a translation of the book *Travels in the Interior Districts of Africa* (1799 edition) by Mungo Park (1771–1806), a Scottish physician, naturalist, and traveler who was famous at the time. The translation was planned for the year of the original's premiere and was originally to be performed by Ludwig Tieck (KGA V/3, 100, 108). In the end, however, he did not take the job and Schleiermacher decided to translate the book in collaboration with Henrietta Herz (who had herself already translated the first part of the book).³² In May 1799, having been asked by the publisher to review Henrietta's partial translation, Friedrich responded thus in a letter: "In the meantime I have read the translation, and if it has any defect, then it is, it seems, too much respect for the original, which is most probably due to unfamiliarity with how such things are done" (KGA V/3, 114). This itself represents a significant comment on the art of translation. Note that it is formulated in the spirit of functionalism and tallies well with Schleiermacher's own translation of Aristotle's *Ethics*, but bears little resemblance to the kind of commitment to foreignizing translation that is quite commonly attributed to him. This is one of many popular opinions about Schleiermacher that urgently need clarification – as I will seek to demonstrate in this book. In any event, the collaborative translation was published in the Berlin publishing house of Haude und Spener, without the names of the translators.³³

Schleiermacher dispatched with his portion of the task conscientiously: he translated carefully, often giving Park's unsophisticated, paratactic style (full of interjections that make reading difficult) the elegance of high literary German. He showed a great deal of independence and inventiveness when it came to translating key terms: for example, he translated "an Arabic version of the Pentateuch of Moses" as "*eine arabische Uebersetzung der fünf Bücher Mosis*" – his choice of "*Übersetzung*" (translation) for Park's "version" here clearly demonstrating that, for him, the kinds of adaptations Park is describing do indeed count as kinds of "translation."³⁴

Undoubtedly, however, the most important event in Friedrich Schleiermacher's "translation biography," an experience that profoundly shaped his views on translation and his career as a translator, was his friendship and collaboration with Friedrich Schlegel. The relationship between the two Berlin-based Romantics was very

---

31 For more on their friendship and correspondence see Marjanne E. Goozé, "Der 'verlorene' Briefwechsel zwischen Henriette Herz und Friedrich Schleiermacher: Freundschaft, Religion und Nachruf," in "*...nur Frauen können Briefe schreiben*" – *Facetten weiblicher Briefkultur nach 1750*, vol. 1, ed. Renata Dampc-Jarosz, Paweł Zarychta (Berlin: Peter Lang, 2019), 177–190.
32 Most likely up to page 149 of the German edition (KGA V/3, 114; cf. KGA IV/2, XLII.).
33 Almost simultaneously, another translation of the book was published by the Campe publishing house in Hamburg (see KGA V/3, 178 and KGA IV/2, XLIX).
34 Mungo Park, *Travels in the Interior Districts of Africa* [...] (London: W. Bulmer, 1799), 314; idem, *Reisen in Innern von Afrika* [...], *aus dem Englischen* (Berlin: Haude und Spener, 1799), 280 (cf. KGA IV/2, 1122). Schleiermacher demonstrates a similar approach to translation a little further on, when the psalms of David are mentioned (281, cf. KGA IV/2, 1122).

dynamic: at first, it was a paragon of the "literary marriage" so idealized by that milieu,[35] manifesting itself in "symphilosophizing" (philosophizing engaged in together, in intellectual symbiosis) and the joint pursuit of daring projects – the most ambitious of these being a critical edition of Plato's complete works in German translation. Later, unfortunately, the harmony between the two men turned into discord and mutual distrust, which made it impossible for their collaboration to continue.[36] Nevertheless, their friendship bore fruit not only in the monumental edition of *Platons Werke* (*Plato's Works*), ultimately edited and translated by Schleiermacher, but also in many other testimonies of their mutual inspiration. A number of these are of considerable importance to translation studies, such as some remarks from Friedrich Schlegel's *Fragments*, Friedrich Schleiermacher's *Hermeneutics,* and their published criticism of various translations. I will devote separate space in this book to these texts, paying particular attention to the translation-studies aspects of the project of *Plato's Works*, conceived by Schlegel and realized by Schleiermacher.

In the shadow of these great enterprises of philosophy and translation, the preacher at the Charité in Berlin was also making some very interesting attempts at translating lyric poetry. They are closely linked to his own poetic writings, which can be described as classicizing stylizations and can hardly be considered successful. This relatively short episode in Schleiermacher's creative biography has been thoroughly analyzed by Hermann Patsch, who also devoted considerable attention to the surviving translations from *Anthologia Graeca*. In this case, the inspiration seems to have come from the older of the Schlegel brothers, August Wilhelm, an excellent literary scholar who was fascinated by ancient metrical forms and experimented with metrical translation of Greek poetry into German.[37] While maintaining in contact with him by correspondence, Schleiermacher prepared over twenty translations of Greek lyric poetry in 1803, of which he published only one.[38] Patsch regards the short lyric forms as the most successful; in the longer ones the translator made numerous departures from the original.[39] Schleiermacher was not satisfied with his translations; when comparing these attempts of his own with the translations of A.W. Schlegel, he could not help but see considerable shortcomings in his lyrical talent.[40]

Schleiermacher devoted an enormous amount of time and creative effort to what would become the six-volume edition of *Plato's Works* published in his translation and with his original commentary in 1804–1809 (a second, corrected edition was

---

35 Cf. Andreas Arndt, *Friedrich Schleiermacher als Philosoph* (Berlin: Walter de Gruyter, 2013), 31–41.
36 I will take up this thread in Chapter III.
37 See Hermann Patsch, *Alle Menschen sind Künstler – Friedrich Schleiermachers poetische Versuche* (Berlin: Walter de Gruyter, 1986), 41.
38 Ibid., 40, 51.
39 Ibid., 52.
40 Ibid., 54–55.

completed in 1828).⁴¹ From the outset, he was aware that he was embarking upon an epic enterprise, so he made no compromises in terms of philological meticulousness, translational conscientiousness, and the philosophical integrity of the project. It is hardly surprising, therefore, that after Platon, he never undertook any other major translation project – only translating occasional short fragments of text (e.g. a minor correction of Luther's bible translation).⁴²

This does not mean, however, that Schleiermacher ceased to concern himself with translation. Rather, he dealt with it both directly and indirectly, at the discursive level, thematizing, analyzing, problematizing, and (re)contextualizing translation relations. This plane will be an equally important subject of study in the present book; the sources analyzed herein include not only Schleiermacher's translation of Plato's *Phaedrus* and his lecture *On the Different Methods of Translating*, but also such texts as his *Speeches on Religion* and his lectures on stylistics, hermeneutics, and dialectics. The connection between the latter works and reflections on translation may not seem obvious, but they do contain extremely important thoughts in this respect, without which the picture of Schleiermacher's discourse would be incomplete.

Obviously, being exhaustive in this regard would require taking a far greater number of Schleiermacher's writings into account, above all his theological work – especially the dogmatic and exegetical-critical writings, on the one hand, as well as his philosophical ethics and aesthetics, on the other. The noticeable absence of references to the former in this book is a result of my conviction that they require a separate study, adopting different analytical priorities. The scant mention of the lectures on ethics and aesthetics, in turn, primarily reflects the fact that at the time the original (Polish) version of this book went to press (in 2020), these sources had not yet been compiled in the critical edition (KGA), whereas the extant editions unfortunately left much to be desired.

3 Signposts to the pathways

To my knowledge, the present monograph is the first in-depth analyses of such a broader range of Friedrich Schleiermacher's works (including various pathways of his philosophical reflection and creative practice) that bear upon the field of translation studies in the wide sense. That is not to say, however, that it was written in a

---

41 Even the first publication of *Platons Werke* (1804–1809) covers a relatively long and important period in Schleiermacher's life. Between 1802 and 1804 he served as preacher in Stolp (today Słupsk in Poland), next accepted a professorship in theology at the University of Halle (1804–1807), and then in 1807, forced by political developments, he returned to Berlin, where he remained until his death in 1834. In the spring of 1809 he was appointed preacher at the Church of the Holy Trinity, and on May 18 he married Henrietta von Willich. A year later Schleiermacher became professor of theology at the newly established Friedrich-Wilhelm University in Berlin.
42 Romans 13:5, in his sermon of 15 January 1809; see KGA III/4, 4.

research vacuum. The last thirty years have seen the publication of many interesting and inspiring works on Friedrich Schleiermacher's translational thought, and the decade 2010–2020 even saw a certain rising vogue for his lecture *On the Different Methods of Translating* – as evidenced not only by its repeated inclusion in numerous anthologies, but also by the appearance of two collective volumes plus one extensive (and methodologically highly eccentric) monograph focusing specifically on it.[43] Yet as recently as the mid-1960s, the leading theorist and historian of translation at that time, Georges Mounin, did not mention Schleiermacher even once an ambitious book presenting almost all aspects of translation.[44] In the same vein, even twenty years later, the 1985 book *The Manipulation of Literature* edited by Theo Hermans, which opened up a whole new chapter in translation studies, likewise contained not a single mention of the Breslau-born theologian.[45]

The change in this state of affairs seems to have been brought about primarily by philosophical hermeneutics, which from the mid-1960s onwards began to exert an increasing influence on the so-called "science of translation" (*Übersetzungswissenschaft*) developing within the structuralist paradigm. As a result, scholars working in this paradigm, leaning more and more towards textual approaches and recognizing the translator's creative autonomy, began to take note of such theoreticians as Schleiermacher.[46] However, an important role was also played by the development of the literary study of translation, taking into account the historical and cultural background, as Schleiermacher's views turned out to be very relevant to such issues as the translator's visibility, the strategy of assimilating what is foreign, and the culture and politics of translation.[47] In parallel, there was dynamic development in translation-studies trends rooted in "pre-scientific" reflection on the phenomenon of translation, which analyzed and creatively interpreted the tradition which Schleier-

---

[43] *Friedrich Schleiermacher and the Question of Translation*, eds. Larisa Cercel and Adriana Şerban (Berlin: Walter de Gruyter, 2015); *Rereading Schleiermacher: Translation, Cognition and Culture*, ed. Teresa Seruya, José Miranda Justo (Berlin: Springer, 2016); Douglas Robinson, *Schleiermacher's Icoses: Social Ecologies of the Different Methods of Translating* (Bucharest: Zeta Books, 2013). The popularity of the lecture is also, for instance, evidenced by the relatively recent emergence of at least four different English translations (listed in the "Note from the translator on texts and translations" in the preface herein).

[44] Georges Mounin, *Problèmes théoriques de la traduction* (Paris: Gallimard, 1963).

[45] Cf. *The Manipulation of Literature: Studies in Literary Translation*, ed. Theo Hermans (London: Croom Helm, 1985). In Hermans' more recent works, on the other hand, Schleiermacher does figure as an important point of reference, e. g. Theo Hermans, *The Conference of the Tongues* (London: Routledge, 2007).

[46] See especially Jiří Levý, *The Art of Translation*, trans. Patrick Corness, ed. with a critical foreword by Zuzana Jettmarová (Amsterdam: John Benjamins, 2011), 85 (first Czech edition 1963).

[47] The German literary scholars Harald Kittel and Andreas Poltermann even go so far as to claim, with considerable exaggeration, that no "fundamentally new approaches" have appeared in this field since Schleiermacher. Harald Kittel, Andreas Poltermann, "The German Tradition," in *Routledge Encyclopedia of Translation Studies*, ed. Mona Baker (London: Routledge, 2001), 422.

macher had been a part of, as an author of translations and commentaries on translation – namely, hermeneutics and the philology of translation.[48]

A detailed discussion of the works that have emerged in the rising wave of interest in Schleiermacher's approach to translation in recent decades would require a separate, very extensive chapter. I will limit myself here to pointing out the most important, in my view, presentations and problematizations that have so far appeared in the field.

For any reader of the twentieth century's most outstanding work on hermeneutics, Hans-Georg Gadamer's *Truth and Method* (1960), the link between Schleiermacher's hermeneutics and translation is clear. "Everything presupposed in hermeneutics is but language" – this quotation from Schleiermacher opens Gadamer's remarks on "language as the medium of hermeneutic experience,"[49] which leads the philosopher to a conclusion very much in the spirit of the lecture *On the Different Methods of Translating*:

> For every translator is an interpreter. The fact that a foreign language is being translated means that this is simply an extreme case of hermeneutical difficulty – i.e., of alienness and its conquest. In fact all the "objects" with which traditional hermeneutics is concerned are alien in the same unequivocally defined sense. The translator's task of re-creation differs only in degree, not in kind, from the general hermeneutical task that any text presents.[50]

This interpretation allows us to look at Schleiermacher as a thinker who combines understanding, language and translation within the space of a philosophy of communication, which is essentially a space of interpretation.

The seeds sown by Gadamer have borne fruit in the works of many eminent scholars of hermeneutics and the art of translation. One of the most creative among them was the American scholar George Steiner, author of *After Babel: Aspects of Language and Translation* (1975). In Steiner's view, the "hermeneutic approach" was "initiated by Schleiermacher" at the dawn of Romanticism, and consists in "the investigation of what it means to 'understand' a piece of oral or written speech, and the attempt to diagnose this process in terms of a general model of meaning."[51] On the basis of this approach, a theory of translation can be developed, which is "a model of the workings of language itself" and through the study of the status of

---

48 See especially Rolf Kloepfer, *Die Theorie der literarischen Übersetzung – Romanisch-deutscher Sprachbereich* (Munich: Wilhelm Fink, 1967).
49 English version taken from Hans-Georg Gadamer, *Truth and Method*, translation revised by Joel Weinsheimer and Donald G. Marshall, 2nd rev. ed. (London: Continuum, 2004), 383. A somewhat more adroit English version of the relevant Schleiermacher passage is offered by Duke and Forstman, as follows: "Language is the only presupposition in hermeneutics, and everything that is to be found, including the other objective and subjective presuppositions, must be discovered in language." Friedrich Schleiermacher, *Hermeneutics: The Handwritten Manuscripts*, trans. James Duke and Jack Forstman (Atlanta: Scholars Press, 1997, 2nd edition), 50.
50 Gadamer, *Truth and Method*, 389.
51 Steiner, *After Babel*, 237.

meaning reveals the essence and limits of translation. It is based on Kant's "rational hermeneutic" and on Schleiermacher's research into the meaning structure and translatability of scripture.[52]

Steiner also gives Schleiermacher credit for noticing the essence of "a special interlingua for translators, a transfer-idiom or hybrid" of the source and target language. In practice, such a symbiosis appears as a result of the "modulation of one's own speech into the lexical and syntactic world of the original."[53] The author of *After Babel* cites Hölderlin's translation of Sophocles as an example of this type of modulation, setting it alongside Schleiermacher's Plato in this respect. This juxtaposition is nevertheless not justified, in my view, as in fact the two cases exhibit quite different translation strategies.

The French scholar Antoine Berman, in turn, devoted much space to Schleiermacher as a theorist of translation, situating him within the overall context of German reflection on translation in the Romantic era. This approach resulted from the specificity of Schleiermacher's research into the "hermeneutics of the translation space," at the center of which he placed the category of experience, understood in the manner of the Romantics.[54] Berman's monograph *L'Épreuve de l'étranger: Culture et traduction dans l'Allemagne romantique* (1985) played a key role, initiating a kind of turn towards Romanticism in modern translation theory and history, of which Schleiermacher was especially a "beneficiary." The starting points of this work are the notions of culture and education (*Bildung*), which the German Romantics imparted with a special meaning, showing their universal dimension. The assimilation of culture and education means, as Berman stresses, "going beyond oneself, leaving behind what is one's own," in order to "experience the foreign, the other," and then returning to one's own self, enriched by that experience.[55] Translation, in this context, is a model of the educational process, as it allows for precisely such experiencing of the foreign. Thus *Bildung* and *Übersetzung* are closely intertwined in the discourse of German Romanticism, forming the basis of a unique translation culture. Schleiermacher was part of this phenomenon, as translator, theorist and critic of translation. A part that represents the whole, because "Schleiermacher's reflection summarizes the experience in the matter of translation of his entire epoch" and also "provides the most accomplished formulation of the law of *Bildung*."[56]

Berman emphasizes that Schleiermacher is the creator of the first modern theory of translation, which is indeed a *theory* a because it precisely defines its object, the

---

[52] Ibid., 414.
[53] Ibid., 266.
[54] This notion appears in the summary of Berman's habilitation claims; citations are given by Irène Kuhn, *Antoine Bermans "produktive" Übersetzungskritik – Entwurf und Erprobung einer Methode* (Tübingen: Gunter Narr, 2007), 24.
[55] After: ibid., 36.
[56] Antoine Berman, *The Experience of the Foreign: Culture and Translation in Romantic Germany*, trans. Stefan Heyvaert (Albany: State Univ. of New York Press, 1992), 152.

broader field within which it is situated, the procedures of translation, and the situation of the translator within a particular culture and linguistic consciousness. Thus defined, it enters into the domain of hermeneutics and criticism.[57] As an example of the close connection between reflection on translation and hermeneutic thought, the French scholar cites Schleiermacher's distinction between authentic and inauthentic translation, which in fact corresponds to the distinction between two kinds of understanding and communication: authentic and inauthentic.[58] In the case of "authentic" translation, there is always the risk of exposing the native language to the influence of the foreign.

What is more, in Berman's eyes Schleiermacher also revolutionized the approach to the translator's work. Thanks to him, translation ceased to be a "naive craft" and became, for the Romantics, a true art that presupposes extensive competences, requires particular responsibility, and encourages philosophical reflection on its principles.[59]

The American scholar Lawrence Venuti, who has long situated Schleiermacher at the very heart of the debate about translation theory's historical identity and tenets, initiated what would become a series of publications that transformed modern translation studies with an article entitled *Genealogies of Translation Theory: Schleiermacher*[60] in 1991. The notions formulated in this article have been consistently developed by Venuti in subsequent works, especially his influential monograph *The Translator's Invisibility: A History of Translation*.[61]

Inspired by the ideas of Nietzsche and Foucault, Venuti postulates a "genealogical" analysis of translation theory. In the light of the prevalence of domesticating translations, whose predominant status is maintained and legitimized by publishers, readers, professional critics, and also translators themselves, such a genealogy may reveal other, alternative ways of thinking about translation, conceptualized as a locus of cultural difference rather than of homogeneity.[62]

Venuti admits that an important step towards pursuing such an agenda was taken by Antoine Berman, who sees the ethics of translation as being linked with the communication of what is different and foreign. A genealogical search for an "antidote" to contemporary homogenization led the French scholar to the German Romantics, to Schleiermacher in particular. Here, however, according to Venuti, the critical impetus of the author of *L'Épreuve de l'étranger* became exhausted:

---

[57] Ibid., 144; Irène Kuhn in: *Antoine Bermans "produktive" Übersetzungskritik*, 39.
[58] Berman, *The Experience of the Foreign*, 145.
[59] Kuhn, *Antoine Bermans "produktive" Übersetzungskritik*, 42.
[60] Lawrence Venuti, "Genealogies of Translation Theory: Schleiermacher" *Traduire la théorie* 4, no. 2 (1991).
[61] Lawrence Venuti, *The Translator's Invisibility: A History of Translation*, 2nd ed. (London: Routledge, 2008).
[62] Venuti, *Genealogies of Translation Theory: Schleiermacher*, 126–127.

Berman finds no poisons in Schleiermacher: he offers a rather deferential treatment that emphasizes what is 'moderne' in Schleiermacher's translation theory – 'le fondateur de cette herméneutique moderne' – and how it can be seen as answering the difficult questions posed by ethnocentric translation in the present.[63]

This perspective, however, is the result of a rather one-sided reading of Schleiermacher that ignores historical differences – Venuti argues – adding that a true genealogical analysis should reveal what possibilities with respect to contemporary translation practices emerge from Friedrich Schleiermacher's discourse. According to the American scholar, his bourgeois cultural elitism and Prussian nationalism, as much as Berman's noted (alleged) critique of ethnocentrism, explain the contemporary shift in discourse from the ethics to the politics of translation.[64]

In his genealogical reading of the lecture *On the Different Methods of Translating* (as contrasted against Berman's reading), Venuti problematizes Schleiermacher's ethics of translation, arguing that the postulate of preserving the linguistic and cultural difference of a foreign text applies to a particular social group – the educated elite to whom translations are addressed.[65] For translation is always ethnocentric, as it cannot escape the hierarchy of cultural values inscribed in the target language. Venuti develops his criticism based on this notion, stating that "Schleiermacher is enlisting his privileged translation method in a cultural political agenda, wherein an educated elite controls the formation of a national culture by refining its language through foreignizing translations."[66] He thus highlights the ideological underpinning of Schleiermacher's argumentation, which is – in his view – a bourgeois elitism with a distinct tinge of nationalism, taking on importance in the context of the struggle for a national German culture, independent of the influence of (aristocratic) Francophile culture.[67]

From the perspective of the Marxist-psychoanalytic critique of ideology, the strategy of foreignization "does not so much introduce the foreign into German culture as use the foreign to confirm and develop a sameness, a process of fashioning an ideal cultural self on the basis of an other, a cultural narcissism, which is endowed, moreover, with historical necessity."[68] Yet at the same time, Venuti perceives another feature of Schleiermacher's reflections, which, running counter to such ideological determinants, nevertheless conveys "the (inadvertent) suggestion that foreignizing translation can alter the social divisions figured in these ideologies, can promote cultural change through its work on the target language."[69] In fact, what we are dealing with here not so much a kind of paradox inherent in Schleiermacher's views as with

---

[63] Ibid., 128.
[64] Ibid., 128–129.
[65] Ibid., 130.
[66] Ibid., 131.
[67] Cf. ibid., 138.
[68] Ibid., 139.
[69] Ibid., 145.

evidence of the weakness of Venuti's own ideology-oriented reading, which – by operating with such key terms as bourgeois individualism, revisionism, narcissism, nationalism, imperialism, and the class system – tries to expose both the false and the true (i.e. progressive) class-consciousness of the author of the lecture *On the Different Methods of Translating*. Only true (progressive) consciousness, the American translation theorist claims, produces theoretical tools that can serve to revolt against the contemporary tyranny of "transparent discourse" in translation, and more broadly: to make us aware of the social conditioning of cultural discourses.[70]

Such an interpretation of Schleiermacher's lecture recurs in other texts by Lawrence Venuti, in which the German theologian usually appears as an ambivalent figure, oscillating between the values the American scholar holds dear and the kinds of views that he consistently combats – between respect for what is foreign and respect for cultural difference, on the one hand, and nationalistic chauvinism and a discourse that homogenizes what is different, on the other.[71] A possible explanation for such ambivalence is the fact that the strategies described by Schleiermacher are situated within "specific cultural formations" within which different discourses clash and struggle.[72]

In Venuti's more recent work, this ambivalence is taken to another level. Re-examining the concept of foreignization in Schleiermacher and Berman, he concludes that it is based on an "instrumental" model of translation:

> Here translation is seen as the reproduction or transfer of an invariant contained in or caused by the source text, whether its form, its meaning, or its effect. For Schleiermacher and Berman, the foreignness of the source text is an invariant that inheres in its lexicon and syntax, style and genre, theme and discourse, and it is this foreignness that the translator must reproduce or manifest by adhering closely to those textual features.[73]

According to this model, foreignness appears as something that can be discovered and transferred into translation. Meanwhile, the foreignness communicated in translation "is never available in some direct or unmediated form; it is a construction that is always mediated by intelligibilities and interests in the receiving situation."[74] Venuti contrasts this negative instrumentalism with an unspecified "hermeneutic model" (or rather, semiotic model) which conceptualizes (and affirms) translation

---

[70] Ibid., 146. Mary Snell-Hornby notes that Venuti "domesticates" Schleiermacher's conceptual apparatus. Cf. Mary Snell-Hornby, "Venutis 'foreignization': Das Erbe von Friedrich Schleiermacher in der Translationswissenschaft?" in *Und sie bewegt sich doch... Translationswissenschaft in Ost und West – Festschrift für Heidemarie Salevsky zum 60. Geburtstag*, ed. Ina Müller (Frankfurt am Main: Peter Lang, 2004), 333–344.

[71] Cf. Venuti, *The Translator's Invisibility*, 83 and 92.

[72] Ibid., 85.

[73] Lawrence Venuti, *Translation Changes Everything: Theory and Practice* (London: Routledge, 2013), 3.

[74] Ibid.

as "an interpretive act, as the inscription of one interpretive possibility among others."[75] This distinction serves as a basis for a reinterpretation of Schleiermacher's lecture in Venuti's new *Genealogies of Translation Theory*, which argues that Schleiermacher's reflection is based, on the one hand, on an instrumental model, referring to an "empirical" theory of language, and, on the other, on a hermeneutic model, connected with a "materialist" conception of language.[76] This, the American translation theorist argues, may explain the "different ideas of autonomy, equivalence, and function for the translated text" that appear in Schleiermacher's lecture.[77] All in all, however, it should be noted that the dichotomy/ambivalence Venuti describes is reducible to the matrix of the "reproductive and creative aspect of translation," problematized by translation scholars since at least Jiří Levý's *The Art of Translation* (1963).

The work of another influential contemporary translation theorist, Anthony Pym, also fits into this critical, or perhaps more precisely, "interrogative" interpretation of Schleiermacher's translation theory. In his article *Schleiermacher and the Problem of Blendlinge* (1995), Pym searches for the sources and underpinnings of the binary approach to translation methods that is posited, in his opinion, by the author of lecture *On the Different Methods of Translating*. Interesting hints in this respect are provided by the metaphors employed by the German theologian to describe the positive and negative paradigm of translation, respectively.[78] Pym's analysis shows that the driving force organizing Schleiermacher's lecture and giving it a certain figurative shape is an aversion to interculturalism.[79] As with other binary theories of translation, here too Pym sees a "refusal to consider the translator, or the place of the translator, as a viable third term."[80] The negative notion of *Blendlinge* (a pejorative term for mixed-race people), to which Schleiermacher refers in his lecture, becomes a metaphor for the translator, who is an intercultural being. By re-evaluating this concept, Pym derives from it the ethos of the translator, as a member of "the community of intermediaries."[81] "The most ethical birth, in this community, is a mixture of cultures"[82] – the Australian scholar polemically concludes.

---

[75] Ibid., 4.
[76] Lawrence Venuti, "Genealogies of Translation Theory: Schleiermacher and the Hermeneutic Model," in *Un/Translatables: New Maps for Germanic Literatures*, ed. Bethany Wiggin, Catriona MacLeod, (Evanston: Northwestern Univ. Press, 2016), 53–54.
[77] Ibid., 54.
[78] Anthony Pym, "Schleiermacher and the Problem of *Blendlinge*," *Translation and Literature* 4, no. 1 (1995), 8, http://usuaris.tinet.cat/apym/on-line/intercultures/blendlinge.pdf (accessed 30 September 2019).
[79] Ibid., 15.
[80] Ibid., 3.
[81] Ibid., 17.
[82] Ibid. Pym's article closes with a sharp polemic against Venuti's criticism formulated in "Genealogies of Translation Theory: Schleiermacher." The crux of this polemic goes as follows: "In defining translation strategies in terms of good and bad, resistant and transparent, Venuti unthinkingly repro-

Pym's reading of Schleiermacher's lecture reveals a certain more general problem in translation-studies scholars' interpretations of the German theologian's thought. As a rule, these interpretations refer to just a single source text (of course, the text of *On the Different Methods of Translating*), focusing on the two options that it presents to the translator, usually referred to as alternative translation strategies. In this situation, it is hardly surprising that Schleiermacher becomes an easy target for criticism. In a more recent version of the aforementioned article, Anthony Pym critiques him by noting that the strategies he posits had already been described earlier (by Bodmer, Breitinger, Herder, and Goethe, among others), and that Schleiermacher resorts to an overly simple argument: "reduce everything to a choice between two methods, and then select one over the other."[83]

However, it is a misunderstanding to accuse Schleiermacher of radical dualism, just as it is a misunderstanding to attribute to him a lack of sensitivity to the dangers inherent in the concept of nation and nationalist discourse – dangers unknown in the Napoleonic era but well recognized today. Without taking into account the fact that Schleiermacher's thinking is immersed in *dialectics*, in the "identity and contradiction of thought,"[84] and that his remarks on translation from his 1813 lecture (to which he himself, besides, did not attach much importance) are just one element of a whole system of knowledge he built up over decades, we will be unable to properly understand Schleiermacher, and even less able to engage in dialog with him. Ultimately, we must ask: How can we possibly discuss the translator's ethics propounded by a professor of philosophy who once rivalled Hegel, without knowing what "ethics" meant to him?

I myself, a philologist and translation-studies scholar, have done my best to avoid such misunderstandings in my analyses, arising from the limitations of a research perspective narrowed by disciplinary intentionality.[85] At the same time, I have sought to show that the perspective of a philologist / translation-studies scholar can also be valuable in the general context of the study of Friedrich Schleiermacher's powerful work. If it is not blind to the extraordinary complexity and interdisciplinarity of

---

duces Schleiermacher's exclusion of intercultural communities. Despite his political support of translators as members of a (receiving) society, Venuti fails to see that a sociology of translators themselves might be the most fruitful exit from Schleiermacher. The key to this sociological rather than theoretical genealogy is to focus on *Blendlinge*, the people in the middle, the intermediaries who form intercultural communities of one kind or another" (Pym, "Schleiermacher and the Problem of *Blendlinge*," 19).

83 Anthony Pym, *On Translator Ethics*, trans. Heike Walker, rev. and updated by the author (Amsterdam: John Benjamins: 2012), 15. Contrary to Pym's claim, the concept of negotiation between opposing methods plays an important role in Schleiermacher's account of translation.

84 An apt expression used by Theodor W. Adorno in *Negative Dialectics*, trans. E.B. Ashton (London: Routledge, 2004), 6.

85 At the same time, I am inclined to understand *philology* broadly, linking it to the study of the products of the human spirit, as August Boeckh did in *Encyclopädie und Methodologie der philologischen Wissenschaften* (Leipzig: B. G. Teubner, 1877), 10.

that work, to which, after all, a vast number of scholarly publications have been devoted, such a perspective can contribute interesting threads to a multi-voiced "monograph" on the Breslau-born cleric, scholar, and translator.

In this book I seek to bridge the gap that exists between translation-studies approaches to Schleiermacher on the one hand, and those fields of study that have systematically taken up Schleiermacher's work without focusing on its translation-related aspects, on the other. That is not to say that translation-studies scholars have not shown any interest in anything beyond the single text that has become a compulsory chapter in almost all "readers" on translation theory. Some of them have indeed mentioned its important contexts, especially Schleiermacher's hermeneutics and criticism.[86] However, they have avoided a broader contextualization of the problem of translation, being reluctant to enter the difficult interdisciplinary landscape, or even – perhaps surprisingly – the broad terrain of Schleiermacher's scholarly and creative biography. Nor does this mean that theologians or philosophers have entirely ignored the question of translation in their study of the German scholar. They have mentioned it in certain contexts, albeit ascribing it a "local" significance and not devoting much attention to it. As a result, even as excellent an interpreter of Schleiermacher's philosophy as Manfred Frank does not notice how important a role the notion of transfer/translation plays in it,[87] and Lawrence Venuti fails to see how the notion of translation is related to the German scholar's dialectics (to just limit ourselves here to two eminent scholars and two exemplary issues). This is all the stranger, given that there are quite a few studies focusing on Schleiermacher's theory of language, which quite simply cries out to be problematized in the context of the broader issue of translation/transference.[88]

In short, this monograph – which represents the outcome of a project carried out largely within the research community in Berlin[89] – aspires to point out a certain new

---

[86] Cf. Christian Berner, "Das Übersetzen verstehen – Zu den philosophischen Grundlagen von Schleiermachers Vortrag 'Ueber die verschiedenen Methoden des Uebersetzens,'" in *Friedrich Schleiermacher and the Question of Translation*, eds. Larisa Cercel and Adriana Şerban (Berlin: Walter de Gruyter, 2015), 43–58.

[87] Cf. Manfred Frank, *Das individuelle Allgemeine – Textstrukturierung und Textinterpretation nach Schleiermacher*, Frankfurt am Main 1977. Frank's approach may come as a surprise because in his monograph he not only focuses on Schleiermacher's "hermeneutical theory of language" (145), but also looks at it through the prism of Derrida's poststructuralism, in the context of which translation plays a key role – see Michał Paweł Markowski, *Efekt inskrypcji: Jacques Derrida i literatura* [The Inscription Effect: Jacques Derrida and Literature] (Bydgoszcz: Homini, 1997), 306–319.

[88] Cf. Hans-Georg Gadamer, "Das Problem der Sprache bei Schleiermacher," in idem, *Gesammelte Werke*, vol. 4: *Neuere Philosophie* II (Tübingen: Mohr Siebeck, 1987), 361–373; Joseph Margolis, "Schleiermacher among the Theorists of Language and Interpretation," *Journal of Aesthetics and Art Criticism* 45, no. 4 (1987): 361–368, and Denis Thouard, "Die Sprachphilosophie der Hermeneutik," in *Friedrich Schleiermachers Hermeneutik – Interpretationen und Perspektiven*, ed. Andreas Arndt, Jörg Dierken (Berlin: Walter de Gruyter, 2016), 85–99.

[89] The first, Polish version of this book was written within the framework of the scientific project "Schleiermachers Übersetzungstheorie aus einer neuen Perspektive," thanks to a grant given to me

direction in the reception of Friedrich Schleiermacher's thought. It consists of six analytical chapters, which take the form of detailed studies of Schleiermacher's most important "pathways of translation"[90] – some of which he travelled alone, others he followed with a companion: Friedrich Schlegel. The chapters are arranged in an order consistent with the chronology of Schleiermacher's thought and work. Chapters III and VI are based on papers delivered at conferences that were organized by German scholars of Schleiermacher's life and work, published (after corrections inspired by many discussions) in German-language collective publications.[91] Here, they appear in a new version, placed in a broader context, re-edited and in many places significantly expanded, and of course for the first time in English.

---

by the Alexander von Humboldt-Stiftung to fund my stay and research work at Freie Universität Berlin. The German scientific partner was Prof. Hans Richard Brittnacher (Institut für deutsche und niederländische Philologie). The project was facilitated by the support of the Schleiermacher research team of the Berlin-Brandenburgische Akademie der Wissenschaften (Berlin-Brandenburg Academy of Sciences) under the direction of Prof. Andreas Arndt, especially by the benevolence of Dr. Sarah Schmidt and Dr. Simon Gerber. This team (Schleiermacher-Forschungstelle Berlin, since 2019 under the direction of Dr. Sarah Schmidt) contributed to the editing of Schleiermacher's KGA and coordinated related research. Dr. Hermann Patsch also provided me with valuable assistance. To all the scholars mentioned here I would like to extend my heartfelt gratitude.

90 The title of the present book is a deliberate reference to the title of Hans Robert Jauss's collection of works *Wege des Verstehens* (Munich: Wilhelm Fink, 1994).

91 The material in Chapter III was originally published as Piotr de Bończa Bukowski, "Zur Übersetzungstheorie bei Friedrich Daniel Ernst Schleiermacher und Friedrich Schlegel in der Zeit ihrer Zusammenarbeit," in *Wissenschaft, Kirche, Staat und Politik: Schleiermacher im preußischen Reformprozess*, ed. Andreas Arndt, Simon Gerber, Sarah Schmidt (Berlin: Walter de Gruyter, 2019), 119–143, whereas Chapter VI is derived from Piotr de Bończa Bukowski, "Schleiermacher und die Frage nach dem Original: Zu einem philologischen und übersetzungswissenschaftlichen Problem," in *Reformation und Moderne: Pluralität – Subjektivität – Kritik. Akten des Internationalen Kongresses der Schleiermacher-Gesellschaft in Halle (Saale), März 2017*, ed. Jörg Dierken, Arnulf von Scheliha, Sarah Schmidt (Berlin: Walter de Gruyter, 2018), 719–732.

II Lectures on Style: Rhetoric, Hermeneutics, and Issues of Translation

1 The significance of the young Schleiermacher's lectures *On Style*

The collected notes of Schleiermacher's lectures *Ueber den Stil* (*On Style*), prepared by the young theologian in early 1791 and published in the first volume of the critical edition of his complete works (KGA), offer very interesting material for scholars of his thought. The main reason is because they inspiringly complicate the widespread image that has accrued to Schleiermacher in contemporary times: as a representative of the Romantic style of thinking about language and literature. Juxtaposing this "pre-Romantic" Schleiermacher[1] against his later writings – e.g. *Ueber die Religion* (*On Religion*) – has led scholars to draw a stark contrast between the views of the young, allegedly still intellectually dependent author vs. those of the already mature scholar. And yet, it appears that if we devote enough time and attention to reading the early considerations on style, avoiding stereotypical preconceptions about his rhetoric and hermeneutics, we will discover important Schleiermacherian tropes of thought already expressed in them – admittedly still in an early stage of development, but nevertheless already clearly crystallized and interconnected.

The fact that the young Schleiermacher's lectures *On Style* constitute a prelude to his broader reflection on anthropological issues was noticed by Wolfgang Virmond, who "rediscovered" them at the end of the last century:

> In Schleiermacher's eyes, reflection on style is something that should concern not only writers or poets, but everyone; it is of general use because communication takes place everywhere: where there is public discussion but also where there is intimate correspondence; it is the domain for living speech as well as for self-reflection, and even for private reading and thinking in its own right. Making oneself intelligible to others and to oneself – these are the processes that can benefit from a hermeneutically grounded science of style [...].[2]

Note that Schleiermacher perceives the issue of translation in a similarly broad cultural and communicative context, as evidenced by his famous lecture at the Royal Academy of Sciences in Berlin, *Ueber die verschiedenen Methoden des Uebersetzens* (*On the Different Methods of Translating*). As we have already noted in the Introduc-

---

[1] Cf. Manuel Bauer, *Schlegel und Schleiermacher – Frühromantische Kunstkritik und Hermeneutik* (Paderborn: Schöningh, 2011), 212.
[2] Wolfgang Virmond, "Bemerkungen zu Schleiermachers Schlobittener Stil-Vorträgen von 1791," in *200 Jahre "Reden über die Religion": Akten des 1. Internationalen Kongresses der Schleiermacher-Gesellschaft, Halle, 14.–17. März 1999*, eds. Ulrich Barth, Claus-Dieter Osthövener (Berlin: Walter de Gruyter, 2000), 258.

tion, that lecture opens with a set of arguments in favor of recognizing translation as an all-pervasive phenomenon. The last of these arguments relates to the need for *self-translation:* "Sometimes we even have to translate our own words, when they feel alien and we want to make them truly our own once again," the published version of the lecture states (DR, 225; KGA I/11, 67). In the younger Schleiermacher's notes *On Style*, we find a formulation that seems to allude to the very same hermeneutical intuition: "[I]n the end, it is as difficult to understand ourselves as it is to explain to others what we mean" (KGA I/1, 367).[3]

The correspondences do not stop there. In both the lectures *On Style* and Schleiermacher's later hermeneutic reflections on translation, two terms which appear in the above-quoted statements play an extremely important role: *Mitteilung* (communication, message) and *Vermittlung* (mediation, conveyance). These are at the same time concepts of key importance in the present monograph. The text *On Style* is, chronologically speaking, Schleiermacher's first significant work in which the issues of language, literature, understanding, and translation, the focus of interest in this book, are all intertwined. And they are intertwined on a very interesting and historically significant plane: that of rhetoric. Many scholars maintain that rhetoric is – perhaps paradoxically – one of the keys to understanding the phenomenon of early German Romanticism (*Frühromantik*). Helmut Schanze contends that:

> Schlegel's progressive universal poetics, Novalis's encyclopedic plan for a universal inventory, and the psychological assumptions of the new style, as well as Hölderlin's concept of "modes of action of the poetic spirit" in the *Homburger Kunstlehre*, and Schleiermacher's hermeneutics and speeches *On Religion* exhibit clear convergences in terms of the objective and the procedures meant to lead to it. They can be seen as transformations of the rhetorical notion of *inventio*.[4]

But is it really only *inventio*, we may ask, or perhaps also the rhetorical notions of *dispositio* and *elocutio*? For a number of reasons, therefore, the lectures *On Style* may be regarded as worthy of deeper analysis and contextual interpretation. In this Chapter I will strive to maintain a broad cognitive perspective, so as to catch hold of as many of the threads appearing here as possible, which I will then follow up on in subsequent parts of this book.

2 Genesis, general shape, and distinctive qualities

Although the biographical context of the remarks on style that are of interest to us in this chapter was quite thoroughly outlined by Wilhelm Dilthey, Schleiermacher's

---

[3] Ibid, 258.
[4] Helmut Schanze, *Rhetorik und Stilistik der deutschsprachigen Länder von der Romantik bis zum Ende des 19. Jahrhunderts*, in *Rhetorik und Stilistik – Ein internationales Handbuch historischer und systematischer Forschung*, ed. Ulla Fix, Andreas Gardt, Joachim Knape, vol. 1 (Berlin: Walter de Gruyter, 2008) (Handbücher zur Sprach und Kommunikationswissenschaft [HSK], 31/1), 137.

most prominent biographer, he nevertheless almost completely ignored the content of his teacher's lectures in this respect.[5] This omission on the part of the author of *Leben Schleiermachers* was rectified in 2000 by Wolfgang Virmond, in a groundbreaking article that, in addition to covering the most important biographical facts, presents a philological and substantive analysis of the content in the lectures *On Style*.[6]

First, however, let us reconstruct their context. Schleiermacher came to Schlobitten (today Słobity in Poland) immediately after studying theology in Halle (1787–1789). After completing his studies, he passed the first of his final examinations in theology in Berlin in 1790, and through the intervention of F.S.G. Sack he obtained a position as an in-house tutor (*Hofmeister*) with Count Friedrich Alexander zu Dohna-Schlobitten at his ancestral seat in East Prussia.[7]

Dilthey vividly describes Schleiermacher's arrival to Schlobitten and his first years there. On 22 October 1790, the young theologian arrived at the then-magnificent (now ruined) palace in Schlobitten, the manor home of a prominent aristocratic family of Prussian patriots. Count Dohna had a military background, having served as an adjutant to the Prince Elector of Brunswick and been engaged in military and political affairs. Dilthey presents an almost idyllic picture of the count's family, which exhibited a combination of cultural refinement and intellectual openness. And so, Schleiermacher entered into a realm of life hitherto unknown to him, life "in a nobler style" (*in edlerem Stil*).[8] This high style of the Dohna family dovetailed in an intriguing way with the subject of Schleiermacher's lectures, contrasting at the same time with the familiar bourgeois world and its values.

Although he was actually meant to become the tutor for the Count's elder son Wilhelm, who was beginning his studies in Königsberg, in the end he was tasked with taking care of the younger children who still lived at the palace. These included girls – the twenty-year-old Countess Caroline, the younger Countesses Friederike and Auguste, and the ten-year-old Christiane – as well as boys – mainly Count Ludwig (Louis), aged fourteen and Schleiermacher's favorite pupil, plus also the Counts Fabian and Fritz, aged nine and six.[9]

We know that the young *Hofmeister* taught school subjects such as geography, history, and French. He also influenced the older and younger members of the household on a spiritual level, as he regularly preached during church services.[10] He prepared scientific lectures for the two young countesses: "That group must look most lovely," his sister wrote to him, "when you are reading out seminars on the fine

---

5 Cf. Wilhelm Dilthey, *Leben Schleiermachers*, vol. I/1: *1768–1802*, 3rd ed., ed. Martin Redeker (Berlin: Walter de Gruyter, 1970).
6 Virmond, "Bemerkungen," 247 ff.
7 Cf. Hermann Fischer, *Friedrich Daniel Ernst Schleiermacher* (Munich: C.H. Beck, 2001), 23.
8 Dilthey, *Leben Schleiermachers*, vol. I/1, 55.
9 Ibid., 56.
10 Ibid., 57; Kurt Nowak, *Schleiermacher – Leben, Werk und Wirkung* (Göttingen: Vandenhoeck & Ruprecht, 2001), 52.

arts or your lectures on style, for then you are a professor standing before an attentive auditorium."[11] The latter lectures were inaugurated by Schleiermacher in January 1791. Commenting on this remark made the theologian's sister, Dilthey informs us that manuscripts of those lectures still formed part of Schleiermacher's unpublished legacy, and suggests that they were of a purely utilitarian nature: "without any claim to originality, they fulfilled their task very well."[12]

It is puzzling that Dilthey failed to appreciate the importance of these lectures, which in essence offer a distinctively *original* interpretation of the sources utilized by the young theologian. Reading the preserved notes makes one wonder whether Schleiermacher's scholarly treatment of the topic did not pose difficulties for his "auditorium," which consisted mostly of young adults and children (although his lectures could also be listened to by adults).[13] The teacher probably spoke from memory, based on notes sketched out earlier, only reading out some of the more important passages. According to Virmond, apart from the final text, the following manuscripts of this composition process have survived: Schleiermacher's own preliminary notes (outlining the schema for the whole), an unfinished draft (fourteen pages), and three versions of listeners' notes. It is probable that Schleiermacher used these listeners' notes when editing his own final draft, for as a lecturer and preacher he was in the habit of speaking off the cuff, relying on very general sketches.[14] The primary source for our analysis here will be Schleiermacher's detailed manuscript, which chiefly presents the content that the author considered most important – not so much from the didactic, but from the substantive standpoint. This substantive aspect must have been important for Schleiermacher, because, as Virmond points out, he held onto the set of materials mentioned here throughout his life.[15]

Schleiermacher's primary source was the lengthy work of Johann Christoph Adelung (1732–1806), a Leipzig scholar, entitled *Ueber den deutschen Styl* (1785–1786), which was highly regarded at the time and reprinted many times, but is almost forgotten today.[16] Virmond describes this work as an uninspiring collection of information, recommendations, and anecdotes, testifying to the author's pedantry and excessive penchant for normativism,[17] but this opinion seems too harsh.

First of all, it should be noted that Adelung was a continuator of the work of Johann Christoph Gottsched (1700–1766), who had promoted a "rational art of rhetor-

---

11 Cited after: Dilthey, *Leben Schleiermachers*, vol. I/1, 57.
12 Ibid.; Dilthey did not consider these materials of scholarly interest, as evidenced by his remark in the appendix to *Leben Schleiermachers*, vol. I/1, 63.
13 See Virmond, "Bemerkungen," 252.
14 Ibid., 250; see Nowak, *Schleiermacher – Leben, Werk und Wirkung*, 53.
15 Virmond, "Bemerkungen," 251.
16 This is evidenced, for example, by a short surviving note from a very productive reading of Adelung: *Notiz zu Adelung "Über den Styl,"* KGA I/14, 49.
17 Virmond, "Bemerkungen zu Schleiermachers Schlobittener Stil-Vorträgen von 1791," 252–253.

ic" (as in the title of his treatise, *Grundriß zu einer vernunftmäßigen Redekunst*, 1729), while working on the project of a uniform German written language.[18] At the foundation of his reform of German was the slogan raised by the proponents of the rational, Enlightenment-era model of rhetoric: "only he who is understood will be able to convince another."[19] Gottscheld's project for the German literary language involved conforming to the norms of speech in line with classical rhetoric: *puritas*, *perspicuitas*, *ornatus* and *decorum*.[20]

Adelung, in turn, set himself the task of completing Gottsched's work, and since this task required further normalization and propaedeutics, he published works that were exemplarily pedantic and prescriptive, as Virmond rightly observed.[21] These included a textbook on linguistics and grammar (*Umständliches Lehrgebäude der deutschen Sprache*, 1782), an extensive dictionary (*Grammatisch-kritisches Wörterbuch der hochdeutschen Mundart*, 1774–1786), and the aforementioned work *Ueber den deutschen Styl*, which Schleiermacher drew upon. As the author of a monograph on style, Adelung was a fairly typical representative of his epoch, the late Enlightenment – a period still dominated, on the one hand, by the rationalist theory of rhetoric, involving concern for the purity, common intelligibility and conceptual clarity of the German language, while on the other hand, a process was already underway whereby stylistics was becoming emancipated as an independent discipline, guided by its own logic.[22] Both this rationalistic element and the focus on proper linguistic expression can be found in Schleiermacher, who adopts the Enlightenment ethos of clarity so evident in Adelung, in some places adhering quite closely to his source. But, as Virmond rightly notes, the young theologian, unlike the author of *Ueber den deutschen Styl*, does not confine himself to the stylistics of the German language, instead greatly expanding his scope of inquiry. In other, mainly propaedeutical aspects, he does narrow his perspective and makes adjustments to Adelung's classification of the properties of good style.[23]

However, by drawing upon Adelung, Schleiermacher situated himself not only, obviously, within the Enlightenment-era tradition of interpreting (ancient) rhetoric, but also within an important cultural project – the codification and dissemination of the principles of a modern German literary language (*deutsche Hochsprache*). In this context, it is easy to understand Schleiermacher's didactic intention. The young *Hofmeister* endeavored to teach the Count's children to speak modern, univer-

---

[18] On Gottsched's vision of rhetoric see Paweł Zarychta, "Tod oder Wiedergeburt? Zur Rhetorik zwischen 1720 und 1760 in Deutschland," *Studia Litteraria Universitatis Iagellonicae Cracoviensis* 1 (2006), 143–144.
[19] Gert Ueding and Bernd Steinbrink, *Grundriß der Rhetorik, Geschichte, Technik, Methode*, 4th ed. (Stuttgart: J.B. Metzler, 2005), 135.
[20] Ibid.
[21] Virmond, "Bemerkungen," 253.
[22] Ueding and Steinbrink, *Grundriß der Rhetorik*, 104 and 111.
[23] Virmond, "Bemerkungen," 253–254.

sal literary German, in accordance with the rules of good style derived from the code of classical rhetoric. While the eighteenth century did see the decline of the dominance of Latin rhetoric (until then taught as a school subject), the art of proper speech did not lose its value, as it became the basis for effective communication in the mother tongue, especially on the level of so-called scholarly discourse, which was by then using Latin only in exceptional cases.[24]

Let us add that the undertaking itself, consisting in preparing (and possibly writing down) a set of lectures on the art of speech to be delivered as part of private tuition, was by no means an extravagant idea, and importantly, the quality of the outcome was certainly not a foregone conclusion. Of a very similar genesis was the contemporary *Theorie und Geschichte der Red-Kunst und Dicht-Kunst* (1757) by Christoph Martin Wieland (1733–1813), prepared by the author, as a private teacher in Zurich, on the basis of selected textbooks as a teaching aid for his students.[25]

Without yet venturing here into the details that will be the subject of our analysis below, let us note that Schleiermacher considers the basis of style to be the comprehensibility (*Verständlichkeit*) of a text/speech and the interest of the recipient (*Interesse*) in the content being conveyed. It is from these that he derives the four basic properties of style: clarity, appropriateness, lightness, and vividness (*Nachschrift*, KGA I/14, 510–511). Even a cursory comparison of the categories discussed by Adelung and Schleiermacher reveals that the latter omits categories associated with aesthetics, such as "melodiousness" (*Wohlklang*) and "unity of style." Rightly noting that the author of the lectures *On Style* does not emphasize, as Adelung does, the unity of expediency and beauty (*Zweckmäßigkeit – Schönheit*), Virmond nevertheless hyperbolizes this difference, claiming that Schleiermacher "abstracts away from the aesthetic quality of the text."[26] But while Schleiermacher does assume, as we shall soon see, that clarity is the basic precondition for successful communication, thus eliminating from the canon of communicative stylistics such essentially ambivalent aesthetic categories as "ambiguity," this does not mean that he constructs an art of expression devoid of aesthetic import.

Virmond therefore tries to present the understanding of style revealed in the lectures in such a way as to demonstrate that, for Schleiermacher, style is something general, supra-individual – something that enables interpersonal communication. At the same time, however, Virmond is unable to link this understanding to the realm of aesthetics, because he does not find in it a direct reference to the notion of beauty.[27]

---

[24] See Dietmar Till, "Rhetorik und Stilistik der deutschsprachigen Länder in der Zeit der Aufklärung," in *Rhetorik und Stilistik* (HSK 31/1), 115. Till, however, seems to overlook the topicality of issues related to rhetoric (especially elocution) in the "post-Latin" era of the emancipation of reason.
[25] Ueding and Steinbrink, *Grundriß der Rhetorik*, 110.
[26] Virmond, "Bemerkungen," 255.
[27] Ibid., 256.

Similarly problematic, in Virmond's view, is the relation of Schleiermacher's stylistics to his hermeneutics. On the one hand, by laying bare the importance of understanding, his stylistics does somehow relate to the concept of general hermeneutics, while on the other hand, by teaching how to make one's speech as comprehensible as possible, it is – in an obvious way – the flip side of hermeneutics.[28] Let us note that without bringing into play the notion of dialectics, the realm of speech and thought, the relationship between the two domains will be construed either in a trivial way (the two doctrines being complementary, with "hermeneutics providing some guidance on how to improve one's style" – as Virmond writes[29]), or as intricate and opaque. Nevertheless, the philological value of Virmond's study of the Schlobitten manuscripts of interest to us is undeniable, as is his identification of Schleiermacher's distinctive stylistics against the backdrop of Adelung's treatise that he made use of.

3 Scientific contextualizations of the lectures *On Style*: hermeneutics, dialectics, dogmatics, and rhetoric

An interesting attempt to appreciate the value of Schleiermacher's lectures *On Style* is presented in Manuel Bauer's monograph. Like Wolfgang Virmond before him, Bauer also considers their relation to Schleiermacher's theory of hermeneutics. Following the suggestion of the publisher of the first volume of KGA, Günter Meckenstock, Bauer states that "themes that will play an important role in [his] later hermeneutics"[30] make themselves felt in in the remarks *On Style*. This mainly concerns the notion of understanding texts, albeit viewed "from the other side," from the perspective of production rather than reception.[31] And herein lies a fundamental difficulty, for the notions of both understanding and misunderstanding figure in the lectures on style in a different context than in the later lectures on hermeneutics, if only because in the former they are linked to a rather rigid norm of correct, that is, communicative style. Merely noting the presence of these concepts in the discourse on style, however, tells us little about this discourse's relation to the discourse on hermeneutics; similarly, asserting the alleged complementarity of Schleiermacher's early stylistics to his hermeneutics does not tell us much.[32] If, in comparing the stylistics of Schlobitten with the hermeneutics of Halle and Berlin, one can speak of a complementarity at

---

28 Ibid., 258.
29 Ibid.
30 Bauer, *Schlegel und Schleiermacher*, 212.
31 Ibid., 213.
32 Ibid., 221.

all, it is primarily due to the explicit references to dialectics, a point to which I will draw attention in the present analysis.[33]

The concept of translation does not appear in the interpretation presented by Bauer, but he does draw attention to Schleiermacher's definition of style – very important in our context – as "*Mitteilung der Gedanken*,"[34] as a vehicle that makes possible "the communication of thoughts." The domain of style, then, would be the transformation of thought into linguistic form. This is, as Bauer stresses, an approach opposite to the hermeneutical theory of language formulated by Schleiermacher in his later years, according to which thinking is identical with speaking.[35] On that later view, language is not something external to thinking, but this is still suggested by the lectures on style, which in this respect fit into the paradigm of classical rhetoric. In this case, however, the argument that the early "rhetorical" Schleiermacher is closely linked to his later, hermeneutical writings would be quite feeble. Bauer's claim that Schleiermacher's conclusions have the character of a "fundamental hermeneutics"[36] would also be questionable, since the young theologian's consideration of the question "how to make oneself intelligible to others?" does not refer to the meaning of the concept of hermeneutics that Schleiermacher later recognized as scientific and worthy of urgent interest.[37]

As is evident, we cannot arrive, by way of simplification, at an interpretation of the lectures *On Style* that would demonstrate the text to be of a proleptic nature. Its relation to Schleiermacher's later works – especially those dealing with the art of interpretation (especially of literary texts) and aesthetics – is often problematic. With regard to the latter, Bauer argues, developing Virmond's point, that the lectures *On Style* almost entirely ignore the aesthetic aspect, which was so crucial to the Romantics.[38] Nevertheless, as we shall see, this aspect is indeed visible, although Schleiermacher does undoubtedly place particular emphasis on clarity of linguistic expression, manifesting his skepticism about the "eccentricities" of so-called *belles lettres*. Bauer is quite right to argue that it is difficult to see Schleiermacher as a Romantic in this respect, although this conclusion seems rather vague and based on a stereotypical image of Romanticism. Other contextualizations of the lectures *On Style* seem more interesting and heuristically productive: I have already mentioned rhetoric, the philosophy of language and dialectics, as well as hermeneutics – albeit viewed

---

33 Dialectics is mentioned by Bauer in passing, when discussing the problem of listening/writing in the lectures on style, emphasizing that Schleiermacher's dialectics, as a "dialogue-oriented philosophy," continues his earlier considerations on stylistics (ibid., 218). This, however, is a considerable simplification of Schleiermacher's dialectics. In any case, however, the idea of dialectics clearly manifests itself in the considerations on style.
34 Ibid., 213.
35 See ibid., 214.
36 Ibid., 216.
37 See Friedrich Schleiermacher, *Hermeneutik und Kritik*, ed. Manfred Frank (Frankfurt am Main: Suhrkamp, 1977), 75.
38 Bauer, *Schlegel und Schleiermacher*, 219–220.

primarily from a stylistic perspective. Translation, closely related to these fields, also appears as an interesting context for these considerations.

In their comprehensive compendium *Grundriß der Rhetorik*, Gert Ueding and Bernd Steinbrink write that Schleiermacher is the author of "many works and lectures inspired by rhetoric," mentioning hermeneutics, criticism, and aesthetics, though they do not further clarify the nature of this inspiration.[39] However, they do so in relation to religious rhetoric and homiletics, pointing out that Schleiermacher as a preacher continued the Enlightenment rhetorical model of "religious speech" understood as a "dialogical process."[40] This remark puts us onto an interesting line of inquiry, for we must remember the connection of *On Style* to dogmatics, bearing in mind that its author was a theologian and pastor. This context is not taken into account by Bauer, although for Schleiermacher intelligibility as a virtue, and the "phantom of incomprehensibility" as a threat, are inseparably inherent in scholarly language in the domain of theology. And it is from this circle of considerations that we can delineate, it seems, the simplest path leading to hermeneutics.

In the context of Schleiermacher's theory of the *Glaubenslehre* (*Christian Faith*), the notion of "critical style" plays an important role, occurring first and foremost as a "conscious stiving for pureness of the language of dogmatics."[41] If discourse on faith, thanks to which it shows itself to be a science (*Wissenschaft*), is to take the form of contemporary scientific reflection, it must exercise self-control, which is a virtue of any work that deserves to be described as scientific (*wissenschaftlich*). This form uses clear and transparent language, maintaining a critical distance from the biblical discourse, which is not always clear and comprehensible. This distance crucially involves a certain dialectically grounded ordering of concepts. That is why, as Scholz reminds us, in the *Christian Faith* we read about the "dialectical character of language," which enables dogmatics to become a science:

> Dialectical language is too sharp for every other religious message [*religiöse Mitteilung*] [...], yet the systematic order would never emerge so clearly (...) if it did not use a language that allows for a strict discourse, similar to the operation of counting, allowing all possible relationships and connections to be tried and checked.[42]

Dogmatics thus enters the world of scientific discourse through the gateway of a critical, analytical style. It demands that theologians should "find, for every fact of

---

[39] In the context of hermeneutics, however, H.-G. Gadamer provides an important clue by linking rhetoric to Schleiermacher's hermeneutics with the Greek concept of *techne* (*Kunstlehre*). See Hans-Georg Gadamer, *Rhetorik und Hermeneutik*, in idem, *Gesammelte Werke*, vol. 2: *Hermeneutik II* (Tübingen: Mohr Siebeck, 1986), 290.
[40] Ueding and Steinbrink, *Grundriß der Rhetorik*, 151.
[41] Heinrich Scholz, *Christentum und Wissenschaft in Schleiermachers Glaubenslehre – Ein Beitrag zum Verständnis der Schleiermacherschen Theologie* (Berlin: Arthur Glaue, 1909), 80.
[42] Cited after: ibid.

pious awareness, the most precise and apt expression."[43] Schleiermacher distinguishes three types of language in which piety can be expressed: lyrical, epic, and didactic. The first of these, born of emotion, arouses enthusiasm, the second appeals also to thought and will, while the third appeals to the realm of reason, because it is oriented towards reaching understanding. This is why the science of faith, which uses such language, is characterized by a "dialectical style."[44] Scholz aptly points out that this tripartite division resembles the division into three levels of thinking in the *Dialectics:* "commercial," "artistic," and "pure," with knowledge being the objective of the latter. Knowledge is also the domain of Christian dogmatics, which is able, if possible, to *translate* the pictorial aspect of faith into the dialectical (for these are, as Schleiermacher taught, two sides of the same coin).[45] The clarity and certainty of style are in this context a precondition for the successful transformation of ambiguous, intuitively comprehensible images into comprehensible and ordered thoughts that can function as elements in the process of religious communication. Style thus conceived constitutes a tool of dialectics, rendering the content of faith verifiable and communicable, moving from the domain of individual experience and poetic expression into the domain of conceptuality, pure thinking, and thus science. In my understanding, the lectures *On Style* lay the preparatory groundwork not only for the subsequent projects of Schleiermacher's *Dialectics*, but also, via philosophical dialectics, for his dogmatics.

This is a good stage – in this particular context and already at this stage of our deliberations – to draw attention to the role that the concept of *translation* plays for Schleiermacher in the realm of human communication. Properly recognized stylistic norms and well-chosen rhetorical devices will make it possible to translate the language of biblical stories into the language of dogmatics, but also – as he stresses – to translate Christianity from the language of dogmatics into the language of the church community (if only in his own sermons, which he himself was a virtuoso at delivering), preserving at the same time the invariant of "intellectual culture" acquired together with theological knowledge.[46]

As I have suggested above, when reading the lectures on stylistics composed in Schlobitten, one should be aware that the connection between Schleiermacher's reflections in them and his later hermeneutics is not so simple and obvious. If, taking our cue from Norbert W. Bolz (and referring back to Goethe's well-known *dictum*), we understand style as a faithful representation of some inner essence of the person expressing themselves, and thus consider it to be an object of interest in hermeneutics, we have to stipulate the reservation that Schleiermacher at that time was not interested in the depths of what is peculiar/idiosyncratic (*eigentümlich*), individual, and

---

[43] Ibid., 80–81.
[44] Ibid., 81.
[45] Ibid., 82.
[46] Ibid., 85. Scholz's particularly apt description of the task facing young theologians is based precisely on the concept of translation and emphasizes the role of intellectual refinement.

demanding of hermeneutical effort, but rather in what is communicable, and thus universal.[47] And it is precisely for this reason that Bolz's claim that "each work creates its own terminology" would be viewed negatively by the author of the notes *On Style*, as a phenomenon that hinders communication and demands to be overcome through the conscious application of transparent style. If, as Schleiermacher argued as a theorist of hermeneutics and criticism, "untranslatability (non-transferability) is the limit of the community" (*die Unübertragbarkeit ist die Grenze der Gemeinschaft*),[48] then in the light of the stylistics he expounded in Schlobitten, the fundamental normative value is translatability, which forms the basis for interpersonal community. In discussing the norms of speaking and writing, Schleiermacher declares his belief in the intersubjectivity of human thinking and experience. As Bolz rightly points out, in Schleiermacher's hermeneutics, what is individual and idiosyncratic is not expressed via the definitions and concepts contained in language, but through sequences of images – such as we encounter in literature.[49] In his stylistics, the same rational forms that would block the expression of individuality are nevertheless a guarantor of intersubjectivity, straightening out what is convoluted in language and illuminating what is opaque.

The problem of translation, as it appears either explicitly or implicitly in the lectures *On Style*, has so far not received due attention. The presence of this problem in Schleiermacher's argumentation is significant in that it makes us aware of the positioning (*die Verortung*) of reflection on translation within the broader framework of the pre-Romantic discourse of the humanities. In fact, as Volker Kapp notes, "until the eighteenth century, translation theory developed in explicit or implicit relation to rhetoric, including by the use of rhetorical categories."[50] Given that one of the oldest and most influential texts on the art of translation is *De otimo genere oratorum* (*The Best Kind of Orator*) by the master rhetorician and rhetorical theoretician Marcus Tullius Cicero, whose influence can be seen in most of the significant texts in early translation theory from Jerome to Luther to Tytler, this connection between *translatio* and *rhetorica* may indeed seem inseverable. Given that the late eighteenth century was a crucial time when the Romantic approach to translation, revolutionary in many respects, was emerging, it is therefore important to observe how rhetoric was then understood, especially in the texts by authors who had a decisive influence on that approach (Herder, Schleiermacher, the Schlegel brothers). One particularly interesting aspect here is that a certain dislike for classical rhetoric is noticeable among the Romantics, related with an aspiration to establish elocutionary rhetoric as a separate discipline in its own right – namely as the discipline of stylistics,

---

[47] Norbert W. Bolz, Friedrich D.E. Schleiermacher: "Der Geist der Konversation und der Geist des Geldes, in *Klassiker der Hermeneutik*," ed. Ulrich Nassen (Paderborn: Schöningh, 1982), 115.
[48] Cited after ibid.
[49] Ibid.
[50] Volker Kapp, "Zum Verhältnis von Übersetzen und Rhetorik," in *Übersetzung – Ursprung und Zukunft der Philologie?*, ed. Christoph Strosetzki (Tübingen: Gunter Narr, 2008), 19.

which was to be based on the science of language.⁵¹ But were such attempts to wrest the craft of elocution out of the framework of classical rhetoric sufficiently justified and fortuitous? This question played an important role in the critical reflection on rhetoric in Romantic texts, giving rise to many interesting observations.⁵² By analogy, we can also ask: Was it really the case that the references to rhetoric mentioned by Kapp no longer appear in the Romantic discourse on translation, because they had lost their *raison d'être* in the "new" (hermeneutic) paradigm of translation theory? It is in this context that Schleiermacher's reflections *On Style* from 1791 make for a very interesting source, especially in comparison with his later views.

4 Style and communication: Analysis of the lectures from Schlobitten

Having examined the context of Schleiermacher's lectures, let us now turn to analyzing their content. Style, he states at the outset, is the art of communicating our ideas by means of signs (KGA I/1, 365).⁵³ We are unable, Schleiermacher contends, to communicate directly anything that flows from the "soul" (*Seele*), neither "thoughts," nor "concepts," nor "sensations."⁵⁴ The language of signs is our only resort. If we wish to set a standard in this domain ("good style"), therefore, it will be a way of properly expressing ideas in the language of signs, that is, a way that makes the recipient understand the sign and relate it to the corresponding "thing" (*Sache*).⁵⁵ Understanding a sign consists in linking it to the "thing" it expresses. This connection must be so expressive that the impression triggered by the sign should immediately evoke an image of that thing in the mind. In terms of this connection, Schleiermacher classifies signs into "natural," "essential," and "arbitrary" types (*natürliche, wesentliche, willkührliche*).⁵⁶ Signs of the first type are the "effect" of the thing signified, those of the second are connected to it by "resemblance," while those of the third type are linked to the thing only by "agreement," by convention (KGA I/1, 365).

The essence of the sciences and the fine arts consists in expressing thoughts and sensations by means of such signs, and so each of them may be ascribed its own style. Gestures and sounds are natural signs of what we experience, and the art of

---

51 Ibid., 18–19.
52 See the work of Paul de Man, especially *The Rhetoric of Romanticism* (New York: Columbia Univ. Press, 1984).
53 The notion of the sign also appears in this context in Adelung's § 7 of his work on style. See Johann Christoph Adelung, *Über den deutschen Styl*, 2nd ed. (Berlin: Vossische Buchhandlung, 1807), 3.
54 The soul also appears in Adelung, cf. ibid., § 30, 12. He does not, however, draw a line between thought and words; errors of speech are errors of thought; see ibid., § 24, 8–9.
55 Cf. here Adelung's general and normative definition of style (ibid., § 23); see also his remark on understanding as the realization of the main intention of speech (ibid., § 30).
56 Adelung here distinguishes only between 'necessary (essential)' and 'arbitrary (accidental)' signs, see ibid., § 8, 3.

appropriate (suggestive) use of such signs makes up "mimical and musical style." Essential signs appear in the domain of painting and sculpture: here the "style of the fine arts" renders experiences visible. Poetry and speech, on the other hand, employ natural language, which, in Schleiermacher's view is based on arbitrary, conventional signs. This is where the "style of the language arts" emerges (*die sprechenden Künste*) – the main subject of the lectures (KGA I/1, 365). These semiotic distinctions thus bring us into the realm of elocutionary rhetoric, i.e. the utterance, which is essentially the art of *translating* thoughts into words.[57]

Natural language is a system of arbitrary signs, which appear in "audible," i.e. phonic, or visible, i.e. graphic form.[58] But only phonic signs directly refer to concepts, because graphic signs refer first to sounds, and only via them to concepts (KGA I/1, 366). There are, therefore, styles of "direct" and "indirect" signs – the style of speech and the style of writing (the terms "grand style" and "small style" appear in the *Postscript*; KGA I/14, 506). This approach shows the influence of Aristotle, who wrote in Περὶ Ἑρμηνείας (*On Interpretation*): "Spoken words are the symbols of mental experience and written words are the symbols of spoken words."[59] Schleiermacher notes on this occasion that each language also has its own internal stylistics, since in each language the ratio of graphic signs to sounds and the impression the latter produce in the recipients is different (KGA I/1, 366). Here there comes into play a key issue in Schleiermacher's thought, namely that of *difference*, which – usually connected with the question of relativism on the level of thought and language – brings up the problem of *translation* (a topic I will discuss in more detail in the final chapter of this book).

As far as written language is concerned, good style means imposing on the writer a rigor which will enable him to express his thoughts in an orderly and clear form that facilitates the reception of the message. Even in intimate correspondence, after all, clarity and appropriateness of expression are important, and misunderstandings resulting from clumsy style are to be avoided. The connection between thinking ("signs in our souls") and speaking/writing is also important: they must be closely connected, otherwise we cannot understand one another properly, or communicate what we have in mind to others (KGA I/1, 367). Another benefit of knowing good style is confidence in the field of literary critique – it refines our sensitivity to beautiful writing, to objective beauty, not to the "illusory splendor" of empty effect (KGA I/1, 367). Here the aesthetic, receptionist aspect of the theory developed by Schleiermacher makes itself evident. Note that he focuses on rational and comprehensible beauty, rather than on beauty that is mysterious, paradoxical, and not susceptible to rational judgement.

Such stylistics teaches us how to manipulate signs so that they remain in proper relation to the things they signify, and in correct relation to one another. It is the art of

---

[57] Jakub Lichański, *Co to jest retoryka?* [What Is Rhetoric?] (Kraków: Wydawnictwo Oddziału PAN, 1996), 19.
[58] This is a development of Adelung's thought from *Über den deutschen Styl*, § 1, 1.
[59] Aristotle, *On Interpretation*, trans. E. M. Edghill (Adelaide: Univ. of Adelaide, 2015), 2.

selecting and ordering signs. But, perhaps surprisingly, it also consists in the proper handling of *thoughts* – selecting and ordering them. Schleiermacher realizes that he exposes himself to criticism here. Is it not the case that "that which concerns only expression [*Ausdruck*] does not belong to style proper"? (KGA I/1, 367). No, he replies, for "individual *thoughts* are also signs, referring to our general state of mind [*Gedankenzustand*]," and are thus subject to selection (KGA I/1, 368). The aim of stylistics is to ensure that what we communicate is clear, intelligible, persuasive, while avoiding unnecessary associations, which are often incomprehensible for the recipients. Note that Schleiermacher problematizes here the definition of elocution as the art of translating thoughts into words. For the order of thoughts is not something given and ready-made, even in the sense in which it manifests itself in the concept of figures of thought, which assumes that they have a natural, "proper" order and deviations therefrom – an "artificial" order justified by persuasive objectives.[60] If there exists a "natural" state that is the initial point for the process of articulation, it is in the form of some stimulus, scheme, or idea that needs to be introduced into the system of communication, translated into the language of signs. The listeners' notes to these lectures indicate that thoughts are "the true signs of a certain source idea [*Grund Idee*]," which "in itself" the speaker is either unable or unwilling to express, depending on "whether it is a sensation [*Empfindung*] or a dry concept [*Trockener Begriff*]" (KGA I/14, 508). If we were to refer in this context to the notion of the "original" content that is being subjected to translation, it would be, on this view, emotional or intellectual content that exists outside the realm of concrete *communication*, which is at the same time the realm of *(mutual) understanding*. This would not be a stage before linguistic conceptualization, but rather the point of departure for the conceptual integration of the message.[61] With some caution, this may be likened to the relationship between a general *topos*, as an "original phenomenon"[62] and a certain already ordered pattern of invention. In sum, Schleiermacher states that for the intelligibility and attractiveness of persuasive utterances, the selection and ordering of thoughts is just as important as the choice and arrangement of words (KGA I/1, 368; KGA I/14, 508).

Note that Schleiermacher here complicates the classical account of the relation of thought to language, which finds its expression in the rhetorical concept of appropriately dressing one's thoughts up in words.[63] First, as we already know, he defines stylistics as "the art of communicating our ideas through signs" (KGA I/1, 365), then observes, "this art would indeed be something inferior if we limited ourselves to merely dressing our raw main thoughts [*Hauptgedanken*] in words" (*Nachschrift*,

---

60 Mirosław Korolko, *Sztuka retoryki: Przewodnik encyklopedyczny* [The Art of Rhetoric: An Encyclopedic Guide] (Warsaw: Wiedza Powszechna, 1990), 112.
61 Vyvyan Evans, *A Glossary of Cognitive Linguistics* (Edinburgh: Edinburgh Univ. Press, 2007), 54.
62 Korolko, *Sztuka retoryki*, 62.
63 Czesław Jaroszyński and Piotr Jaroszyński, *Podstawy retoryki klasycznej* [Foundations of Classical Rhetoric] (Warsaw: Wydawnictwo Sióstr Loretanek, 1998), 54.

KGA I/14, 507; cf. KGA I/1, 370). The young theologian is here invoking a simple model of communication, based on the metaphor of Latin *vestire:* here the speaker/writer dresses his thoughts up in appropriate words (signs), while the hearer/reader discovers his thoughts by correctly interpreting the words (decoding the signs).[64] In Schleiermacher's view, this process of transformation goes deeper and is more complex, as it also applies to the matter of thought itself, which is thus incorporated into the space of communication. In his later reflections, he would try to link thinking and speaking even more closely, following his intuition that we identify our thoughts as elements functioning in the space of signs (language), which has an intersubjective character, being a *common* space.[65]

Let us return to the lectures *On Style*. The function of stylistic devices, according to Schleiermacher, is to get the recipient to "grasp our thoughts," that is, to *understand* us and, moreover, to *take an interest* in what we want to convey (KGA I/1, 369). We must, therefore, choose our signs in such a way as to objectify our ideas and impressions and to ensure that they exert the proper impact. What evokes certain feelings in us, via our individual way of translating thoughts into signs, may not necessarily be understandable and effective in communication with others. We should therefore turn what is subjective, referring only to ourselves, into what is objective, referring to mankind in general (KGA 1/1, 369).

How does style emerge? Every art composes its works out of component parts: Schleiermacher calls these the *means* of that art, which taken together comprise the *potential* (*Vermögen*) of that form of art. Just as harmony and melody make up the potential of music, so the potential of the *art of expression* in writing and in speech is constituted by the choice and arrangement of one's words and sentences and – as we already know – of one's thoughts themselves (KGA I/1, 370).

The art of good style, in Schleiermacher's view, is the art of successful *transfer:* If we cannot organize our thoughts and objectify them in such a way (by relativizing what is closest and most important to us) that they become comprehensible and interesting to the recipient, the act of transfer will be a failure and we will not get our message across to the receiver. The writer must also take into account that not everything that is meaningful and interesting to him or her will be considered so by the readers. Looking at this issue from the perspective of the recipient, Schleiermacher contends: "Here, too, he [the writer] must transfer his interest to me – either by generalizing his case so that it might concern me myself, or by means of stimulating in me an interest in participation [*das Interesse der Theilnahme*]" (KGA I/1, 372). The key word here is *Übertragung*, meaning transfer, transmission, and at the same time translation, not only etymologically but also conceptually related to this process, because translation is a type of transfer overcoming difference. It is worth noting already at this point that the notion of transfer will play a very important role in Schleiermach-

---

64 Max Black, *The Labyrinth of Language* (New York: Mentor, 1968), 65–66.
65 Schleiermacher, *Hermeneutik und Kritik*, 361.

er's later philosophy – especially his ethics and psychology. Transfer is linked, not only in this case, to understanding, which in turn is linked to the relation between the subjective and the objective and to the difference that defines these two domains. For Schleiermacher, the possibility of understanding and being understood by another person are key issues[66] related to the transfer of knowledge, impressions and emotions, which draw together hermeneutics, dialectics, rhetoric, psychology, and ethics.

Reflecting on the problems connected with optimal communication of our ideas, i.e. the kind of communication that results in understanding and interest on the part of the recipient, Schleiermacher interestingly describes a certain mechanism of misunderstanding:

> Certain ideas have an effect [*Nachdruck*] on us which they do not have on other people. We want to communicate the same to them. We do not think that it will be difficult to find suitable signs for them, and make use of a quite ordinary ones, the first that come to mind, which are certainly sufficient for us, as a characteristic to remind us of an idea which has great clarity and vividness for us, but not for others to instill this idea in them in the first place. I convey to them a subjective idea, whose objective meaning does not reach them […] (KGA I/1, 371–372).

There is, therefore, a fundamental mismatch here between an intention to objectivize some conceptual content and the incomprehensible, subjective message that actually reaches the recipient. This mismatch results from the unfortunate selection of signs which, though they are meant to evoke a specific idea in the recipient's mind, fail to do so, resulting in obscurity and unsuccessful transfer. Similar misunderstanding can also occur at the level of drawing detailed connections between ideas and concepts. Schleiermacher speaks here of "confusing the subjective with the objective" (KGA I/1, 372). This problem can be seen not only on the level of understanding, but also in terms of arousing the interest of the audience in receiving the message. The author of the utterance must *transfer* his own engagement in the subject (*das Interesse […] übertragen*), arousing empathy in the recipient, he must draw him or her into the subject, objectifying what is to become the subject of the recipient's interest (KGA I/1, 372).

Style is also strongly influenced, Schleiermacher argues, by the mutual relation of the three "rules" (*Gesetze*) which shape the content of our ideas: senses, reason, and imagination (KGA I/1, 373). The senses are oriented towards what surrounds us, reason concentrates on a fixed point that ensures conceptual unity, whereas imagination essentially knows no bounds. The latter is the least disciplined "rule," and it operates even when we think we remain within the domain of perceived reality or the rational point of reference we have chosen. The limits of imagination "are set by the whole stock of our concepts, which gives it a free field of action." (KGA

---

[66] See Wilhelm Dilthey, *Die Entstehung der Hermeneutik*, in *Materialien zur Ideologiegeschichte der deutschen Literaturwissenschaft*, Band 1, ed. Gunter Reiß (Tübingen: Max Niemeyer-Verlag, 1973), 55–68.

I/1, 373). At the same time it has, as Schleiermacher says, a combinatorial character, not a truly creative one, because it only creates "new combinations of old ideas" (KGA I/1, 373). This is not, therefore, the same imagination of which the Romantics usually spoke.[67] Nevertheless, it has the power to produce sequences of secondary ideas or connotations (*Nebenvorstellungen*). Since imagination does not always submit to the rigors and laws of our reason, neither does it always follow the reason of another human being. This obviously affects our reading and comprehension:

> It therefore sometimes happens that, during the assimilation of individual representations [*beim Lesen von einzelnen Vorstellungen*] our imagination takes the opportunity to develop, according to its own laws, new sequences of them which, interweaving with the original ones, counteract the main ideas [*Hauptideen*] and divide the attention of the audience. The craft of writing consists in keeping them under control and being able to play with them (KGA I/1, 373).

Note how modern is Schleiermacher's approach to the process of reading, and more generally to the poetics of production and reception. The reader's imagination organizes the message according to its own "laws," develops its own strings of associations and connotations, and enters into a dialogue with the main ideas of the text, often gaining the upper hand in this dialogue. A good writer is able to foresee and capitalize on this property of imagination, which is in fact an integral part of the reception process, inviting it into a (controlled) game (*das Spiel*).[68] We are talking here about one of the foundations of narrative art – the mechanism of *lector in fabula*.[69] Following in the footsteps of Schleiermacher, one might add that the translator is an "amplified" reader and author, being simultaneously receiver and sender in the process of transfer.[70] His activity is a kind of game with the differentiating mechanisms of

---

67 See on this subject Jean Starobinski, "Jalons pour une histoire du concept d'imagination," in idem *L'oeil vivant II* (Paris: Gallimard, 1970), 173–195.
68 By referring to the concept of game/play, Schleiermacher becomes part of the German aesthetic discourse employing the notion *das Spiel* – a discourse co-shaped by Kant and Schiller, *inter alios*. For the philosopher from Königsberg, play in the domain of literature is the opposite of a persuasion-oriented, prearranged rhetorical game, just as freedom is the opposite of compulsion based on manipulation – Immanuel Kant, *Critique of Judgement*, trans. Werner S. Pluhar (Indianapolis, Hackett, 1987), 197 (§ 53). Schleiermacher, however, does not write about manipulation, but rather about influencing the reader's imagination. His understanding of the rhetoric of writing is reminiscent of the somewhat later concept of Friedrich Schlegel, who distinguishes between the "analytical writer," who draws the empirical reader into his game, and the "synthetic writer," who "constructs and creates a reader as he should be." At the same time he does not want "to make a specific impression on the reader, but enters into a [...] relationship of [...] sympoetry" – idem, *Friedrich Schlegel's Lucinde and the Fragments*, trans. Peter Firchow (Minneapolis: Univ. of Minnesota Press, 1971), 157.
69 Cf. Umberto Eco, *Lector in fabula* (Milan: Bompiani, 1979).
70 The concept of the amplification of the output product of creative work was, of course, further developed by the Romantics, who thematized reflection, criticism, and indeed reading itself as amplified in the act of creative reception. Novalis perceived the "true reader" as an amplified, or "extended author" (*der erweiterte Autor*), someone who works creatively upon the material provided to

transfer, including those about which the young theologian writes (subjective–objective, denotation–connotation).[71]

Thus, Schleiermacher concludes, if we take the above-mentioned difficulties – those of defining the objective and the subjective, and of mastering the element of connotation – and juxtapose them with the main intentions of style (intelligibility and suggestiveness), we arrive at four general properties of style: "clarity" (*Klarheit*), "appropriateness" (*Angemessenheit*), "lightness" (*Leichtigkeit*) and "vividness" (*Lebhaftigkeit*) (KGA I/1, 373–374). *Clarity* of style, in Schleiermacher's view, consists in the ability to express oneself in such a way that no doubts arise as to the meaning of the ideas conveyed. If, in turn, the thoughts are expressed in such a way that no associations arise that run contrary to the author's intentions, then we are dealing with *appropriate* style. Schleiermacher situates these two qualities of style in the domain of the imagination. The next two qualities are related to suggestiveness, in other words, arousing the recipient's interest. For when ideas are expressed in such a way that the recipient may recognize them as his or her own, we can speak of *lightness* of style. If, on the other hand, certain associations (connotations, images) arise that serve to enhance his or her interest, this is indicative of a *vivid* style (KGA I/1, 374).

These qualities of style are related to the four virtues of expression in classical rhetoric, which are usually taken to include correctness (*latinitas*), perspecuity (*perspicuitas*), appropriateness (*aptum*), and ornamentation (*ornatus*)[72] and are considered to have their source in distinctions drawn by Aristotle. And indeed, in the Stagirite's *Rhetoric* we do find categories that seem to be the model for Schleiermacher's set of distinctions. According to Aristotle, clarity, or perspicuity, is "one of the chief merits" of style (in his discourse, style is *lexis*),[73] because "speech, if it does not make the meaning clear, will not perform is proper function"[74]; at the same time it should be distinguished by *appropriateness* with respect to its object, that is, it should correspond to its quality (triviality, commonality, sublimity, etc.).[75] Appropriateness is therefore in this context the key to the credibility of the reality presented. Both Schleiermacher and Aristotle, in speaking of appropriateness, are concerned with the proper reception of a message, i.e. one that is essentially consistent with the code of the speaker. If dissonant elements appear in it, that means imperfect style

---

him by the author – Novalis, *Fragmente I*, ed. Carl Seelig, Herrliberg-Zürich 1945 (*Gesammelte Werke*, vol. 2), 44.

71 Cf. in this context Fritz Paepcke's remarks on the translator's game as a kind of heuristic: Fritz Paepcke, *Übersetzen zwischen Regel und Spiel*, in *Im Übersetzen leben – Übersetzen und Textvergleich*, ed. Klaus Berger, Hans-Michael Speier (Tübingen: Gunter Narr, 1986), 127.

72 Korolko, *Sztuka retoryki*, 99.

73 Aristotle, *Rhetoric*, trans. J. H. Freese, in *Aristotle in 23 Volumes*, vol. 22 (Cambridge, MA: Harvard Univ. Press, 1926), 351 (1404b), in *Perseus Digital Library*, ed. Gregory R. Crane. Tufts University. www.perseus.tufts.edu (accessed 20 May 2022).

74 Ibid.

75 Ibid.

has led the recipient astray (either by means of deviant associations, or through a sense of oddness or strangeness of the presented things).[76] Aristotle also introduces two other categories that can be perceived as counterparts to *lightness* and *vividness* in Schleiermacher's taxonomy. Firstly, *naturalness* of speech, appearing in the rhetoric as the opposite of artifice in prosaic style (the Stagirite here gives examples of inappropriate use of lexical means of expression, thus distinctly linking artifice with the category of inappropriateness),[77] and secondly, *picturesqueness* of style. The latter is created by means of "words that signify actuality," (Gr. ἐνέργεια) which "set things before the eyes,"[78] mainly through "proportional metaphor." Aristotle, like Schleiermacher after him, also speaks about the dynamism of a story, meant to surprise and interest the viewer.[79] As an example of a vivid style, Aristotle cites passages from Homer. This effect of pleasant surprise, for example, by means of an apt metaphor, is connected, for the author of *Rhetoric*, with the effect of teaching the hearer something, through the mechanism of thwarted expectations,[80] which, in turn, is connected with the hermeneutical effort required to read metaphorical expressions correctly. Understanding thus intermingles with suggestive influence.

5 Obstacles to communication: vagueness, ambiguity, and incomprehensibility

Schleiermacher's lectures offer a detailed discussion of particular determinants of good style and means of achieving the desired stylistic effects, but the author also points very clearly to the consequences of deviations from the rules that he considers normative. Such deviations pose obstacles (*Hindernisse*) to communication, rendering it ineffective, and as a result, cause misunderstanding and miscommunication between the speaker and the hearer. Adherence to the norms of clear style is required by the pragmatics of communication, but also by a sense of elementary respect for the hearer. For it cannot be, as Quintilian ironically observed in his *Institutio Oratoria*, that "we regard it as a real sign of genius that it should require a genius to understand our meaning."[81]

Schleiermacher here invokes an important theme of reflection in which rhetoric is intertwined with dialectic, the art of clearly communicating ideas interwoven with the art of thinking, of operating with clear ideas. The basis of this affiliation is, on the one

---

76 Ibid., 353 (1404c).
77 Ibid., 359 (1405b).
78 Ibid., 405–7 (1411b).
79 Ibid., 408–9 (1412a).
80 Ibid. In such cases, Aristotle writes, when a conclusion "turns out contrary" to the hearer's expectations, his "mind seems to say, 'How true it is! but I missed it." Ibid., 408–9 (1412a).
81 Quintilian, Institutio Oratoria, Loeb Classical Library edition, vol. III, 1920. https://penelope.uchicago.edu/Thayer/E/Roman/Texts/Quintilian/Institutio_Oratoria/8A*.html (accessed 20 May 2022)

hand, the Platonic tradition of dialectics as the science of understanding ideas, and on the other hand, Aristotle's analytic of rational (*logical*) thinking.[82] This intertwining clearly comes to the fore already in the oldest stylistic treatises, for example in Περί ιδεών λόγου (*On the Ideas of Speech*) by Hermogenes of Tarsus, the title of which is often translated as *On the Types of Style*.[83]

The subject in question had been taken up by philosophers interested in the problem of human thought, and in particular language as a medium of rational discourse. Already St. Augustine emphasized that the purpose of speech is to support successful communication, an effective exchange of thoughts based on understanding.[84] The real challenge for the participants involved in communication is to overcome the distance between "the world of ideas and the material body, which is the main obstacle in the process of communication."[85] An important role is played here by the material sign, which is the word – the carrier of meaning.[86] Thus, as the Polish scholar Ryszard Pankiewicz remarks, the success of communication is determined primarily by "the moment of choosing the sign," as "language does not automatically imply unanimity in the way words are received."[87] Pankiewicz writes, commenting on Augustine's views:

> The ideal is for [...] the way the speaker understands his own speech to be received and understood by the hearer in the same way, despite the fact that regardless of the intention, the sound of the mouth differs fundamentally from the image created in the mind, not to mention its distorted reflection in the memory [...].[88]

In Augustine's writings it is very clear that stylistic norms, which are the foundation of successful communication, have their relevance in the context of dialectics, which can be (metonymically) understood as a treatise on the problem of (verbalized) incongruence of thought. Since the times of Socrates, such incongruence has been inscribed in the domain of communication, dialogue whose object is knowledge. In this domain, dialectics is not only a tool of communities building the foundations of knowledge, but also – as Schleiermacher stresses – a means which "conditions com-

---

[82] See the entry "Dialektik" in *Historisches Wörterbuch der Philosophie*, vol. 2, ed. Joachim Ritter (Basel: Schwabe, 1972), 165.

[83] Hermogenes of Tarsus, *Hermogenes' On Types of Style*, trans. Cecil W. Wooten III (Chapel Hill, UNC Press, 1997); cf. Andrie du Toit, "Galatians and the περὶ ἰδεῶν λόγου of Hermogenes: A Rhetoric of Severity in Galatians 1–4," HTS Theologiese Studies 70, no. 1 (2014), http://www.scielo.org.za/scielo.php?script=sci_arttext&pid=S0259-94222014000100049 (accessed 7 December 2018).

[84] Ryszard Pankiewicz, *Sztuka rozmawiania z Bogiem – Modlitwa a teoria komunikacji* [The Art of Talking to God – Prayer and the Theory of Communication] (Kraków: Wydawnictwo WAM, 2009), 228.

[85] Ibid.

[86] Augustine, *On Christian Doctrine, in Four Books* (Grand Rapids, MO: Christian Classics Ethereal Library), 25. http://www.ntslibrary.com/PDF%20Books/Augustine%20doctrine.pdf (accessed 1 April 2022).

[87] Pankiewicz, *Sztuka rozmawiania z Bogiem*, 228.

[88] Ibid.

munication, the exchange of ideas" (*die Mitteilung, den Umtausch der Ideen bedingt*).[89] In this context, the question of language and its mediating role in the process of communicating thoughts becomes a fundamental problem. What is more, it is connected with the issues of interlingual communication and translation, because congruence of ideas is very difficult given the incommensurability of various (arbitrary) sign systems (their "irrationality," as Schleiermacher put it).

St. Augustine was already well aware of this, since, writing about the obstacles to understanding the signs of Scripture (and thus also to *teaching* such understanding), he draws attention to the untranslatability of expressions functioning in different languages. At the same time, interestingly, he adds that the variety of translation solutions "would assist rather than hinder understanding" and "examination of a number of texts [different translations] has often thrown light upon some of the more obscure passages."[90] Understanding is, in the eyes of the Doctor of the Church, the supreme value, which style is meant to serve: clarity or correctness have their justification as virtues of style insofar as they lead the reader (of a translation of Scripture) to an understanding of the Word of God.[91] The study of the principles of speech, of rhetoric, does not bring us closer to understanding itself (logic and dialectics are more important here), but it can help people declare intelligible ideas, which is of great importance for communication itself, the exchange of "the feelings of their minds, or their perceptions, or their thoughts."[92]

For Schleiermacher's reflections, another modern context – or rather *intertext* – that makes us aware of the connections between stylistic issues and the problems of language, communication, and knowledge, situated within the realm of the philosophy of cognition, can be found in John Locke's remarks on the use of words in his *An Essay Concerning Human Understanding* (1690). This is an especially interesting line of inquiry in that the British empiricist's name has not figured very prominently in the context of research on Schleiermacher's work.

Locke's intention was to create a description of the workings of the human mind that could "liberate people from fruitless metaphysical wranglings" (J.D Peters) and set them on the path of rationality.[93] In Book III of his *Essay Concerning Human Understanding*, Locke writes about the obstacles to communication that have their source in the imperfection of language and the unskillful use of words, leading to misunderstandings and ambiguities.[94] According to Locke, language is supposed to serve the purpose of a quick and simple exchange of "thoughts" or "ideas," which

---

[89] Friedrich Schleiermacher, *Dialektik (1811)*, ed. Andreas Arndt (Hamburg: Felix Meiner, 1986), 6.
[90] St. Augustine, *On Christian Doctrine*, 30.
[91] Ibid., 56.
[92] Ibid., 25.
[93] John D. Peters, "John Locke, the Individual and the Origin of Communication," *Quarterly Journal of Speech* 75, no. 4 (1989): 389.
[94] John Locke, *An Essay Concerning Human Understanding*, ed. Peter H. Nidditch, The Clarendon Edition of the Works of John Locke (Oxford: Oxford Univ. Press, 1975), 490. (Book 3, Ch. X, § 1).

5 Obstacles to communication: vagueness, ambiguity, and incomprehensibility

aims to convey knowledge about the world.[95] If it does not fulfill this task, that means it is "abused or deficient."[96] Note that Locke introduces stylistic norms guided by considerations relevant to dialectics, which presupposes optimal communication and the attendant understanding of others' words and the ideas they are linked to, which enable confusion to be avoided when the discussion concerns human concepts and artificial obstacles that "impose upon our understandings."[97] The danger of the misuse of words is great, because language is, the philosopher argues, arbitrary, consisting of signs connected to ideas in human minds, not to things – as, for example, St. Augustine believed.[98] Importantly, they are linked "not by any natural connexion" (as in that case there would be a single common language), but "by a voluntary imposition."[99] Since "words in their primary or immediate signification stand for nothing but the ideas in the mind of him that uses them,"[100] we are often inclined to think (wrongly) that a misunderstanding at the level of words must signify some fundamental differentiation at the level of concepts and things, rather than a problem related to signifying itself.[101]

Of particular interest in the context of Schleiermacher's lecture are Locke's remarks on rhetoric, with which he closes his argument about the "abuse of words." The philosopher writes here about "figurative speeches," about operating with allusions.[102] Well, if our aim is to speak about "things as they really are," rhetoric, teaching eloquence based on artificiality and figurativeness, is not useful, and it can even be harmful.[103] Only its teaching of the "order and clearness" of speech can be considered useful here.[104] Other rhetorical devices can lead us to the wrong ideas, for example by stirring our emotions and leading to false judgments. These are "arts of deceiving," writes Locke.[105]

And so, wherever *truth* and *knowledge* are concerned, rhetoric should be used with utmost caution – especially elocutionary rhetoric, which teaches poetic style. Nevertheless, the question of elocution, of style, is very important in the context

---

[95] Ibid., 504 (Book 3, Ch. X, § 23). At the same time, an idea, which Locke calls a "determined" (or in other words, "clear and distinct") idea, is meant "to signify some immediate object of the mind, which it perceives and has before it, distinct from the sound it uses as a sign of it" – ibid., 13 (Book 1, "Epistle to the Reader").

[96] Ibid., 504 (Book 3, Ch. X, § 23).

[97] Ibid., 488 (Book 3, Ch. IX, § 21). Cf. also § 22, explaining that ancient writings, "though of great concernment to be understood, are liable to the unavoidable difficulties of speech, which [...] is not capable, without a constant defining the terms, of conveying the sense and intention of the speaker, without any manner of doubt and uncertainty, to the hearer."

[98] Peters, *John Locke*, 390–91.

[99] Locke, *An Essay Concerning Human Understanding*, 404 (Book 3, Ch. II, § 1).

[100] Ibid., 405 (Book 3, Ch. II, § 2).

[101] Peters, *John Locke*, 390–92.

[102] Locke, *An Essay Concerning Human Understanding*, 508 (Book 3, Ch. X, § 34).

[103] Ibid., 405 (Book 3, Ch. II, § 2).

[104] Ibid., 508 (Book 3, Ch. X, § 34).

[105] Ibid.; cf. John D. Peters, *John Locke*, 397.

of Locke's views, since he writes often about the relation between thought and its (linguistic) expression, suggesting that specific content may be expressed in different ways, by different (linguistic) forms, according to the choice of the speaker. This line of thought comes to the fore, in my opinion, in the following passage of the "Epistle to the Reader" that opens the *Essay Concerning Human Understanding:*

> There are few, I believe, who have not observed in themselves or others, that what in one way of proposing was very obscure, another way of expressing it has made very clear and intelligible; though afterward the mind found little difference in the phrases, and wondered why one failed to be understood more than the other. But every thing does not hit alike upon every man's imagination. We have our understandings no less different than our palates; and he that thinks the same truth shall be equally relished by every one in the same dress, may as well hope to feast every one with the same sort of cookery.[106]

Locke writes here about stylistic variants, which Nils Erik Enkvist defines as "different ways of expressing the same content."[107] Their existence is conditioned by a kind of "mental dualism," implying the possibility of choosing between different forms in which a given thought can be *dressed*, a choice that defines the style of the utterance.[108] Note that this approach opens the way to considerations of ambiguity, near-synonymy, precision and opaqueness of terms, which were an important part of normativist stylistic treatises such as Schleiermacher's. Moreover, it prompts deliberation about the issues of linguistic expression and the transfer of thought (which are present in Schleiermacher's *Dialectics*)[109] and, relatedly, translation. To sum up, it is worth noting that in Locke we are dealing with a critique of rhetoric from the point of view of an empiricist philosopher who dreams of substantive communication uncontaminated by the imperfections of language.[110] On the one hand, this criticism refers *de facto* to the idealistic assumptions of Plato's dialectics (with obvious conceptual differences), understood as a critical analysis of concepts "aimed at bringing about the truth of knowledge or discussion."[111] On the other hand, it is based on Aristotle's concept of meaning, according to which it is the result

---

106 Locke, *An Essay Concerning Human Understanding*, 8 (Book 1, "Epistle to the Reader").
107 Nils Erik Enkvist, *Stilforskning och stilteori* (Lund: CWK Gleerup Bokförlag, 1973), 99.
108 Ibid.
109 It is worth mentioning in this context that in his *Dialectics* of 1814/15 Schleiermacher was critical of the skeptical (as he put it – but in fact: pragmatic) belief that people can communicate with each other while having different ideas about the object of communication. Commentators on this passage of the *Dialectics* relate these words to Locke's *An Essay Concerning Human Understanding*, although there is no direct evidence in support of such a connection (*Dialektik 1815/15*, KGA II/10.1, 178).
110 See Peters' remarks on the utopia of undistorted communication through natural science: Peters, *John Locke*, 393.
111 Wojciech Chudy, "Dialektyka" [Dialectics], in *Powszechna encyklopedia filozofii* [General Encyclopedia of Philosophy], ed. Andrzej Maryniarczyk et al., vol. 2 (Lublin: Katolicki Uniwersytet Lubelski, 2001), 562.

5 Obstacles to communication: vagueness, ambiguity, and incomprehensibility — 47

of an agreement, which means that words "are neither true nor false by their nature"; rather, they can be used properly or not.[112]

Schleiermacher's stylistics is dominated by a rational element, and there is an evident intention to subject the elements of language to conscious control, so that words used incorrectly or inopportunely do not evoke "wrong ideas" (*falsche Ideen*; KGA I/1, 375). When Schleiermacher speaks of "incorrect words, which do not express what we want to express through them" (KGA I/1, 374), it is hard not to associate his concern that language can deceive us and lead communication astray with Locke's remarks outlined above.

Gottfried Wilhelm Leibniz – whose views on language later interested Schleiermacher[113] – also demonstrated a critical evaluation of the role of language as a medium in communication, the subjects of which are ideas. Leibniz overtly critiqued Locke (while at the same time polemicizing with that criticism) in his *New Essays on Human Understanding* (written 1704, published 1765), composed in the form of a dialog. Speaking through the "empiricist" Philalethes, Leibniz offers a rebuttal to Locke's *Essay*:

> words interpose themselves to such an extent between our mind and the truth of things, that we may compare them with the medium, across which pass the rays from visible objects, and which often spreads a mist before our eyes; and I have tried to think that, if the imperfections of language were more thoroughly examined, the majority of the disputes would cease of themselves, and the way to knowledge and perhaps to peace would be more open to men.[114]

Leibniz's Philalethes then continues this argument by discussing the most common ways in which words are misused, most notably: the habit of linking words to vague ideas, giving colloquial terms "unusual meanings," the belief that words correspond to real things, and misuse as "figurative terms or allusions"[115] The latter refer, as in Locke, to the art of rhetoric. Philalethes claims that "all the art of rhetoric, all these artificial and figurative applications of words, serve only to insinuate false ideas, to excite the passions and seduce the judgment, so that they are nothing but pure frauds."[116] Here he repeats Locke's argument from the *Essay on Human Understanding*. Such a harsh criticism of rhetoric is mitigated by his interlocutor, Theophilus (who can be identified in many ways with Leibniz himself), who reminds us that "certain rhetorical ornaments are like Egyptian vases, which you could use in the worship

---

[112] Kazimierz Leśniak, "*Wstęp tłumacza*" [Translator's Introduction], in Aristotle, *Hermeneutyka*, in *Dzieła wszystkie* [Collected Works] vol. 1 (Warsaw, PWN, 1990), 67.
[113] See his lecture at the meeting of the Prussian Academy of Sciences on 7 July 1831 (KGA I/11, 709–717).
[114] Gottfried Wilhelm Leibniz, *New Essays Concerning Human Understanding*, trans. A. G. Langley (London: Macmillan, 1896), 375.
[115] Ibid., 389; cf. ibid. 376, 378, 380.
[116] Ibid., 389.

of the true God."[117] Rhetoric, like the art of painting and music, can be "usefully employed" to "render the truth clear" and to "make it effective."[118] This is the compromise conclusion, one might say, that Leibniz arrives at, appreciating the role of rhetoric, and in particular of elocution and of style in communication (Theophilus even draws attention to the stylistic and discursive function of obscurity in Pythagoras).[119] This point seems to be the philosophical basis of Schleiermacher's considerations, in which the key role is played by "intelligibility" (*Verständlichkeit*) and "interest" (*Interesse*) (KGA I/1, 374). The whole artistry of stylistics consists in mastering the elemental nature of words so that they act as an effective intermediary between the minds engaged in communication. An effective mediator stimulates understanding and growth of knowledge, seeking to avoid misunderstanding and uncertainty. Finally, there is a hermeneutical and philological dimension to this ethics of discourse: "if it is difficult to understand the meaning of the terms used by the people of our time, it is much more difficult to understand the *ancient books*," notes Leibniz's Philalethes.[120] This is the track that Friedrich Schleiermacher would follow in his later inquiries.

Clarity, in Schleiermacher's analysis, is the most important stylistic feature of an intelligible utterance and at the same time the basis of good style (KGA I/1, 374). As the theologian explains, clarity stimulates comprehension – it makes the recipient understand our thoughts, as if he himself had derived them from the given thing. Clarity can be achieved through the proper selection and appropriate arrangement of the parts of speech, that is, words and sentences. In selecting words, we consider their importance with respect to other words; mistaken choices here lead to obscurity and incorrect argumentation, and therefore to "intellectual incomprehensibility."[121] Obscurity is caused by words whose meaning is "inappropriate," "uncertain," and "unknown" (KGA I/1, 374). Thus they stand in the way of mutual comprehension, as hermeneutical obstacles on the path to understanding.

We express ourselves unclearly when, for instance, the matter to which we refer is foreign to us or when we have to use new words, borrowed from other languages. Here it often happens that we associate a word with an inappropriate idea (KGA I/1, 375), lapsing into error and introducing confusion into our communication. Errors can also be caused by the very process of the constitution of new knowledge on the basis of the still forming language, which has to keep pace hitherto unknown conceptual distinctions, creating new terms, performing internal (intralingual) transfer or borrowing words from other languages (KGA I/1, 376).

---

117 Ibid., 390.
118 Ibid., 390.
119 Ibid., 379.
120 Ibid., 371 (italics in original).
121 Jerzy Ziomek, *Retoryka opisowa* [Descriptive Rhetoric] (Wrocław: Zakład Narodowy im. Ossolińskich, 1990), 129.

5 Obstacles to communication: vagueness, ambiguity, and incomprehensibility — 49

Semantic ambiguity is above all an important problem of the art of translation. Schleiermacher notes:

> most often this kind of ambiguity arises in the course of translation, when one comes across a word in the language from which one is translating that can have several meanings. Then one often reaches for a word in the target language which in this case does not match the meaning – not because of misunderstanding, but because it is too easy to assume an analogy of expression in the two languages. And so complex expressions in one language must have a completely different compositional form in the other language in order to make similar sense and to be similarly understood (KGA I/1, 376).

This brings up the issue of the differences between languages in the realm of expression. A failure to take into account the fact that different languages express particular ideas in different ways leads to translation errors at the level of re-expression, which is largely at the level of style. The correct approach here would be to recognize not identity, but *difference* in means of expressing meanings and to search for a linguistic expression that ensures adequate understanding on the part of the recipients of the translation. Languages differ from one another, they are not rational creations, and so they are not structured in the same way. Schleiermacher later expanded upon this thought in his lectures on dialectics (beginning in 1811), grappling with the problem of the relativity of knowledge (*Relativität des Wissens*).

The observation in question here, then, leads to the conclusion that assuming an analogy on the level of expressions (especially word-compounds) can lead the translator astray. Schleiermacher knew very well what he was writing about, since he himself had produced translations into German, and had certainly not steered clear of difficult texts, such as Aristotle's *Nicomachean Ethics* and *Metaphysics* (1789; see KGA I/1, 47–125 and 167–175). It seems that drawing upon his own practical experience was natural for him, and at the same time cognitively stimulating, as the rhetorical (stylistic) context shed interesting light on the problem of translational re-expression, revealing the key significance of the stylistic impact of the translated text and the resulting reception of the translation. The latter may be perceived either as a "bright" text, or as a "dark" one, incomprehensible and so of little value. I would venture to say here that this very contextualization, or in other words, attempt at a scientific problematization of the art of translation, became the starting point for the reflection that led Schleiermacher, on the one hand, to what would become his penetrating remarks on the linguistic aspects of translation, and on the other – perhaps even more importantly – to a practice of translation that was marked by functionalism, which he demonstrated with virtuosity in his translations of Plato's dialogues. I will come back to this issue, but already here I would like to underline the connection between the functional method of translation and the rhetorical tradition,[122] especially with the norms of proper articulation (*elocutio*), and the aware-

---

[122] See on this subject Piotr de Bończa Bukowski, "Słowo w retorycznej teorii przekładu" [The Word

ness of this relationship that is evident in Schleiermacher's lectures on style from 1790/1791.

In Schleiermacher's (and also Adelung's) view, an important source of the ambiguity of an utterance lies in the *polysemy* of expressions, the ambiguity of those having two or more meanings (KGA I/1, 376).[123] Often a single word denotes different concepts that are linked by resemblance, sometimes it happens that a word undergoes so many shifts over time that its meaning merges with an originally different expression. It is also often the case that on the level of concepts there is a transfer (*Übertragung*) of one semantic domain to another, which can cause confusion for the reader. This kind of ambiguity related to polysemy is somehow a natural affliction of language and occurs everywhere. Locke, whom we cited earlier, would consider them to be the result of the "imperfection of words."[124] Because multiple senses are often inherent in fairly common expressions, such as those describing relationships, a language user may not even realize that he or she is lapsing into ambiguity, thinking that the expression he or she has used is sufficiently clear, or at least becomes so in context. Nevertheless, this approach is mistaken, because it

> assumes a great understanding between the hearer and the speaker, whereas one should rather assume a proclivity for misunderstanding, because even when some clarification appears here, it is usually too late, and so what follows will not be understood either, since what preceded it was not understood (KGA I/1, 377).

Schleiermacher here formulates the initial thesis of his later hermeneutics: that every act of communication is burdened with the risk of *misunderstanding* to such an extent that such misunderstanding has to be presumed as a fact.[125] Acknowledging this fact is the beginning of the path to *understanding* all speech. From the perspective of text production, this risk can be reduced by resorting to explication, which consists in illuminating the thought that is "darkened" by language itself (KGA I/1, 377). Note that ambiguity is an important problem for dialectics because it deals with the transfer of ideas,[126] thereby facilitating the process of understanding. It also teaches us how to construct ideas correctly – that is, in such a way that their truthfulness

---

in the Rhetorical Theory of Translation], in *Słowo – kontekst – przekład* [Word – Context – Translation], eds. Joanna Dybiec-Gajer, Anna Tereszkiewicz (Kraków: Tertium, 2014), 15–26.

123 This source was pointed out in classical rhetoric, see for example Aristotle, *Rhetoric for Alexander*, trans. E.S. Forster, in *The Works of Aristotle*, ed. W.D. Ross (Oxford: Oxford Univ. Press, 1924), § 25, 1435b.

124 John Locke, *An Essay Concerning Human Understanding*, ed. Peter H. Nidditch, in The Clarendon Edition of the Works of John Locke (Oxford: Oxford Univ. Press, 1975), 490. (Book 3, Ch. X, § 1).

125 See *Allgemeine Hermeneutik 1809/10*, KGA II/4, 73; AB 227: "Hermeneutics rests on the fact of the non-understanding of discourse."

126 In Thomas Pfau's terms: "the discursive mediation of different representations": Thomas Pfau, "Immediacy and the Text: Friedrich Schleiermacher's Theory of Style and Interpretation," *Journal of the History of Ideas* 51, no. 1 (1990): 65.

5 Obstacles to communication: vagueness, ambiguity, and incomprehensibility — 51

and usefulness in constructing knowledge can be assessed.[127] Difficulties (theoretical and practical) are caused here by all changes and manifestations of instability in the meaning of words on the intralingual plane and by the lack of semantic symmetry on the interlingual plane.[128] The latter is obviously a problem of translation, one aspect of which is polysemy.

Schleiermacher continues his argument by pointing out that words whose meaning is not known to everyone, such as foreign words, archaisms, provincialisms, and neologisms, may also give rise to difficulties in understanding (KGA I/1, 378). Words borrowed from foreign languages can become established in the target language if, having been in common use for a long time, they gain a kind of naturalized status. Thus, borrowings are linguistic migrants of a sort, incomers from a foreign world, whose presence is justified when there are no native words conveying the same meaning. They appear most often when foreign influences penetrate the native culture, as happened in Germany in the second half of the eighteenth century:

> Foreign words had to penetrate our language, for we were so quickly inundated with fashionable French thought that our language, which lacked the proper fashion, could not keep up and find expression for all those subtleties and concepts which had suddenly become familiar to a large share of our nation. At the same time, this was taken too far, without good reason or benefit, using foreign words for which equally beautiful and expressive synonyms could be found in the treasury of the mother tongue – only to avoid being accused of ignorance of foreign thought (KGA I/1, 378).

Note that Schleiermacher presents the French influence as a rather negative phenomenon: it is no accident that he speaks of an "inundation" of French culture, challenging the natural development of language and the equally natural formation of new concepts. In addition to necessary borrowings, related to cultural development or the existence of lexical gaps, there are always unjustified borrowings, the result of fashion, snobbery, ignorance of the native language or laziness. On this ambivalent ground grows the common phenomenon of the "mixing of languages" (*Vermischung der Sprachen*), which – not least because of the association with the Tower of Babel – has clearly negative connotations. Schleiermacher would develop this idea in a very interesting way later, in his lecture on the art of translation (*On the Different Methods of Translating*, delivered at the Prussian Academy of Sciences), in which, speaking of the challenges of foreignizing translation, he refers to the concept of language "mixing," juxtaposing its negative connotations with a certain positive cognitive effect:

> Who would not want his native language [*Muttersprache*] to appear in the resplendence most characteristic of his people and of each individual genre? Who would willingly breed mongrels [*Blendlinge*] when he could instead sire loving children in the pure image of their father? (DR 232; KGA I/11, 81)

---

127 See *Dialektik, Kolleg 1811 (Nachschrift Twesten)*, KGA II/10,2, 8.
128 See *Dialektik, Aufzeichnungen zum Kolleg 1811*, KGA II/10,1, 58.

The exaggerated, unjustified borrowing of foreign words often provokes a reaction in the form of purism, seeking to prevent the phenomenon of language-mixing – Schleiermacher notes (KGA I/1, 378). Purists want to eliminate all foreign words from the native tongue, striving for purity of style, which consists in being predominantly uniform and familiar. Schleiermacher recognizes the usefulness of purism, stressing that a native-tongue equivalent of a foreign word has two important advantages: flexibility in word-formation (which is important for the creation of compounds) and a kind of neutrality on the connotative level, whereas borrowings "always evoke a connotation of foreignness," often against the speaker's intentions (KGA I/1, 379). Nevertheless, he takes a rational position in this context, bearing in mind the principles of communication and knowledge construction: for if a foreign word is widely used while its native equivalent is not widespread, a borrowing will convey the concept in question with greater clarity than the native equivalent (KGA I/1, 378).

In Schleiermacher's view, a language that is still developing will adopt many foreign words, while discarding from time to time words that are no longer adequate for its current level of refinement (*Bildung*). This means archaic words, dating back to earlier stages of the language's evolution. However, too hastily disposing of native words, combined with too much susceptibility to foreign impulses, may attest to a certain weakness of a national language, and thus of the nation itself. Schleiermacher cautions the Germans:

> a nation such as ours, which has received so much from outside, and in whose case the imitative drive [*der Nachahmungstrieb*] ran so clearly ahead of its own good sensibility, consequently had to become acquainted with the character and predominance of its language and, while disposing of what was bad, also disposed of good things as well (KGA I/1, 379).

His reflections on style are thus part of broader political reflection about what is native vs. what is foreign. As in the case of translation, it becomes necessary to consider the overall tally of gains and losses involved in opening up to foreignness. The "imitative drive" does not discredit a nation, after all, it may even help strengthen it, by absorbing and integrating valuable foreign elements into the native stock. In fact, this may even fortify its intellectual power and moral greatness (as a *hospitable* nation). This idea had been developed by Herder, Goethe (through the concept of *Weltliteratur*) and the Romantics. At the same time, as the discourse under discussion shows, this tendency should be cultivated in such a way that it does not counteract the formation of what can be called, following Schleiermacher, the nation's "own good sensibility."

This essentially metaphysical quality guarantees the coherence and identity of the language and the nation that uses it. A wise national policy, therefore, should also be based on maintaining the right balance between embracing what is foreign and cherishing what is familiar – tradition and memory. To this day, this still remains one of the most important tasks of German liberal-national policy. For centuries, one

5 Obstacles to communication: vagueness, ambiguity, and incomprehensibility

of its main slogans has been the enriching assimilation of valuable foreign spirituality into the domain of the German language, a strategy that consists in stimulating the development of the German spirit through borrowing and imitation. In *On the Different Methods of Translating*, Schleiermacher emphasizes the special role of translation in this process of building and consolidating German cultural supremacy, stating:

> it seems that our respect for the foreign and our mediatory nature together destine the German people to incorporate linguistically, and to preserve in the geographical center and heart of Europe, all the treasures of both foreign and our own art and scholarship in a prodigious historical totality, so that with the help of our language everyone can enjoy, as purely and as perfectly as a foreigner can, all the beauty that the ages have wrought. This seems, in fact, to be the true historical goal of translation for all people in all periods, as it already is for Germans today. (DR 238; KGA I/11, 92)

It is not difficult to see how consistently the author of these words, starting from his youth, addresses the problems of national culture, while at the same time remaining free of nationalistic rapture in the style of Fichte.

But which words in a language should be deemed archaic, outdated; which should be avoided in stylistically sophisticated texts? According to Schleiermacher, the basic criterion here is comprehensibility (*Verständlichkeit*): therefore words that refer to outdated and forgotten concepts, which in their anachronism are difficult to grasp and sound foreign to modern speakers of German, are bad choices (KGA I/1, 379–380).[129] The use of such words usually contradicts the main aim of stylistics, as understood by the theologian, i.e. the clear, understandable, and at the same time effective exposition of a thought.

This same criterion underlies Schleiermacher's negative opinion of provincialisms; they, too, can interfere with the understanding of utterances, because they are used by regional communities and usually fall within a low linguistic register (colloquial language). Although provincialisms are often components of a comic style in which spoken language is mixed with written language, for an educated audience it is more important for the content of a mental picture to be clear and intelligible than for a colloquial style to be imitated with precision (KGA I/1, 380). Here again, the motif of the mixing of languages – in this case colloquial and standard language, and thus also low and middle and high style – appears in Schleiermacher's discourse. Even in the domain of "comic novels" he is reluctant to accept hybridization, "mixing." Above all, he fears that the audience will be unable to understand the "attitudes," "(world)views" (*die Gesinnungen*) of the characters speaking. For if they are presented in an obscure, unclear, inconsistent form, they may be misunderstood or not understood at all.

---

[129] Schleiermacher borrows examples of such words from Adelung.

Schleiermacher also analyses the stylistic value of specialized language, involving the use of words "defining concepts [...] which belong to the system of a certain science or art" (KGA I/1, 380). These concepts can also be expressed in more commonplace ways, but because of the economy of language, which tends towards using simple signs for complex concepts, specialized nomenclature continually gets developed. If specialized words make it easier to understand the state of affairs being described, the use of such words, Schleiermacher feels, is by all means justified. Moreover, it may even be necessary, so as "not to hinder their understanding through the use of paraphrases and neologisms" (KGA I/1, 381). This is most often the case with scientific dissertations. However, if such words have an illustrative or erudite function and are referred to or quoted in a figurative discourse, then they often explain "something incomprehensible in terms of something else incomprehensible" (KGA I/1, 381) and so are undesirable.

In this context, Schleiermacher criticizes the ludic use of specialized languages in fiction, even in the form of pastiche, as in the plays of August von Kotzebue and the prose of Laurence Sterne. "It is likewise prohibited," we read in his lecture notes, "to seek to be witty by spinning long allegories out of unfamiliar terms and neologisms, or to induce characters to speak in such a way, purporting to be characteristic. Kotzebue. Yorik Tristram" (KGA I/1, 381). This second example from fiction is particularly interesting, as it is not at all explicit. In a footnote to this passage, the KGA editors assume that Schleiermacher is referring here to both of Sterne's major works, *A Sentimental Journey through France and Italy [By Mr. Yorick]* and *The Life and Opinions of Tristram Shandy, Gentleman* (KGA I/1, 381). The figure of Yorick, widely recognized as an *alter ego* of Sterne himself, does indeed appear in both works. But, the former text appeared in Johann Joachim Christoph Bode's translation into German under the title *Yorick's empfindsame Reise durch Frankreich und Italien* (1769), which would justify the abbreviation "Yorick" in Schleiermacher's lecture notes. The same translator published a translation of the second work, as *Tristram Schandis Leben und Meinungen*, in 1774, which had gained fame and found its way into the hands of Goethe and Herder, among others.[130] And so, while Schleiermacher may have read these texts in the original, it is more likely that he relied on the acclaimed popular translations.

The interesting thing about this example is that – put as succinctly as possible – this is literature that takes, as its theme, human communication itself, and at the same time also rhetoric and dialectics. Sterne makes direct reference, especially in *Tristram*, to Locke's *Meditations*, showing how the misuse of words and the attendant associations of ideas hinder human communication. Some scholars have even seen *Tristram* as a "fictionalized and often comic illustration of Locke's *Essay on Human Understanding*."[131] Sterne's characters blunder through the world of words and ideas,

---

130 See Zofia Sinko's, introduction to the Polish edition: Laurence Sterne, *Podróż sentymentalna przez Francję i Włochy* [A Sentimental Journey through France and Italy], trans. Agnieszka Glinczanka, ed. Zofia Sinko, 2nd edition (Wrocław: Zakład Narodowy im. Ossolińskich, 2009), LXXI–LXXII.
131 Ibid., XXVII.

while being critiqued by an ironic narrator, who "considers their bizarre thought structures [and arguments] to be an excellent source of amusement."[132] Thus, the reader is confronted with a kind of rhetoric-gone-awry, which makes us realize that language, "being the great conduit, whereby men convey their discoveries, reasonings, and knowledge," (J. Locke)[133] can also be a source of confusion, ambiguity and "darkness" (*Dunkelheit* in Schleiermacher's discourse), which can be intriguing, amusing, but also sometimes irritating. In this light, an alternative, often more effective way of communication is offered by the language of gestures, actions, glances, the "short hand" of "turns of looks and limbs" that Sterne writes about in *A Sentimental Journey*, claiming that it can be translated into the words of "any civilized language."[134]

Looking from Schleiermacher's perspective, we will notice many examples of such "allegories" constructed by the author of *Tristram*, using strange neologisms whose meaning is at the very least unclear. We can mention the discussion of rhetorical arguments in Book I of *The Life and Opinions of Tristram Shandy, Gentleman*, where one type is described as *Argumentum Fistulatorium* (i.e. "argument by piping"), or point to the character of a bitter and unkind traveler, a scholar who is given the name "Smelfungus" (actually a caricature of Tobias Smollett).[135] In both novels, however, such neologisms serve a derisive function and encourage reflection about the role of knowledge and erudition in life and their meaning when juxtaposed against "ordinary facts." They can thus be considered an element of Sterne's critical, subversive literary strategy, in fact convergent with Schleiermacher's stylistics, viewed through the prism of dialectics.

With these examples Schleiermacher concludes his analysis of words which, by their incomprehensibility (*unverständliche Worte*), can deprive a text of clarity and legibility (*Deutlichkeit*). He goes on to point out that not only the quality but also the quantity of words is of stylistic importance. Both omissions (ellipses) as well as over-explanations and redundancies can have a negative impact on the reception of a text. As in the case of single words, the process of identifying meanings and synthesizing sense, and consequently also the mental (re)construction of the transmitted knowledge, may be disrupted. The audience may, for example, incorrectly combine various "ideas" or misperceive their development (KGA I/1, 382–383). The result will be "darkness and confusion" (*Dunkelheit und Verwirrung*) (KGA I/1, 382) instead of clear understanding and ordered knowledge. In this way, Schleiermacher's lecture on good style takes a form that pre-signals his lectures on hermeneutics and dialec-

---

132 Ibid., XXXI.
133 John Locke, *An Essay on Human Understanding*, Book 3, XI, § 5.
134 Laurence Sterne, *A Sentimental Journey through France and Italy* (London: Becket and De Hondt, 1769), 67 (from the sketch tellingly entitled "The Translation"); see also Zofia Sinko, "Introduction," XLIX.
135 Laurence Sterne, *The Life and Opinions of Tristram Shandy, Gentleman* (London: Methuen, 1894), Book 1, Ch. XXI; *A Sentimental Journey through France and Italy*, 33.

tics – which indicates, I think, Schleiermacher's mental coherence and consistency, as a methodical and systematic thinker, not lapsing into dogmatism or speculative "everything-ism" (as Hegel did, for example).

In Schleiermacher's view, correct style (*der korrekte Styl*) is based on the correct choice of words, i.e. one that takes into account their mutual relations on a syntactic level (KGA I/1, 383). Again, it is inadvisable to mix together what is heterogeneous and sometimes even contradictory, such as two mismatched figurative expressions (KGA I/1, 384). Even if two expressions are linked by a thread of association, the effort that the recipient has to make to understand the author's intention must be borne in mind. "Often an expression of some kind does indeed fit with an earlier one, but the reader has to look too far to find this resemblance, so it does not express things as clearly as it should – at least not for everyone," state the young theologian's notes (KGA I/1, 384). Here the risk of misunderstanding and failed communication is very great.

Schleiermacher distinctly favors the clarity and legibility of a thought conveyed in words over innovation and linguistic creativity, manifested in surprising juxtapositions of images (omitting, of course, linguistically incorrect juxtapositions and anacoluthons) (KGA I/1, 384). The poetic effect arising from the semantic tension between different images/words, i.e. from the intriguing "mixing" of incompatible elements, for him is *not* of sufficient value to justify the violation of communicative conventions and the norms of good style. Such a "poetic" style results, in his opinion, from a multitude of uncoordinated thoughts and signs that are difficult to coordinate with them. Locke writes in this context about "subtlety" as a false virtue of style.[136]

Likewise, all idiosyncrasies and individual stylistic peculiarities are for Schleiermacher a potential source of misunderstanding – especially on the level of syntax, when only the speaker of an utterance can explain the sense of one particular ordering of words, rather than another (KGA I/1, 385). The audience, on the other hand, often gets lost in ambiguous constructions, unsure of the correct interpretation (KGA I/1, 386). Schleiermacher supposes that among languages German is the most prone to errors resulting from incomprehensible syntactic constructions. The German language leaves its users a lot of freedom in this field, but the limits of this freedom are set by the intelligibility of the sentence. That is why Schleiermacher warns against using syntactic constructions that are at odds with the nature of the German language. These very often arise due to the influence of a foreign language and the resulting exoticization of style. "Here the temptation is great, as in our country foreign languages are often read and a lot of foreign books are translated," Schleiermacher explains (KGA I/1, 387). The author is, of course, referring here primarily to the French language, whose influence on German was linked to the interest in Enlightenment literature, in the original and in translation. In connection with this, a conviction spread – one criticized by Schleiermacher – that everything "per-

---

[136] Locke, *Reflections on Human Reason*, Book 3, Ch. XI, § 5.

mitted in French" is also "worthy of imitation" in German (KGA I/1, 387). This is, however, a more general problem: any exoticization of style, consisting in the imitation of foreign linguistic constructions, appears in this light as an unnecessary complication, an unnecessary "mixing" of linguistic and stylistic idioms. It makes the target text incomprehensible, unclear. Such is the outcome of both "French" and "Greek" style applied to the German language: "And so Wieland's prose is full of French phrases; Klopstock, the Stolbergs, Voß and others multiply Greek syntagms, most of which are of no use," Schleiermacher contends (KGA I/1, 387).

This harsh assessment of the "Greek" style of Friedrich Gottlieb Klopstock, the brothers Friedrich Leopold and Christian Stolberg, and Johann Heinrich Voß offers much food for thought. These authors share an interest in the Greek metrical form, including an ambition to translate Greek hexameter into German. The first such attempt was made by Friedrich Gottlieb Klopstock, who published his *Messiah* (1773), in which he tried to imitate the form of the Homeric epic. Friedrich Leopold Graf zu Stolberg, in turn, was not only a poet and novelist (cf. KGA I/1, 387), but also a translator of the *Iliad* (1778). His brother Christian translated Sophocles' dramas,[137] while Voß, probably the most famous translator of ancient literature of those times, gained recognition for his translation of the *Odyssey* (1781) and later also of the *Iliad* (1793), being at the same time an esteemed author of poems in the ancient style. Klopstock's Christian imitation of the Homeric epic was not received with enthusiasm by everyone; for instance, the work failed to please Ludwig Tieck, who, after hearing the author recite it, criticized it for its "incomprehensible verses" and lack of panache.[138] This incomprehensibility was most probably due to a multitude of Greek syntagms, such as Schleiermacher was discussing. Besides, the theologian did not spare Klopstock any criticism; referring to his imitation of ancient poetic meters, he said years later: "we always feel foreign here and have to regret that such a great lyrical talent has resorted to such an indigestible form."[139] Starting from a similar conviction as Tieck, Schleiermacher also emphasizes in the context of Klopstock's *Oden:* "If we do not understand a certain stanza at once, we lose much of the impact of the whole."[140] Time would eventually prove the young Schleiermacher right as a critic of the otherwise brilliant Voß: in an extensive and detailed review of the *Iliad* and the *Odyssey* published in 1793, August Wilhelm Schlegel re-

---

137 The *parodos* in *Oedipus Rex*, for example, is largely written in dactylic hexameter; cf. Sophocles, *Oedipus rex*, ed. Roger D. Dawe (Cambridge: Cambridge Univ. Press, 2006), 205.
138 Karl Schön, *Über Klopstocks Epos Messias*, after: https://de.wikipedia.org/wiki/Messias_(Klopstock) (accessed 1 October 2019).
139 Friedrich Daniel Ernst Schleiermacher, *Ästhetik (1819/1825). Über den Begriff der Kunst (1831/1832)*, ed. Thomas Lehnerer (Hamburg: Felix Meiner, 1984), 145. I quote here from the "Niederschrift 1825 (B)". It was, until recently, erroneously believed to be Schleiermacher's own handwritten notes. However, this anonymous lecture postscript documents Schleiermacher's 1825 lecture on aesthetics (11.04.-09.09.1825). The text has not been included in the KGA II/14 edition. Cf. KGA II/14, LXX-LXXI (the editor's itroduction).
140 Ibid.

proached Voß for many errors and unnatural, incomprehensible solutions on the level of linguistic constructions and syntax.[141]

Schleiermacher was averse to unnatural, bizarre imitations, although he was quite tolerant of imitations of ancient poetic meters, accepting (albeit with some reservations) even Voß's rather radically exoticized solutions. At the same time, however, he had doubts as to whether these solutions, which all too often crossed the limits of linguistic naturalness, would win readers' approval.[142] This problem preoccupied Schleiermacher throughout the entire period of his scholarly activity, and it seems that with time he increasingly perceived its more general dimension, incorporating it within the framework of his philosophical reflection. In his lecture on aesthetics in 1825, this issue appears in the context of the characterization of the novel as one of the verbal arts (*redende Künste*). "Nothing is more common than a novel which shows the reader nothing foreign [...]"[143], Schleiermacher remarks at the beginning of his reflections. And he continues a little further on:

> The more poets established themselves in their own language, contributing to its development while manifesting a direct knowledge of ancient works of art, the more the question must have come to mind: to what extent is it possible to compose poetry according to ancient models? On this, we [Germans] have undoubtedly achieved the most. This also applies to translation. To see how far a language can be extended and bent without losing its specific character, however, is an issue for art and does not have to relate to the accuracy with which words can be rendered in another language, but rather has to do with the musical treatment of artistic language and with liberation from rhyme [...].[144]

Excessive adaptation of the native language to a foreign (literary) speech convention may lead to greater foreignness and the related impression of unnatural speech. As an example, Schleiermacher cites the translations of Sophocles by Karl Friedrich Ferdinand Solger (1st ed. in 1808), who tried to render the original metrical measure exactly, at the same time severely straining the reader's ear.[145] Schleiermacher next refers to the translations of the Stolberg brothers, the same ones he mentioned in his lectures on style: "The way in which the Stolbergs solved the problem – by simply adopting other lyric stanzas in their entirety, for example from Horace, in order to translate the choruses – is an example of excessive arbitrariness. But this only proves the difficulty of the problem," Schleiermacher concludes, "for translation requires the

---

[141] August Wilhelm Schlegel, *Homers Werke, von Johann Heinrich Voss*, in *Dokumente zur Theorie der Übersetzung antiker Literatur in Deutschland seit 1800*, ed. Josefine Kitzbichler, Katja Lubitz, Nina Mindt (Berlin: Walter de Gruyter, 2009), 27–28. In this context Schlegel wrote: "He [Voß] wished to adhere everywhere to the Greek order, but not as close as is possible in our language (which would be praiseworthy), but as close as is not possible" (ibid., 28).
[142] See Hermann Patsch, *Alle Menschen sind Künstler – Friedrich Schleiermachers poetische Versuche* (Berlin: Walter de Gruyter, 1986), 66–67.
[143] Friedrich Daniel Ernst Schleiermacher, *Ästhetik*, 143.
[144] Ibid.
[145] Ibid.

deepest insight into a foreign language, the most certain feel [*das bestimmteste Gefühl*] for how one language may be reflected in another, and no less artistic talent."[146]

This is one of the central problems in the German theologian's thought, one which will accompany us in this study. Artistic talent is not only an asset for writers, but equally, or perhaps even more so, a gift that allows the translator to penetrate the essence of a foreign language, to understand it, to grasp it and – without betraying the essence of his own language – to re-fashion this foreign linguistic creation out of new, familiar substance. It is a difficult challenge, but one that can be met. In this spirit, Schleiermacher notes in his lectures on aesthetics:

> I would like to believe, therefore, that just as it has been possible in our language to produce translations in which the original language shines through and shines out in all its nature, we can all the more grant to our language the right to move in the ancient form and other foreign forms in a way that is natural and does no harm.[147]

He reminds us that in the case of "literary composition," form is always "fused" with content, thanks to the "sensual power of language" which means that form is not the "poetic clothing" of the thought, but its function.[148] The key relationship in classical rhetoric, appropriateness (*Angemessenheit*) is thus not based on convention (be it ethical or aesthetic), but on the organic need for conformity between the thought and the *type of form* of expression (*Typus der Form*). This conformity cannot be lost in the act of literary communication, for that would threaten to separate and thus dissociate form from content. Unfortunately, however, this is what happens all too often in the translation of foreign texts. The result is an impression of "unnaturalness" (F. Schleiermacher)[149] or "incomprehensibility" (L. Tieck on *Messiah*). Its source is often a lack of stylistic competence, ignoring the rules of good communication or a lack of awareness of how good style stimulates the understanding of a linguistic message. These are issues discussed in great detail in the lectures *On Style* from Schlobitten. Later, in his lectures on aesthetics, Schleiermacher would reflect on these issues in even more depth, searching for an answer to the question of what style, understood as the choice of a certain form of linguistic expression, actually consists in.

Schleiermacher was inclined to believe that all experiments with the linguistic assimilation of "foreign forms" should be subjected to the reader test, i.e. a test of real communication. Experiments that produce degenerate (as the accusation of unnaturalness entails), hybridized creations fail, because in their hybridity they remain incomprehensible to almost everyone except the author himself. Schleiermacher would in principle remain faithful to this assumption, though later as a translator

---

146 Ibid., 144.
147 Ibid., 147.
148 Ibid., 145.
149 Ibid., 144.

he would here and there bend German to foreign principles, sympathizing with the maxim of *fremde Ähnlichkeit,* and as a translation theorist he would emphasize in his famous lecture what a difficult and thankless task translation in a "foreignizing" spirit is. It often involves stretching the substance of language to the limits of naturalness, which is why it often meets with criticism from readers, who complain "that this kind of translation will certainly negatively affect the purity of the language and its peaceful, inherent development" (KGA I/11, 82). But if we are dealing with a situation in which the reader is skilled in understanding things foreign, and the target language is sufficiently malleable to yield to the pressure of the foreign speech without harm, such a translation makes sense and has value (see KGA I/11, 83–84).

In his lectures *On Style,* Schleiermacher lastly moves on to the highest plane of stylistic analysis, which involves sentences – their proper selection and order – in relation to the ideas conveyed in the text (KGA I/1, 388). This is the final element in Schleiermacher's analysis of "the teaching of clarity" (*Lehre von Klarheit*). He ascribes stylistic relevance to sentence units as long as they contain "thoughts and concepts" that contribute to "clarifying, supplementing, and developing the main ideas" of the discourse (KGA I/1, 388). The explanatory function is realized by sentences that appeal to the reader via the latter's "power of judgment" (*Urteilskraft*), or "imagination" (*Einbildung*) (KGA I/1, 388). The former refers to general principles of reason, while the latter involves what Schleiermacher calls "images," understood as "all those sentences which, through a similar kind of relation, can explain the property of a given thing" (KGA I/11, 390). They are not meant to assert anything, because they do not have such power – rather, their task is, by means of similarity, to make the thing in question more graphic, more vivid (*anschaulich*) and thus also more interesting in the eyes of the audience (see KGA I/1, 359). True stylistic craftsmanship is evidenced by the aptness and legibility of the chosen images, but also by their wit (*Witz*; KGA I/1, 390). The relationship of similarity, which is crucial here, should be easily grasped by the reader, because – in Schleiermacher's notion of style – it is not an end, but rather a means: it does not create a thing, but brings it closer to the reader. Therefore ambiguity should be avoided and the order of sentences should stimulate the understanding of the text, which is the case when the sentences follow one another in such a way that each preceding one "makes the following one (if it is connected with it) more comprehensible" (KGA I/1, 390). Note that effective persuasion here is closely related to intelligibility, which has to do with the effort to translate the arrangement of conceived ideas into discourse such that it can reach the mind of the recipient in an optimal, undistorted way. The thesis that there is a dialectical dominant to Schleiermacher's stylistics, i.e. as a science that paves the way for many other considerations in which dialectics, as the basis of communication in the domain of "pure thinking"[150] plays a central role or is of vital importance, is thus confirmed here.

6 *Elocutio* and *translatio* – an attempt to summarize and contextualize

In bringing our consideration of Schleiermacher's lectures on style to a close, it will be useful to expand our perspective somewhat and reflect on their significance in the context of translation theory. The relationship between elocutionary rhetoric and translation has emerged several times in the course of our analysis: at more specific points, but also in general terms. It is hard not to notice here the basic similarity between a good rhetor and a good translator, which Rainer Kohlmayer in his study *Rhetorik und Theorie der Literaturübersetzung* examines in a multifaceted way: both perform a certain transfer, as they strive to convey a certain message (*Botschaft*).[151] Modifying Kohlmayer's discourse a bit, we might say that in both cases, a strategy of laying out the optimal route to the audience is important. Words are the vehicle here; thoughts, concepts are the object being transferred. Yet it is not always the case (despite appearances) that the orator puts his own thoughts into words, whereas the translator searches for the most appropriate expression of someone else's thoughts. Topica is not, in principle, the domain of originality, and the original, in order to be grasped in the hermeneutic act, must undergo schematization. Kohlmayer rightly writes that the purpose of both transfers is "persuasive" in nature.[152] At the same time, the point of communiation is, as rhetoric scholar Chaïm Perelman argues, "to influence one or many people, to direct their thinking," and thus to gain command of their imagination and emotions.[153] "If we want to persuade the hearer, we must first know what capacity or readiness for reception he possesses," Perelman adds elsewhere, writing about the speaker and his audience.[154] In the same way, the translator has to know the conditions under which his or her work will be received, to know to what kind of reader his or her translation is addressing, because the choice of the translation strategy depends on it. In the case of translating Plato – a challenge that Schleiermacher took on at the instigation of Friedrich Schlegel (as will be discussed in subsequent chapters) – the question can be formulated as fol-

---

[150] *Einleitung zur Dialektik 1833*, KGA II/10,1, 568: "Dialectics presents the principles of skilled conversation in the field of pure thinking."
[151] Rainer Kohlmayer, "Rhetorik und Theorie der Literaturübersetzung – Überlappungen und Differenzen," in *Unterwegs zu einer hermeneutischen Übersetzungswissenschaft – Radegundis Stolze zu ihrem 60. Geburtstag*, eds. Larisa Cercel, John Stanley (Tübingen: Narr, 2012), 135.
[152] Ibid.
[153] Chaïm Perelman, *L'empire Rhetorique: Rhetorique et Argumentation* (Paris: Vrin, 1977), 117.
[154] Cited from: Chaïm Perelman, *Logik und Argumentation*, ed. and trans. Freyr Roland Varwig (Weinheim: Beltz Anthenaum, 1994), 86.

lows: will the reader be an expert, or rather a layman for whom all signs of foreignness (e.g. Greek terms in the original spelling) will be an obstacle to understanding the work? How, in the latter case, can "the reader's thinking be directed" so that he or she can encounter Plato's thought? Or maybe the philosopher's thinking should be reshaped in such a way that it might reach the contemporary reader without too many obstacles? This is the basic dilemma that would be considered by Schleiermacher in his famous lecture *On the Different Methods of Translating* – a lecture which, as I have been seeking to demonstrate in this book, becomes fully understandable only in the light of other important texts by its author.

The art of expression, or style, plays a key role in the translation process. Kohlmayer claims, referring to the five divisions of rhetoric, that translators of fiction start their work at the level of *elocutio*, while adopting the original theme and composition of the work (*inventio* and *dispositio*).[155] This, he argues, is what distinguishes translation from adaptation or elaboration, where transformation takes place at the level of theme and/or composition. However, in many cases a translator does perform a transformation on all three levels of the text/speech produced in the original language, primarily in view of the intended recipient of the translation. There are many examples: for instance, the different (often controversial) names of the chapters of the Bible in different translations, which are not a result of the adaptation of the original. Schleiermacher's Plato, too, is perceived by many critics as the result of such a transformation of the original text, justified by philological and philosophical research, in the course of which it was transformed at the level of the statement of the problem and the argumentation, thereby becoming a fully autonomous work (as is well illustrated, for example, by the translation of the *Phaedrus*).[156]

Nevertheless, one must grant Kohlmayer's point when, taking his lead from theoretical rhetoric, he argues that the "five-canon model of rhetoric" is indeed useful if we want to create a functional schema of the translation difficulties that translators have to deal with. These difficulties (perceived by Kohlmayer as resistance that the source text presents to the translator) arise at the level of *inventio* (e.g. themes, realities of the original), *dispositio* (e.g. specific genre conventions), *elocutio* (e.g. poetic meters, dialects, jargons), as well as *memoria* and *actio* (problems of medium and implementation).[157]

Note that these difficulties, or this resistance manifested by the original in various ways, have a *hermeneutic* dimension, allowing us to link hermeneutics to rhetoric. I will look at this issue more closely in the next section. At the same time, it is clear that Schleiermacher's lecture on elocutionary rhetoric, focusing on

---

[155] Kohlmayer, *Rhetorik und Theorie der Literaturübersetzung*, 141.
[156] Giovanni Reale, *A History of Ancient Philosophy II: Plato and Aristotle*, trans. John R. Catan, 1st ed. (Albany, New York: State Univ. of New York Press, 1990), 8–11.
[157] Kohlmayer, *Rhetorik und Theorie der Literaturübersetzung*, 143–144. See in this context Joachim Knape, *Was ist Rhetorik?* (Stuttgart: Reclam, 2000), 58, whose notion of "communicative resistance" (*kommunikativer Widerstand*), informed Kohlmayer's approach.

the regulative value of fortuitous communication between sender and receiver, illuminates the two basic phases of the translation process: the (hermeneutic) phase of understanding, and the phase of re-expression. However, it is also relevant in the context of another important phase – verification.

In the domain of *elocutio*, the concept of appropriateness (*aptum*) plays an important role, which has already appeared above in our analysis of Schleiermacher's lectures on style, in the context of the "four virtues of expression." It is closely related to adequacy, defined in the context of translation theory as functional appropriateness.[158] "Adequacy or appropriateness," explains Jörn Albrecht, "[...] corresponds to an old concept from ancient rhetoric (Greek το πρέπον; Latin *aptum*). It concerns the relationship between the linguistic means of expression and the circumstances and objectives of speaking and writing."[159] This relationship can be seen as "the equivalence of style."[160] Classical rhetoric pointed out certain norms in this regard (e. g. *perspicuitas*), which could, however, be violated under certain (persuasive) circumstances.[161] Albrecht, drawing a distinction between his understanding of functional adequacy in translation and the concept of adequacy for a given purpose, as advocated by adherents of Skopos Theory,[162] clarifies: "adequacy means the same as appropriateness in terms of the 'function of the target text.'"[163] He emphasizes that this function must be, as it were, "read out" of the text, it is not simply given, but rather recognized in the hermeneutic act.[164] Adequacy, linking translation to the notion of a norm by making reference to classical rhetoric, makes us realize the importance of the communicative context of translation, situating the translator in the role of a sympathetic intermediary between the author and the reader. According to the rhetorical concept of "internal appropriateness," the speaker's role is to ensure the compatibility (or adequacy) of the thought/thing (*res*) and the word (*verbum*)[165] – to ensure the correct *translation* of thoughts into words[166]; the translator should, for the sake of this compatibility, choose words in such a way that they

---

158 Mark Shuttleworth and Moira Cowie, *Dictionary of Translation Studies* (London and New York: Routledge 1997), 5.
159 Jörn Albrecht, *Übersetzung und Linguistik* (Tübingen: Gunter Narr, 2015), 34.
160 As Stefanie Arend writes in the context of Goethe's stylistics: *Rhetorik, Stil und Verstehen: Theoriegeschichte der "Angemessenheit" (aptum) von der Antike über Goethe und Kayser bis zur linguistischen Pragmatik*, in *Gutes Übersetzen – Neue Perspektiven für Theorie und Praxis des Literaturübersetzens*, ed. Albrecht Buschmann (Berlin: Walter de Gruyter, 2015), 130.
161 "Central is the requirement of legibility and clarity, or *perspicuitas*. One should avoid any 'darkness,' *obscuritas*. The latter, however, can be used intentionally, in order to achieve a certain effect" – Arend, *Rhetorik, Stil und Verstehen*, 121.
162 See Katharina Reiss, Hans J. Vermeer, *Grundlegung einer allgemeinen Translationstheorie* (Tübingen: Max Niemeyer, 1984), 139.
163 Albrecht, *Übersetzung und Linguistik*, 35.
164 Ibid.
165 Korolko, *Sztuka retoryki*, 51.
166 Lichański, *Co to jest retoryka?*, 19.

best express the original thought and communicative intention, and most effectively reach the audience. When Johann Christoph Adelung's textbook (which, as I have already mentioned, inspired Schleiermacher) dealt with appropriateness, he argued that the writer's task is to "illuminate" a given object or thought through appropriate style.[167] The hermeneutic translator also faces a similar task: he illuminates the thought of the original by re-expressing it in the target language. In a broader sense, the tendency to explicate, clarify, and complete the original text in translation seems to be rooted in the persuasive paradigm of communication, which is pragmatic in nature and clearly recipient-oriented. If we link this paradigm to the anthropological interpretation of rhetorical theory as a repertoire of basic cultural competences,[168] the tendency takes on the character of a kind of translation *universal*.

In discussing the principle of appropriateness, Mirosław Korolko points out that in rhetoric it embraces the issues of aesthetics, stylistics, and ethics.[169] The latter plane is stressed by Alberto Gil in his considerations on the "hermeneutics of appropriateness" and translation, subordinating *aptum* together with *pulchrum* (appropriateness together with beauty) to the superior notion of *decorum*, which in his eyes synthesizes many values.[170] One of these is an awareness of the ethical dimension of communication, especially mediated communication. This encompasses a conviction that the role of the mediator is to bring about dialogue and understanding between the author and the reader of the translation. There are many routes to such understanding; Schleiermacher discusses them in his lecture *On the Different Methods of Translating*, describing the translator as someone who leads the author to the reader or the reader to the author (DR 229; KGA I/11, 74). However, for the sake of communication, the translator should not put too much emphasis on his own person. Gil puts this thought this way: "The more visible the translator wants to be, revealing his or her own *creativity*, the less transparent the message becomes, because in this way the translator becomes a veil (*Blende*) between the reader and the translator."[171] The aim here is not to depreciate the creative approach to the translation problems that proliferate while working with the original, but to keep in check the desire to display one's own creativity against *decorum* – that is, against what befits the translator and what is "purposeful" and "functional" in a given communication situation.[172] And so the method of translation based on the ancient (Roman) principle

---

167 Quoted in: Stefanie Arend, *Rhetorik, Stil und Verstehen*, 127.
168 See Peter L. Oesterreich, *Spielarten der Selbstfindung – Die Kunst des romantischen Philosophierens bei Fichte, F. Schlegel und Schelling* (Berlin: Walter de Gruyter, 2011), quoted in: Rainer Kohlmayer, *Rhetorik und Theorie der Literaturübersetzung*, 143.
169 Korolko, *Sztuka retoryki*, 50.
170 Alberto Gil, "Hermeneutik der Angemessenheit – Translatorische Dimensionen des Rhetorikbegriffs *decorum*," in *Übersetzung und Hermeneutik / Traduction et herméneutique*, ed. Larisa Cercel (Bucharest: Zeta Books, 2009), 319–320.
171 Gil, "Hermeneutik der Angemessenheit," 326.
172 Cf. Korolko, *Sztuka retoryki*, 50.

of emulation, once so popular, should be avoided, as it boils down to a rivalry between the translator and the author and is rooted in the agonistic concept of rhetoric.[173]

Note that Schleiermacher's lectures *On Style* carry a similar message when it speaks of stylistic eccentricities that obscure the message and hinder communication. In fact, as we shall see, the lecturer himself adhered to this when later translating Plato: he avoided exaggerated, brilliant creativity, exhibiting it where the author's linguistic creativity required it, and where an analogous solution was possible without excessive embellishments that might obscure the original thought. Referring back to Albert Gil's statement, we may surmise that Schleiermacher was aware "that translation as an act on the level of *parole* is ultimately interlingual rhetoric [*interlinguale Rhetorik*]."[174]

7 The further pathways of Schleiermacher's reflection: Rhetoric and style in the hermeneutic perspective

The lectures *On Style* occupy a special place in Schleiermacher's work; they seem to be an introduction to his mature philological and philosophical reflection, although – as I have tried to show – they do already contain thoughts and problematizations that would recur in his later works, in which language and communication play an essential role. The importance of Schleiermacher's reflections on the notion of style can be seen by looking at his lectures and writings on hermeneutics.

In his first known remarks on the art of interpretation (*Auslegungskunst*), Schleiermacher situated this art in a theological context, seeing it, however, as a "philological discipline" based on precisely formulated principles.[175] This first stage of his work on hermeneutics is evidenced by the preserved aphorisms *Zur Hermeneutik* (1805 and 1809) and the sketch known as *Hermeneutik – Erster Entwurf* (1810–1819). Characteristic of Schleiermacher's conception is a firm conviction that a *general* hermeneutics needed to be constructed, whose rules can be applied whenever we are dealing with a particular language or a particular genre of speech or text.[176] As Heinz Kimmerle aptly points out, this position leads to an important shift in perspective: both the Bible and the classical texts of antiquity – hitherto treated in a special way – lose their privileged position in the light of a general hermeneutics, since they "must now be understood according to essentially the same principles as all other written and oral expressions of man."[177] Therefore, even if a

---

173 Bukowski, "Słowo w retorycznej teorii przekładu," 16.
174 Gil, "Hermeneutik der Angemessenheit," 325.
175 Heinz Kimmerle, "Einleitung," in Fr[iedrich] D.E. Schleiermacher, *Hermeneutik*, ed. Heinz Kimmerle (Heidelberg: Carl Winter Universitätsverlag, 1974), 15.
176 Ibid.
177 Ibid., see KGA II/4, 6.

special *biblical hermeneutics* can be applied to Scripture, it will be based on the rules of a *general hermeneutics* (see *Erster Entwurf*, KGA II/4, 37), because the interpretation of divinely inspired texts is based on the same rules of understanding that stem from the specific nature of the communicative process: thinking, speaking/writing and understanding.

One of the most important principles of text interpretation, especially of ancient texts, consists in reconstructing the original communicative situation, including the mental horizons of the author and the reader. Schleiermacher writes about this in one of his notes: "One must try to take on the role of the original reader in order to understand the allusions, as well as the power and the particular scope of the comparisons [and also parables]" (*Zur Hermeneutik*; KGA II/4, 8). Here the scholar touches upon the question of style, which will soon prove to be an important test for the theory of interpretation. Identifying oneself with the "reconstructed" recipient of the analyzed message, as he was imagined by the sender, allows one to understand the motivation for the linguistic shape of the utterance, and thus its sense. But the road to such identification leads through rhetorical (and especially stylistic) analysis, which assumes an awareness that regardless of whether we are dealing with the Gospel or with a philosophical essay, the speaker always wants to get his message across to the hearer, ordering his thoughts, arranging them in optimally connected sequences and choosing the right, suggestive words. Schleiermacher expresses this thought clearly, for instance when opposing over-interpretations of Christ's words which indicate that the original communicative situation resulting from the text is being ignored:

> With any style it is necessary for the speaker to take into account how his hearer relates the thoughts and how he understands them, and so this applies in the New Testament as well as in other writings. Nothing may be formulated in such a way that the hearer could not possibly understand [...] (KGA II/4, 27).[178]

In his 1819 *Hermeneutics*, attempting to chart out the relationship between rhetoric, dialectics, and hermeneutics, Schleiermacher notes that speaking (*Reden*) is the communication (*Vermittlung*) of thought, both collectively and individually (KGA II/4, 120). Rhetoric is the art of the optimal coupling of thought and speech by the speaker for the sake of a specific communicative purpose, whereas hermeneutics is its opposite, the art of revealing the thoughts that have been expressed in speech. In the sense in which both these arts have within their scope of vision the process of

---

[178] This is in reference to the exegesis of Mt 8:20 undertaken by T.F. Stange in his work *Über Christi Armuth*, which was completely detached from situational context. Schleiermacher joined in the critical reviews of this author's exegetical argument published in *Jenaische Allgemeine Literatur-Zeitung* in 1805 (see the publisher's commentary in KGA II/4, 27).

"the becoming of knowledge" (KGA II/4, 120), they are dependent upon dialectics.[179] It is clear, therefore, that on Schleiermacher's approach, the concepts of classical rhetoric will be interpreted in terms of general hermeneutics.

This is evident already in his first aphorisms, in which he *rewrites* the classical theory of elocutionary rhetoric in the spirit and perspective of hermeneutics, keeping in mind his reflections on dialectics and the necessary connection between dialectics and hermeneutics. Under the umbrella of hermeneutics, he includes reflection on rhetorical semiotics (the figurative form of thought as *signifié* – the element signified; KGA II/4, 8), as well as contrastive stylistics (barbarisms; KGA II/4, 9), the theory of the three styles (KGA II/4, 11), the theory of tropes (KGA II/4, 11, 12) and problems of stylistic clarity (KGA II/4, 33). Why is such meticulous analysis of stylistic issues important to Schleiermacher? Well, because, as he himself writes, "[t]he diversity of styles nevertheless gives rise to different rules of interpretation" (KGA II/4, 13); and so an inadequate interpretation of style can lead interpretation in general astray (e.g. by attributing ambiguity to Plato where there is none).[180]

In later, fuller versions of his writings on hermeneutics (*Hermeneutics 1819* and the recovered transcript of *General Hermeneutics 1809–10*),[181] Schleiermacher seeks to deepen his analysis of style by relating it to the dialectic of the general vs. the particular in language (*eigenthümliche Sprachbehandlung*, see KGA II/4, 32, cf. *Eigenthümlichkeit des Styls*, KGA II/4, 31). Already from the first notes of *Zur Hermeneutik*, a division emerges between grammatical vs technical interpretation (cf. KGA II/4, 20),[182] the principles of which are more fully presented in the sketch *Hermeneutik – Erster Entwurf* (1805). There Schleiermacher draws a clear division: hermeneutics "starts from two quite different points: understanding in the language and under-

---

[179] "Speaking is the communication of the communal character of thinking, and from this arises the connection between rhetoric and hermeneutics and their common relation to dialectics" (KGA II/4, 120). It is of course possible – taking Radegundis Stolze's lead – to find in this passage an outline of the project of a "hermeneutical science of translation," in which understanding is connected with "formulation," but it should be remembered that Schleiermacher's project was concerned with much broader issues, situated in the space marked out by the coordinates of rhetoric, hermeneutics and dialectics – cf. Radegundis Stolze, *Die Wurzeln der hermeneutischen Übersetzungswissenschaft bei Schleiermacher*, in *Friedrich Schleiermacher and the Question of Translation*, eds. Larisa Cercel and Adriana Şerban (Berlin: Walter de Gruyter, 2015), 145.

[180] Schleiermacher criticizes the interpretation Ludwig Friedrich Heindorf gives in the footnotes to *Charmides* and *Gorgias* of two phrases used by Plato. These examples probably occurred to him because Schleiermacher was then finishing the revision of another portion of his own translations of Plato. See KGA II/4, 13.

[181] Both of these versions are cited herein in English translation from the volume *Hermeneutics and Criticism and Other Writings*, ed. Karl Ameriks and Desmond M. Clarke, trans. Andrew Bowie (Cambridge: Cambridge Univ. Press, 1998), (hereafter cited in text as "*AB*").

[182] He would later refer to technical interpretation using the term 'psychological' instead, cf. KGA II/4, 121. See Hendrik Birus, *Die Aufgaben der Interpretation – nach Schleiermacher*, in *Friedrich Schleiermachers Hermeneutik – Interpretationen und Perspektiven*, ed. Andreas Arndt, Jörg Dierken (Berlin: Walter de Gruyter, 2016), 59 and 72.

standing in the speaker," or in other words, "grammatical and technical understanding" (KGA II/4, 38). The interpreter focuses in the former case on the language itself (as a sign system), and in the latter case, on the author as a creative user of language. Of course, one-sidedness is undesirable here; in interpretive practice these two perspectives are intertwined and even interdependent (see KGA II/4, 39 and 54).

"The main point of grammatical interpretation is the elements by which the central object is defined; the main point of technical interpretation is the broad context and its relation to general principles of combination," Schleiermacher explains (KGA II/4, 38). "Grammatical" here refers us to a "common, collective schema" (*gemeinschaftliches Schema*; KGA II/4, 40), while "technical" refers to the particularized thought of the individual, shaping its substance (KGA II/4, 54). Applying this characterization to the issues of stylistics, we may hazard the claim that in the grammatical domain there is style understood in a *functionalist* way (as a supra-individual, social entity, constituted by a clear reference to the linguistic norm and typicality), while in the technical domain there is style construed *individualistically* (as a form of the creative expression of the individual).[183] "In the same way as spirit is the manner of thought, style is the manner of representation," states the transcript of *General Hermeneutics 1809/10* (AB 255; KGA II/4, 102). And so a lot of space in his notes and lectures will be devoted by Schleiermacher to style understood as "particularity of representation" (*die Eigenthümlichkeit der Darstellung*) (KGA II/4, 55).

In technical interpretation, the ideal, in his view, would be to understand style by fully knowing the character of the speaker ("In the technical method, style can only be understood through the fullest knowledge of character," KGA II/4, 56), which, however, is not possible, since in the field of understanding we are limited to making approximations (*Annährungen*). "Particularity," on account of which individual style exists, cannot, according to Schleiermacher, be reduced to a functional level, by assignment to specific forms of expression (as classical poetics seems to postulate). He is aware of the advent of a new epoch in which the classical model of normative rhetoric, subjected to the pressure of the aesthetics of genius, experiencing a certain dissociation, and from it emerges the Romantic doctrine of individual style, which cannot be reduced to any particular form, since its domain is the very diversity of forms of expression (see KGA II/4, 57). We thus witness a (successively) ongoing shift in the historical paradigm and the birth of a modern non-normative stylistics, casting off the corset of the rules of the old science of expression. This change will clearly influence the perception of translation, linking translation more firmly with hermeneutic *divination* as a method of interpretation (see the next chapter).

Similarly, a conviction was maturing in Schleiermacher that style is something much more than just a certain (distinctive) use of language. In his lecture on Hermeneutics of 1819 he writes: "We are used to understanding, by styles, only the treat-

---

183 Dorota Zdunkiewicz-Jedynak, *Wykłady ze stylistyki* [Lectures on Stylistics] (Warsaw: PWN, 2008), 14–15.

ment of the language. But thought and language everywhere combine with each other, and the particular manner of grasping the object combines with the ordering and thus also with the treatment of the language" (AB: 91; KGA II/4, 156). Thus the three basic branches of rhetoric constitute an inseparable unity. Moreover, if it is so difficult to separate thought from language (in other words: if these two elements are so strongly conditioned by one other), the interpretation of texts becomes an extremely difficult challenge, and translation – if it is to be adequate – can be seen as downright impossible.

A crucial assumption underlying the Schleiermacherian viewpoint is the author's creative originality, for "[e]very writer has his own style" (KGA II/4, 57).[184] If he does not have his own "individuality," he blends into the masses, forming a collective, a medium of objectification and schematization of speech (KGA II/4, 57). Meanwhile, the essence of having "one's own style" lies in transforming the universal, the common, into the individual, into an individually expressed sense.[185] This type of individualistic theory of style is exemplified in the account we find in Karl Philipp Moritz's *Vorlesungen über den Styl*, written just three years later than Schleiermacher's treatment:

> As deviant as this may sound from the common approach, strictly speaking, there are no rules of style. For by style one usually conceives of certain peculiar features, by means of which one recognizes a certain person's manner of writing, and because of which we can speak of a manner of writing at all; but, after all, it is impossible to find a rule for what is particular [*das Eigenthümliche*].[186]

Moritz posits this clearly in the spirit of pre-Romantic aesthetics, but the radicalism of his approach is weakened by a conviction that proper style must be the result of clear thought, as "otherwise all that remains is empty bombast and the clanging of words that deceive us."[187] Thus the regulative idea of clarity and legibility of the message as the basis of communication between sender and receiver returns here – and with it, the dialectical dimension of the science of style, extremely important (as we already know) for Schleiermacher. For an individual style of expression must, in its "particularity" (*Eigentümlichkeit*), be legible to the recipient. The conviction of the individuality of expression (not only artistic expression) goes hand in hand here with the conviction that this individuality nevertheless has to be *communicable* – otherwise it will be devoid of content, empty, illusory.

How can one recognize and characterize a person's style? The answer may be surprising in the context of Schleiermacher's earlier assertions concerning stylistics as an independent domain. Style can be grasped interpretatively, he explains, by jux-

---

184 In the recovered transcript of *General Hermeneutics 1809/1810*: "Every utterer has an individuality of style, which appears everywhere." (AB: 256; KGA II/4, 103).
185 Pfau, "Immediacy and the Text," 65.
186 Quoted after Arend, *Rhetorik, Stil und Verstehen*, 127.
187 Ibid., 128.

taposing the individual use of language with the "composition," that is, with "the idea" that it expresses (KGA II/4, 59; cf. KGA II/4, 103). It is not difficult to see that this approach links back up to classical rhetoric, in which an utterance is the outcome of an idea or a topic, and thus of *inventio*, ensuring the integrity of the speech/text. Schleiermacher, as we recall, spoke of the proper ways of expounding a given theme in his lectures on style, often employing the concept of *Hauptgedanke*, which he identifies in the first draft, *Hermeneutik – Erster Entwurf* (1810–1819), as "the idea and thesis of the work" (KGA II/4, 67).

Importantly, originality (and thus individuality) is not, in Schleiermacher's view, a feature of the thesis itself, but of the way it is presented and articulated.[188] This is also the direction in which the author of *Hermeneutics* argues when he notes: "The author's idea attests only to his own *dignity* [*Dignität*], not to his individuality, which is indicated by the way in which he presents this idea [...]" (KGA II/4, 59). A little further on Schleiermacher writes that in the case of two different writers expressing the same idea, different "particularities" (of style) will manifest themselves (KGA II/4, 61);[189] this remark, too, is in keeping with the spirit of classical rhetoric, contrasting the schematicity of *res* against the individual character of its linguistic realization, *verba*.[190] Schleiermacher also refers to these concepts in his lectures, using the German terms *Sache* and *Wort* (*General Hermeneutics* 1809/1810; KGA II/4, 76). It may be worth noting in this context that in the old rhetoric, *res* and *verba* were the basic elements of a work (*opus*), whose creation or "emergence" was an art (*ars*) based on specific rules. Similarly, in Schleiermacher's view, hermeneutics is the rule-based "art of understanding," which, as he wrote in a later compendium, can be seen as a mirror image of the "art of speech" (KGA II/4, 120).

It goes without saying that knowledge of the rules of rhetoric is indispensable for the hermeneuticist. The examples Schleiermacher cites from the New Testament are telling in this regard: the rhetorical shortcomings of the apostles' writings (e.g. the uncoordinated ideas of St. Peter in the realm of *res*, and the elliptical style of St. John in the realm of *verba*) explain the specific hermeneutical difficulties that are encountered by their interpreters (the "places difficult to explain," KGA II/4, 68). No less characteristic in this respect is the remark in *General Hermeneutics 1809/10* on the recognition of "secondary ideas" (*Nebenvorstellungen*) that "emerge of their own accord," which recalls the principles of communicative style taught in Schlobitten:

> For if the writer wants the secondary ideas then he also wants to be sure, and must do something for the people who could be less inclined to find them themselves. But given that he

---

188 See Korolko, *Sztuka retoryki*, 54.
189 But when, on the other hand, different works are penned by the same author, he is recognizable precisely for this stylistic "particularity"; cf. KGA II/4, 103.
190 Heinrich Lausberg, *Handbuch der literarischen Rhetorik – Eine Grundlegung der Literaturwissenschaft*, 3rd ed. (Stuttgart: Franz Steiner, 1990), 47.

must actually try to counteract all ideas which insinuate themselves as distractions, he can only want them in order to achieve something specific. (AB 250–251; KGA II/4, 97).

This is how Schleiermacher instructs students of the art of interpretation, essentially encouraging them to adopt the author's point of view, that is, in this context, the subject of linguistic actions aimed at the desired persuasive effect.[191]

An extremely important element of Schleiermacher's study of style, as seen from the perspective of hermeneutics, is figurative language. His *General Hermeneutics 1809/10* states: "In order to assess figurative expressions correctly, one must bear in mind the whole sequence of changes in the area in question and thus also the character of the writer" (AB 252; KGA II/4, 98). Thomas Pfau rightly notes in this context that Schleiermacher contends that a full determination of someone's style implies a complete knowledge of the person in question,[192] which seems to be a kind of regulative fiction. However, knowledge of patterns and types of linguistic choices is indeed indispensable. The link between these two aspects is revealed during the analysis of the structure and interpretation of figurative speech, which is based on comparing the "proper" vs. the "foreign," i.e. figurative, meaning.[193] For we are dealing here with a "separate," unique, individual sense, which, after all, grows out of universal principles – out of conventions, without whose consideration that sense is incomprehensible.[194] "For any opening of new semantic space, which constitutes the operative core of 'style,' must simultaneously lay bare the rupturing of the existing syntactic and semantic universals," Pfau aptly comments.[195] Since figurations are constituted by a certain awareness and its accompanying intentionality, the act of interpreting figuration (and style in general) will always be a difficult task, based not only on comparison, but also on *divination*.[196]

Analyzing Schleiermacher's notion of style in the context of the theory of language, Manfred Frank, an eminent interpreter of Schleiermacher's thought in a poststructuralist spirit, notes that here grammar represents the "system of the totality of the language" whereas rhetoric – which "provides a theory of the art of speech" – refers to what is "particular" and, in its particularity, "untranslatable" (*Unübertragbar*).[197] Thus, on the one hand, "signs that are elements of the linguistic code are also a function of a certain 'untranslatable' projection of meaning," yet on the other hand, "the individual act of thinking – even if it, in a certain fashion, escapes 'lin-

---

[191] A little later in a similar context he states: "But one must admittedly have first placed oneself in the same sphere as the utterer" (AB 253; KGA II/4, 100).
[192] Thomas Pfau, *Immediacy and the Text*, 66.
[193] Ibid., 69–70.
[194] Cf. ibid., 70
[195] Ibid.
[196] Cf. ibid., 72. See also KGA II/4, 157.
[197] This term plays an important role in Schleiermacher's thought, meaning "non-translatability," including in the very broad sense of "non-transferability."

guistic law' – nevertheless should be able to be constituted linguistically."[198] This is a kind of paradox, aptly pointing us towards the very essence of language as an "individual universal" (*ein individuelles Allgemeines*).[199] This means, as Frank stresses, that linguistic signs are not "only the external re-presentation of something internal,"[200] since thinking is already linguistic to a certain extent, and thus does not constitute some substrate of content that can be easily transferred from one linguistic container to another. This thesis, which Schleiermacher himself had already pointed out to us, is of great importance for translation theory, showing its relativistic starting point.

In Frank's view, Schleiermacher's concept of language as an "individual universal" managed to capture the creative, meaning-creating energy of speech, which "sees the purest expression" as lying in figurative, "poetic use of language."[201] This is because it breaks conventionalized forms (schemas), opening up a new sense to the audience. This sense soon accrues cognitive (hermeneutic) and communicative value. "If the originally simply individual image is appropriated by the recipients of an act of speech," Manfred Frank writes, "then this image has thereby ceased to be exclusive or private and exists as a virtual universal schema or possibly as a rule for language use [...]."[202] This reconstruction of Schleiermacher's views is, in Frank's opinion, the essential context that allows us to understand the concept of "divination," a concept incorporated into Schleiermacher's concept of style.

Let us return to the relevant section of *Hermeneutics (1819)*. Frank emphasizes the above-cited passage from the section on "technical interpretation"[203]; let us repeat its crowning conclusion: "thought and language everywhere pass into one another and a particular way of treating an object passes into the composition and thus also into the use of language" (KGA II/4, 156). Frank here draws an analogy to "the metaphorical 'new description' in as far as stylistic modification challenges the general schematic posture of language with a speaker's initially untranslatable 'thought'".[204] By using metaphorical language and thus "producing new meaning," the speaker "forces his individuality onto language, an individuality which has not yet been codified and is in this sense ineffable" through the "particular combinatory structure" of style.[205] It goes beyond what is imposed by conventions, rules, schema, creating its

---

[198] Manfred Frank, "The Text and Its Style: Schleiermacher's Hermeneutic Theory of Language," trans. by Richard Hannah, and Michael Hays, *Boundary 2* 11, no. 3 (1983): 19–20.
[199] Ibid., 22.
[200] Ibid., 20.
[201] Ibid., 23.
[202] Ibid., 23
[203] In the edition of *Hermeneutik und Kritik* prepared by Manfred Frank, the term used instead is "psychological" interpretation – meant to be more in accordance with the 1832 lecture and, in Frank's view, with the logic of the concept itself; see Friedrich Schleiermacher, *Hermeneutik und Kritik*, 167 and 236–237.
[204] Frank, "The Text and Its Style," 23
[205] Ibid., 24

own sense on the basis of universal signs.[206] Of course, this sense can be grasped and understood, but never in its entirety, because, as Schleiermacher states, the inner "unity" of style is impossible to describe, and is graspable only as "harmony."[207] Thus, Frank concludes, "it is then impossible to characterize the 'complete understanding of style' with expressions which are oriented toward the metaphorics of decoding [...] There is no continuous passage from a system to its application [...]."[208] Seen from this perspective, style does indeed seem to possess some kind of *untranslatable essence* that escapes the comparative method, operating in the domain of "ordinary sense," and cannot be rationalized in an act of intuitive divination.[209]

When we enter the domain of untranslatability, we enter the realm of Romantic reflection in which the mysterious language of poetry, caught up in various contradictions and paradoxes, becomes the main point of reference for the theory of language and interpretation. It is in this paradigm of thought that Manfred Frank wishes to situate Schleiermacher. Nevertheless, one should remember that the hermeneutician was a philosopher not just of difference, but also of synthesis, the latter being at least as characteristic of Romanticism as the former. Paul Ricoeur, in turn, views Schleiermacher's theory of style in synthetic terms: "it marks the union of thought and language, the union of the common and the singular in an author's project," the French philosopher writes. Style, Ricoeur continues, "displays a singularity inside the common resources of language, and, above all, in the style the formal aspect of the work's structure is joined to the psychological aspect of the author's intention."[210] Good style does indeed conceal some mystery difficult to grasp, but at the same time it creates this "unity," "harmony."

Style is something more than just ornamentation – Schleiermacher already knew this when he was teaching in Schlobitten. It is, as Hans-Georg Gadamer writes in his sketch *Reading is Translation*, "one of the factors of legibility – and thus a separate task in translation."[211] The task is a difficult one, because such translation is not just the outcome of good technique or "craftsmanship"[212] – but rather an art. Legibility is comprised of many features, often different ones depending on the genre of speech or text; not only clarity, so important in elocutionary rhetoric, but also the appropriate structure of meaning, distinctive sound, etc. It seems that it is in the hermeneutic

---

206 Ibid.
207 "As a unity, individuality cannot be reproduced. It always remains indescribable, and can only be characterized as harmony" (Friedrich Schleiermacher, *Hermeneutik und Kritik*, 177, English translation after Pfau, "Immediacy and the Text," 68).
208 Frank, "The Text and Its Style," 25
209 Cf. ibid., 25–26. Elsewhere, Frank writes about the "indivisibility" and "incommunicability" (*un-teilbar/un-mitteilbar*) of this essence, as a certain kind of elementary particle of individuality. See Manfred Frank, *Stil in der Philosophie* (Stuttgart: Reclam, 1992), 17.
210 Paul Ricoeur, "Schleiermacher's Hermeneutics," *The Monist* 60, no. 2 (1977): 188.
211 Hans-Georg Gadamer, "Lesen ist wie Übersetzen (1989)," in idem, *Gesammelte Werke*, vol. 8, Ästhetik und Poetik I. (Tübingen: Mohr Siebeck, 1999), 279–285.
212 Ibid.

act – which is essentially an act of translation, or more precisely, the initial phase of interlingual translation – that style becomes recognizable and thus takes on its own kind of legibility.

III Schleiermacher's and Schlegel's Contributions to the Theory of Translation

1 Assumptions and preliminary remarks

The way the title of this chapter is formulated may be taken to suggest that Friedrich Schleiermacher and Friedrich Schlegel developed the foundations of a "theory of translation" in the modern sense. However, this term is quite a problematic one to apply in the context of the early German Romantics' work. If we take the approach adopted by Radegundis Stolze in her monograph *Übersetzungstheorien*, and thus define a "theory" in strictly scientific terms as "an attempt to represent the multifaceted structures and relations of states of affairs by means of an abstract model,"[1] it would in this respect be difficult to lump the ideas of Schleiermacher, the Schlegel brothers, or Wilhelm von Humboldt into the same category alongside those of modern translation-theorists such as Eugene Nida or Hans Vermeer. For similar reasons, Werner Koller, in his classic work *Einführung in die Übersetzungswissenschaft*, is also cautious about such "theoretical reflections" offered by translators themselves, which, in his opinion, "can be regarded as pre-scientific explorations about the problems of translation."[2] It is from this perspective that Koller discusses Schleiermacher's lecture *On the Different Methods of Translating*, which he sees, along with Martin Luther's *Circular Letter on Translation*, as "reports" (*Rechenschaftsberichte*) in which translators merely seek to justify the choices that they themselves have made in practicing their craft.[3]

We can safely surmise that neither Schleiermacher nor Schlegel saw themselves as translation scholars or as precursors of a science of translation (*Übersetzungswissenschaft*). While the German theologian has indeed been hailed – at a colloquium on Schleiermacher and translation studies held at the Berlin Seminar in 1993 – as "the scholar who raised the call for translation studies to become an independent discipline,"[4] subsequent research eventually made it apparent that the pioneering postulate of a "comprehensive treatment of translation theory" attributed to him had in fact been formulated by someone else (the rather marginal classics scholar Karl Heinrich Pudor).[5] Schleiermacher, the Schlegel brothers, Novalis, and the other German Romantics indeed have little in common with representatives of the

---

1 Radegundis Stolze, *Übersetzungstheorien – Eine Einführung*, 5th ed. (Tübingen: Narr, 2008), 9.
2 Werner Koller, *Einführung in die Übersetzungswissenschaft*, 4th ed. (Heidelberg: Quelle & Meyer 1992), 34.
3 Ibid., 39.
4 Heidemarie Salevsky, "Schleiermacher-Kolloquium 1993," *TEXTconTEXT* 9 (1994): 159.
5 Cf. Klaus Schubert, "'So gewiß muß es auch eine Uebersetzungswissenschaft geben' – Erweiterte Recherchen zur ersten Forderung nach einer wissenschaftlichen Beschäftigung mit dem Übersetzen," *trans-kom*, 8 no. 2 (2015): 560–617.

contemporary German school of translation studies, especially those who apply scientifically rigorous research paradigms.

However, I would like to venture the claim that the Romantics would not have shied away from being called translation theorists if we instead adopted the notion of "theory" that was once advocated by the ancient Greeks, i.e. as referring to philosophical musings inspired by observation.[6] It is in this sense that Schleiermacher, Goethe, Herder, Novalis, August Wilhelm Schlegel, and Friedrich Schlegel, who were important translation scholars in the German tradition, contributed to the rediscovery of translation and the significant growth of interest in literary translation during the *Sturm und Drang* (*Storm and Stress*) period and then Romanticism.

The views and ideas to be examined in this chapter originated during Schleiermacher's years of friendship and cooperation with Friedrich Schlegel. I will therefore discuss their reflections on translation primarily in connection with their joint projects: the journal *Athenaeum* and the endeavor to translate Plato's complete works. The contributions that Schlegel and Schleiermacher did make to translation theory are, of course, intellectually rooted in the period of early German Romanticism. Schleiermacher's widely discussed and acclaimed 1813 lecture at the Prussian Academy of Sciences, *On the Different Methods of Translating*, which the author himself described as "a rather trivial thing,"[7] is in my opinion best viewed as a late fruit of the early Romantic concept of translation, shaped considerably by philosophical sketches and discussions among the authors of the *Athenaeum* circle, by literary criticism of specific translations, and by the experience of translating Plato.[8] In this chapter, therefore, I will try to present the important circumstances that preceded Schleiermacher's famous lecture, and hence to reconstruct its underlying premises. Though not itself being a subject of analysis here, the lecture on translation will as such provide a certain proleptic point of reference for the discussion through this chapter.

2 Schlegel's influence

In the second volume of Wilhelm Dilthey's monumental *Leben Schleiermachers*, when tracing the development of Schleiermacher's "method of practicing philological art," the biographer turns his attention to Friedrich Schlegel. Dilthey calls the author of

---

6 Angelica Nuzzo, "Theorie," in *Enzyklopädie Philosophie*, vol. 2, ed. Hans Jörg Sandkühler (Hamburg: Felix Meiner, 1999), 1621.
7 Letter from Schleiermacher to his wife, 21 June 1813 – quoted after: *Kritische Gesamtausgabe* I/11, XXXIII.
8 Cf. in this context Adam Schnitzer, "A History in Translation: Schleiermacher, Plato, and the University of Berlin," *The Germanic Review: Literature, Culture, Theory* 75, no. 1 (2000): 53–71. Schnitzer attempts here to draw a controversial link between Schleiermacher's translations of Plato and lecture on translation (1813), on the one hand, and the Prussian university reforms, on the other.

Lucinde "a leader of Romanticism," whose significance becomes evident at the level of "philological art."[9] The method of aesthetic interpretation developed by Schlegel was to have a direct impact on Schleiermacher's methodology and hermeneutical theory.[10] In this context, Dilthey points to Schlegel's unfulfilled greatness:

> Out of a kind of infinite agility and ease at combining things, there arose in him an extraordinary ability to perceive the veins of metal running beneath the surface of scholarly craftsmanship. But this natural talent and literary posture would prove disastrous, for they prevented him from the kind of consistent mining that would allow the metal so discovered to be exploited.[11]

Dilthey may be right here, but in order to properly understand Schlegel's thought and its influence on his contemporaries, it should be borne in mind that his project was not actually aimed at tapping into those deepest "veins of metal," of knowledge. Rather, his goal was progress in and of itself; Schlegel trusted in the "propelling force of becoming"[12] and rejected almost everything that impeded dynamic thinking and lead to stagnation. This attitude was accompanied by a certain epistemological skepticism: Schlegel absorbed more than he produced, and was often critical even of his own bold ideas and concepts. He always displayed great intellectual humility towards a world marked by contradictions, as is evident in his contributions to hermeneutics.

Schlegel's hermeneutical ideas have been repeatedly compared to Schleiermacher's works and examined from the genetic and typological perspectives.[13] Schlegel's importance in the history of hermeneutics has been widely noted, especially how the concept of understanding sketched out in his notes for his planned *Philosophy of Philology* influenced Schleiermacher's general hermeneutics.[14] It is often emphasized, however, that it was thanks to Schleiermacher that the art of interpretation "gained a universal audience."[15]

---

9 Wilhelm Dilthey, *Leben Schleiermachers*, vol. II/2: *Schleiermachers System als Theologie*, ed. Martin Redeker (Göttingen: Vandenhoeck & Ruprecht, 1966), 670.
10 On Dilthey's interpretation, see Manuel Bauer, *Schlegel und Schleiermacher – Frühromantische Kunstkritik und Hermeneutik* (Paderborn: Schöningh, 2011), 26 ff.
11 Dilthey, *Leben Schleiermachers*, vol. II/2, 671.
12 Berbeli Wanning, *Friedrich Schlegel – Eine Einführung* (Wiesbaden: Panorama, 2000), 9. Cf. also Jure Zovko, *Verstehen und Nichtverstehen bei Friedrich Schlegel – Zur Entstehung und Bedeutung seiner hermeneutischen Kritik* (Stuttgart: Frommann-Holzboog, 1990), 145.
13 See especially Hermann Patsch's insightful study, "Friedrich Schlegels 'Philosophie der Philologie' und Schleiermachers frühe Entwürfe zur Hermeneutik," *Zeitschrift für Theologie und Kirche* 63, no. 4 (1966): 434–472.
14 The extent of this influence is disputable, see Andreas Arndt, *Friedrich Schleiermacher als Philosoph* (Berlin: Walter de Gruyter, 2013), 299. Michael N. Forster argues strongly that Schlegel's ideas concerning interpretation "go beyond anything in Schleiermacher's hermeneutics" and "are all in fact more continuous with Herder then anticipative of Schleiermacher" – Forster, *German Philosophy of Language: From Schlegel to Hegel and Beyond* (Oxford: Oxford Univ. Press, 2011), 15.
15 Jean Grondin, *Hermeneutik*, trans. Ulrike Blech (Göttingen: Vandenhoeck & Ruprecht, 2009), 2.

Schlegel's ideas and reflections, which bear eloquent testimony to the "unceasing heuristic process,"[16] do not seem to offer the basis for a coherent hermeneutical theory.[17] However, as Hermann Patsch aptly observes, the author of *Lucinde* was not concerned with "developing a hermeneutical theory, like Schleiermacher, but with critically determining the relation between philosophy and philology, for which the hermeneutical problem seems to be a secondary theme."[18] Themes which are of fundamental importance for both general hermeneutics and the hermeneutical theory of translation do nevertheless recur in Schlegel's reflections: precise understanding (of the text), non-understanding (*das Nichtverstehen*), better understanding (das *Besserverstehen*), reconstructing (*das Nachkonstruieren*), and reproducing (*das Wiedererzeugen*).

Schleiermacher in a certain sense "systematized and carried out"[19] Schlegel's ideas on hermeneutics, while at the same time reinterpreting them. The most important point of reference for his critical reflection may have been the concept of dialectics correlated with hermeneutics, which emerged out of confrontation with Schlegel's philosophical dialectics and invoked the notion of pure thinking, independent of circumstances.[20]

Schlegel's hermeneutics – designed as a hermeneutical critique[21] – is characterized by ambivalence: "nonunderstanding" is evaluated positively (*wird positiviert*)[22] by being presented in an ironic context, while "better understanding" is conceptualized as gradually honing in on an intricate, nebulous sense suspended between the individual and the infinite.[23] While Schleiermacher constructs a general theory of interpretation that presupposes a study of understanding based on rationality and commonality of thought (with nonunderstanding evaluated negatively),[24] Schlegel maintains that understanding also embraces the unconscious and the vague, actually entering the domain of magic ("That a man understands another man is philosophically inconceivable, yet magical"),[25] which human reason cannot avoid confronting.

---

16 Patsch, *Friedrich Schlegels "Philosophie der Philologie,"* 444.
17 See ibid.; Bauer, *Schlegel und Schleiermacher*, 33.
18 Patsch, *Friedrich Schlegels "Philosophie der Philologie,"* 445.
19 Ibid., 465.
20 See especially Arndt, *Friedrich Schleiermacher als Philosoph*, 312–313, 322–323, and Ingolf Hübner, *Wissenschaftsbegriff und Theologieverständnis – Eine Untersuchung zu Schleiermachers Dialektik* (Berlin: Walter de Gruyter, 1997), 22 ff.
21 See Friedrich Schlegel, *Hefte "Zur Philologie,"* ed. Samuel Müller (Paderborn: Schöningh, 2015), 124.
22 Harald Schnur, *Schleiermachers Hermeneutik und ihre Vorgeschichte im 18. Jahrhundert – Studien zur Bibelauslegung, zu Hamann, Herder und F. Schlegel* (Stuttgart-Weimar: Metzler, 1994), 149.
23 Zovko, *Verstehen und Nichtverstehen bei Friedrich Schlegel*, 144.
24 This negative formulation of the task of hermeneutics explains, in Zovko's view, Schleiermacher's constructive reinterpretation of Schlegel's idea of non-understanding and divination (see ibid., 164).
25 Friedrich Schlegel, *Kritische Friedrich Schlegel Ausgabe* [KFSA] XVIII: *Philosophische Lehrjahre 1796–1806; nebst philosophischen Manuskripten aus den Jahren 1796–1828*, vol. 1, ed. Ernst Behler

He posits that the basis of understanding is divination, creative thinking by means of analogy, and allegoresis, rather than rational analysis. His reflection on language and understanding leads him towards esotericism, thereby bringing hermeneutics close to hermeticism. This could explain Friedrich Schlegel's unusual theoretical reflections on translation, such as his Parisian notes on theosophy and translation (1802).[26] This distinctive aspect of Schlegel's thought, reflected in his statements on understanding, sheds light on the differences between his and Schleiermacher's approaches to translation.

The significance of the holistic principle in Schlegel's hermeneutical discourse is very clearly emphasized by Dilthey. "The first condition of all understanding," Schlegel writes in *Lessings Geist*, "and therefore also of the understanding of a work of art, is the perception of the whole."[27] The objective is to reconstruct someone's thinking "down to the subtler peculiarities of its totality."[28] The essence of the whole lies hidden in the form, which is why Schlegel is interested in the *forms of thought*, which remain in constant motion. It seems that this abstract idea of dynamic forms of thought can only be translated into the symbolic language of "spatial images" (*Raumbilder*), as was done for Lessing and Plato. What Dilthey calls the germ of the "schematic game" in the field of philosophy[29] is the conceptual basis for Schlegel's theory of translation, which led him to express original ideas that influenced all the representatives of the *Athenaeum* circle, especially including Friedrich Schleiermacher.

3 Rediscovering translation: Schlegel, *Athenaeum*, and the framework of ideas

In 1796, while in Jena, Schlegel acquired notebooks so as to jot down his thoughts on literature and philosophy.[30] Inspired by Chamfort, he experimented with an open, fragmentary form that reflected his awareness of the shortcomings and preliminary

---

(Paderborn: Schöningh, 1963), 297. See also Reinhold Rieger, *Interpretation und Wissen – Zur philosophischen Begründung der Hermeneutik bei Friedrich Schleiermacher und ihrem geschichtlichen Hintergrund* (Berlin: Walter de Gruyter, 1988), 119.

26 See, for example, F. Schlegel, KFSA XVIII: *Philosophische Lehrjahre*, 452. Cf. in this context H. Jackson Forstman, "The Understanding of Language by Friedrich Schlegel and Schleiermacher," *Soundings: An Interdisciplinary Journal* 51, no. 2 (1968): 160, who writes: "Schlegel's meditations about language lead him to the mystic tradition of Böhme and Franz von Baader, to astrology, theosophy, hieroglyphics, the Cabbala and ultimately to absolute esotericism."

27 Dilthey, *Leben Schleiermachers*, vol. II/2, 672; Friedrich Schlegel, *KFSA III, Charakteristiken und Kritiken II. 1802–1829*, trans. Hans Eichner (Paderborn: Schöningh, 1975), 56.

28 F. Schlegel, KFSA III: *Charakteristiken und Kritiken II*, 60.

29 Dilthey, *Leben Schleiermachers*, vol. II/2, 674.

30 Cf. the footnotes to *Kritische Fragmente*, in Friedrich Schlegel, *Werke in zwei Bänden*, vol. 1 (Berlin: Aufbau, 1980), 335.

character of his own ideas and projects, while at the same presenting what is finite and delineated, in a shape that nevertheless made it possible to intuit the mystery of its unlimitedness and infinity. This is how the *Athenaeum* project was born, but it is also where the history of the Romantic fragment as a form of thought and art begins. This approach would, on the one hand, stimulate Romantic thought, propelling it towards its most daring experiments and projects, and on the other hand, it would inhibit the development and maturation of ideas, which all too often ended up abandoned at an embryonic stage. This tendency can also be observed in the early Romantic reflection on translation.

The first collection of Schlegel's fragments, described in their title as "critical," appeared in the journal *Lyceum der schönen Künste*. It contained several important remarks on translation, for which the motto could be this thought-provoking remark from his notes for the *Philosophy of Philology:* "We do not actually yet know at all what translation can be."[31] Schlegel sees translation as a "truly φλ [philological] art,"[32] which could be described as productive, critical and progressive. For Schlegel, as Ellena Polledri aptly notes, productive translation begins with the recognition of "understanding as a challenge to philological thought."[33] Schlegel's reflection is essentially rooted in the hermeneutic tradition. He speculates on the understanding and translation of classical texts, while at the same time making the dialectical turn characteristic of his ironic stance: "A classical text must never be entirely comprehensible,"[34] for it is precisely in their incomprehensibility, uniqueness and strangeness that classical texts appear as inexhaustible sources of wisdom. Schlegel thus turns against the historical criticism of the Enlightenment, which was based on the axiom of the ordinary and the commonplace, and which attempted to eradicate the unusual, the extraordinary and the alien, following the principle that "just as things are within us and around us, so they must be everywhere").[35] This kind of approach ignores the "basic distance between the familiar and the foreign," neglecting the problem of non-identity between the original and the translation, and thus rejecting the new, creative model of translation that appealed to Schlegel, and later Schleiermacher.[36]

But what is the essence of translation? According to Schlegel, true translations are not "mythical" (idealistic) or "mystical" (ahistorical and uncritical) but should

---

31 F. Schlegel, *Hefte "Zur Philologie,"* 97.
32 Ibid., 132.
33 Elena Polledri, "'Übersetzungen sind φλ [philologische] Mimen' – Friedrich Schlegels Philologie und die Übersetzungen von Johann Diedrich Gries," in *Friedrich Schlegel und die Philologie*, eds. Ulrich Breuer, Remigius Bunia, Armin Erlinghagen (Paderborn: Schöningh, 2013), 167, 168.
34 Friedrich Schlegel, "Critical Fragments" in idem, *Friedrich Schlegel's Lucinde and the Fragments*, trans. Peter Firchow (Minneapolis: Univ. of Minnesota Press, 1971), 144.
35 Ibid., 8. See also Peter L. Oesterreich, *Spielarten der Selbstfindung – Die Kunst des romantischen Philosophierens bei Fichte, F. Schlegel und Schelling* (Berlin: Walter de Gruyter, 2011), 79.
36 Elena Polledri, "Übersetzungen sind φλ [philologische] Mimen," 171 and 168.

rather be seen as "mimic" since they appear as "philological mimes."[37] This characterization perfectly captures the early Romantics' proclivity for analogical thinking. Note that analogy itself also constitutes a kind of translation. Most scholars link this particular analogy to the conception of translation as a philologically grounded critical activity (e.g. Antoine Berman).[38] But what translation also has in common with musical notes, mentioned by Schlegel in the same context,[39] is that it is a genre of art, embodying its own mode of representation, which Friedmar Apel describes as "improvised play."[40] Reproduction is essentially a kind of creative reenactment – an inventive, critical reproduction that means setting the text in motion. Translation maintains the historical vitality of poetic texts, thanks to the ongoing work of renewing meanings.[41]

In his *Critical Fragments* (*Kritische Fragmente*) Schlegel takes the question of translation seriously, problematizing translation to the same extent as he problematizes other arts, which he links to philosophy (or even transforms into philosophy) in order to show that the latter is an art. Schlegel attempts to critically examine translation, to describe it with metaphors, and to reduce it through analogies to a philosophical formula. In this sense, he theorizes translation, at the same time showing awareness of the imperfections of his analysis since "each translation is an indeterminate and incomplete task."[42] It needs maximal freedom, including in order to test its possibilities.

* * *

Friedrich Schleiermacher met Friedrich Schlegel when the latter arrived in Berlin in the summer of 1797. They immediately took a liking to one other, as if "they were struck by a thunderbolt of intellectual empathy."[43] "He is a young man of twenty-five years, with such extensive knowledge that it is difficult to comprehend how one can know so much at such a young age," Schleiermacher wrote to his sister Charlotte, declaring immediately: "since I have become intimately acquainted with him, a

---

37 F. Schlegel, *Hefte "Zur Philologie,"* 97. Perhaps the author is referring here to Greek folk theater, in which mythological content underwent an updating transformation. See Friedmar Apel, *Sprachbewegung – Eine historisch-poetologische Untersuchung zum Problem des Übersetzens* (Heidelberg: Universitätsverlag Winter, 1982), 96.
38 Antoine Berman, *The Experience of the Foreign: Culture and Translation in Romantic Germany*, trans. S[tefan] Heyvaert (Albany: State Univ. of New York Press, 1992), 106 ff.
39 Cf. F. Schlegel, KFSA II: *Charakteristiken und Kritiken 1796–1801* (Paderborn: Schöningh, 1967), 156: "Notes are philological epigrams; translations are philological mimes [...]."
40 Friedmar Apel, *Virtuose in der historischen Form – Philologie und Übersetzung bei Friedrich Schlegel*, in *Übersetzung antiker Literatur – Funktionen und Konzeptionen im 19. und 20 Jahrhundert*, eds. Martin S. Harbsmeier et al. (Berlin: Walter de Gruyter, 2008), 22.
41 See Friedmar Apel, *Sprachbewegung*, 96.
42 F. Schlegel, *Hefte "Zur Philologie,"* 122.
43 Kurt Nowak, *Schleiermacher – Leben, Werk und Wirkung* (Göttingen: Vandenhoeck & Ruprecht, 2001), 83.

new period has begun, as it were, for my existence in the philosophical and literary world."⁴⁴ This letter heralds a "literary marriage" that began with shared lodgings and a communion of thought, and ended with unsuccessful collaboration and a painful rift.⁴⁵ At the end of 1797 Friedrich Schlegel founded the journal *Athenaeum*. Between 1798 and 1800, three annual volumes (six issues) of the journal were published, which rapidly won recognition for effectively disseminating and putting into practice the bold ideas of the early Romantics. The primary vehicle for these ideas were the "fragments," which were initially intended to be Schlegel's own contributions, but later appeared as the outcome of collaborative work, or "symphilosophizing." "The more fragments, the less monotony and the greater the popularity," Friedrich put it frankly in a letter to August Wilhelm and his wife Caroline.⁴⁶ To ensure variety, Schlegel invited Schleiermacher, Novalis and, of course, his own brother⁴⁷ to collaborate. Most noteworthy from our perspective is the fact that in certain of the fragments published in *Athenaeum* Schlegel expanded upon his analysis of translation issues, paying due attention to their hermeneutical dimension.

"Interpretations are frequently insertions of something that seems desirable or expedient, and many a deduction [*Auslegen*] is actually a traduction [*Einlegen*]," the insertion by the reader of their own wishes and goals⁴⁸ – notes Schlegel in *Athenaeum* Fragment 25. In other words, the translator's activity can be described as interpreting a foreign text against the backdrop of his own ideas. The hermeneutic theory of translation stems precisely from such reflection on the peculiarities of this interpretation process – with Schleiermacher often being unfairly credited with its authorship. In fact, it was Herder who claimed that "the best translator must also be the best interpreter,"⁴⁹ while Schlegel picked up on and problematized this assertion. Hermeneutic competence is, from Schlegel's perspective, crucial for the translator. Understanding encompasses the literary system of the target language and that of the original text alike. The historical distance between these two systems invariably poses a challenge to the translator. "In order to translate perfectly from the classics into a modern language, the translator would have to be so expert in his language that, if need be, he could make everything modern; but at the same time he would have to understand antiquity so well that he would be able not just to imitate it

---

44 Letter from Friedrich Schleiermacher to Charlotte Schleiermacher (KGA V/2, 177).
45 See especially Arndt, *Friedrich Schleiermacher als Philosoph*, 31–41. In Schleiermacher's eyes, Friedrich Schlegel's conversion to Catholicism placed the final seal on their parting, i.e. the severing of a community of thought that had lasted several years. Cf. in this context the letter from Schleiermacher to F. Schlegel of 24 February 1809 (KGA V/11, 91–293).
46 Quoted after the notes to *Kritische Fragmente*, in Friedrich Schlegel, *Werke in zwei Bänden*, vol. 1, 338.
47 Cf. Nowak, *Schleiermacher – Leben, Werk und Wirkung*, 90.
48 F. Schlegel, "Athenaeum Fragments" in *Friedrich Schlegel's Lucinde and the Fragments*, 164.
49 Johann Gottfried von Herder, *Fragmente zur deutschen Literatur – Zweite Sammlung, Sämmtliche Werke*, part 2 (Tübingen: Cotta, 1805), 41. Bauer sees the problematization of interpretation in fragment 25 as a critique of "naive" hermeneutics, cf. Bauer, *Schlegel und Schleiermacher*, 136–137.

but, if necessary, re-create it,"⁵⁰ says *Athenaeum* Fragment 393. Translation as making something anew, re-creation (*Wiedererschaffung*), is an artistic act based on deep understanding. Understanding is also the condition for any creative reconstruction of a literary work in another language. As Schlegel notes elsewhere, "every translation is [...] actually a new linguistic creation [*Sprachschöpfung*]" and "Only translators are artists of language,"⁵¹ suggesting that once a foreign work has been understood, it should reveal itself in the form of amplified literature. Only translation appears as the true art of language, because it is "the literature of literature." The hermeneutic competence and literary artistry of the translator can *re-create* the original and revive its spirit in the new language of the present time.⁵² This naturally leads us to the theoretical foundations for the translation of Plato, which will be addressed later in this book.

However, understanding is not a simple task. The translator must embrace the paradoxical essence of comprehension and use it for their own purposes. Both non-understanding (*Nichtverstehen*) and better understanding (*Besserverstehen*) can be seen as extreme moments in the hermeneutic motion.⁵³ The translator oscillates between the self-understanding of words (which "often understand themselves better than do those who use them"⁵⁴) and the self-understanding of the speaker.⁵⁵ In *Athenaeum* Fragment 401, Schlegel has this to say on the subject: "In order to understand someone who only partially understands himself, you first have to understand him completely and better than he himself does, but then only partially and precisely as much as he does himself."⁵⁶ This ironic figure of thought, probably a reference to Kant's interpretation of Plato, in which Schlegel's holistic epistemology comes to the fore, is echoed in Schleiermacher's 1805 draft of his hermeneutics: "One should understand as well as, and better than the author" (KGA II/4, 39), and also in the 1819 draft: "This task is also to be expressed as follows: to understand the utterance at first just as well [as,] and then better than its author" (KGA II/4, 128).⁵⁷ As Harald Schnur notes, however, "Schleiermacher's account of the notion of better comprehension in hermeneutics differs from Schlegel's on a fundamental point, namely,

---

50 F. Schlegel, "Athenaeum Fragments," 226.
51 F. Schlegel, KFSA XVIII: *Philosophische Lehrjahre*, 71.
52 "Schlegel demanded that the prerequisite for practicing the art of translation was a combination of artistic ability and hermeneutical competence," Willy Michel aptly observes in his *Ästhetische Hermeneutik und frühromantische Kritik – Friedrich Schlegels fragmentarische Entwürfe, Rezensionen, Charakteristiken und Kritiken (1795–1801)* (Göttingen: Vandenhoeck & Ruprecht, 1982), 70.
53 See George Steiner, *After Babel: Aspects of Language and Translation* (New York and London: Oxford Univ. Press, 1975): 296–413.
54 F. Schlegel, "On Incomprehensibility," in *Friedrich Schlegel's Lucinde and the Fragments*, 260.
55 Cf. here Hermann Patsch's remarks on the distinction between *intentio auctoris* and *intentio operis* in Schlegel, in Hermann Patsch, *Friedrich Schlegels 'Philosophie der Philologie,'* 456 ff.
56 F. Schlegel, "Athenaeum Fragments," 227–228.
57 Friedrich Schleiermacher, *Hermeneutics and Criticism*, ed. Andrew Bowie (Cambridge: Cambridge Univ. Press, 1998), 23.

where 'understanding as well as' precedes understanding that surpasses [the author]."⁵⁸ The latter kind of understanding can bring to consciousness what may have remained unconscious for the creator.⁵⁹ As Gunter Scholtz suggests, a better understanding may actually be facilitated by distance, allowing the interpreter to see what the author could not see from closer up.⁶⁰ Even more important in this context, however, is the path of rationalization charted out by Schleiermacher – as Jure Zovko writes: "Schleiermacher's 'better comprehension' leads through the mediation of 'speech' and 'understanding' of that speech, from the individuality of the original thought back into the generality."⁶¹

Simply put, there are two ways of thinking about the problem of understanding that can be teased apart: the first – exploiting analogies, assuming a holistic and synthetic perspective, combining the conscious with the unconscious, the clear with the abstruse, the spirit with the letter, and the second – adopting a methodical, systematic, rational, and transfer-oriented perspective. This difference is also manifest in Schlegel's and Schleiermacher's attempts to theorize translation. A point made by Bauer appears to be particularly relevant here, namely that Schleiermacher always starts "from an intermediary instance" (*vermittelnde Instanz*) and treats "hermeneutics as an act of translation," whereas Schlegel does not seem to need a "translating intermediary" (*dolmetschender Vermittler*").⁶² Schlegel formulates questions and ponders aporias in order to identify the fundamental problems of translation theory and practice, rather than to establish a coherent axiom-based scientific translation theory. *Athenaeum* Fragment 402 states: "In trying to see if it's possible to translate the classical poets, the important thing is to decide whether or not even the most faithful German translation isn't still Greek."⁶³ The postulate of fidelity and linguistic purity formulated by readers is being questioned here. Does it lead to comprehension or rather miscomprehension of a foreign work? Does an "absolute" translator (such as Voß) destroy the original?⁶⁴ Schlegel's philological criticism is devoted to these problems, a criticism "whose substance can only be the classical and absolutely eternal" which may never be understood.⁶⁵ The classical and the eternal elude understanding, reducing the status of translation to a preliminary work flawed by deficiencies. The pathos of alienation and distance, which resounds so radically in Friedrich

---

58 Schnur, *Schleiermachers Hermeneutik und ihre Vorgeschichte im 18. Jahrhundert*, 151.
59 See KGA II/4, 128; cf. also Sarah Schmidt, *Die Konstruktion des Endlichen – Schleiermachers Philosophie der Wechselwirkung* (Berlin: Walter de Gruyter, 2005), 250.
60 Gunter Scholtz, *Ethik und Hermeneutik – Schleiermachers Grundlegung der Geisteswissenschaften* (Frankfurt am Main: Suhrkamp, 1995), 145.
61 Zovko, *Verstehen und Nichtverstehen bei Friedrich Schlegel*, 162.
62 Bauer, *Schlegel und Schleiermacher*, 342.
63 F. Schlegel, "Athenaeum Fragments," 228.
64 See Schlegel, *Hefte "Zur Philologie,"* 163.
65 F. Schlegel, "Athenaeum Fragments," 228.

Hölderlin's translation of Sophocles, casts a shadow over the hermeneutic theory of translation.

Schlegel expands the notion of translation so that it fits into his transdisciplinary project.⁶⁶ He proposes that "musical compositions" can be seen as "merely translations of poems into the language of music."⁶⁷ Also "copying by painters," "composing by musicians," and "declamation by actors" are akin to translation for Schlegel,⁶⁸ next to "characterization," i.e. "critical mimicry," and "explanation."⁶⁹ On this view, translation appears as a semiotic practice in which different ways of interpreting signs can be distinguished: into signs of the same linguistic system, into signs of another linguistic system, or into signs of an extralinguistic system, such as music or the fine arts.⁷⁰ This concept seems to have influenced Schleiermacher and prompted him to analyze various forms of intralingual translation using the concepts of hermeneutics in his well-known lecture before the Prussian Academy of Sciences in June 1813 (DR 226; KGA I/11, 67). But shortly after the publication of the second volume of *Athenaeum*, intersemiotic translation would also become the subject of his considerations, as evidenced in this letter sent from Stolp (Słupsk) to Henrietta Herz on 9 June 1803:

> [...] and I would like, among other things, to have you, in *Athenaeum*, compare the treatise *Die Gemälde* with the sonnets attached to it, and let me know whether you see any resemblance here to the paintings themselves as regards character and impression. This kind of translation is central to my theory and I would like to know how well it works. I am also studying Friedrich's thoughts on painting in *Europa*, especially Raphael and Correggio, quite closely. Then I will see if I can clarify and communicate my thoughts on the matter.⁷¹

Schleiermacher is referring here to the text signed by August Wilhelm Schlegel and Caroline Schlegel, *Die Gemählde – Gespräch* (*The Paintings – A Conversation*), which appeared in the first issue of the second volume of *Athenaeum* in 1799. The text was inspired by the artistic excursions of German Romantics, who visited the Dresden Gallery together in the summer of 1789.⁷² The titular conversation (*Gespräch*) takes place among fictional characters: the wordsmith Waller, the draughtsman Reinhold, and the art aficionado Louise, who voice their opinions on the relations between the arts, the material with which they work, and their modus of imitation. Es-

---

66 See Marike Finlay, *The Romantic Irony of Semiotics: Friedrich Schlegel and the Crisis of Representation* (Berlin: Mouton de Gruyter, 1988), 209.
67 F. Schlegel, Friedrich Schlegel, "Athenaeum Fragments," 226.
68 F. Schlegel, *Philosophische Fragmente*, in KFSA XVIII: *Philosophische Lehrjahre*, 262.
69 Ibid., 386.
70 See Roman Jakobson, "On Linguistic Aspects of Translation," in Reuben A. Brower ed., *On Translation* (Cambridge, Mass.: Harvard Univ. Press, 1959), 233
71 Letter from Friedrich Schleiermacher to Henrietta Herz, 9 July 1803 (KGA V/6, 409).
72 See Lothar Müller, "Nachwort," in August Wilhelm Schlegel, *Die Gemählde – Gespräch*, ed. Lothar Müller (Amsterdam-Dresden: Verlag der Kunst, 1996), 175 ff.

pecially noteworthy are Louise's highly imaginative comparisons and analogies. She likens a translator of Pindar or Sophocles to a copyist making sketches of ancient sculptures.[73] Just as the translator struggles to recreate the works of the Greek writers by shaping the material of the German language, so too the draughtsman seeks to render the form of a sculpture on paper by means of black and white contrasts. The similarity is that in both cases, original works are re-represented in a form alien to them.

In this dialogue, various artistic experiences are thus juxtaposed and reduced to a common denominator, with the notion of translation leading to a deeper reflection on different systems of representation. Louise, for example, reflects on the linguistic shape of her aesthetic experiences and raises the issue of their verbalization. It involves, as she puts it, the translation of impressions or feelings into discourse.[74] Schleiermacher, too, took a keen interest in this issue, which was closely related – as should be noted – to hermeneutical reflection, devoting to it considerable attention in his 1805/1806 notes on language, thoughts and feelings, written for his lectures on ethics.[75] In those notes he characterizes the concept of non-translatability or non-transferability (*Unübertragbarkeit*) derived from the principle of the individual/peculiar nature of feelings (*Eigentümlichkeit des Gefühls*). The peculiar, however, requires an illustrative translation in order to become communicable, hence the communication of an untranslatable feeling in art,[76] just as the kinds of foreign and alienated speech Schleiermacher focuses on in his lecture on translation need to be translated in order to take the form of meaningful linguistic expressions and nullify their state of non-identity (*Nichtidentität*).[77]

In another part of that conversation, to which Schleiermacher directly refers to in his letter, the topic of "the relation of the fine arts to poetry" is discussed. This is, undoubtedly, a theme well established in the aesthetic reflection of the time. Let us mention here two influential works: Lessing's *Laokoon oder über die Grenzen der Malerei und Poesie* (1766) and Wackenroder and Tieck's *Herzensergießungen eines kunstliebenden Klosterbruders* (1796). The young Romantic Wilhelm Heinrich Wackenroder, inspired by Raphael, wrote a text entitled *Zwey Gemähldeschilderungen*, in which

---

[73] A.W. Schlegel, *Die Gemählde*, 15. Here I will refer the reader to my own detailed analysis: Piotr de Bończa Bukowski, "Zwischen Platon und christlicher Kunst: Zu Friedrich Schleiermachers Verständnis der Übersetzung in seinen frühen Jahren," in *Odysseen des Humanen: Antike, Judentum und Christentum in der deutschsprachigen Literatur – Festschrift für Prof. Dr. Maria Kłańska zum 65. Geburtstag*, eds. Katarzyna Jaśtal, Paweł Zarychta, Anna Dąbrowska (Frankfurt am Main: Peter Lang, 2016), 195–204.
[74] A.W. Schlegel, *Die Gemählde*, 17 ff.
[75] See Friedrich Daniel Ernst Schleiermacher, *Brouillon zur Ethik (1805/06)*, ed. Hans-Joachim Birkner (Hamburg: Felix Meiner, 1981), 21–26.
[76] Ibid., 22. On the concept of untranslatability (*Unübertragbarkeit*) see Bukowski, "Zwischen Platon und christlicher Kunst," 200 ff. Cf. also Michael Moxter, "Arbeit am Unübertragbaren: Schleiermachers Bestimmung des Ästhetischen," in *Schleiermacher und Kierkegaard – Subjektivität und Wahrheit*, ed. Niels Jørgen Cappelørn et al. (Berlin: Walter de Gruyter, 2006), 53–72.
[77] KGA I/11, 67.

he presented dramatized poetic descriptions of two paintings depicting the Virgin Mary together with the Infant Jesus and the three Magi. He preceded them with a short introduction, stating that "it is virtually impossible to describe [...] a beautiful painting," thus explaining the unusual form he had chosen to strive to lyrically and dramatically recreate the reality depicted on the canvas.[78]

Similarly, Schlegel's Waller exhibits the "transformation of images into poems,"[79] which materializes in seven sonnets describing masterpieces of Christian painting. A literary description of works of art, referred to as ekphrasis, may be considered one of the various types of translation.[80] In an essay on the draughtsman and sculptor John Flaxman, published in *Athenaeum*, August Wilhelm Schlegel wrote about the translation (*Dolmetschen*) of the "charming language of lines and forms" into the poetic "dialect."[81] He was however cognizant of the problematic character of this kind of translation, in which a writer faces the task of "painting a picture with words."[82] Despite the availability of various techniques for ekphrasis, such as narrative or musical ones, the result is usually disappointingly inadequate.[83]

Friedrich Schlegel also wrote ekphrases. His visits to Dresden and numerous conversations about paintings with Ludwig Tieck and Philipp Otto Runge inspired him to write essays on art, in which he reflected upon the perception of visual works. During his stay in Paris, Schlegel visited the Louvre and other places, subsequently presenting descriptions of selected masterpieces, in which he attempted – to use Berbeli Wanning's words – "to translate what he saw into words and thus make it visible again to the mind's eye of the reader."[84] The hermeneutic intent of these translations should not be overlooked, the main aim of Schlegel's descriptions of the Old Masters being to make them understandable.[85] His ekphrases, or reflections on painting, were

---

78 Wilhelm Heinrich Wackenroder, "Herzensergießungen eines kunstliebenden Klosterbruders: Zwey Gemähldeschilderungen," in idem, *Sämtliche Werke und Briefe*, vol. 1, eds. Silvio Vietta, Richard Littlejohns (Heidelberg: Carl Winter Universitätsverlag, 1991), 82–85.
79 A.W. Schlegel, *Die Gemähdle*, 108 ff.
80 Cf., for example, Seweryna Wysłouch, "Ekfraza czy przekład intersemiotyczny?" [Ekphrasis or Intersemiotic Translation?] in *Ruchome granice literatury – W kręgu teorii kulturowej* [Moving Boundaries of Literature – In the Circle of Cultural Theory], eds Seweryna Wysłouch, Beata Przymuszała (Warsaw: PWN, 2009), 48–64, and Lawrence Venuti, "Ekphrasis, Translation, Critique," *Art in Translation* 2, no. 2 (2010): 131–152.
81 August Wilhelm Schlegel, "Über Zeichnungen zu Gedichten und John Flaxman's Umrisse," *Athenaeum* 2, no. 2 (1799): 203.
82 A.W. Schlegel, "Fragment (177)," *Athenaeum* 1, no. 2 (1798): 46.
83 See Yvonne Al-Taie, *Tropus und Erkenntnis – Sprach und Bildtheorie der deutschen Frühromantik* (Göttingen: V&R Unipress, 2015), 255. Cf. also the author's comments on Schlegel's understanding of the notion of *Dolmetschen* in the context of the mutual illumination and explanation of visual arts and literature (258–259).
84 Wanning, *Friedrich Schlegel*, 103.
85 See Friedrich Schlegel, *Nachricht von den Gemälden in Paris*, in KFSA IV: *Ansichten und Ideen von der christlichen Kunst*, ed. Hans Eichner (Paderborn: Schöningh, 1959), 21 ff.

published in the journal *Europa*, which he himself had founded, and Schleiermacher read with great interest what he called "Friedrich's thoughts on painting."

It is therefore not difficult to demonstrate that this particular kind of translation certainly inspired Schleiermacher in 1803. Yet, there is no simple answer to the question of exactly what form such a theory of the translation of pictures into words should take, with several hypotheses being possible. There are many indications that such a theory was involved in Schleiermacher's aesthetics, as I have argued in an earlier publication.[86] In his late lectures on aesthetics (1825), in which he summarizes his previous research, Schleiermacher distinguishes between verbal art (*redende Kunst*) and fine art (*bildende Kunst*), the former being the result of "the process of generating thought," and the latter the result of "generating pictures and images, which is natural for humans."[87] This distinction is not absolute, however, because, as Schleiermacher himself admits, we can describe imaginary figures by means of which the process of generating images engenders verbal art.[88] The generation of thought here seems to be secondary with respect to the primordial concepts of perception and sensation. From this perspective, verbal art is, on the one hand, related to "mimicry and music" (sensations), and on the other hand to fine art (perception).[89]

If we consider translation from one mode of art into another, the key issue is how the formative element present in the original is represented in the translation. In the case of ekphrasis, visual perception is of fundamental importance. According to Schleiermacher, the visual sphere corresponds with the domain of "objective poetry," comprising primarily epic and dramatic works, for which the perception rather than the sensation provides a point of departure.[90] Lyrical poetry, too, can sometimes describe images and characters, but it leans towards subjectivity or the sphere of sensations. Such is the case of the Romantic translations of religious images that Waller presents in *Die Gemählde*. The musical and subjective elements in the form of synesthetic sensations often come to the fore, for example in the sonnet *Die Himmelfahrt der Jungfrau* ("Assumption of the Virgin"), which is a translation of Guido Reni's painting *Himmelfahrt Mariae* (1642).[91] The intersemiotic translator thus created a new piece – a poetic interpretation of a visual work. Using the potential of poetic lan-

---

[86] Bukowski, "Zwischen Platon und christlicher Kunst," 203 ff.
[87] Friedrich Daniel Ernst Schleiermacher, *Ästhetik (1819/25). Über den Begriff der Kunst (1831/32)*, ed. Thomas Lehnerer (Hamburg: Felix Meiner, 1984), 132. On the relationship between Schleiermacher's typology of the arts and his general theory of aesthetics see Thomas Lehnerer, *Die Kunsttheorie Friedrich Schleiermachers* (Stuttgart: Klett-Cotta, 1987), 194–213, 323–337. Lehnerer closely explains the dialectics of image and thought and the dialectical relationship of fine arts and literature in Schleiermacher's aesthetics.
[88] Schleiermacher, *Ästhetik*, 132.
[89] Ibid.
[90] Ibid., 133.
[91] A.W. Schlegel, *Die Gemählde*, 113–114.

guage, he tried to capture the sense of the original in his own fashion.[92] Was his interpretation comparable in terms of character and impression? From the point of view of Schleiermacher's aesthetics, the character of the work has changed as a result of the transfer. Taking this into consideration, the key significance must be attributed to the impression, that is, the impact of the work, which, as Yvonne Al-Taie notes, August Wilhelm Schlegel saw as an invariant value in his theory of ekphrasis as translation.[93] The impression, understood as an adequate aesthetic effect, hinges not only on the rhetorical skills of the translator, but also, by and large, on the recipients and their sensitivity to imagery, that is, on their special ability to "feel the images," and to "see the words."[94]

We can sum up this section with the conclusion that the problem of poetic ekphrasis as a special kind of poetic expression, fascinating the early Romantics, including the Schlegel brothers and Friedrich Schleiermacher, is of vital importance for their hermeneutical reflection. As Gottfried Boehm notes, the interpretive relation linking image and language appears to be a fundamental hermeneutical problem, not only in art history, but also, as should be emphasized, in aesthetic communication in its broadest sense.[95]

4 The "German Plato" project

Schleiermacher's collaboration with Friedrich Schlegel on a project to translate the complete works of Plato, which ultimately strained their friendship to the point of conflict, has already been studied and critically examined a number of times.[96] Similarly, Schleiermacher's unparalleled accomplishments as a translator of Plato's dialogues have also been closely examined and critiqued, as have the rationale, execution, and impact of this work.[97] As such, I will focus here on certain important

---

[92] Gottfried Boehm, "Zu einer Hermeneutik des Bildes," in *Seminar: Hermeneutik und die Wissenschaften*, ed. Hans-Georg Gadamer, Gottfried Boehm (Frankfurt am Main: Suhrkamp, 1978), 455.
[93] Al-Taie, *Tropus und Erkenntnis*, 259.
[94] See Gottfried Boehm, "Zu einer Hermeneutik des Bildes," 454.
[95] Ibid., 447.
[96] Cf. in this context, for example, Wilhelm Dilthey, *Leben Schleiermachers*, vol. I/2: 1803–1807, 3rd edition, ed. Martin Redeker (Berlin: De Gruyter, 1970), 37–75; Nowak, *Schleiermacher – Leben, Werk und Wirkung*, 131–138; Jan Rohls, Schleiermachers Platon, in *Schleiermacher und Kierkegaard*, 709–732; Christoph Asmuth, *Interpretation – Transformation: Das Platonbild bei Fichte, Schelling, Hegel, Schleiermacher und Schopenhauer und das Legitimationsproblem in der Philosophiegeschichte* (Göttingen: Vandenhoeck & Ruprecht, 2006), 187–244; Arndt, *Friedrich Schleiermacher als Philosoph*, 263–274. Many promising new lines of research are explored by Julia A. Lamm in her recent book *Schleiermacher's Plato* (Berlin: Walter de Gruyter, 2021).
[97] E.g. Jörg Jantzen, "Zu Schleiermachers Platon-Übersetzung und seinen Anmerkungen dazu," in Friedrich Schleiermacher, *Über die Philosophie Platons*, ed. Peter M. Steiner with Andreas Arndt, Jörg Jantzen (Hamburg: Felix Meiner, 1996), XLV–LVIII.

aspects of this project that bear upon Schlegel's and Schleiermacher's contributions to translation theory. In Chapter VI of this book, in turn, I will try to illuminate Schleiermacher's Plato from a slightly different angle by offering an analysis of one specific case, namely his rendering of the dialogue *Phaedrus*.

Embittered by Schlegel's accusations that he had allegedly made use of Schlegel's ideas in his translation of Plato, Schleiermacher recounts in one of his letters to August Boeckh (dating from 1808) the entire history of their collaboration from his own perspective, emphasizing the substantive differences between himself and Schlegel (mostly concerning the arrangement of the dialogues). Exhibiting great rhetorical skill, Schleiermacher begins his narrative as follows:

> It must have been *anno Domini* 1798 when, during one of our philosophical conversations, which often concerned Plato, Friedrich Schlegel expressed the thought in passing that, given the contemporary state of philosophy, there was a need to set Plato right, and therefore to translate him fully.[98]

However, as Andreas Arndt has shown, Schleiermacher had not focused on Plato in much detail prior to this "symphilosophical" fellowship with Friedrich Schlegel,[99] thus we can conclude that it was indeed Schlegel who drew the young theologian into his own fascination with Plato and encouraged their joint efforts.

Friedrich Schlegel, on the other hand, certainly exhibited both a philosophical and a literary captivation with Plato.[100] He admired Plato's manner of writing and literary style, identifying the "dithyrambic character" of his work as its poetological dominant, as the domain in which Plato's work "is most Platonic."[101] Schlegel even perceived a kind of "language within language" in the philosopher's dialogues, a language that is essentially esoteric, "enlivened by enthusiasm."[102] Here again Schlegel's dynamic reasoning becomes evident: he tends, in the fashion of later structuralists, to describe meaning *in statu nascendi*, as an open process of revelation.[103] And it is in this progression of thinking, in the "movement" of ideas, in

---

[98] Letter from Schleiermacher to August Boeckh, Berlin, probably between late April and 16 August 1808 (KGA V/10, 116 ff.).
[99] Arndt, *Friedrich Schleiermacher als Philosoph*, 263 ff.
[100] On the origins of this fascination, see Zovko, *Verstehen und Nichtverstehen bei Friedrich Schlegel*, 61–62.
[101] Friedrich Schlegel, *KFSA II: Charakteristiken und Kritiken I*, 119.
[102] Ibid., 184. However, Schlegel rejects the assumption that there is an unwritten (esoteric) doctrine of Plato. See Bärbel Frischmann, "Friedrich Schlegels Platonrezeption und das hermeneutische Paradigma," *Athenäum – Jahrbuch für Romantik* 11 (2001): 78.
[103] See Peter V. Zima, *Literarische Ästhetik – Methoden und Modelle der Literaturwissenschaft* (Tübingen-Basel: Francke, 1995), 275.

the "becoming, creation and development" that, in his opinion, the "proper unity of the Platonic dialogues" manifests itself.[104]

In Schlegel's eyes, Plato's "political science of art" has Romantic qualities. "This is due to its universality," he explains in his *Philosophical Fragments*, meaning that it invokes the universal, that is to say, the infinite.[105] Plato's "mode of reasoning" may also be dubbed Romantic: "it is always based on analogy; it departs from concrete data, to point towards the mystical."[106] Schlegel also noticed a correspondence between his own understanding of philosophy and Plato's perception of transcendence. The infinite and the divine were, in his opinion, brought nearer in the dialogues through the use of symbols and myths. Hans Krämer remarks that these "symbolic-allegorical means of representation, as well as the whole form of Plato's discourse, reflect, from Schlegel's perspective, the philosopher's characteristic principle of the relative non-representability of the supreme."[107] In Schlegel's view, therefore, "the supreme, the infinite, the divine, cannot in Plato's philosophy be described philosophically, explained, or adequately represented; it can at most be suggested in an indefinite way."[108]

Friedrich Schlegel's genuine fascination with Plato led him to develop plans to translate all of the philosopher's works. Most probably as early as 1797, when he published a review of a German translation of selected dialogues by Plato in the journal *Philosophisches Journal einer Gesellschaft Teutscher Gelehrten*, he pondered whether he should present his own understanding of the philosopher's works in the form of a German translation of them.[109] In this review – which we should add was highly critical of the translator, Count Stolberg – hermeneutic and translation issues come into contact. "In order to make the German reader sense the value of Plato's Socrates, one should first of all concentrate on explaining not so much the individual words as the spirit of his teaching," Schlegel writes, anticipating his later hermeneutical remarks on the principles of coherence in Plato's work.[110]

---

104 So Friedrich Schlegel wrote in his *Charakteristik des Plato* within the *Wissenschaft der europäischen Literatur* (1803–1804), KFSA XI: *Wissenschaft der europäischen Literatur: Vorlesungen, Aufsätze und Fragmente aus der Zeit von 1795–1804*, ed. Ernst Behler (Paderborn: Schöningh, 1958), 118–120.
105 F. Schlegel, KFSA II: *Charakteristiken und Kritiken I*, 284.
106 Ibid., 285.
107 Hans-Joachim Krämer, "Fichte, Schlegel und der Infinitismus in der Platondeutung," *Deutsche Vierteljahrsschrift für Literaturwissenschaft und Geistesgeschichte*, 1988, Vol. 62 (4), 601.
108 Ibid.
109 Friedrich Schlegel, *Rezension der Auserlesenen Gespräche der Platon*, trans. Friedrich Leopold Grafen zu Stolberg, in KFSA VIII: *Studien zur Philosophie und Theologie*, eds. Ernst Behler, Ursula Struc-Oppenberg (Paderborn: Schöningh, 1975), 38–40.
110 Ibid., 39. Among other shortcomings, Schlegel also accuses Stolberg of lacking critical sense and misunderstanding of his contemporaries. Cf. Michel, *Ästhetische Hermeneutik und frühromantische Kritik*, 328. The observation of the anachronism of previous interpretations/translations of Plato in relation to the "spirit of the times" was an important premise for Schlegel's concept of a new translation of the philosopher's dialogues. See Zovko, *Verstehen und Nichtverstehen bei Friedrich Schlegel*, 64.

According to Dilthey, even before 1799 Schlegel "had begun to translate *Lysis* and was thinking about translating the *Laws*."[111] Reflecting on the essential nature of Plato's legacy, around 1800, in his sketches *Grundsätze zum Werk Platons* he noted: "There is a visible thread connecting a number of the dialogues, indeed all of them, some original intentional connection."[112] This leads us directly to Schlegel's claim about the unified essence of Plato's works, which Schleiermacher adopts in its most general form. In the course of Schleiermacher's correspondence with Schlegel, however, it becomes clear that Schlegel achieves this unity by means of radical exclusion.[113] Those dialogues "not authored by Plato" are rejected, so that the remaining ones, as Schlegel writes in a letter dated 25 February 1802, "will be all the more strongly connected with one another."[114] The key role is played here by Plato's own train of thought, the development of ideas, which is the thread binding the various works and ensuring the unity of his philosophy. For Schlegel, it does not lie *outside* the dialogues, but *in* them (H. Krämer).[115]

For scholars of translation, Schleiermacher's manuscript *Zum Platon* also makes for interesting reading. It contains reflections on the translation project, both conceptual (in the spirit of Schlegel) and substantive, i.e. referring to specific fragments of text.[116] Here philological textual criticism takes the form of an analysis of the source text in preparation for its translation, which involves working with the meta-contexts of the translation.[117] The most difficult and risky task in this case, however, concerns the original itself, because it has to be (re)constructed, that is, put together through thorough philological reading, comparing editions, and establishing a reading.

In order to turn the "disarray" of the *Corpus Platonicum* into a "natural sequence of Platonic works," it was necessary, Schleiermacher stresses in his introduction to *Platons Werke*, "to clarify beforehand which writings are of Plato's authorship, and which are not."[118] Only after this can there be a *re-interpretation*, a *re-expression* of the thoughts expressed in the original text. In this, Schleiermacher finds it important to avoid a modernizing, "philosophical translation" of Plato. As he makes clear in his review of Friedrich Ast's *De Phaedro*, the interpretation of thoughts must "remain a

---

111 Dilthey, *Leben Schleiermachers*, vol. I/2, 42.
112 F. Schlegel, *KFSA XVIII: Philosophische Lehrjahre*, 526.
113 See Friedrich Schlegel, Philosophie des Plato, in idem, *Schriften zur Kritischen Philosophie 1795–1805*, ed. Andreas Arndt, Jure Zovko (Hamburg: Felix Meiner, 2007), 208. On Schlegel's conclusions regarding the authorship and periodization of Plato's dialogues see Frischmann, "Friedrich Schlegels Platonrezeption und das hermeneutische Paradigma," 84–85.
114 Letter from Friedrich Schlegel to Schleiermacher, 25 February 1802. (KGAV/5, 333). On the order of the dialogues see Rohls, Schleiermachers Plato, 714.
115 Krämer, "Fichte, Schlegel und der Infinitismus in der Platondeutung," 605.
116 See Günter Meckenstock, Einleitung, KGA I/3, XCVII.
117 Krzysztof Lipiński, *Übungstexte zur Methodologie der literarischen Übersetzung* (Kraków: Wydawnictwo UJ, 1986), 20.
118 Friedrich Schleiermacher, Einleitung, in *Platons Werke*, vol. I/1, 3rd. ed. (Berlin: Georg Reimer, 1855), 22; cf. KGA IV/3, 40.

translation, so that no foreign sense is brought into the translated passages" (KGA I/3, 474).[119] As such, as Jörg Jantzen notes, "a German duplicate of a thought originally expressed in Greek" can be produced in the end.[120]

In his notes on *Zum Platon*, one can sense a conviction that such an extensive and philologically ambitious project requires a particularly solid explanation, and consequently a theoretical justification for the translation. Schleiermacher notes: "In the introduction there must be something about the assumptions behind the translation of particular words and the difference it makes whether they are nouns and figure in some particular terminology" (KGA I/3, 344). The translator is thus interested in words, in their function, meaning and how they fit into the broader conceptual system (terminology).

Schlegel, too, in a hastily written announcement of the forthcoming publication of Plato's works, promised his readers an informative introduction of his own. However, in his conception, this text was meant to provide a scholarly justification for the German edition of Plato; musings about the theory of translation were not in the plans. On the subject of translation itself, Schlegel expressed himself briefly and, of course, optimistically: "this difficult task for the art of translation" appears to be solvable "at the point of development which the German language is now beginning to approach."[121] It was precisely this image of the German language striving towards perfection, that intensified the Romantic zeal to translate.

However, to claim that Schlegel's contribution to the joint translation project was limited solely to the conceptual plane because he made no attempt at translatological analysis of the text would be incorrect. In his *Grundsätze zum Werk Platons*, for example, he pointed out that Plato's favorite thoughts appear "often in the same phrases"[122] – important information for a translator. Schlegel's interest in translational analysis is also evidenced by a comment in a letter to Schleiermacher of 1 May 1801, concerning the latter's translation of the *Phaedrus*:

> I think the language and the manner of imitation are good and excellent. I also completely agree with your assumptions; I was only struck by the word games. The one with *Wahn* and *Wahrsagkunst*, however, is very hard. The one with Τυφων I would possibly still try to reproduce differently, but the sense could then take on slightly different nuances than in your version.[123]

Schleiermacher, in turn, noted in Berlin: "Plato's word games are a truly dialogical ingredient and should be worthily imitated where a concept is explained through

---

119 Cf. also Rohls, *Schleiermachers Plato*, 715, and Julia A. Lamm, "The Art of Interpreting Plato," in *The Cambridge Companion to Friedrich Schleiermacher*, ed. Jacqueline Mariña (Cambridge: Cambridge Univ. Press, 2005), 95.
120 Jantzen, *Zu Schleiermachers Platon-Übersetzung und seinen Anmerkungen dazu*, LI.
121 Quoted in Dilthey, *Leben Schleiermachers*, vol. I/2, 63.
122 F. Schlegel, *KFSA XVIII: Philosophische Lehrjahre*, 529.
123 Letter from Friedrich Schlegel to Schleiermacher, 1 May 1801. (KGA V/5, 111 ff.). On the imitations mentioned in the letter (*Phaedrus* 244c and 230a) see the notes of the editors of the volume (111 ff.).

such play," and on this point the two friends were in complete agreement (KGA I/3, 293).

Note that Schlegel's views on Plato's language and style, as expressed in his lecture *Philosophie des Plato* (1804/1805), were closely related to his analysis of translation. In this text, he argued that "pure thinking and knowledge of the supreme, the infinite" – which is, after all, the very essence of philosophy – can never be adequately represented, that is, translated into equivalent "form and language." Since the "supreme" can only appear in disguise, Plato's thinking assimilated the language and terminology of each of the "arts and sciences of the time."[124] This is why Plato's dialogues are not only polyphonic but also multilingual.[125] His philosophical language consists, as Schlegel argues, of "expressions, phrases and words" that come from "all genres and branches of human knowledge," moreover: it varies in its form from rhetorical to dialectical, from political to poetic-physical.[126] This has to do with the aforementioned principle of "relative irrepresentability," and the *untranslatability* of the supreme and infinite, out of which specific linguistic problems of translation arise.

Schlegel's and Schleiermacher's notes and correspondence about translating Plato demonstrate that their reflections were to a large extent parallel – even partly addressing the very same problems. Differences of opinion naturally manifest themselves as regards the authenticity of certain dialogues and their "arrangement," as well as specific proposals for their interpretation. The latter, however, were primarily due to Schlegel's unwillingness to devote time to the practical pursuit of the project, that is, to work on the translation itself: "Translation is not my strong point, I suppose. I have no real inclination for it." This excuse from a letter to Schleiermacher from Paris dated 5 May 1803 is often quoted in this particular context. Less often cited, however, is the immediately following explanation offered by Schlegel, that this shortcoming is connected with "a special regard for substantive commentary."[127]

This statement can be understood in the sense that, for Schlegel, translating Plato was too closely related to his own (ambitiously planned) critique of Plato's works[128] to be put into practice freely. Of course, the statement can also be taken as an attempt at simply making an excuse, since Schlegel was already aware that he would not be able to complete his work, not even partially. A letter Schlegel sent from Paris, in which he inundates Schleiermacher with ideas and proposals

---

124 F. Schlegel, *Philosophie des Plato*, 209 ff. Cf. also idem, KFSA XI: *Wissenschaft der europäischen Literatur*, 124.
125 Mikhail M. Bakhtin, "Aus der Vorgeschichte des Romanwortes," in *Die Ästhetik des Wortes*, ed. Rainer Grübel, trans. Rainer Grübel und Sabine Reese (Frankfurt am Main: Suhrkamp. 1979), 301–337; Julia Kristeva, "Word, Dialogue and Novel," in idem, *The Kristeva Reader*, ed. Toril Moi (New York: Columbia Univ. Press, 1986), 51–2.
126 F. Schlegel, *Philosophie des Plato*, 210.
127 Letter from Friedrich Schlegel to Schleiermacher, May 5, 1803 (KGA V/6, 363).
128 Friedrich Schlegel wanted to publish *Critique of Plato* as a "separate publication" (ibid.).

for rescuing their joint project, also contains reflections that aptly characterize his own attitude to the practice of translation. Schlegel writes that his and Schleiermacher's methods of translation "differ so much from one other" that this entitles the author of *Lucinde* to undertake a "new experiment" with his own translations of the *Parmenides*, *Cratylus*, *Timaeus*, and *Critias*.[129] A little further on he writes: "I am so dissatisfied with my translation of the *Phaedo* that I have already wanted to throw it out many times."[130]

It seems, therefore, that Schlegel, practicing the early Romantic mode of criticism,[131] strove for a synthetic translation meant to express his own "overall critical-systematic view of Plato"[132] and at the same time setting the Platonic texts in motion, creating them anew. For only in a mimic translation, which is creative, critical and dynamic-progressive, can the dialogues realize their educational potential (*Bildungspotential*).[133] Such a translation, however, is only possible as an experiment, as a project – a preliminarily and imperfectly developed commentary.

Despite his propensity for speculation, Schlegel was not willing to enter into theoretical discussion about translation. In a letter dated 20 October, 1800, Schleiermacher informed his friend: "we still have to agree upon many things about the theory of translation (*Übersetzungstheorie*), and only then will I be able to begin translating."[134] There is every indication, however, that no concrete "agreements" of this kind were ever reached.

And so neither Schlegel, who in the end abandoned the project, nor Schleiermacher ever explained in detail the assumptions underpinning their new German translation of Plato. Schleiermacher, who ultimately became responsible for the project on his own, explains this situation in the introductory foreword to the first volume of the translation as such: "The principles according to which this translation has been produced will be readily recognized by everyone; to defend them would

---

129 Ibid., 363 ff.
130 Ibid., 365.
131 Cf. Bauer, *Schlegel und Schleiermacher*, 345.
132 Hermann Patsch, "Friedrich Asts Eutyphrion-Übersetzung im Nachlass Friedrich Schlegels. Ein Beitrag zur Platon-Rezeption in der Frühromantik," *Jahrbuch des Freien Deutschen Hochstifts* (1988): 123.
133 Schleiermacher's different point of view is emphasized by Andrea Follak in her dissertation *Der "Ausblick zur Idee" – Eine vergleichende Studie zur Platonischen Pädagogik bei Friedrich Schleiermacher, Paul Natorp und Werner Jaeger* (Göttingen: Vandenhoeck & Ruprecht, 2005), 49.
134 Schleiermacher's letter to Friedrich Schlegel, 20 October 1800 (KGA V/4, 299 ff.). Andreas Huyssen argues that this mention of a "theory of translation" suggests that Schleiermacher was already thinking about the shape of a general theory of translation at this time, whereas the fact that it was not until thirteen years later that he formulated his contributions to it is explained by his specific style of work. However, it seems that the author of the letter was concerned with the theoretical premises of translating *Plato*. Andreas Huyssen, *Die frühromantische Konzeption von Übersetzung und Aneignung – Studien zur frühromantischen Utopie einer deutschen Weltliteratur* (Zürich: Atlantis Verlag, 1969), 51.

be partly superfluous, partly futile."[135] In the successive prefaces to the individual dialogues Schleiermacher likewise gives essentially no information about the theoretical aspects of his translation.

In several introductions and a large number of footnotes, however, he does discuss specific cases of the difficulty or impossibility of faithful translation, developing a discourse in which he skillfully involves his readers. He not infrequently expresses an awareness of linguistic relativism or – as Schleiermacher himself put it, the "irrationality" of languages – that it is not true "that that any given word in one will correspond precisely to one in the other, or that an inflection in one will unify the same complex of relationships as any conceivable counterpart in the other" (DR 227; KGA I/11, 70). This is how Schleiermacher sums up the essence of this irrationality in his lecture *On the Different Methods of Translation*, emphasizing:

> For how infinitely difficult and intricate the business becomes [...]! What accurate knowledge, what command of both languages it [...] requires! And how often, with a similar sovereign command of the subject matter and the languages involved, and sharing the belief that no perfect equivalent can be found, do two translators differ as to which rendering most closely approximates the original (DR 227; KGA I/11, 71).

This remark applies both to "the most vivid poetic images" and to "the most inward and universal scholarly terms" (DR 227; KGA I/11, 71). Schleiermacher is certainly referring here to his experience with translating Plato.

In spite of numerous difficulties, conditioned by the "irrationality" of languages, i.e. systemic differences, Schleiermacher went to great lengths to provide an "appropriate" translation of "Hellenic" expressions into German, especially of the most important philosophical terms, such as sophrosyne (σωφροσύνη: Besonnenheit 'prudence', 'restraint') in *Charmides*.[136] His commentaries prove his high philological competence. One has to admit here that Dilthey is right when he claims that Schleiermacher, a theologically educated translator, "thanks to his close collaboration with Heindorf, became an insightful philologist."[137] The key concept in this context is that of appropriateness (*Angemessenheit*), once analyzed by Schleiermacher as a rhetorical concept, which appears here as a principle or goal of translation and also refers to foreignness. In the preface to the *Cratylus*, Schleiermacher writes of "this etymological part" of the dialogue that "has been the *crux* of the translator and it was [a]

---

135 Schleiermacher, "Vorerinnerung," in *Platons Werke*, vol. I/1, V. Cf. KGA IV/3, 7.
136 Friedrich Schleiermacher, "Einleitung zu Charmides," in idem, *Platons Werke*, vol. I/2, 3rd ed. (Berlin: Georg Reimer, 1855), 6.
137 Dilthey, *Leben Schleiermachers*, vol. I/2, 50. This is confirmed by Julia A. Lamm, noting that "the philological method for Schleiermacher involves close grammatical and comparative work within the text" (Lamm, *Schleiermacher's Plato*, 29)

matter of long and perplexing deliberation with him how to extricate himself from the difficulty."[138] What did this difficulty involve? The translator explains:

> The introduction generally of the Greek words appeared [to be] an intolerable expedient, and it seemed better to let the Socrates who was speaking German once for all derive German from German. On the other hand, it was not possible to do this with the proper names – in these it was necessary to preserve the original tongue; and since both methods now stand in company with one another, the reader will at all events have occasion to congratulate himself that no one exclusively pervades the whole.[139]

What Schleiermacher is addressing here is, in today's terms, the problem of foreignization vs. domestication. He does not apply a radical theory of foreignization (in which a consistently foreignized German is meant to evoke the foreignness of the original, as, for example, in Friedrich Hölderlin's translations), but takes into account the perspective of the recipient of the translation.[140] Hence the careful balancing of foreignness in the Germanized text. Schleiermacher speaks of "ways of proceeding" (*Verfahrungsarten*) of the translator and thus clearly articulates a *pragmatic* translation strategy. This attitude to translation can be seen as the starting point of the discourse on translational "methods" and "foreign semblance" (*fremde Ähnlichkeit*) in his later lecture at the Prussian Academy of Sciences in 1813 (DR 232; KGA I/11, 81).[141]

In one of his letters to Schleiermacher, Schlegel also referred to the difficult passages in the *Cratylus*. As a possible solution to the issue of translating the derivations quoted by Socrates, Schlegel proposed "German derivative words," which admittedly lead to a "lack of correspondence." In essence, however, such a translation is not, as Schlegel argues, about equivalence, but about "conveying the image of the work."[142] Nevertheless, he advised: "In derivations from Scythian [actually from the language of the Phrygians] [...] precisely the Hellenistic words should be preserved."[143] Schleiermacher, on the other hand, opted for a domesticating translation.[144] From the standpoint of modern translation theory, one can see that Schleiermacher largely applies here the principles of functionalism in translation, at the same time antici-

---

138 Friedrich Schleiermacher, "Einleitung zu Kratylos," in *Platons Werke*, vol. II/2, 3rd ed. (Berlin: Georg Reimer, 1857), 15. English version from *Introductions to the Dialogues of Plato*, trans. William Dobson (Cambridge: Pitt Press, Deighton, and Parker, 1836), 244.
139 Ibid., 244–45.
140 On the target audience of *Platons Werke* see Hermann Patsch, "Schleiermacher und die philologische Bibelübersetzung", in *Übersetzung – Translation – Traduction: Ein internationales Handbuch zur Übersetzungsforschung*, vol. 3, ed. Harald Kittel et al. (Berlin: Walter de Gruyter, 2011), 2401.
141 Cf. in this context the analysis of poetic imitation in Schleiermacher's translation of Plato in: Hermann Patsch, *Alle Menschen sind Künstler – Friedrich Schleiermachers poetische Versuche* (Berlin: De Gruyter, 1986), 68–76.
142 Letter from Friedrich Schlegel to Schleiermacher, 12 April 1802 (KGA V/5, 375).
143 Ibid.
144 See Friedrich Schleiermacher, *Kratylos*, in *Platons Werke*, vol. II/2, 48.

pating the theories of foreignization oriented towards empirical and aesthetic empirics and the aesthetics of reception. In the lecture *On the Different Methods of Translating*, he presents the problems of text mediation in translation as follows:

> But what paths are open to the true translator, one who would bring those two utterly unconnected people together, the source-language author and the target-language reader – and would aid the latter, without banishing him from the sphere of the target language, in attaining as accurate and thorough an understanding and enjoyment of the former? (DR 229; KGA I/11, 48).

Hans J. Vermeer, the most important representative of German functionalism in translation studies, saw this statement of the problem as a confirmation of his own pragmatic, target-text-oriented theory of translation: "This foreignization, this bringing of the reader to the author, is also foreignization within one culture," he wrote. "The recipient does not actually step out of his culture [...]. He does not give up his culture; the translator has expanded it for him."[145] Schleiermacher thus proves himself to have been a pioneer of creative, "culturally sensitive" (*kultursensitiv*) translational action, aiming at an effective cultural mediation.[146]

Here an important difference between Schleiermacher's and Schlegel's understanding of translation makes itself apparent. The former tends towards approaches that focus on process and transfer, firmly grounding them in practice.[147] The latter, on the other hand, prefers to comprehend translation in its potentiality, understanding it as a thinking tool, a mode of philological criticism, a way of potentializing the original, also as an image, a metaphor, a unity in heterogeneity, and finally as poetry, creation in itself. Therefore, André Lefevere is right when he observes, writing about Schlegel's theory of translation: "Friedrich Schlegel most radically conceives of translation as a category of thought rather as an activity connected with language or literature only."[148]

A significant difference between Schleiermacher's and Schlegel's intentions can also be seen on the hermeneutical plane of the project of publishing Plato's works in German. Both wanted, it seems, to perpetuate and disseminate their own understanding of Plato's philosophy, but also, conversely, both wanted to arrive at a more complete understanding of Plato through the translation project. However, while Schlegel focused mainly on synthesizing methods that revealed the "eccentric peculiarity of the whole"[149] (indicating the open-ended character of his thinking), Schleiermacher approached his material analytically, following the idea of a "seed

---

145 Hans J. Vermeer, "Hermeneutik und Übersetzung(swissenschaft)," *TEXTconTEXT* 9 (1994): 174.
146 See Ibid., 173.
147 As Christoph Asmuth notes, Schleiermacher "repeatedly points out to Schlegel the need for a practice-oriented theory of translation, as well as a clear conception of Plato's evolution, so as to take this as a point of departure when working on Plato" (Asmuth, *Interpretation – Transformation*, 199).
148 André Lefevere, *Translating Literature: The German Tradition* (Assen: Van Gorcum, 1977), 58.
149 F. Schlegel, *Grundsätze zum Werk Platons*, in *KFSA II: Charakteristiken und Kritiken I*, 530.

draft" (*Keimentwurf*), which ensures the unity of Plato's work, while at the same time perfecting his hermeneutical skills. Therefore, he could already in 1803 formulate the conclusion: "not only can much be explained in Plato, but Plato is also the right author for illuminating the question of understanding."[150]

While examining Friedrich Schleiermacher's philosophical relationship with Friedrich Schlegel, Andreas Arndt points out that three concepts essential to the former's philosophical discourse – "briefly put: Plato, hermeneutics, dialectics" – were being worked out by Schlegel during the time of his friendship and collaboration with Schleiermacher.[151] This extraordinary meeting of minds gave rise to translation-theoretical concepts and translation solutions, which remained in close connection with hermeneutics and dialectics. Their influence can be seen in Schleiermacher's subsequent thinking, particularly in his reflections on dialectics, and especially where he considers the problem of the "linguistic circle" (*Sprachkreis*) and the linguistic differences that lead to untranslatability and difficulties in communication.[152] But it also reveals itself in Schleiermacher's aesthetics.[153] It can be concluded, therefore, that his collaboration with Friedrich Schlegel had a significant impact on Schleiermacher's entire subsequent intellectual output.

---

[150] Schleiermacher's letter to Georg Andreas Reimer (KGA V/7, 393).
[151] Arndt, *Friedrich Schleiermacher als Philosoph*, 40.
[152] See the introduction to Schleiermacher's *Vorlesungen über die Dialektik* (KGA II/10,1, 404–408). On the notion of *Sprachkreis* see Sarah Schmidt, "Wahrnehmung und Schema: Zur zentralen Bedeutung des bildlichen Denkens in Schleiermachers Dialektik," in *Schleiermacher und Kierkegaard*, 78 ff.
[153] See Schleiermacher, *Ästhetik*, 143 ff. Cf. also Patsch, *Alle Menschen sind Künstler*, 76.

IV The Dead Letter and Living Spirit of Mediation

1 Introduction: Schleiermacher's "ingenious" *Jugendwerk*[1]

While Schleiermacher's *Hermeneutics* came into being gradually and accumulatively, only eventually gaining the status of an epoch-making work in the eyes of his contemporary listeners and readers, his equally groundbreaking speeches *On Religion* were written very differently: in response to a single a creative impetus, without any prior plans or outlines. One would be hard pressed to find even a hint of any such plans in Schleiermacher's extraordinarily rich correspondence, which otherwise abounds in intimate confessions and detailed reports about his ongoing work on successive texts.[2]

However, as Wilhelm Dilthey rightly notes, one can quite precisely identify the intellectual milieu from which the speeches *On Religion* sprang: the inspirations, readings and creative attempts of Schleiermacher's time in Berlin – the most important of which concerned Plato, whom he had "discovered" thanks to Friedrich Schlegel. The young theologian also then reworked his earlier influences, combining them with new ones into a whole that took on an independent shape. Dilthey points out:

> Expressions like 'the finite' [*das Endliche*], 'the infinite' [*das Unendliche*], 'the eternal' [*das Ewige*], 'the Universe' [*das Universum*] were taken by Schleiermacher from Spinoza, Shaftesbury, Hemsterhuis, Jacobi. But their intended sense, as depicted in the context of his own worldview, needs to be guessed at by often boldly linking together various fragments.[3]

This is particularly true of the philosophy of Baruch Spinoza, which Schleiermacher profoundly transformed in his speeches *On Religion* in the spirit of the post-Kantian transcendental philosophy. In this context, following Martin Jay's suggestion, we can speak of Schleiermacher's *translation* of the theses of the author of the *Ethics* into the language of Romantic expressionism.[4] Unlike Spinoza, the German theologian claimed, for example, that the universe (*das Universum*), that is, "the world in a higher sense, opens up to him through the mediation of the Spirit in the spiritual

---

[1] The speeches *On Religion* were dubbed his "*genialische Jugendwerk*" by Hermann Fischer, *Schleiermacher, Friedrich Daniel Ernst (1768–1834)*, in *Theologische Realenzyklopädie*, vol. 30, ed. Gerhard Müller et al. (Berlin: Walter de Gruyter, 1999), 153.

[2] Wilhelm Dilthey, *Leben Schleiermachers*, vol. I/1: *1768–1802*, 3rd ed., ed. Martin Redeker (Berlin: Walter de Gruyter, 1970), 389.

[3] Ibid., 323.

[4] Martin Jay, *Songs of Experience: Modern American and European Variations on a Universal Theme* (Berkeley: Univ. of California Press, 2005), 97.

world."⁵ It is worth emphasizing here the concept of mediation (*die Vermittlung*), which will play a key role in our analysis of the speeches *On Religion*.

With regard to Schleiermacher's private life, Dilthey notes that the moment the speeches *On Religion* came into being falls during the best period of his youthful years, which was simultaneously a watershed time in his life: "all those life circumstances of this youthful period reach their apogee, the heart is filled with a feeling of spiritual richness, although, on the other hand, there are the first signs that the position he took amongst the Berlin milieu might jeopardize his future career."⁶

Dilthey speculates that Schleiermacher had been discussing religion with Friedrich Schlegel and Henrietta Herz since the spring of 1798, and had become increasingly immersed in the subject.⁷ Although he did not explicitly declare his writing plans, by the end of the year it was clear to all his friends that he was already developing a work devoted to religion. "Schleiermacher, who is not so much an apostle, but rather a born reviewer of all the sublime biblical sayings, and to whom a single word from God is enough to compose a powerful sermon, is also working on a treatise on religion," Friedrich Schlegel wrote to Novalis.⁸

There is much to suggest that between November 1798 and February 1799 Schleiermacher worked on his speeches *On Religion* with an intensity that was unusual even for him. Dilthey notes that during this time he did not even answer his letters. It was then, during his stay in Potsdam, that the first two speeches were written, evidencing the utmost creative vigor and inspiration. Later, professional obligations led Schleiermacher to pause writing for some time. When he returned to the project, however, it turned out that his inspiration had waned – the third speech did not manage to achieve the same level of dazzling rhetoric and intellectual inno-

---

5 Dilthey, *Leben Schleiermachers*, vol. I/1, 340; see also other differences: ibid., 339–341. On Schleiermacher's stance on Spinoza, cf. also Konrad Cramer, "'Anschauung des Universums' – Schleiermacher und Spinoza," in *200 Jahre "Reden über die Religion: Akten des 1. Internationalen Kongresses der Schleiermacher-Gesellschaft, Halle, 14.–17. März 1999*, ed. Ulrich Barth, Claus-Dieter Osthövener (Berlin: Walter de Gruyter, 2000), 118–141, and Sarah Schmidt, *Die Konstruktion des Endlichen – Schleiermachers Philosophie der Wechselwirkung* (Berlin: Walter de Gruyter, 2005), 26–39 and 81–84. Many scholars, I believe, exaggerate the influence of Spinoza on Schleiermacher's speeches *On Religion*. It is worth remembering, however, that in fact, Spinoza's metaphysics was alien to the hermeneutics of experience that was important to Schleiermacher. This is probably the reason why, almost 30 years after the publication of the speeches *On Religion*, when the fashion for Spinoza the mystic had waned, Schleiermacher categorically denied that he had ever been a follower of the philosopher – letter of 2 January 1827 to Delbrück, *Aus Schleiermachers Leben – In Briefen*, ed. Wilhelm Dilthey, vol. 4 (Berlin: Georg Reimer, 1863), 375.
6 Dilthey, *Leben Schleiermachers*, vol. I/1, 389. On Schleiermacher's youthful experiences and their influence on the speeches *On Religion* see Siegfried Müller, *Die Erfahrung des jungen Schleiermacher als Grundlage seines philosophisch-theologischen Denkens*, in *Internationaler Schleiermacher-Kongreß Berlin 1984*, ed. Kurt-Victor Selge, sub-vol. 1 (Berlin: De Gruyter, 1985), 153–161.
7 Dilthey, *Leben Schleiermachers*, vol. I/1, 389–390, see also KGA I/2, LIV, *Einleitung*.
8 Friedrich Schlegel, KFSA XXIV: *Die Periode des Athenäums (25. Juli 1797 – Ende August 1799)*, ed. Raymond Immerwahr, Paderborn 1986 (Abt. 3: Briefe), 206.

vation, a fact its author was aware of (cf. KGA I/2, LVI). He worked on the fourth and fifth speech at an uneven pace, sometimes rather laboriously, correcting them quite a lot.[9] Finally, on 15 April 1799 he finished: "let it go out into the world, we'll see how it fares," he wrote to Henrietta Herz, when sending her the last part of the work (KGA V/3, 90).[10] As it would happen, these speeches *On Religion* were to become one of the most important and most lively debated works of Romanticism.

Not long before the work made its premiere (finally in the summer of 1799), it was still functioning under the title *Ueber die Religion: Reden an die aufgeklärten Verächter derselben* (*On Religion: Speeches to its Enlightened Despisers*). Ultimately, however, the anonymous work was published under the title *Über die Religion: Reden an die Gebildeten unter ihren Verächtern* (*On Religion: Speeches to its Educated Despisers*). It is easy to notice that, with this move, Schleiermacher opted out of the idea of exposing the supporters of the Enlightenment (*die Aufklärung*) as opponents of religion, instead deciding on a broader generalization. This was probably because among the "enlightened" Berliners he himself was acquainted with, there really were few declared enemies of religion.[11] The book was accepted by the Berlin publisher Johann Friedrich Unger and it appeared in the summer of 1799. Subsequent editions were no longer published anonymously, and differed from the first. Schleiermacher submitted edited versions of the text to Georg Reimer's publishing house in 1806, 1821, and 1831, and ultimately "the fourth edition, which was also included in *Sämmtliche Werke*, barely resembled the first version, thereby condemning it to a long period of nonexistent reception."[12] The reason for these alterations was most likely the desire to align the speeches *On Religion* with his other theological works, and especially with the *Christian Faith* (*Glaubenslehre*). Interest in the original text was rekindled by the eminent religious scholar Rudolf Otto, who republished the speeches in the same form as their first edition in 1799.

The book met with great interest and was very warmly received by "educated" readers sympathetic to Romanticism, although outside this circle the publication did not arouse much enthusiasm.[13] Friedrich Schlegel was the earliest (due to his comments on the manuscript) and probably the fairest reviewer of the work. He made many pertinent analytical remarks about the speeches *On Religion* in a specially dedicated "Note" published in the journal *Athenaeum* (KGA I/2, LXVIII-LXIX). Such prominent thinkers as Goethe, Jean Paul, Schelling, and Hegel also commented on

---

9 Dilthey, *Leben Schleiermachers*, vol. I/1, 392.
10 He sent the parts he finished to friends in Berlin, and Schlegel forwarded them Johann Friedrich Unger to be prepared for printing, see KGA I/2, LIV–LV.
11 Andreas Arndt, "Kommentar," to Friedrich Schleiermacher, *Schriften*, ed. Andreas Arndt (Frankfurt am Main: Deutscher Klassiker Verlag, 1996), 1146; see also Kurt Nowak, *Schleiermacher – Leben, Werk, Wirkung*, Göttingen 2001), 99.
12 Arndt, "Kommentar," 1144, cf. KGA I/2, LXXVIII.
13 On the reception of the speeches *On Religion*, cf. Günter Meckenstock's detailed report in KGA I/2, LXI-LXXVIII.

the work, appreciating its significance. This interest is hardly surprising, since with this work Schleiermacher made a contribution to the philosophical discourse on religion that had been playing out in Germany since the Enlightenment, and had already given rise to fundamental texts by Lessing, Jacobi, Kant, Fichte, Schelling, and Hegel. A year before the publication of the speeches *On Religion*, the courageous writings of Friedrich Karl Forberg and Johann Gottlieb Fichte had touched off the so-called "atheism dispute" (*Atheismusstreit*), which was an important context for Schleiermacher.[14] In 1793 Immanuel Kant had taken an important stand on religion, publishing in Königsberg his *Religion within the Limits of Reason Alone*. Kant served as the main point of reference for Schleiermacher in the speeches *On Religion*, who in his polemics with Kant invokes the aforementioned Spinozian inspirations and develops a theory of religion which in time, contrasted against Kant's religion of reason, would come to be described as Romantic.[15]

Also of fundamental importance for understanding the author's intentions is his polemic exchange with his censor, who also happened to be an acquaintance: Oberhofprediger Friedrich Samuel Gottfried Sack. In a letter to Schleiermacher of June 1801, Sack made no secret of his disappointment with this work:

> Unfortunately, after a careful reading of the book, I cannot see it as anything other than a spiritualized apology for pantheism, as a speech-like representation of the Spinozian system. [...] Nor do I understand how an adherent of such a system can be a reliable teacher of Christianity; for no sophistical or rhetorical artistry can convince a reasonable man that Spinozism and the Christian religion can be reconciled (KGA I/2, LXII).

Sack warns Schleiermacher that with this work he is contributing to an unfortunate transformation of traditional religious concepts, whereby they evolve into speculative and poetic ones – that he is translating, as it were, the natural, comprehensible language of Christian religion into a Spinoza-inspired, new-fashioned philosophical and poetic jargon (KGA I/2, LXIII).[16]

---

14 Controversy arose primarily over two articles published in *Philosophisches Journal* (1798), one by Forberg (*Entwickelung des Begriffs der Religion*) and the other by Fichte (*Über den Grund unseres Glaubens an eine göttliche Weltregierung*). Fichte's critical analysis of the foundations of faith in the divine order of the world led him to be accused of propagating atheism among the youth and dismissed from the University of Jena. See Folkart Wittekind, "Die Vision der Gesellschaft und die Bedeutung religiöser Kommunikation: Schleiermachers Kritik am Atheismusstreit als Leitmotiv der 'Reden,'" in *200 Jahre "Reden über die Religion,"* 397–415.
15 Hermann Fischer, *Friedrich Daniel Ernst Schleiermacher* (Munich: C.H. Beck, 2001), 51. Elsewhere, Fischer writes about the speeches *On Religion* as a Romantic project in response to Kant's Enlightened concept (see idem, *Schleiermacher, Friedrich Daniel Ernst*, 154).
16 An important context for this polemic is, of course, the so-called "Spinoza dispute" (*Spinozastreit*, or *Pantheismusstreit*), which was touched off in Germany by Friedrich Heinrich Jacobi in his letter *Über die Lehre des Spinoza in Briefen an den Herrn Moses Mendelssohn* (1785). Jacobi suggested that atheism and fatalism are obvious consequences of Spinoza's rationalism. But with his appeal for opposition to "Spinozism," Jacobi nevertheless contributed to the growing interest in Spinoza's

Schleiermacher responds to these accusations with a detailed self-commentary, contained in a letter written probably also in June 1801. He protests against being accused of adopting a Spinozian perspective. After all, he writes, he does not make any claims in *On Religion* that might support this:

> All I said was that religion does not depend on whether, in our abstract thinking, we assign the predicate "person" to the infinite, supra-sensory cause of the world or not. In this context, not being a Spinozian, I have cited Spinoza as an example, for there is a prevailing mood in his *Ethics* that can only be described as pious (KGA I/2, LXIII-LXIV).

Some ascribe personhood to God, while others do not, Schleiermacher notes, formulating a thought that is important in the context of our considerations in this chapter: "Here we must make the distinction that without a certain dose of anthropomorphism, nothing in religion can be put into words [...]." A little further on he writes: "The dominant concept of God today is compound, consisting of such qualities as supra-worldliness [*die Außerweltlichkeit*], personality and infinity, which become annihilated if just one of them is subtracted." And he concludes: "In the present storm of philosophical views, my ultimate aim has been to properly present and justify the independence of religion from any metaphysics" (KGA I/2, LXIV). In a letter to Sack, Schleiermacher also rejects the unpleasant accusation that he had betrayed his own vocation: he considers himself a deeply religious man, responsible in his faith, who nevertheless holds his own views on the role of the Church and preachers in the modern world (KGA I/2, LXV).

It is hard to deny that Schleiermacher has a point; after all, his work is perfectly defensible as a modern Protestant apologetics, which aims to defend religious faith from critics by demonstrating its essence, justification, and place in the present times. In the final tally, it is about even more than just religion: the ambition of the speeches *On Religion* is to affirm religion (in particular, Christian religion) as a value constitutive for culture.[17]

Attention has repeatedly been drawn to the extraordinary persuasive power of the speeches *On Religion*. Kurt Nowak points out that they allude to the kinds of speeches delivered by orators before democratic assemblies.[18] In them, Schleiermacher develops a rhetorical style that seems to be a synthesis of the classical, Rousseauian, and early Romantic traditions. He creatively draws upon his intensive studies of elocutionary rhetoric, as was evident in the lectures *On Style* that we discussed in the first part of this book, as well as upon his inspirations and experiences in Ber-

---

thought (which resulted in new editions of his works). See Fritz Mauthner, "Einleitung," in *Jacobis Spinoza-Büchlein nebst Replik und Duplik*, ed. Fritz Mauthner (Munich: Georg Müller Verlag, 1912), XVIII–XIX.

17 See Karl Barth, *Die protestantische Theologie im 19. Jahrhundert – Ihre Vorgeschichte und ihre Geschichte*, 5th ed. (Zürich: Theologischer Verlag Zürich, 1985), 392 and 394.

18 Kurt Nowak, *Schleiermacher: Leben, Werk und Wirkung*, 98.

lin – "symphilosophizing" among a circle of friends, discussions with Friedrich Schlegel, studying Plato, and engaging in lively correspondence. He believed that this was necessary, as the lofty and difficult subject of religion required the utmost virtuosity: "the communication of religion [*die Mittheilung der Religion*] must occur in a grander style, and another type of society, which is especially dedicated to religion, must arise from it. It is proper that the whole fullness and magnificence of human speech be expended on the highest which speech can attain," he wrote in the fourth speech *On Religion*. And he concluded: "Thus it is impossible to express and communicate [*auszusprechen und mitzutheilen*] religion other than verbally with all the effort and artistry of language, while willingly accepting the service of all skills that can assist fleeting and lively speech" (RC 74; KGA I/2, 268–269).[19]

In this chapter, I will analyze the first edition of the speeches *On Religion* from the perspective of the discourse developed herein, which is built around the concept of translational transfer, as applied to the problems of communication in the religious sphere. I will be interested, above all, in how this rhetoric of translation, through specific schematizations and valuations, profiles the realm of religious experience to which the young theologian's book is devoted. This analysis stems from my own understanding of the speeches *On Religion:* as an attempt, embedded in hermeneutics, to capture the essence of religious faith and translate it into a language comprehensible to contemporary society and to the cultural community constituted on its basis.[20]

2 *Apology:* mediation and transfer

And yet, this work that installed Schleiermacher among the pantheon of German Romanticism would appear not to discuss translation at all. Rather, the topic the speeches *On Religion* address is the problem of religious experience, trying to identify what is it inside us that constitutes religion – that is to say, how the Infinite enters into our own, finite world. Nonetheless, I claim – and seek to demonstrate in this chapter – that the issues raised by the young theologian are in fact closely related to the problem of translation, in the broad sense of the Romantics' scope of interest.

---

19 As for the point made here, see also Karl Barth, *Die Theologie Schleiermachers*, ed. Dietrich Ritschl (Zürich Theologischer Verlag Zurich, 1978) (*Gesamtausgabe*, II.11), 439. More generally, all citations from *Reden ueber die Religion* are taken from Richard Crouter's translation of the original 1799 edition in German (Friedrich D.E. Schleiermacher, *On Religion: Speeches to its Cultured Despisers*, trans. and ed. Richard Crouter, Cambridge Univ. Press, 1988), hereafter cited in text as "*RC*," followed by the page number, then followed by the KGA page number for the 1799 edition in German.
20 See Marek Szulakiewicz, *Filozofia jako hermeneutyka* [Philosophy as Hermeneutics] (Toruń: Wydawnictwo Naukowe UMK, 2004), 253, who writes that on the level of religion and theology, hermeneutics plays "an important role of updating and 'translating' faith appropriately to the given situation" and thus "creatively develops tradition, emphasizing the dynamic (rather than static) status of truth in religion" (ibid.).

On this view, translation is a fundamental tool of cognition, manifesting itself in the processes of conveying ideas and emotions. In religion, as perceived by Schleiermacher, transfer is the principle of contemplating the world of phenomena as a representation of the infinite, thus invoking the conceptual idea (impossible in real terms) of the language of phenomena being translated into the language of the infinite, of the absolute.[21] In this context, the figure of the *mediator* is also of great importance, bringing together two, often very distant, opposing poles (such as man, on the one hand, vs. "humanity," infinite in its essence, on the other).[22] His role is hermeneutic in nature: he brings things closer by initiating understanding, by leading those who are open to his mediation towards understanding.

In the speeches *On Religion* the problem of translation is linked above all with the figure of the *mediator* (*Mittler*), who is the *translator* (*Dolmetscher*) of the will and works of the *Deity* (*Gottheit*) (RC 6; KGA I/2, 192–193). However, the mediator also appears in the context of the question of the very possibility of conveying various religious ideas. But let us first try to clarify who this mediator is and what function he plays in Schleiermacher's vision of religion. To illustrate this, let us look at the first speech, entitled "Apology," which presents an image of the world as a play of opposing "primal forces of nature": interiorization and exteriorization (RC 5; KGA I/2, 191). As such, each human soul is "merely a product of two opposing drives," the first of which is an urge to absorb and assimilate what is external, while the second is an urge to express, to spread its own inner self so that it penetrates the external world (RC 5; KGA I/2, 191). It is not easy to achieve a state of harmonious interplay between these extremes; indeed, it seems to "the Speaker" (the voice Schleiermacher adopts in the speeches *On Religion*) that he is surrounded by individuals who are clearly inclined towards one of the two poles: either overly self-centered or lost in self-expression. There is, however, a point of "perfect balance" between these extremes which is a place of power and harmony, an almost inaccessible place. It appears as the great mystery of human existence. This is why, Schleiermacher writes,

> at all times the deity sends people here and there in whom both tendencies are combined in a more fruitful manner, equips them with wondrous gifts prepares their way with an all-powerful word, and employs them as translators of his will and its works and as mediators of what would otherwise remain eternally separated (RC 6; KGA I/2, 192–193).

---

21 See Inken Mädler, Friedrich Schleiermacher: "Sinn und Geschmack fürs Unendliche," in *Kompendium Religionstheorie*, eds. Volker Drehsen, Wilhelm Gräb, Brigit Weyel (Göttingen: Vandenhoeck & Ruprecht, 2005), 15–26.
22 See Barth, *Die Theologie Schleiermachers*, 439, 442. Kurt Nowak writes that Schleiermacher often drew upon "the philosophical scheme of polarity and mediation [*Polarität und Vermittlung*]"; this is, as one can easily see, a scheme fundamental to the speculative idealist philosophy of German Romanticism (with Schelling and Hegel at the forefront); Kurt Nowak, *Schleiermacher und die Frühromantik – Eine literaturgeschichtliche Studie zum romantischen Religionsverständnis und Menschenbild am Ende des 18. Jahrhunderts in Deutschland* (Berlin: Walter De Gruyter, 1986), 164.

These creative individuals, using the gifts of the Deity, shape the world as "heroes," "lawgivers," "inventors" or "benevolent genies." By their very existence such individuals "prove themselves to be ambassadors of God and mediators [*Mittler*] between limited man and infinite humanity" (RC 7; KGA I/2, 193). But what does this mean? They demonstrate to "the inactive, merely speculative idealist" the value of what he was abstracting away from: the material world, the earth which is home to men; "they explain to him the misunderstood voice of God" (*sie deuten ihm die verkannte Stimme Gottes*, RC 7 52; KGA I/2, 193). But Schleiermacher writes that such individuals are needed even more by "merely earthly and sensual people" because they teach the latter to understand what is loftier in humanity, its higher "elemental force" (RC 7; KGA I/2, 193).

The figure of the mediator which the Speaker / Schleiermacher introduces is significant from the point of view of the phenomenology of religion. He belongs to the category of "sacred men," representing the "historical form" of religious experience.[23] Mediators are holy men who, through their representation, "ensure the relations between power and man."[24] "But in the truest sense he is a mediator [*Mittler*] whose whole being is mediation, who surrenders his own life as the 'Means' for power," Gerardus van der Leeuw emphasizes in his *Phänomenologie der Religion*.[25] In contrast to the figure of the teacher (*Lehrer*), the *Mittler* acts through himself and his (religious) experience, not through doctrine.[26] This difference was extremely important for Schleiermacher, because he placed his mediator in the domain of freedom, far from dogma.[27] Similarly, the aspect of the figure's presence in historical space was very important an essential element of the Schleiermacherian concept.[28]

The mediators mentioned in the speeches *On Religion*, being "instruments" of power, are also "translators" (*Dolmetscher*) of the will or works of God and, and at the same time "interpreters" (*Deuter*) of His voice. Their task is therefore of a hermeneutical nature and consists in clarifying the sense of an incomprehensible content.[29] Note that the message here is the will of the Deity, His works, and the voice that demands proper understanding. Is this explanation a translation? In hermeneutical terms, yes, because both concepts are included in the meaning of the Greek word *hermeneuein*, which, as Hans Robert Jauß reminds us, "includes three directions of

---

[23] Gerardus van der Leeuw, *Religion in Essence and Manifestation: A Study in Phenomenology*, trans. John Evan Turner (London: George Allen & Unwin, 1938), 650.
[24] Ibid., 666.
[25] Ibid.
[26] See ibid., 662.
[27] Paul Seifert, *Die Theologie des jungen Schleiermacher* (Gütersloh: Gütersloher Verlagshaus Gerd Mohn, 1960), 139.
[28] Nowak, *Schleiermacher und die Frühromantik*, 165.
[29] See Manuel Bauer, *Schlegel und Schleiermacher – Frühromantische Kunstkritik und Hermeneutik* (Paderborn: Schöningh, 2011), 231–232.

meaning: to express (utter), to explain (construe), to translate (transfer)."[30] The scholar also draws attention to the sacred context in which the word is used: "and so the dark language of the oracle required not only that the divine will expressed by it should be clarified through interpretation, but also that what was proclaimed should be translated into the current situation."[31] Thus, expressing, explaining, and translating were combined at the dawn of hermeneutics into a single *realm of mediation*.

Translation is, in the words of Jean Grondin, "a fusion of horizons between the foreign meaning and its interpretation-translation in a new language, horizon and situation, where the meaning resonates."[32] Interpretation, on the other hand, is (dialectically) connected with expression, so that understanding, following the trajectory of the content, is in the first case directed internally, while in the second case there is an outward understanding of the inner content.[33] Both expressing and interpreting, and also translating, aim to reveal and convey meaning (*Sinnvermittlung*); one could say that through the mediation of the *hermeneut*, or mediator (*Mittler*), a meaning that has hitherto remained outside the realm of understanding becomes grasped. Lack of comprehension is usually a function of distance; "a 'hermeneut' or translator is demanded […] by Homer's poetic work, which, having become far away in time, is no longer immediately comprehensible" (*nicht mehr unmittelbar verständlich blieb*) as the aforementioned Jauß writes.[34] Schleiermacher himself begins his later lecture on translation by enumerating a number of communicative situations in which people can understand one another only through linguistic mediation (*Vermittlung*).[35]

But getting back to Schleiermacher's "Apology" (the first of the speeches *On Religion*), one may ask how this initially "infinite" meaning is actually conveyed to "limited" people. Schleiermacher here presents a second image of the mediator (dialectically related to the first), showing such interpreters as creators who communicate their knowledge of the language of the infinite in inspired "pictures or words," "as poets and seers, as orators or as artists" (RC 7; KGA I/2, 193). "Endowed with mystical and creative sensuality [*Sinnlichkeit*], his spirit moves towards the infinite, so that, struggling for images and words, it returns from it to our finitude," Karl Barth comments on Schleiermacher's thought.[36] The translator must, after all, as Schleiermacher argues, bring the self-communicating deity "closer" to people immersed in the fi-

---

[30] Hans Robert Jauß, *Ästhetische Erfahrung und literarische Hermeneutik* (Frankfurt am Main: Suhrkamp, 1991), 367.
[31] Ibid.
[32] Jean Grondin, "Hermeneutics," in *New Dictionary of the History of Ideas*, ed. Maryanne Cline Horowitz, vol. 3 (New York, Thomson Gale, 2005), 982–987; also Jean Grondin, *Introduction to Philosophical Hermeneutics*, trans. Joel Weinsheimer (New Haven: Yale Univ. Press, 1994).
[33] Ibid.
[34] Hans Robert Jauß, *Ästhetische Erfahrung*, 367.
[35] KGA I/11, 67; see Manuel Bauer, *Schlegel und Schleiermacher*, 231.
[36] Karl Barth, *Die Theologie Schleiermachers*, 441.

nite world. How else might meaning drawn from the infinite and eternal world be brought closer, other than through artistic translation, in the full sense of the word? Other than through inspired visions, sublime prophecies, works of sacred art? The mediator thus belongs to a "higher priesthood" that "proclaims the inner meaning of all spiritual secrets" (RC 7; KGA I/2, 194). In portraying this image of the translator/mediator, endowed with the gift of the suggestive representation of the almost unrepresentable, Schleiermacher invokes the Romantic figure of the artist-priest. In the Romantic imagination these roles shared a dialectical bond. The priest, and often also the prophet, acquired the traits of the artist, while the artist, subjected to sacralization, was endowed with the features of the priest, the prophet.[37]

In Schleiermacher's imagination the mediator is, it seems, at the same time priest and prophet: for in the speeches *On Religion* we read of "true priests of the Most High," but also of "ambassadors of God" (RC 7; KGA I/2, 193). Priesthood in the domain of the Judeo-Christian religion is connected with the idea of election/appointment by God (the Levites), as well as mediation (there is a continuity here from Moses to Christ). The prophets, too, are God's chosen ones, through whom the Most High communicates His word to the people. In communicating the word of Yahweh, they become "interpreters of God"[38] who, using their charisma, communicate His message. But unlike priests, prophets were called upon (summoned) to serve individually, personally. They were sent by God – often against their will – to become his mouthpiece and denounce transgressions of the Law.[39] Priests also exercised, and still do exercise, the ministry of the word, but of a different kind: standing guard over the Lord's temple, they interpret His Word (the Torah of Moses, the New Torah of Christ). They are empowered to interpret the Word, to interpret what has been written down or transmitted.[40] Nevertheless, mediation is connected, in the case of both priests and prophets, with *translation:* either of the "living," intervening Word, or of the Word already "dwelling" among men, albeit often unknown.[41] At the same time, Schleiermacher's "ambassador of God" is, in the Hellenistic tradition,

---

37 See, for example, Paul Bénichou, *Le Sacre de l'écrivain (1750–1830)* (Paris: Joseph Corti, 1973), 467–474.
38 So writes, following Philo of Alexandria, Johannes Lindblom in *Prophecy in Ancient Israel* (Oxford: Blackwell, 1963), 29. The sense in which prophets are "interpreters of God" is explained in detail by Spinoza in his *Tractatus Theologico-Politicus*, a work well known to Schleiermacher. The Hebrew term *nabi*, which as Spinoza explains is "commonly translated Prophet, signifies orator or interpreter, but is always used to signify an interpreter of the Divine will." Unlike Schleiermacher, however, Spinoza emphasized the importance of the moral content of the message of the prophets – Benedict Spinoza, *Theological-Political Treatise*, ed. Jonathan Israel, trans. Michael Silverthorne and Jonathan Israel (Cambridge: Cambridge Univ. Press, 2007), Chapter 1.
39 *Dictionary of Biblical Theology*, 468–474 (entry for "Prophet").
40 Ibid., 359–364 (entry "Priesthood").
41 See also the entry "Mediator" in the *Dictionary of Biblical Theology*, 344–348.

Hermes, the son of Zeus and Maia, who conveyed the will of the gods to people.[42] Many scholars maintain that the Greek term for interpreter, *hermêneus*, is a direct reference to the person and function of Hermes.[43] In this context, Plato is usually quoted, who claimed, while analyzing in the *Cratylos* the content of the name "Hermes" by Socrates, claims that it "has to do with speech, and signifies that he is the interpreter, or messenger."[44] Hermes is seen in the Greek tradition as an eloquent mediator, a master of rhetoric; nevertheless, as Gerhard Funke aptly observes, "it is not the wealth of words that enables him to achieve the goal of communication, but rather his ability to make the meaning of the missive he is meant to transmit [...] precisely adequate for the intentions of [...] his principals, and at the same time understandable to the recipients."[45] Therefore, as the German scholar writes elsewhere, he is "the master of language, the master of speech and the word, the one who is meant to translate to people the often hidden and coded decisions of the gods and is able to put them into a form comprehensible to people."[46] Thus, Hermes can be seen as a "functional" translator, reconciling the intention of the sender with the perspective of the receiver.

The image of the divine mediator sketched out here is connected in early Christianity with the priest-prophet tradition, which is evidenced by the episode in the Acts of the Apostles when Paul and Barnabas preach the word of God and perform signs in Lycaonia. Paul, speaking in Lystra, is called "Hermes" by the crowds (Acts 14:12), and not without reason, since he explained the meaning of the Good News to the gathered people. He spoke under the inspiration of the Holy Spirit, who is after all the interpreter (exegete) of the Son, revealing and illuminating his words, allowing them to resound in all languages.[47]

In the Protestant traditions the gift of interpretation is very clearly, and sometimes also suggestively, linked with the person of the Holy Spirit. In the classic work of Puritanism, *The Pilgrim's Progress* (1678) by John Bunyan, the figure called

---

42 Pierre Grimal, *Dictionary of Classical Mythology*, trans. A. R. Maxwell-Hyslop (Oxford: Blackwell, 1996), 209–211 (entry for "Hermes").
43 See Alexander Gross, *Hermes – God of Translators and Interpreters: The Antiquity of Interpreting: Distinguishing Fact from Speculation*, https://www.translationdirectory.com/article340.htm (accessed 01 April 2022): "Basically, what the ancient Greeks were saying when they used this verb, *hermêneuo, hermêneueis, hermêneuei* could be duplicated in English only if our verb for to translate or interpret went 'I hermese, you hermese, he or she hermeses.' Or more colloquially, 'I make like Hermes, you make like Hermes, etc.'" On Hermes and the origins of *hermeneutics*, cf. Richard E. Palmer, *Hermeneutics: Interpretation Theory in Schleiermacher, Dilthey, Heidegger, and Gadamer* (Evanston: Northwestern Univ. Press, 1969), 13–14.
44 Plato, *Cratylus*, trans. Benjamin Jowett, in *The Dialogs of Plato* (New York: Macmillan, 1892), 351.
45 Gerhard Funke, "Auslegen, Deuten, Verstehen," *Sprachforum* 3/4 (1959/60), 236.
46 Gerhard Funke, "Glaubensbewußsein. Hermeneutik als Sprachlehre des Glaubens," in idem, *Zur Signatur der Gegenwart* (Bonn: Bouvier 1990), 361.
47 See René Laurentin, *L'Esprit Saint – 1. Cet Inconnu, découvrir son expérience et sa personne* (Paris: Fayard, 1997).

the *Interpreter* is an allegorical representation of the Holy Spirit, who appears as the Hermeneut, because he enables the pilgrim Christian to understand the true sense of the choices he makes in life. He translates accidental, "dead" literalness into the structures of spiritual meaning, which is through unusually suggestive allegorical images, in which the transformation of eternity into its temporal representations takes place.[48]

The notion of the mediator as the interpreter of the Deity, responsible for the transfer between the finite and the infinite, appealed very strongly to the Romantics.[49] Even before the publication of Schleiermacher's speeches *On Religion*, Novalis had already invoked it. In one of the fragments published in *Athenaeum* (1798, from the cycle *Blüthenstaub*), he writes about an indispensable element of every "true religiousness," which is the "intermediary link [*Mittelglied*] that connects us to the deity."[50] In Novalis' view, this mediator (*Mittler*) is an "organ of the Deity" in the world of the senses, a link between the sensual and the extra-sensual.[51] Religiousness consists precisely in the free choice of the mediator and in defining our relation to him.[52] Novalis reverses the perspective here in an interesting way, looking from the point of view of "limited people" seeking contact with the Deity, with the Infinite. "Educated people" make, according to Novalis, an independent choice of translator-mediator, enabling them to understand and know God.[53] As man's self-reliance increases, these "mediating links" become more and more sophisticated. Over time, the difference between "pantheism" and "monotheism" in the domain of "true religion" is also revealed. Novalis sees pantheism as the idea "according to which everything can be an organ of the deity, an intermediary [*Mittler*], if I give it this rank."[54] Thus, for the pantheist, everything can, to refer to Schleiermacher's term, explain the will and works of the Deity, whereas for the monotheist, there is only one "organ" of God corresponding to "the idea of the mediator." In the case of Christians, this mediator is the "God-Man" (for Novalis: *Gottmensch*), Jesus Christ, in fact, revered as the "Sole Mediator," the "Mediator of the New Covenant."[55] A necessary condition for the

---

48 Bunyan, John, *The Pilgrim's Progress*, ed. Roger Sharrock and James Blanton Wharey (Oxford: Oxford Univ. Press, 1975).
49 See Paul Seifert, *Die Theologie des jungen Schleiermacher*, 138–139.
50 Novalis, *Fragmente I*, in Carl Seelig, ed., *Gesammelte Werke*, vol. 2 (Herrliberg-Zürich: Bühl, 1945), 26.
51 Novalis, *Fragmente I*, 27. The essence of religious mediation was also sought by Friedrich Schlegel, who, inspired by Schleiermacher's speeches *On Religion*, dedicated a separate passage to the figure of the mediator in his collection *Ideas* (1800). "A mediator [*Mittler*]," that passage states, "is one who senses the Divine element in himself and relies entirely on it in order to proclaim, communicate and represent the Divine" (Friedrich Schlegel, *Werke in zwei Bänden*, vol. 1 (Berlin: Aufbau, 1980), 268).
52 Ibid., 26.
53 Ibid.
54 Ibid., 27.
55 *Dictionary of Biblical Theology*, 344–348 (entry for "Mediator"); see also 1 Tim 2:5.

realization of His redemptive mediation is the existence of *communication* among the community of believers. For it is in this context that the most perfect – so to speak – competences of Christ as a reliable interpreter (Schleiermacher's *Dolmetscher*) of the will and deeds of the Most High are revealed. It is no coincidence that Jesus is often called the "hermeneutic,"[56] the one who "interprets God" (*Auslegung Gottes*).[57]

Schleiermacher felt that Christ was aware of his divinity and at the same time of his "office of mediator" (*Mittleramt*), the essence of which is the truth which he communicates – that no one knows the Father except the Son, who shares in his infinite divine nature and has the power to reveal it according to his will.[58] Christ therefore shares in both the divine nature and the temporal, human nature – which emerges as a necessary condition for his supreme mediation (RC 120; KGA I/2, 322). He is, as Jochen Hörisch writes, commenting on Schleiermacher's discourse, "the Infinite that wants to communicate [*vermitteln*] a finite being so that any mediation [*Vermittlung*] in the face of direct participation may find its fulfillment, abolishing itself.[59] We will come back to this issue later, when considering the thoughts on mediation that Schleiermacher develops in the fifth and last speech *On Religion*.

The specificity of Schleiermacher's interpretation of the person of Christ the Mediator is related primarily to the vision of the advent described by an "old prophecy" of the time when all mediation will "cease," for then "all will be taught by God" (RC 8; KGA I/2 194). Schleiermacher develops here an idea inspired by the Old Testament promise of the kingdom of God, in which God's people would live in direct contact with their Creator. It appears in Leviticus, where we read of Yahweh's promise: "And I will set my tabernacle among you: and my soul shall not abhor you. And I will walk among you, and will be your God, and ye shall be my people" (Leviticus 26:11–12).[60] Later, this vision recurs in the prophets, first in Isaiah, then in Jeremiah and Ezekiel. The motif of God teaching his people without intermediaries appears in Isaiah (54:13), whose author, describing the beauty and safety of the New Jerusalem, says that all its sons will become disciples of Yahweh (in the Luther Bible: "*und alle deine Kinder gelehrt vom HERRN*).[61] Jeremiah, on the other hand, in his vision of the revival of God's people, prophesies: "At the same time," Yahweh proclaims, "will I be the God of all the families of Israel, and they shall be my people" (Jer 31:1). God, in establishing the New Covenant, will place the law within the people and write it on their hearts (Jer 31:33), "And they shall teach no more every man his neighbour, and

---

[56] Bernd Springer, *Die antiken Grundlagen der neuzeitlichen Hermeneutik* (Frankfurt am Main: Peter Lang, 2000), 155–159.
[57] Herbert Braun, *Jesus – der Mann aus Nazareth und seine Zeit* (Stuttgart: Kreuz, 1984), 161.
[58] RC 120; KGA I/2, 322: "Niemand kennt den Vater als der Sohn, und wem Er es offenbaren will."
[59] Jochen Hörisch, *Die Wut des Verstehens – Zur Kritik der Hermeneutik* (Frankfurt am Main: Suhrkamp, 1988), 53.
[60] Bible quotations in English taken from the King James Bible.
[61] Quotes from Luther's Bible taken from: *Die Bibel – Mit Apokryphen, nach der Übersetzung Martin Luthers (revidierter Text 1975)* (Stuttgart: Deutsche Bibelstiftung, 1978).

every man his brother, saying, Know the LORD: for they shall all know me, from the least of them unto the greatest of them, saith the LORD: for I will forgive their iniquity, and I will remember their sin no more (Jer 31:34). (Luther Bible: "*und wird keiner den andern noch ein Bruder den andern lehren und sagen: 'Erkenne den HERRN', sondern sie sollen mich alle kennen, beide, klein und groß, spricht der HERR*"). Ezekiel later writes of the new spirit breathed into the people of Israel and their new heart. It will be a spirit of obedience and faithfulness to the Torah: "And ye shall dwell in the land that I gave to your fathers; and ye shall be my people, and I will be your God" (Ez 36:28). This theme recurs in Paul's letters: 2 Corinthians and the Epistle to the Hebrews, where we read that Christ is the High Priest of a new and "better covenant," which is meant to be underpinned by the quotation of Yahweh's promise from the Book of Jeremiah (Heb 8:1–13). Finally, this image becomes part of the vision of the New Jerusalem in John's Apocalypse: "And I heard a great voice out of heaven saying, Behold, the tabernacle of God is with men, and he will dwell with them, and they shall be his people, and God himself shall be with them, and be their GOD" (Rev. 21:3).

When God dwells with men, there will be no need for mediators, interpreters of His will and His acts. Sin, which alienates people and distances them from God, will be overcome and there will be a time of full understanding with the Creator. The explanation of this is found in the words of Jesus the Mediator, which are recorded in the Gospel of St. John: "It is written in the prophets, And they shall be all taught of God. Every man therefore that hath heard [the call], and hath learned of the Father, cometh unto me. Not that any man hath seen the Father, save he which is of God, he hath seen the Father" (J 6:45–46). The promised kingdom of God is already revealed with the faith that leads to understanding the word of Yahweh-the-Father.

Schleiermacher elaborates on this promise conveyed by "ancient prophecy" by linking together images from the Old and New Testaments. "If the holy fire burned everywhere, firey prayers would not be needed beseech it from heaven, [...] it would probably not break out in dreaded flames, but its sole striving would be to put the inner and hidden glow into balance among everyone" (RC 8; KGA I/2, 194). Using the symbolism of fire, Schleiermacher draws a vision of complete understanding and agreement, when "the office of mediator will cease" and the priesthood of man will rise to a higher level of realization. The images of this element are combined into a clearly syncretic whole, made up of images drawn from Greek religion, Judaism, and Christianity. However, biblical images predominate, from both the New and the Old Testament. "Holy fire" changes its character, or, more precisely, the way in which it makes itself present. "Fiery prayers," bringing down "terrible flames" from heaven, are a reference to, among other things, the initiation of the priestly ministry of Aaron (the "interpreter" of Moses), when "there came a fire out from before the Lord, and consumed upon the altar the burnt offering and the fat" (Leviticus 9:24), but also to other moments involving a similar kind of theophany (see 1 Kings 18:38–39 and 2 Kings 7:1–3). According to the logic of the New Covenant, this violent theophany of Yahweh's fire, which strikes fear into the faithful, is replaced by the image of an internal, personal fire, shared by all who dwell in love. Of this Jesus spoke, revealing the essence of his mediation: "I am come to send fire on the earth; and what will I, if it be already kindled?" (Lk 12:49).

"Justly distributed" internal "fire" with which "individuals would then light the way for themselves and for others" (RC 8; KGA I/2, 194), is associated with Pentecost, when "as if tongues of fire" appeared over the apostles' heads and they began to speak in "strange tongues" (Acts 2:1–4), reaching all those around them with their message. The confusion of tongues and the dispersion of the people, whose origin is explained in the story of the sin of the generation of the tower of Babel (Gen 11:1–9), were thus overcome. Through the action of the Holy Spirit as mediator, people were able once again to understand one another and thus to unite as participants in religious communication.

And indeed this is the direction that seems to be taken by the Speaker's (Schleiermacher's) argument, in which fire is transformed into holy light, appearing as a medium for the transfer of "holy thoughts and feelings" (religiousness): "Individuals would then light the way for themselves and for others, and the communication [Mittheilung] of holy thoughts and feelings would consist only in the easy game of now unifying the different beams of this light and then again breaking them up, now scattering it and then again concentrating here and there on individual objects" (RC 8; KGA I/2, 194). This is an image of a mystical model of communication, a voiceless language of angels, or rather, a visual code that makes understanding possible, removing the problem of ambiguity and uncertain reference of words where they have to face the Unnameable. But with the universal "gift of mediation," ordinary conversations would also take on another dimension. Schleiermacher writes: "The softest word would be understood, whereas now the clearest expressions do not escape misinterpretation" (RC 8; KGA I/2 194).

This state of affairs seems to indicate that all the sins of humanity, which have consequently led to the alienating and universally prevailing lack of understanding (of thought and speech), have been overcome. This "hermeneutical paradise," we might say, of spiritual understanding should actually mean the abolition of hermeneutics, which as the science of "non-understanding" (das Nichtverstehen)[62] ceases to be necessary under these conditions. What is the use of hermeneutics and translation, after all, when what is sacred and infinite is given directly to all people – the close-knit participants of a free sociability (die Geselligkeit), unfettered by misunderstandings and alienation? This "longing for communication [die Mittheilung] and for sociability" (RC 8; KGA I/2, 195) appears as a longing for a world without polarity and therefore without the difficulty of mediation/translation.

Schleiermacher describes a utopia of understanding, a universal priesthood, a mediation that would satisfy our longing for a sociability untainted by the interpretive fallacy that results from not understanding the speech of religion. The corre-

---

[62] See Schleiermacher's *Zur Hermeneutik 1806 und 1809/10*, KGA II/4, 6.

spondence between the terms *Mittler* and *Mitteilung* is clearly revealed in his discourse. A universal priesthood implies the replacement of the interpreter of the infinite (*Mittler*) by the universal proclamation of religion, that is, by the communication (*Mitteilung*) of religious experience. Such a message cannot fall into a vacuum or exist in a vacuum, for it is the emanation of a specific community, which feels the need to "exchange completed ideas" (WIS 8; KG I/2, 194). On the day of Pentecost, the Holy Spirit called into being a community of people who understand and proclaim the Gospel, who communicate their doctrine and their experience without any additional mediation. This communication (*Mitteilung*) broke the barrier of the foreign word, crossed the boundary of foreign culture, in the name of the universality made real by the Holy Spirit, the translator of the Son of God.

In Schleiermacher's description, a "holy" community is brought to life, open to all who wish to listen and bear witness. The religious experience thus communicated has the power of the *kerygma*; for those who comprise the circle of understanding, it means to "jointly penetrate into the interior of the sanctuary" (RC 8; KGA I/2, 194), a source of joy, whereas for others, distant from that community, it seems a "scandal or folly" (*ein Ärgerniß oder eine Thorheit*) (RC 9; KGA I/2, 195). It is difficult not to associate these last words with the teaching of St. Paul, who wrote in 1 Corinthians: "But we preach Christ crucified, unto the Jews a stumblingblock, and unto the Greeks foolishness" (1 Corinthians 1:23; Luther Bible: "*den Juden ein Ärgernis und den Griechen eine Torheit*"). To many, then, it is foolishness and a scandal to preach a religion that penetrates through very being of he who experiences it and wishes to express it, guided by a "longing for understanding and sociability." With his message, the Speaker / Schleiermacher addresses the community of rational representatives of the people, which he sees – following the example of Paul – as a community in search of a truth that transcends "the common standpoint of humanity" (RC: 11; KGA I/2, 197).

Schleiermacher's vision of understanding, which is the consequence of communication (*Mitteilung*), pursued in an environment of people testifying and listening to testimonies in a common language, also has its antithesis. The opposite of understanding is misunderstanding, which usually stems from a lack of closeness and community, from linguistic, cultural, and moral alienation.

One is forced to admit that here, the argumentation of the Speaker / Schleiermacher quite surprisingly takes an abrupt "negative turn." His very clear-cut references to the community of the Holy Spirit ultimately imply universalism, an endeavor to overcome foreignness, to transcend barriers while preserving one's own cultural identity. Yet this is how Schleiermacher delineates the borders of this "paradise of understanding," so to speak, closing its circle:

> Where else will there be listeners for my speech? Is it not blind partiality for my native soil or for my companions in disposition and language that makes me speak thus, but the deep conviction that you are the only one capable, and thus also worthy of having the sense for holy and divine things aroused in you (RC 9; KGA I/2, 195).

Already in the very next sentence we are told about those who will never, because of their cognitive deficiencies, join the community of those who understand. First and foremost it is the British, "those proud islanders," whom many people of reason "venerate so unduly," but who "know no other watchword than to profit and enjoy." Their "zeal for the sciences," for wisdom, for freedom is – in the Speaker's eyes – only an "empty sham battle," and thus religion, when inscribed in this world of "lamentable empiricism," becomes but "a dead letter, a holy article in a constitution in which there is nothing real" (RC 9; KGA I/2, 196).

As is plain to see, the Speaker is averse to what we may call, with some simplification, British empiricism and liberalism. For Schleiermacher, religion being reduced to the earthly order of positive law demonstrates that it is being misunderstood. The British misunderstanding of spirituality (the key words here are: emptiness, dead letter, nonreality, sensuality) means that when they speak about religion they use a different language, rejecting the message of the new priest-mediators. It seems that this language lacks equivalent concepts or even thoughts, capable of expressing those "complete ideas" whose exchange characterizes an ideal community. Here, a barrier of concepts/words thwarts any chance of communication.

No lesser barrier separates the Speaker from the "Franks," although he turns away from them for other, even more serious reasons. It turns out that "in every act, in every word" the French "all but trample on [the] most holy laws" of religion. This attitude is influenced by their innate "frivolous indifference," "witty levity," and incapacity for piety (RC 9; KGA I/2, 196). "And what does religion abhor more than the unbridled arrogance with which the rulers of people defy the eternal laws of the world?" asks Schleiermacher's Speaker, leaving no illusion that above all he has in mind Napoleon Bonaparte (RC 9–10; KGA I/2, 196). Religion grows out of "circumspect and humble moderation," which is why, as we shall soon learn, it flourishes in the German people and not in the French. The French do not understand religion, and "in the intoxication of blindness" they cannot read what is most sacred to religion – the language of the punishing Nemesis (RC 10; KGA I/2, 196). What follows from these remarks is that those for whom religion is "scandal and folly," who close themselves off from it, who do not wish to know the idea of "mediation," are excluded from the community of understanding.

As it turns out, the limits of an ideal community of understanding and agreement allegedly coincide with the borders of the Speaker's Germanic homeland:

> Here, in my ancestral land is the fortunate climate that denies no fruit completely; here you find everything scattered that adorns humanity, and everything that prospers fashion itself somewhere, at least individually, in its most beautiful form; here neither wise moderation nor quiet contemplation is lacking. Here, therefore, it must find a refuge from the coarse barbarism and the cold earthy sense of the age (RC 10; KGA I/2, 196).

And so, we have a fortunate Germany, a land containing within itself all the richness of a diverse world, where every value finds its realization in individuals – in maximal amplification. Germany understands religion and gives it shelter, whereas modern barbarians and skeptics persecute it. In portraying the Germans as the last trustees of religious sensibility and their society as the center of world spirituality, the Speaker / Schleiermacher comes close to a thought that he would later clearly express in his 1813 lecture on the methods of translation, *Ueber die verschiedenen Methoden des Uebersetzens* (*On the Different Methods of Translating*). In the latter, he speaks of the Germans as having a "special calling" to cultivate the foreign, often exotic fruits of the Spirit (DR 232; KGA I/11, 92) – a vocation whose value can be seen particularly clearly when it is contrasted against the Frankish lack of pietism towards the products of spirituality. This issue is of great importance in the context of Schleiermacher's reflection on interlingual translation. It turns out that the Germans have a vocation to *mediate*, to make the invisible visible, to make the absent present. In a sense, this is an activity similar to sowing, planting, transplanting, cultivating – as seems to be indicated by the metaphors Schleiermacher uses in his *Akademierede* on translation. Near the end of it, he states:

> concomitantly with this, it seems that our respect for the foreign and our mediatory nature [*seiner vermittelnden Natur*] together destine the German people to incorporate linguistically, and to preserve in the geographical center and heart of Europe, all the treasures of both foreign and our own art and scholarship in a prodigious historical totality (DR 238; KGA I/11, 92).

Here, in the German land the universal Spirit grows and brings forth its fruits, and the diligent workers of the Lord's vineyard gather and spread His gifts. Note: the German people not only know what mediation is, but even have it in their very nature (*vermittelnde Natur*).[63]

From among this people, the Speaker distinguishes a still more elite group – those who strive for understanding, who do not stop at the superficial. These individuals are able to rise above the "common standpoint of humanity," and orient themselves towards "the depths of human nature" (RC 11; KGA I/2, 197). It is these people that the Speaker wants to lead "to the pinnacles of the temple," to the innermost reaches, from which religion speaks to the affections. He wants to induce them to speak about religion, to study its essence instead of disparaging it and passing over it. These are the eponymous "educated" opponents of religion, to whom Schleiermacher directs his speeches and to whom it is he offers his mediation.[64] Can this value-focused community (shaped by the German idea of *Bildung*) be transformed into a community of those who understand the speech of religion? A proposal

---

[63] An extensive analysis of Schleiermacher's "nationalist" discourse in relation to his reflections on the two methods of translation is presented (from the perspective of neo-Marxist criticism) by Lawrence Venuti in his monograph *The Translator's Invisibility: A History of Translation* – 2nd ed. (London: Routledge, 2008), 83–98. On the same topic see also idem: *Translation Changes Everything: Theory and Practice* (London, Routledge, 2013), 125–131.

[64] See Christian König, *Unendlich gebildet – Schleiermachers kritischer Religionsbegriff und seine inklusivistische Religionstheologie anhand der Erstauflage der Reden* (Tübingen: Mohr Siebeck, 2016), 78.

is made for an in-depth hermeneutics of religion: to examine its "inner essence," as it were, "from its center," as "a product of human nature" (RC 12; KGA I/2, 198). This is how Schleiermacher arrives at his famous definition of the essence of religion. And it begins where man's enslavement to the "scholastic and metaphysical spirit of barbaric and cold times," the spirit of discourse, argument, and system, ends (RC 13; KGA I/2, 199). It is, one might say, the *letter*, not the *spirit* of religion. "Where [religion] is present and effective it must so reveal itself that it moves the mind in a peculiar manner, mingling or rather removing all functions of the human soul and resolving all activity in an astonishing intuition of the infinite" (RC 13; KGA I/2, 200). Religion, therefore, being a feeling, is the "spiritual material" of religious systems.

> In all of them something of this spiritual material lies latent, for without it they could by no means have arisen. But those who do not know how to release it, no matter how finely they dissect it, no matter how thoroughly the investigate everything, always retain in their hands only the dead cold mass (RC 13; KGA I/2, 200).

Religions are thus mutually translatable, because in spite of their different "surface structures," we might say, they share a common "deep structure," that living core which is the feeling born out of confrontation with the infinite. The distinctive *tertium comparationis* here is experience, religious experience.[65]

In this context, the previously introduced distinction between *spirit* and *letter* recurs. The spirit is the most sensitive, elusive part of the religious message. It is the element that is most easily lost in translation – it rests on the "discoverers," the "heroes of religion," "those who have brought down some new revelation" (RC 14; KGA I/2, 201), while it often escapes or hides in the shadows in translation, where the revealed word is translated into systematic discourse. Schleiermacher's speaker speaks of theologians "of the dead letter" who believe that salvation is hidden in "the new garb of their formulas" (RC 14; KGA I/2, 201). The Word of the Deity rarely speaks through the systematic interpretation of these theologians. "Heavenly sparks," arising when "a holy soul is stirred by the universe" (RC 14; KGA I/2, 201), are extinguished upon contact with the cold, alien word of religious teaching.

Born in the soul of the individual, religion also loses out when it is subjected to another kind of impoverishing transfer, namely when it is transferred into the realm of morality (*Sittlichkeit*). In this domain, religion is "something foreign" and thus retains "its lofty and alien colors" (RC 16; KGA I/2, 203). Here Schleiermacher emphasizes that "it also shows the greatest contempt for religion to wish to transplant it into another realm and expect it to serve and work there" (RC 16; KGA I/2, 204). Thus, what might be called the translation of religion into life practice is in fact

---

[65] The paradox that is present in Schleiermacher's reflection and is theorized by him, related to the necessity of mediation (*vermitteln*) in the realm of what is direct (*unmittelbar*), i.e. religious experience, is analyzed by Dalia T. Nassar in "Immediacy and Mediation in Schleiermacher's 'Reden über die Religion,'" *The Review of Metaphysics* 59, no. 4 (2006): 807–840.

its profanation, since such a transformation deprives it of its very essence (of this "spirit"), making it the handmaid of temporality. The purpose (*skopos*) of such a translation is clear: "utility" (RC 17; KGA I/2, 204). A translation of this kind appears to Schleiermacher's Speaker as a constant transfer of useful values, an "eternal cycle of general utility in which they allow everything good to perish" and all (spiritual) meaning escapes, because from this cycle "no person who even wishes to be something for himself understands a sound word" (RC 17; KGA I/2, 204). This is in fact a very serious accusation, because every translation, being a transfer and making the sense present, should aim at understanding, rather than incomprehensibility and confusion.

Religion, Schleiermacher writes, has "its own province in the mind"; its transfer from one soul to another is possible and desirable (RC 17; KGA I/2, 204). It appears as a quest for understanding, a path towards a community of understanding, whose ideal fulfillment is the paradise of understanding, the temple of understanding. In this paradise there will be no need for translation, because thoughts and feelings relating to the infinite will reach people together with the omnipresent light of the Spirit. The "province" of religion grows in communities of people who open their feelings and thoughts up to the influence of the infinite. Schleiermacher regards the German people as such a community. Among Germans, religion finds its place and its refuge in the "free city" of those who understand. In contrast, the transfer of religion from the world of the "stirrings of the heart" to the world of temporal necessities is undesirable and, indeed, even impossible. To transfer religion beyond the boundaries of its native "province," especially in order to legitimize other discourses (including religious discourse!), is to distort what is most precious about it, namely its value and identity. Its spirit gets lost in such translation, and all that remains is the dead letter, its alienation making us aware of the impossibility of "taming" the infinite.

3 On the essence of religion: spirit and letter

Explaining the essence of religion at the beginning of the second speech ("On the Essence of Religion"), Schleiermacher invokes an interesting figurative analogy. "Spiritual things," and among them religion, are similar to a "particular disposition [*Sinnesart*] of various cultivated peoples" (RC 19; KGA I/2, 207). Since contacts between nations have become "more many-sided" and, thanks to more intensive communication, "what they have in common has increased," their particular mental idiolects ("dispositions") have become blurred, hardly legible "in individual actions" (RC 19; KGA I/2, 207). They have become "dispersed" and "mixed with much that is foreign" and only – we read – our imagination is able to "grasp the entire idea behind these qualities" (i.e. of the various ways of thinking which characterize individual nations), that is, to distill out, as it were, what has been lost in the element of the mingling of different languages, which are, after all, always an expression of ways of thinking.⁶⁶ In the case of other "spiritual things" too, including religion, the separate spiritual qualities have become blurred; within the human soul there has been a confusion of "the soul's powers," so that none of them "now acts among us distinctly, as much as we like to think of them as distinct" (RC 19; KGA I/2, 207). Here, too, the cause is communication (which is the basis of the synthesizing "sociability" and "friendliness"), in the course of which what is one's own is mixed with what is foreign, thus an exchange takes place, a transfer of values – a *translation*. Forces influence each other; by cooperating they interpenetrate each other, and "one looks around vainly in this cultured world for an action that could furnish a true expression of some capacity of spirit, be it sensibility or understanding, ethical life or religion" (RC 19; KGA I/2, 207). Formerly, these powers of the spirit found their faithful expression in human action, whereas in Schleiermacher's contemporary world, made up of a community of educated people, words and actions are the expression not of one but of many powers – for example, of religion and at the same time of morality, which is alien to it in terms of sources. In the case of every representation (the prototypical case being a translational representation), a lack of faithfulness raises hermeneutical problems, and so here, too, unfaithfulness leads to misunderstanding. To understand means to relate to the source – this seems to be the essence of hermeneutics.

Writing about the disturbance in the relation between source and expression, Schleiermacher raises the problem of understanding. Note: in "more childlike times" national characters were "distinct and individual" (RC 19; KGA I/2, 207). and thus well understood; in the new times, in which processes of mixing and intermingling prevail, ideas lose their individuality and legibility, which can lead interpretation astray. The same is true of religion, which used to express itself directly in words and other actions, making them legible and understandable. Via these words and actions, religion could be accessed. As this relationship became murky, their interpretation has become difficult, as has the answer to the question of the very essence of religion, i.e. its explanatory source.

Schleiermacher analyzes the essence of religion, wishing above all to purge religion of elements foreign to it which render it incomprehensible. For "metaphysics and morals" have "invaded religion on many occasions, and much that belongs to religion has concealed itself in metaphysics or morals under an unseemly form" (RC 19; KGA I/2, 208). This unfortunate transfer has clouded the pure "characters" or "natures" of these disciplines, making them hardly intelligible. The Speaker responds to this state of affairs by arguing for differentiation: each of the domains, including especially religion, which is dear to his heart, should treat its subject matter "completely differently, express or work out another relationship of humanity to it," (RC 19; KGA I/2, 208), all the more so if that subject matter is common to them in

---

66 In the *Dialectics*, as we shall see later, Schleiermacher returned to this issue, but highlighted it from a different angle.

many respects.⁶⁷ Religion, in its modern form, appears to the Speaker precisely as a function of confused domains which should be separated from one another. And it should return to its source, which means first of all withdrawing from the domain of metaphysics (and therefore of transcendental philosophy), that is, from "the tendency to posit essences and determine natures," (RC 20; KGA I/2, 208). The same is true of the domain of morality, which "develops a system of duties out of human nature and our relationship to the universe" – here, too, religion must not enter: "it must not use the universe in order to derive duties and is not permitted to contain a code of laws" (RC 20; KGA I/2, 208).

In modern times, the Speaker notes with irony, theorists of religion turn out to be metaphysicians, practitioners of religion prove to be moralists, with clear leanings towards metaphysics. He addresses his learned readers:

> You take the idea of the good and carry it into metaphysics as the natural law of an unlimited and plenteous being, and you take the idea of a primal being from metaphysics and carry it into morality so that this great work should not remain anonymous, but so that the picture of the lawgiver might be engraved at the front of so splendid a code (RC 20; KGA I/2, 208).⁶⁸

This is, however, playing an "empty game," because the domains between which the transfer is practiced are too different, even incommensurate. The definitions of religion and religiousness thus become a mere "compilation," "shameful plagiarism" (RC 20; KGA I/2, 209). "Where, then, is the unity in this whole?" the Speaker asks rhetorically.

Thus begins Schleiermacher's search for religion in its pure form, without "extraneous parts that cling to it" (RC 21, 210). By differentiating these domains, he concludes that religion does not want to "determine and explain the universe according to its nature" as metaphysics does, nor does it want to "shape and finish" it as morality does. And here the Speaker comes to an important conclusion: "Religion's essence is neither thinking nor acting, but intuition and feeling [*Anschauung und Gefühl*]" (RC 22; KGA I/2, 211).⁶⁹ Religion is a pious intuiting of the universe, surrendering to the universe's influences with "childlike passivity"; it perceives in man that which is a reflection, a representation of the infinite. Schleiermacher's Speaker cites

---

67 Schleiermacher here proposes a maximally general account of the common object of religion, metaphysics and morality: "the universe and the relationship of humanity to it" (RC 19; KGA I/2, 207).
68 "Taking" and "carrying" (in the original: "*nehmt Ihr aus der Metaphysik und tragt sie in die Moral*") suggests *Übertragung* – transfer, translation.
69 This notion of intuition is close in some respects to Kant's understanding, who associated *Anschauung* with an intuitive (rather than discursive) and comprehensive (rather than sequential) way of apprehending the object of cognition – see the entry "Anschauung" in *Historisches Wörterbuch der Philosophie*, vol. 1, ed. Joachim Ritter (Basel: Schwabe, 1971), 342. Schleiermacher, however, did not associate intuition with the interpretative activity of the subject, but with its receptivity, resulting from its opening up to the infinite. Schleiermacher's *Anschauung* is therefore not the same concept as appears in Fichte or Schelling (see König, *Unendlich gebildet*, 259–260).

here a whole list of differences pertaining to the specific perspective from which religion looks at reality, at entities and values. All this to demonstrate that it "maintains its own sphere and character," going beyond the domain of metaphysical speculation and moral practice (RC 23; KGA I/2, 212). "Praxis is an art, speculation is a science, religion is the sensibility and taste for the infinite" [*Sinn und Geschmak fürs Unendliche*], concludes Schleiermacher through the words of his Speaker (RC 23; KGA I/2, 212). Although religion conditions and elevates metaphysics and morality with its discourse, it remains separate, uncontaminated by extraneous thinking and valuations.

The highest formulation of religion, the semantic core of religious discourse, is, according to Schleiermacher, "intuition of the universe" (*Anschauen des Universums*, RC 24; KGA I/2, 213). Such intuition consists in religious persons being inclined to "accept everything individual as a part of the whole and everything limited as a representation of the infinite" (RC 25; KGA I/2, 214). Schleiermacher then draws another line: between religion and mythology. A description of intuiting the universe, in which a transcendent principle is established that binds this universe into unity – this is what religion is. However, theogonic narratives, however, are not religion, for they belong to mythology.[70]

Thus, while "to present all events in the world as the actions of a god" is religion, "brooding over the existence of this god before the world and outside the world" is "only empty mythology," constituted by the transfer of individual, singular insight, of individual feeling into the domain of generalizations, of "abstract thought" (RC 25–26; KGA I/2, 214). Can individual intuitions of the infinite be put into a system? – the Speaker asks. No, intuitions are not amenable to the rational language of generalizations. They can be translated into the language of images. This language is a living language; within the language of images everything is "indeterminate and endless," for images remain "something purely arbitrary and highly changeable" (RC 26–27; KGA I/2, 215). The expressivity of religion requires translation into the language of images and symbols (as well as sounds), which retain the trait of individual experience and are therefore wonderfully diverse and ambiguous. Hence religion is tolerant, open to the multiplicity of experiences and the symbols representing them; a system, on the other hand, is intolerant, a rigid order of concepts (RC 27; KGA I/2, 217).

Here Schleiermacher links his reflection to the concept of mediators and priests. The true language of religion has an epiphanic power – the "seer" who speaks it be-

---

[70] Schleiermacher's understanding of mythology has little in common with Romantic thought (e.g. F. Schlegel's "new mythology" or Schelling's "mythology of reason"). Mythology is involved, the author of the speeches *On Religion* explains in a footnote to a later edition, "when a purely ideal object is presented in a historical form" (KGA I/12,134). Schleiermacher is thus much closer to Rudolf Bultmann's hermeneutics and its concept of myth. On this relationship see Gerhard Gloege, *Mythologie und Luthertum – Recht und Grenze der Entmythologisierung* (Göttingen: Vandenhoeck & Ruprecht, 1963), 69–71.

comes "a new priest, a new mediator [*ein neuer Mittler*], a new mouthpiece" (RC 28; KGA I/2, 212). That is, as we remember from the "Apology," an interpreter of the speech of the divine infinity. Schleiermacher identifies the proponents of systematizing the language of religion with papal Rome, contrasting it with "ancient Rome," which was, in his view, "hospitable to every god and so it became full of gods" (RC 28; KGA I/2, 217). By individualizing the language of religion, emphasizing its symbolic, arbitrary, non-systematic character, and at the same time linking it with religious tolerance and hospitality, Schleiermacher (consciously or unconsciously) evokes the world of "liberal" polytheism, which operated with mutually translatable languages of the sacred.[71] The birth of Yahwistic religion, its development, codification, and *systematization* (the Mosaic Torah) became a "scandal" for polytheists, who perceived belief in a single, unrepresentable God as *a(poly)theism*. The religion of the Old Testament was for the protestants at once close and very distant – they saw it as a religion distrustful of images and skeptical of individualism, oriented toward orthopraxy and shutting itself up in a system of commands and prohibitions. Schleiermacher, like many of his brothers in faith, did not have much esteem for Judaism and did not take a particular interest in it, although he was keenly interested in the issues of the emancipation of the German Jews.[72] He expressed his opinion about the Jewish religion in the fifth speech, which we will return to later. At this point, however, it is worth noting that the Old Testament faith usually serves as a negative point of reference for Schleiermacher.[73] It seems that here too, when he speaks of its "systematizers" with their prohibitions and precepts, and immediately afterwards he once again refers to the opposition of the letter and the spirit, he has in mind the legacy of the Old Testament.[74]

It is probably in this context that the speaker's harsh words against "the adherents of the dead letter that religion casts out" should be read. It is they who have "filled the world with criers and tumult," while "the true contemplators of the eternal have ever been quiet souls [...] happily granting his own way to everyone who only understood the mighty word" (RC 28; KGA I/2, 217). The latter are *hermeneuts*, creating a great community of understanding, unlimited by artificial divisions. This thought directly refers back to the "Apology," to the image of a community of people who understand "the softest word" of God (cf. RC 8), of open souls and minds attuned to the speech of the Infinite.

---

[71] See Jan Assmann, *Moses der Ägypter – Entzifferung einer Gedächtnisspur* (Munich: Carl Hanser, 1998), 73–82.
[72] See Nowak, *Schleiermacher – Leben, Werk und Wirkung*, 95–97.
[73] An interesting analysis of the problem of anti-Judaism in Schleiermacher's theology (including his *Speeches on Religion*) is offered by Matthias Blum in his monograph *"Ich wäre ein Judenfeind?" Zum Antijudaismus in Friedrich Schleiermachers Theologie und Pädagogik* (Köln: Böhlau, 2010), 16–30.
[74] Cf. 2 Cor 3:6: "Who also hath made us able ministers of the new testament; not of the letter, but of the spirit: for the letter killeth, but the spirit giveth life."

This opposition between the spirit vs. the letter of religion is an obvious reference to the discussion about the interpretation of Scripture, and, consequently, to the disputes about the essence of a good translation.[75] Religion reduced to the letter is dead, and it also dies when we translate it into the language of obligations – a system of commandments and prohibitions, i.e. the Law. It remains alive, however, in the domain of the spiritual *experiencing* of the word of the infinite Deity and of its individual *understanding*. Here we can perhaps again draw on the image of the miracle of Pentecost – a multitude of languages, or linguistic images of the word, arising in the hearts and minds of mediators-translators inspired by the Holy Spirit. And each of them bore witness to their own individual inspiration and mission. Without the gift of the Holy Spirit and without their mediation, the Gospel would have remained a dead letter. Thus it is evident that Schleiermacher remains within the circle of Protestant sensitivity to the source of the *kerygma*, proclaimed among a community of individuals. We will return to this issue later.

Schleiermacher's Speaker, remaining in harmony with the worldview of Romantic poetry, criticizes "whoever only thinks systematically," claiming that only intuition turned toward the infinite "places the mind in unlimited freedom" (RC 28; KGA I/2, 217). And so it is precisely religion that saves us from the "most ignominious fetters of opinion and desire." In the eyes of the religious man, every element of reality that stimulates his feeling and produces in him an inner transformation becomes holy and precious (RC 29; KGA I/2, 218). Depending on how he sees the universe around him, this is the character of his religion; the more intense the feelings aroused in him, the greater the degree of his religiosity (RC 29; KGA I/2, 219). Religious feeling can be kept to oneself, or also communicated – but it cannot be translated into action (RC 29–30; KGA I/2, 220–221). For religion, in order to remain itself, must remain in the domain of intuition and feeling, not action.

Unlike morality, religion does not individualize, does not divide, but unites. Therefore it sees not individuals but humanity itself, "eternal humanity" in which the infinite is reflected. This humanity is revealed most directly in those "holy men" who are mediators (*Mittler*) between the limited human way of thinking and the "eternal limits of the world" (RC 41; KGA I/2, 232). Schleiermacher thus returns here to the central figure of the speeches *On Religion* – the mediator. The mediator can help those who identify with him to understand what humanity is. He can therefore be, in this sense, an interpreter of the infinite, as it allows those who receive it to discover "eternal humanity," that is, in essence, the infinite within, in the depths of one's own self (RC 41; KGA I/2, 232). "In whomever religion has thus worked back

---

75 See especially Jerome, "On The Best Kind of Translator," trans. H.M. Hubbell, in *Western Translation Theory: From Herodotus to Nietzsche*, ed. Douglas Robinson (Manchester: St. Jerome, 1997), 23–30, and also Martin Luther, "Circular Letter on Translation (*Sendbrief vom Dolmetschen*)," trans. Douglas Robinson, in Robinson, *Western Translation Theory*, 84–89; the original of the latter can be found in Martin Luther, *Werke – Kritische Gesamtausgabe*, vol. 30, Abt. 2 (Weimar: Hermann Böhlau, 1909), 627–646.

again inwardly and has discovered there the infinite," Schleiermacher writes, "it is complete in that person in this respect; he no longer needs a mediator for some intuition of humanity and he himself can be a mediator for many" (RC 41; KGA I/2, 232). To intuit humanity in its becoming, to observe how it is directed by the Spirit, is here to contemplate history, whose true source lies in religion (RC 42; KGA I/2, 233). And indeed: thoroughly religious is the belief in "the calm and uniform progress of the whole," that "the lofty world spirit [*Weltgeist*] smilingly strides across all that tumultuously opposes it" (RC 43; KGA I/2, 234). We also find this belief in Schelling and Hegel.

Schleiermacher admits that he only lightly sketches "some of the prominent religious intuitions from the realms of nature and humanity" (RC 43; KGA I/2, 234), for it is impossible to grasp the boundless whole. Nor is it possible to express the Unity he strives for – here words fail: "any further word about it would be an incomprehensible speech," Schleiermacher's Speaker explains to his religion-skeptical audience (RC 44; KGA I/2, 235). Because the One is ultimately inexpressible, in attempting to translate it into words or images, we make only allusions to the incomprehensible Whole. They are comprehensible only through the intuition possessed by all those who have religion. Those who have no religion, for whom the religious view is foreign, remain blind and deaf. In Schleiermacher's view incomprehension means, as in the teaching of Christ recorded in the Gospels, a lack of spiritual vision flowing from faith, an inability to see the spirit in letters and images, which are allusions rather than faithful representations.

Religion, the Speaker argues, is an individual matter, but is realized through communication, the expression of a religious feeling that "really communicates itself [*sich mittheilt*], so that the intuition of the universe is transferred to others" (RC 49; KGA I/2, 241).[76] Such action is in fact *translation*, and it comes from a source that is inspiration (*Eingebung*). Everything takes place in the domain of freedom, which is a dialectic of *reception* and *expression*. To be religious thus means: to belong to oneself, but also to know and become through others. We read in the second speech: "Except for a few chosen ones, every person surely needs a mediator [*eines Mittlers*], a leader who awakens his sense for religion from its first slumber and gives him an initial direction" (RC 50; KGA I/2, 242). Such a mediator – as we recall, an *interpreter* of the Deity – is needed until we have learned to "see with our own eyes," to learn, as it were, the language of religion and to master it to such an extent that we can communicate in it. If we remain blind, we become mere imitators, reproducers of religion. The latter include those who "cling to a dead document" that guides their choices, "by which they swear and from which they draw proof" (RC 50; KGA I/2, 24). Schleiermacher's Speaker is very harsh on them, as "every holy writing is merely

---

[76] In this way, communication becomes causal: "Communication as community-creation is the determination of what is indeterminate, in other words, the bringing of the infinite universe into the finite world, or mediation" (Nassar, "Immediacy and Mediation," 838).

a mausoleum of religion, a monument that a great spirit was there that no longer exists" (RC 50; KGA I/2, 242). For if it still existed, it would not attach importance to "the dead letter, that can only be a weak reproduction of it?" Whoever makes use of such an imperfect translation – a literal translation of the intimate, individual reality of the Spirit – misses his own vocation, which is creativity. "It is not the person who believes in a holy writing who has religion, but only the one who needs none and probably could make one for himself" (RC 50; KGA I/2, 242).

Once again the dichotomy of spirit and letter returns here, this time clearly related to Scripture. The source of this dichotomy lies, as Bernhard Kaiser explains, in the thinking of the ancient Greeks:

> One could generally say that the human word, the concept, always appears to the ancient Greek as a this-worldly, limiting quantity. The spirit can indeed be connected with the word, the letter, but it must be fundamentally separated from it, because the word is something foreign to the spirit. The spirit is rather to be classified in the realm of the supra-corporeal, ecstatic and directly animating. If we transfer this thinking to the Holy Scriptures, then the Holy Spirit must also be divorced from the word. Then, as it were, the word remains on a lower, this-worldly level, while the spirit enters as an animating, stirring or existentially claiming quality.[77]

It is this discourse that coincides fundamentally with the Speaker's/Schleiermacher's line of thinking. At the same time – importantly – it does not necessarily coincide with the Lutheran approach to this problem. For, as the author of the above quotation emphasizes, the "connection between the Word and the Spirit was not very problematic from Luther's perspective, because he valued the Word as a creaturely quality and saw no contradiction in the fact that God as Creator used something finite to communicate His infinite gifts."[78] In this context, Scripture appears as a kind of medium through which the gift of the saving grace of the Holy Spirit reaches man. Hence the special importance and dignity of the letter of Scripture. According to Luther, it guards the universality and accessibility of the Holy Spirit, contradicting the fantasies of the "dreamers" claiming that the "Holy Spirit speaks through them unmediated" [*unmittlelbar*].[79] However, this "subjectivist" current of Reformation thought remained vibrant and, based on a misinterpretation of Paul's opposition of the Letter (i.e. the Law condemning one to sin) and the Spirit (i.e. the Gospel saving one from sin), over time it became more and more insistent on valuing the inter-

---

[77] Bernhard Kaiser, *Die Scheidung von Geist und Buchstabe in der Heiligen Schrift – ihr geistiger Hintergrund und ihre praktischen Folgen*, Institut für Reformatorische Theologie, 1. http://www.irt-ggmbh.de/downloads/scheidunggeistwort.pdf%20 (accessed 6 June 2019) (originally printed in *Bibel und Gemeinde* 1994, 94, 34–51).
[78] Ibid., 2.
[79] Ibid.

nal, the living Spirit at the expense of the external, the Letter.[80] Kaiser comments on this tendency, seeing it as a precursor of Pietism:

> However, where the bringing to life by the Spirit is sought in the realm of inner experience that can no longer be captured in words, the boundary of mysticism is crossed, and we no longer have the biblical faith, but the imagined birth of God in the soul, commonly called rebirth.[81]

German Pietism, standing in conflict with Enlightenment rationalism, was picked up by the Romantics (often under its influence) who, while recognizing (in the spirit of philology) the historical character of Scripture, sought direct access to its universal message.[82]

And this is where Friedrich Schleiermacher, informed by Pietism, the Enlightenment and early Romanticism,[83] appears with a theology he develops of the non-conceptual experience of the Holy Spirit that facilitates Christians' spiritual communication with God and with one another. Kaiser suggests that in this approach, believers make a spiritual *translation* of the Gospel of Jesus Christ into the language of human feelings.[84] A foreshadowing of just such a theology, which Schleiermacher presented in *Der christliche Glaube* (1821–1822), can be found in the speeches *On Religion*. Kaiser criticizes this work, reproaching its author for ignoring Scripture and depriving the Christian faith of its foundation.[85] In essence this is an apt accusation, but it is nevertheless out of synch with the intentions of the author of the speeches *On Religion*, who was anxious to salvage the autonomy of religion and to rescue it from the deadly blade of rational criticism by "educated" skeptics, including philologists, historians and philosophers.

Speaking through the mouth of the Speaker, Schleiermacher sees religion not as the contemplation of the Letter, but as *creativity* inspired by the Spirit and sharing

---

[80] The Spirit becomes in this view the domain of freedom and originality: "The Spirit is originality and spontaneous enthusiasm – the wind blows where it wishes (John 3:8). The letter is a futile attempt to contain the Spirit, to enclose Him in formulas and schemes, to determine His form, to plan His action. That is how one can get rid of the Spirit, creating at the same time a being alien to Him, annihilating spirituality and reproducing one's own soullessness" – Simon Gerber, "Geist, Buchstabe und Buchstäblichkeit – Schleiermacher und seine Vorgänger," in *Geist und Buchstabe: Interpretations- und Transformationsprozesse innerhalb des Christentums – Festschrift für Günter Meckenstock zum 65. Geburtstag*, ed. Michael Pietsch, Dirk Schmid (Berlin: Walter de Gruyter, 2013), 106.
[81] Kaiser, *Die Scheidung von Geist und Buchstabe in der Heiligen Schrift*, 2–3.
[82] In this aspect the Romantics sympathized with the ideas propagated by Lessing, who (according to Heine) wanted to liberate Christianity from the Lutheran "tyranny" of the Word, or the Letter; "The letter, said Lessing, is the last shell of Christianity and only after the destruction of this shell will the spirit come forth" – Heinrich Heine, *Zur Geschichte der Religion und Philosophie in Deutschland*, in *Heines Werke in fünf Bänden*, vol. 5, ed. Helmut Holtzhauer (Berlin: Aufbau, 1981), 88–93.
[83] See Andreas Arndt, *Die Reformation der Revolution – Friedrich Schleiermacher in seiner Zeit* (Berlin: Matthes & Seitz, 2019), 11–46.
[84] Kaiser, *Die Scheidung von Geist und Buchstabe in der Heiligen Schrift*, 5.
[85] Ibid., 6.

Him.[86] In Schleiermacher's understanding, the "dead Letter" or "dead Scripture" refers to a religion squeezed into a rigid system of laws and obligations, a mechanically performed ritual (including the letters and words of Scripture read over and over again in the same way),[87] standing in opposition to the living Spirit in the words of the Living God, who himself did not write them down "dead letters." The words of Christ would in this view be a testimony to the living and working Spirit.[88] Proof of this can be found in the fact that these words retain their holiness even when expressed in other letters, in other languages. And even, in different intuitions (see RC 52; KGA I/2, 244). This juxtaposition will recur in other contexts.

The extent to which Schleiermacher is concerned to assert the sovereignty of the Spirit in opposition to the claims of the dead Letter is evidenced by the remarks on the idea of God and immortality that conclude the second speech. Rhapsodic thoughts here revolve around the divine unity of the universe and the multiplicity of God's images.[89] Since this unity is constituted in man's imagination (fantasy), which creates the world around us, also the idea of God is shaped by imagination turning to the infinite. If imagination depends on our consciousness of freedom, it will "personify the spirit of the universe" (RC 53; KGA I/2, 245) as a personal God. Schleiermacher's speaker is concerned to inscribe God into the dynamics of "the divine life and activity of the universe" and prevent him from becoming the God of Scripture, "existing and commanding," or the God of "the physicist or moralist" who lives in "misunderstandings" (RC 53; KGA I/2, 245). For understanding according to the Letter is indeed misunderstanding.

How can one establish a bond with the infinite, come into contact with it? This is one of the central questions of Schleiermacher's speeches *On Religion*. Through broadening one's intuition, through intensification of the imagination, through losing oneself and uniting with the infinite One – this is the answer Schleiermacher suggests.

---

[86] The rhetoric of stressing the immediacy of spiritual influence connects here with the metaphor of artistic creation showing the Spirit to be the living essence of a work of art, in its universality embracing all humanity (see Simon Gerber, *Geist, Buchstabe und Buchstäblichkeit*, 107). For Fichte, this essence appears as an emanation of the artist's emotionality (see Johann Gottlieb Fichte, *Ueber Geist und Buchstab in der Philosophie*, in idem, *Gesamtausgabe der Bayerischen Akademie der Wissenschaften*, Reihe I: *Werke*, vol. 6: *1799–1800*, ed. Reinhard Lauth, Hans Gliwitzky (Stuttgart: Frommann-Holzboog, 1981), 336, 356). Roland Barthes' remark that a departure from the regime of the letter is a precondition for liberating the language of symbols is relevant in this context; see Roland Barthes, *Erté: oder an den Buchstaben*, in idem, *Der entgegenkommende und der stumpfe Sinn. Kritische Essays III*, trans. Dieter Hornig (Frankfurt am Main: Suhrkamp, 1990), 121–122.

[87] Günter Bader, *Spirit and Letter – Letter and Spirit in Schleiermacher's Speeches 'On Religion'*, in *The Spirit and the Letter: A Tradition and a Reversal*, ed. Paul S. Fiddes, Günter Bader (London: T&T Clark, 2013), 135.

[88] It was already emphasized by Luther, in contrasting the Old Testament with the Gospel, that the latter is originally oral in character (as the Good News proclaimed), and thus its "letter" is immersed in the living word. See Gerber, *Geist, Buchstabe und Buchstäblichkeit*, 117.

[89] The inspiration of Spinoza's philosophy, in the light of which "the universe manifests itself as totality, as unity in multiplicity," is evident. (RC 52; KGA I/2, 245).

However, the road here leads across the threshold of paradox: for we are meant, "in the midst of the finite" to attain a bond with the infinite, tireless in action, eternal, immortal. In constructing this opposition, Schleiermacher highlights incommensurability, alienation, incomprehensibility, and untranslatability. It reaches its climax when he allows the infinite to speak with words alluding to the words of Christ: "Whoever loses his life for my sake shall find it, and whoever would save it will lose it."[90] He extorts: "But try to yield up your own life out of love for the universe" (RC 54; KGA I/2, 246). Detached from the letter of human language, the "spirit of the universe," stripped of its being and free from any moral influence, becomes pure emotion. This, however, reaches listeners as rhetorical exaltation. In this way, religion becomes speech *about* religion – made up of quotations, evocations and attributions. The desire to imitate the Spirit's speaking in tongues often leads to glossolalia, difficult to understand. Understanding in accordance with the Spirit is replaced by the ecstasy of identifying with the essentially foreign "infinite" (RC 54; KGA I/2, 247).

For those familiar with the Enlightenment concept of religion, Schleiermacher's clear affirmation in the second speech of the freedom that comes with uniting with the universal and the infinite, the freedom that makes it possible to expand one's personality, will sound familiar. Indeed, all too often it seems that Schleiermacher is not writing his own "poem," but is to some extent translating the Enlightenment dreams into the ecstatic language of the dreams of the Romantics. Thus, much like Denis Diderot, he calls for the "tearing down of the walls" that "hamper" our ideas, for "setting God free" so that we "see him everywhere, as he is everywhere."[91] As Ernst Cassirer explains, "in contrast to the narrow-mindedness of dogma," this literature "strives for the freedom of an all-comprehensive, a truly universal awareness of God."[92] This is the truth of religion, which does not rest on external proof, but can only, as Lessing argues, be "demonstrated inwardly," in its creative action; its testimony is written in man "by the hand of God" and not by human hands in the form "on parchment and marble."[93] The Enlightenment called this spiritual inscription the testimony of natural religion, the truthfulness of which its believers feel "immediately within themselves."[94] Schleiermacher sharply attacked natural religion in his fifth speech, accusing it of being thoroughly imbued with philosophy and moralism (RC 109; KGA I/2, 296–297). While strongly associating it with the objectivist paradigm of the Enlightenment, he failed to see the similarities linking Diderot's and Lessing's project with his own – for example, the postulate of the interiorization of

---

90 See Mt 16:25; Mk 8:35; Lk 9:24, and also Jn 12:25.
91 So writes Denis Diderot in his "Philosophic Thoughts": idem, *Diderot's early philosophical works*, trans. M. Jourdain (Chicago: Open Court, 1916), 43.
92 Ernst Cassirer, *Philosophy of the Enlightenment*, trans. Fritz C. A. Koelln and James Pettegrove (Princeton: Princeton Univ. Press, 1951), 166.
93 Ibid. 170
94 Ibid.

religion and opposition to the domination of the dead letter.[95] But Goethe himself noticed them and, according to testimonies, he liked the *Second Speech* very much because it sounded decidedly familiar.[96]

4 The transmission of insight and the problem of understanding

The paradox of all religious teaching is, the Speaker tells us, that intuition of the infinite cannot be directly conveyed to someone who does not have it. Judgments can be conveyed through words, as it were, taken over into them (*übertragen*); however, words do not suffice for the transfer of intuitions – they are only "shadows of our intuitions and feelings" (RC 57; KGA I/2, 250). If the recipient of our words does not share our religious experience, expressed in images and feelings, they would remain in the realm of nonunderstanding, far from the "original light of the universe" (RC 57; KGA I/2, 250). Incommensurability here results in untranslatability. How then to achieve commensurability, where to look for equivalence?

It is possible, by direct influence on other people, to "arouse the mimetic talent of their imagination" so that they produce in themselves feelings corresponding to our feelings, that "remotely resemble" them in their eyes (RC 57–58; KGA I/2, 250). But this is not yet, according to Schleiermacher, religion. For there is no medium through which the "sense for the universe" which is the basis of religious feeling can be communicated. Comparing it with the "artistic sense," the Speaker observes that people to whom religious feelings have been communicated (helping them to achieve a "passive religiousness") are similar to artistic audiences who, while not artists themselves, do experience aesthetic feelings, albeit only under the influence of extraneous discourse on works of art ("commentaries," "imaginative interpretations"). These people are then unable to express their feelings – when confronted with a work of art they can, "in a language that is poorly understood," only "stammer a few inappropriate words that are not their own" (RC 58; KGA I/2, 250–251). For there is no transformation here of the foreign into the personal, of someone else's spark into one's own flame.

Religion is ascribed by Schleiermacher to the realm of problems of Kantian esthetics: the subjective aesthetic experience cannot be simply transferred from one person to another, because it must be created within the individual, developed from the impulse received by him. Since religion is not a science, it cannot be con-

---

[95] Although some scholars find an 'element of affirmation' in the Speaker's remarks on natural religion – e.g. David E. Klemm in his article *Culture, Arts, and Religion*, in *The Cambridge Companion to Friedrich Schleiermacher*, ed. Jacqueline Mariña (Cambridge: Cambridge Univ. Press, 2005), 259.
[96] Cf. Günter Bader, *Spirit and Letter*, 135. Goethe's positive opinion of the first three *Speeches* was communicated to Schleiermacher in a letter by F. Schlegel, who at the same time reported that the apology for Christianity had not appealed to the author of *Werther* (see *Briefwechsel 1799–1800*, KGA V/3, 212).

veyed in the form of a discursive, rational *kerygma*, some sort of formula of faith.[97] For that would be merely the Letter, not the Spirit, which must be truly born in the individual. In the domain of religion, the essence of the pupil-master relationship is not blind imitation, but the creative stimulation of the inner impulse. Travestying the Gospel, Schleiermacher writes: disciples "are not disciples because their master has made them into this; he is rather their master because they have chosen him as that" (RC 58; KGA I/2, 251). Why does the speaker reverse the meaning of Christ's words (Jn 15:16)? To show, it seems, that by arousing a religious impulse in others, we open up to them the way to freedom: "as soon as the holy spark flares up in a soul, it expands into a free and living flame that draws its sustenance from its own atmosphere" (RC 58; KGA I/2, 251). Note that in this approach it is not the (discursive) content of the doctrine that is important: what is important is intuition, the inspiring image which, absorbed by another soul, becomes the source of religious flame, igniting it and releasing the energy of that soul's own views and feelings. Such is the logic of the Spirit, juxtaposed by Schleiermacher against the logic of the Letter, of Law, of Reason, of the Word. It seems that by pointing to this logic he reinterprets Christian doctrine in the spirit of Romanticism. Such a reinterpretation may stir controversy, since it leads the Speaker to invert the sense of the evangelical "Logia"; however, its basic intention seems to be a peculiar deverbalization of the message, which makes it possible to leap across the abyss of contradictions and misrepresentations (as revealed by the contemporary philological criticism, with which Schleiermacher was excellently familiar) and to move into the true Kingdom of the Spirit, which is not of this world, but of the realm of the Divine Infinite. We shall return to the related problem of the expressibility of religious spirituality towards the end of this chapter.

According to Schleiermacher's Speaker, the capacity for religion is given to everyone from birth. The sense of religion, unless it encounters an obstacle, develops individually, inspired by other individuals. The most serious hindrance to this development is, in the Speaker's view, the "rage of the understanding" (*die Wuth des Verstehens*, perhaps better rendered as "the fury of those who understand") (RC 59; KGA I/2, 252). It is this that prevents the sense of the infinite from developing, binding man instead to the finite. This thought has already been the subject of serious discussion, touching upon the very sources of Schleiermacher's hermeneutics.[98]

---

[97] Its foundation is also not common sense, which for Kant is the basis for the intersubjectivity of the feeling of aesthetic pleasure. Cf. Immanuel Kant, *Critique of Judgement*, trans. Werner S. Pluhar (Indianapolis: Hackett, 1987), 159 (§ 39).
[98] See Hörisch, *Die Wut des Verstehens*, 50–56. Hörisch tries to show that the young Schleiermacher was skeptical about understanding, expressing this in his speeches *On Religion*. In first edition he used the term *Die Wut des Verstehens,* only to change it later, in the second edition of 1806, to *Wut des Berechnens und Erklärens*. On this view, understanding mediates, reduces the infinite to the finite. It seems, then, that religiousness excludes hermeneutics. Hörich has drawn attention to an interesting motif in Schleiermacher's reflections, but he has interpreted it in a shallow and in many respects inaccurate way, as has been pointed out by experts on the subject. Cf. here especially Manuel Bauer's polemic in his *Schlegel und Schleiermacher*, 224–227.

Is Schleiermacher speaking negatively here about hermeneutics, which will soon become one of the main objects of his thought and work? It seems not; rather, we should ask who these furious understanders are, obstructing the inner nature that "wishes to bring religion forth" in man. And they are, as the Speaker explains, "prudent and practical people" (*die Verständigen und praktischen Menschen*), who are the "counterbalance to religion" and with their great numbers overwhelm those who wish to develop their religious sense. By exerting a negative influence on the upbringing of young people, they "suppress their striving for something higher" (RC 59; KGA I/2, 252). Here Schleiermacher is clearly constructing a thoroughly Romantic opposition: imagination and the "longing of young minds" vs. skepticism and narrow, practical rationalism. *Die Wuth des Verstehens* is correlated with the "finite and determined," with practical reason and with the analytic-synthetic method of thinking, which has the ambition of conclusively *demystifying the world*, depriving it of "the miraculous and supernatural" (RC 59; KGA I/2, 252).[99] The nature that brings religion forth, in the view of these "understanding" individuals, appears as a *de-divinized* nature.[100]

Meanwhile, the voice of religion cries out from the shadow zone: this "secret, incomprehensible intimation" (*unverstandene Ahndung*, thus in essence: "uncomprehended") drives people "go beyond the richness of this world," towards another world (RC 60; KGA I/2, 252). The awakening of religious sensitivity and the opening to the infinite becomes possible when the mind is free from "the yoke of understanding and disputation" (RC 60; KGA I/2, 253), which turns religious feeling and imagination into a universally rational discourse on religion, and every stirring of the Spirit is translated into the Letter. Thus "everything supernatural and miraculous is proscribed and the imagination is not to be filled with empty images. In the meantime one can just as easily get real things into it and make preparations for life" (RC 60; KGA I/2, 253). Instead of religion we obtain morality, just as instead of experiencing art, prudent and practical people offer us a discourse on beauty. In the light of the bourgeois ethics cited by Schleiermacher, incomprehension appears as "indolence" and laziness of the mind, which should, after all, be constantly acting, subjecting the whole (visible) reality to its power.

The imperative of understanding is opposed to faculty of sense (*der Sinn*). The latter, having found objects for itself, "approaches them and offers itself to their embraces"; it wants to see itself in them, its own creativity. Understanding, on the other hand, is not concerned with the source of objects, since in its view they appear as "a

---

[99] Max Weber wrote about the disenchantment of the world as a result of the triumph of the regime of calculation. Cf. Max Weber, "Science as a Vocation," trans. Rodney Livingstone, in *The Vocation Lectures* (Indianapolis: Hackett, 2004), 13.

[100] A reference to Friedrich Schiller's poem *Die Götter Griechenlands: die entgötterte Natur*, or "de-divinized nature" ("Gleich dem toten Schlag der Pendeluhr, / Dient sie knechtisch dem Gesetz der Schwere, / Die entgötterte Natur!," Friedrich Schiller, *Die Götter Griechenlands* (1788), http://www.friedrich-schiller-archiv.de/gedichte-schillers/highlights/die-goetter-griechenlands/ (accessed 18 July 2019).

well-acquired, inherited possession" long since "enumerated and defined" (RC 60–61; KGA I/2, 254). Sense "strives to grasp the undivided impression of something whole," its special, unique character, whereas understanding is wholly unconcerned with this. In understanding, the whole is broken up into parts, because "it is supposed to be understood singly, and this or that thing [is to] be learned from torn-off pieces" (RC 61; KGA I/2, 254) – above all, the objective of the object under study.

Schleiermacher does not, as it seems, reject the idea of understanding; he reinterprets it in the spirit of Romantic gnoseology. In order to perceive how individual things participate in the whole, his Speaker teaches, one must ask about their "unique nature" and "highest perfection" (RC 62; KGA I/2, 255). In order to grasp a thing's place in the universe, therefore, it is necessary to consider it "not only from an external point of view" – as proponents of the power of reason do – "but from its own center outward and from all sides in relation to the center, that is to say, in the thing's differentiated existence, in its own essence" (RC 62; KGA I/2, 255). This is a manifesto of the *multi-perspective* intuition (and understanding), striving for "all points of view for each thing" instead of "one point of view for everything" (RC 62; KGA I/2, 255).

Friedrich Schleiermacher presents, in his third speech, the impressive project of a Romantic *hermeneutics of sense and feeling*, standing opposed to the Enlightenment hermeneutics of theoretical and practical understanding. The latter is the antithesis of the former: instead of sense, it sees a goal, instead of an organic whole, it sees mechanically separated parts, an "encyclopedic dashing about" (RC 67; KGA I/2, 260). It forcefully imposes a single perspective, supposedly shedding the light of understanding on all things. It omits, therefore, what is peculiar and thus important in things. It thus reduces the basic conditions of the process of understanding: multiple perspectives, progressivity, non-closure, and preliminariness (with respect to "the myriad ways" objects are "able to put themselves in touch with human beings"; RC 67; KGA I/2, 260).[101]

Here we see the source of the Romantic ethics of foreignness (whose paradigm is the "foreign work of art"), which demands an understanding intuition. It will become one of the important parts of Schleiermacher's hermeneutics, as well as his reflection on translation. This ethics patronizes those approaches in the contemporary hermeneutics of translation which see text as a mysterious organism, which is part of the infinite universe of constantly renewing sense, and the translator as a *co-feeling* creator.[102]

In the speeches *On Religion*, foreignness is valued positively: the "acknowledgement of another realm" (*Anerkennen des Fremden*), appears as a sign of wisdom,

---

[101] See Hans-Georg Gadamer, "Text and interpretation," in *Dialogue and Deconstruction: The Gadamer-Derrida Debate*, ed. Diane P. Michelfelder, Richard E. Palmer, trans. Dennis J. Schmidt; Richard E. Palmer (Albany, NY: State Univ. of New York Press, 1989), 21–51

[102] See Ralph-Rainer Wuthenow, *Das fremde Kunstwerk – Aspekte der literarischen Übersetzung* (Göttingen: Vandenhoeck & Ruprecht, 1969), 10.

transcending obstacles and limitations (RC 67; KGA I/2, 261). Going beyond one's own finiteness is necessary for finding the infinite universe – for finding it also within oneself. On the level of translation, too – as Schleiermacher would speak about at the Prussian Academy of Sciences – recognition of the value of what is foreign makes it possible to glimpse a way of thinking and sense previously unknown to us.[103]

A hermeneutics based on sense demonstrates its superiority most fully where a hermeneutics of encyclopedic reason fails most. There exists "an object to which the understanding, which is in inimical to sense, only loosely clings": this is the inner world of man. All rational "explanatory psychology" (*die erklärende Psychologie*) capitulates before it, incapable of comprehending the religious man, who "has surely turned inward with his sense in the process of intuiting himself" (RC 64; KGA I/2, 257). Here, religion is safe from the fanatics of reason and their "rage of the understanding." This is the domain of experiences which cannot be translated into the language of reason: first of all, mysticism. It was raised "to the highest pinnacle of divinity and humanity" by Plato (RC 69; KGA I/2, 262)[104] – a philosopher to whose works Schleiermacher would devote his attention in the years following the publication of the speeches *On Religion*.

5 The social element

Already from childhood, according to Schleiermacher, man wishes to communicate, to transmit (*mittheilen*) his intuitions and feelings to others. Interestingly, this communication-oriented "endeavor" does not concern concepts (which would seem natural), but sensory content: man "wants to have witnesses for and participants in that which enters his senses and arouses his feelings" (RC 73; KGA I/2, 267). He wants to transmit to others "the influences of the universe," to "communicate the vibrations of his mind to them." He must therefore speak, aware that the object of his speech, religion, is inexhaustible; he must speak while listening, because that object always needs to be supplemented, perceived "through another medium." The most important thing, however, is that such communication is has a defect, for "too much of the original impression is lost in this medium in which everything is slurred over that does not fit into the uniform signs in which it shall go forth again" (RC 74; KGA I/2, 268). Here the "varied life" of religion is forced to hide itself "in dead letters," in books made up of these letters (RC 74, 142; KGA I/2, 267). And so the familiar opposition between the living Spirit vs. the dead letter returns. There is

---

[103] "If [...] readers are to understand, they must grasp the spirit of the language native to the author, they must be able to gaze upon the author's inimitable patterns of thinking and meaning" – *On the Different Methods of Translating*, DR 228; KGA I/11, 72–73.

[104] Cf. Giovanni Moretto, "Schleiermachers 'Reden' und die Mystik," in *200 Jahre "Reden über die Religion,"* 371.

also the recurring problem of the *untranslatability* of the fluid matter of sensual experiences, perceptions and feelings into the medium of language, which uses "uniform signs," "dead letters." Language is also (or perhaps above all) an organized discourse, closed in its finiteness, taking on the shape of a scholarly argument or "common conversation." How could this discourse express and explain to others the vast depths of an individual's inner experiences; make an impossible attempt to speak of the universe? And yet, such impossible communication actually occurs every day, it is realized. To express, to communicate religion – this is the supreme challenge for human speech, which, wanting to face it, harnesses all its possibilities. The regularities and aporias of human communication would absorb Schleiermacher's attention for many years to come, and he would devote to them interesting theoretical discussions in his lectures on dialectics and elsewhere.

In his speeches *On Religion*, Schleiermacher approximates this communication with images and imagery familiar from the writings of the German Romantics: inspired speech instills or unleashes a "sacred feeling" in its listeners, and comes close to music, that "speech without words" which appears as the best comprehensible expression of spirituality (RC 75; KGA I/2, 269). Hence the mutual affinity of music and religion, to which I will devote particular attention in the last part of this chapter. Singing provides a "natural eternal association" of religious people, creating a heavenly bond. This relationship is the basis of a democratic religious community: by communicating our feelings, by interacting with one another, we become part of a "priestly people" in which "each follows in the other the same power that he also feels in himself and with which he rules others" (RC 76; KGA I/2, 270). The fact that a community of religious people strives to communicate with one another entails its unity, which is not disrupted by individual religious confessions. Religion is *one*, it is a whole in which all its adherents share.[105]

The community of religious people is oriented towards communication, the content of which is individual intuitions of the infinite. Schleiermacher's speaker sees them as equal, since they all participate in a "flowing, integrating part of the whole." They are communicable within a community in which religious feeling is not something alien (as they "already have religion"). For infinity cannot be communicated to someone who feels no connection with it. It cannot be translated into the common language of general concepts – because such concepts do not exist in the case of religion. There is only the particular, the individual (RC 77; KGA I/2, 271).

The mutual communication (*Mittheilung*) of religious people is based on expressing what is one's own and assimilating what is foreign; the two acts are inseparable (RC 79; KGA I/2, 274). In a religious community, communication that is not based on mutual interaction is not true religion, that is, living, actively interacting religion

---

[105] Gräb emphasizes that this communication occurs between free individuals: Wilhelm Gräb, "Der kulturelle Umbruch zur Moderne und Schleiermachers Neubestimmung des Begriffs der christlichen Religion," in *200 Jahre "Reden über die Religion,"* 176.

(RC 80; KGA I/2, 276). What is alive is only the language of individual experience (of individual "intuitions and feelings"), of "high and free enthusiasm" (RC 81; KGA I/2, 276), while all abstractions, "dead" concepts, certainties, external symbolic actions belong to the domain of the dead Letter, which is an obstacle to religious communication. And if the Church, as a religious community, fails, it fails above all on the level of communication. It mediates it by imposing an objectified language and itself as interpreter-mediator who, by introducing its own inter-discourse, destroys the community based on equality and unity. Such an interpreter acts in favor of systematic understanding, usually valued more than "intuition and feeling." Once again Schleiermacher refers here to the kind of understanding that imposes its violence upon the individual view. He speaks of an understanding that invokes concepts and abstractions, leading in the realm of religion to misunderstanding (RC 82; KGA I/2, 278).

There is, however, an understanding that can be called *true* – one that is shared by the members of a community of religious people. Each of these people knows that he "is a part and a creation of the universe, that its divine work and life reveals itself also in him" (RC 94; KGA I/2, 291). Therefore every human existence is a revelation of the universe, shown in the shape of concrete humanity. And as such, it communicates itself to the other (*sich Jeder dem Andern mittheilt*), binding itself to him in the unity of "sense and understanding" that characterizes "humanity" as such (RC 94; KGA I/2, 291). This unity presupposes an interpenetration of the consciousness of individuals ("none is conscious of himself alone, but each is simultaneously conscious of the other"), signifying a full understanding of self and other (RC 94; KGA I/2, 291). The metaphysical basis for this brotherhood of understanding seems to be the equivalence of individuals immersed in the sacred and the divine. If understanding means overcoming the strangeness that causes illegibility, that "one-sided communication" of which Schleiermacher writes, then its basis is the spirit that allows for a profound reading of the book of the macrocosm and the microcosm, in which we are all legible signs (for ourselves and for others) (RC 93; KGA I/2, 290).

6 On religions and the dynamics of the Christian faith

Speaking through the mouth of his Speaker, in his fifth speech *On Religion* Schleiermacher assumes that the multiplicity of religions is "necessary" and "unavoidable" (RC 96; KGA I/2, 294), because religion, as something infinite on the plane of phenomenal existence, individuates itself in order to become an object of perception. It must therefore, as the Speaker asserts, manifest itself in a multiplicity of finite (denominational) forms (RC 98; KGA I/2, 296). These are, as it were, variable forms of what is eternal and unchangeable – forms formed by the formative will of man. This concept may give rise to certain doubts – Schleiermacher's metaphor suggesting a metaphysical source of religion, situated somewhere in the "womb of the universe," is not a very fortunate one (RC 98; KGA I/2, 296). However, he is concerned with the "self-individuation" of the object of consideration,[106] experienced by us as something infinite and immeasurable, so that this object becomes perceptible to us and graspable by reason. Elsewhere, Schleiermacher adds another aspect, which is the plurality of individual views of the infinite, requiring a plurality of forms of their expression (RC 100; KGA I/2, 299). Nevertheless, in discussing the notion of positive religion, Schleiermacher gets caught up in a nearly Gnostic metaphorical drama of the holy Religion *descending* from its ineffable empire into the realm of finitude, temporality, and mortality (RC 99; KGA I/2, 298).

According to the Speaker, those who are to blame for the bad reputation that religions have are those "who have forced religion out of the depths of the heart and into the civil world," forcing it to take on "imperfect raiment" (RC 99; KGA I/2, 298). This is how the finite came to rule over the infinite. In essence, what is being talked about is the process of the *translation* of a certain "inner," spiritual content – images and intuitions – into a system of material carriers of that content, or "letters," meaning here beliefs and practices. This is why the Speaker emphasizes that beneath the "code of empty customs," the "system of abstract notions and theories," that is to say, beneath the extinguished "dead slag," a sensitive mind can also perceive "the glowing outpouring of the inner fire that is contained in all religions" (RC 99; KGA I/2, 298). So once again the crucial juxtaposition in the *Speeches* resurfaces: beneath the dead Letter, lies concealed the flame of the (individual) Spirit. It is important, therefore, that educated people be able to "distinguish the inner from the outer, the native from the borrowed and foreign, the holy from the profane" (RC 100; KGA I/2, 298), and thus to separate the inner source from the outer, schematized expression.

This inner source must always remain active: immobility and dogmatic rigidity are characteristic of "sectarianism" and therefore alien to the true "spirit of religion"

---

[106] "[...] in accord with its concept and essence religion is infinite and immeasurable, even for the understanding; it must therefore have in itself a principle of individualization, for otherwise it could not exist at all and be perceived" (RC 97; KGA I/2, 296).

(RC 102 ; KGA I/2, 301). For it is constantly developing, dissolving its branches, intertwining them and creating complex forms. These can be divided into types (e.g. deism, pantheism, polytheism), although they are interwoven and do not yet define the essence of religion itself. On an individual level, some "particular intuition of the universe" becomes "the center of the whole of religion" (RC 104; KGA I/2, 303) to which everything is related. This "central intuition" defines the boundaries of positive religion, which is given "in the totality of all forms that are possible according to this construction" (RC 104; KGA I/2, 303). If man, embraced by his own original view of the universe, does not find himself in the orbit of any other dominant view, he is able to "cultivate a religion according to his own nature and sense" (RC 105; KGA I/2, 304), and thus: to create his own religious language by which he articulates his soul.

Schleiermacher is fascinated by the very moment of the birth of religious feeling, when man "first enters into the realm of religion" (RC 106; KGA I/2, 305).[107] Under the influence of an external stimulation (the Speaker here suggests the influence of the "deity" himself), his "sense for the universe" is activated (*Organ fürs Universum*), which generates a certain "religious view" (RC 106; KGA I/2, 305) one might say: a principle of religious perception and interpretation of reality. This is why the initial moment is so important, described in the fifth speech in the manner of the mystics: as the embrace of the soul by the universe or the "marriage of the infinite with the finite" (RC 107; KGA I/2, 306). It is in this extraordinary way that the "religious individuality" arises, the source of which Schleiermacher sought – in line with the Romantic paradigm – in the childhood of the individual, that is, at the dawn of its history. This individuality is a particular expression of being, since, as we read:

> Each being that arises in that way can be explained only from itself and can never be completely understood, if you do not go back as far as possible to the initial expressions of free choice in earliest times. In the same way each religious personality is also a completed whole, and your understanding of it rests on your seeking to fathom its first revelations (RC 107; KGA I/2, 307).

One can treat this assertion as a kind of hermeneutical *credo*. Only by going back to the initial moment, to the act of spiritual inspiration, already an expression of the "singularity" of man,[108] will allow us to understand the closed world of individual meaning. This seems to apply both to the "religious personality" with its "all kinds of idiosyncrasies of sensitivity and peculiarities of temperament" (*Idiosynkrasien der Reizbarkeit und Eigentümlichkeiten der Stimmung*) as well as to its creative expression (RC 107; KGA I/2, 307–308). Ultimately, what is at stake is the clarity of the spiritual sense of what appears to us as foreign.

---

107 Here Schleiermacher means positive religion, not natural religion.
108 This "religious personality" is in the original "*ein eigenthümliches geistiges Leben*" (RC 107; KGA I/2, 307): Schleiermacher uses here the concept *Eigentümlichkeit*, "peculiarity, distinctiveness, individuality," which would soon become one of the key concepts in his philosophy (see for instance his lectures on dialectics).

How is it possible to discover and fully understand the true spirit of religion? – Schleiermacher asks, debating against the proponents of natural religion. Certainly not by looking for what is common to all religions, or by getting lost in their detailed features: for one must first of all "find its basic intuition," for only then, in the light of the Whole, will all similarities and differences become intelligible (RC 112; KGA I/2, 312). But even after having learned this principle of explanation (that is, the foundation of religious hermeneutics), we will be exposed to errors and misunderstandings, if only due to the historical character of religious people. This historicity is connected to the moment in which the individual is "filled" with the religious intuition (which gives religious meaning to his life), believing most often that he is in the realm of the immediate influence of the Deity. This "seeing of the infinite in the finite" is generalized, going beyond the individual and entering the world of religion and religious culture (RC 112; KGA I/2, 313). Nevertheless, it invariably remains the causal force and meaning of this world.

The greatest mistake, the most serious misappropriation of the principle of the hermeneutics of "religious individuality" sketched out by the Speaker, is to identify religion with dogma. And in both the negative and positive sense. For one can identify religion with a set of dogmas, eliminating the life within it, its becoming, its inner dynamics (orthodoxy and heterodoxy), but one can also consistently reject everything discursive in it as the domain of the dead letter, "in order to set off toward the indeterminate" (RC 113; KGA I/2, 314). Some Schleiermacher calls "rigid systematizers," others "superficial indifferentists" – what they have in common is that they do not understand "the spirit of religion." This brings us to an important point: contrary to popular opinion, it is not some kind of irrationalism, some undefined spiritual matter escaping all attempts at understanding, that the author of the speeches *On Religion* proposes to the critics of religion in lieu of rigid dogmatics. As we have already mentioned, religion does not exclude understanding, although religious experience does deprive us of "the illusion" that we might be "able to embrace it completely" (RC 113; KGA I/2, 314).

But even when maintaining the caution recommended by Schleiermacher and remaining alert to the various pitfalls, understanding religion still remains an extremely difficult task. Can one understand religion by situating oneself outside of its domain? – ponders the Speaker, wondering if his listeners will be able to comprehend something that, in essence, "can only be understood through itself" (RC 113; KGA I/2, 314), that is, by participating in it. And the understanding of ancient, "exotic and strange" religions is less important here, as the key problem for Schleiermacher is the understanding of what is close. And that presupposes finding the right point of view.

The Old Testament religion is not close to us; on the contrary, it appears to the Speaker as distant and foreign. Judaism is, he says, "long since a dead religion" (RC 113; KGA I/2, 314). Even its adherents seem to understand this, lamenting the mummified corpse of a religion that has lost its "beautiful, childlike character," becoming "a remarkable example of corruption" and the disappearance of the spiritual element that constitutes the vitality of any religion (RC 114; KGA I/2, 315). Why such a harsh judgment? Schleiermacher proposes a phenomenological analysis: let us strip Judaism of those aspects that are not related to what constitutes the essence of religion, namely the political superstructure, the moral code, and the social dimension. Then we will see that the religious core of Judaism, and at the same time the "idea of the universe" that shines through it, turns out to be "the idea of universal immediate retribution [*Vergeltung*]" (RC 114; KGA I/2, 315), which characterizes the relation of the infinite to the arbitrary, finite individual.[109]

The God of Moses punishes and rewards the individual by relating to what is singled out within the individual person. This is the "religious spirit of Judaism" (RC 114; KGA I/2, 315), which was, moreover, transcended in the teaching of Christ. Judaism is, as the speaker emphasizes, a religion of conversation between God and man which, passing through various phases, leads through the phenomenon of prophecy to the messianic promise. The context of this conversation is "the sacredness of the tradition" that requires "initiation" (RC 114–115; KGA I/2, 315). At some point this dialogue ceased and the holy books of Judaism were closed.[110] Its continuation (in the form of rabbinic Judaism) is an "unpleasant" sight for the Speaker, for it involves the practice of a religion that "after the life and spirit had long since departed" (RC 115; KGA I/2, 316). A higher level of spiritual maturity is represented, in Schleiermacher's view, by "the original intuition of Christianity," because it has a universal dimension as "the intuition of universal straining of everything finite against the unity of the whole [*die Einheit des Ganzen*]" (RC 115; KGA I/2, 316). In this striving, conflicts and contradictions are bridged primarily by mediation (*Vermittlung*).[111] This notion seems crucial to understanding the Christian view, which is for Schleiermacher "more glorious, more sublime, and worthy of adult humanity" than Judaism (RC 115; KGA I/2, 316). In Christianity, God "reconciles the enmity directed against" him, by not allowing his creation to stray too far from him. Even though he continues stubbornly to move towards that which is contrary to the infinite, to truth and to good, even though its individual nature "tears itself loose from relationship with the whole," God does not withdraw from history (RC 115–116; KGA I/2, 316–317). On the contrary, the deity makes "ever-new arrangements" and therefore

> ever more splendid revelations issue from the womb of the old; it places ever more sublime mediators [*Mittler*] between itself and the human being, in every later ambassador it unites the deity more intimately with humanity so that through them and by them we might learn to recognize the eternal being (RC 116; I/2 KGA, 317).

---

109 See Blum, *"Ich wäre ein Judenfeind?,"* 25–28.
110 On this concept see Arnulf von Scheliha, "Schleiermacher als Denker von Pluralität," in *Reformation und Moderne: Pluralität – Subjektivität – Kritik: Akten des Internationalen Kongresses der Schleiermacher-Gesellschaft in Halle (Saale), März 2017*, ed. Jörg Dierken, Arnulf von Scheliha, Sarah Schmidt (Berlin: Walter de Gruyter, 2018), 31–32.
111 See Joseph W. Pickle, "Schleiermacher on Judaism," *The Journal of Religion* 60, no. 2 (1980): 118.

Herein lies, in Schleiermacher's understanding, the secret of Christianity's spiritual vitality; its essence is God's *communication* with creation, aimed first at uniting, linking together what is separated, then at revealing "the image of the infinite in every part of finite nature" (RC 116; KGA I/2, 317), and finally at overcoming alienation. Such is the purpose of God's signs, messengers and mediators.

In Judaism, however, communication between the Infinite and human beings soon became illusory, because it was closed within the rigid framework of tradition. The prophets stepped outside this framework; it was not coincidental that the last word in this dialogue was a prophecy about the Messiah, who was to restore Zion "where the voice of the Lord had grown silent" (RC 115; KGA I/2, 316). The ensuing silence and stillness contrast against the vitality of Christianity, in which God self-reveals his infinity in communication with his created finite being. Stillness is thus contrasted against movement, represented by the figure of the Mediator-Hermes-Translator, but also realized through the constant movement of concepts and judgments: through polemics (the New Torah of Jesus Christ), unveiling, unmasking (of false morality).[112]

From Schleiermacher's perspective, Christianity is able – like no other religion is – to purify itself inwardly, rejecting what is finite and dead. The faith of Christ does not allow itself to be dominated by idle verbal disputes "concerning the dead matter that living religion does not assimilate" (RC 118; KGA I/2, 319). Neither can it be immobilized, for it is oriented toward the infinite. The feeling which, the Speaker asserts, does not allow the Christian to rest in the indolence of complacency, is "holy sadness" (*die heilige Wehmut*) – the "dominant tone" of his religious feelings (RC 119; KGA I/2, 319). For the Founder of the Christian religion himself remained in this mood, as the Speaker convinces us, as his preserved words testify.

This sentiment takes us on a straight path to the idea that reveals the universal principle of the connection between the Infinite and the finite. Christ shows us that "everything finite needs a higher mediation [*Vermittlung*] in order to be connected with the divine" (RC 120; KGA I/2, 321). Without such higher mediation, the finite would drift further and further away from the infinite universe, sinking into nothingness and emptiness; the link with the universe would be broken. This powerful Mediator, able to maintain such a bond, a communication between man and the Infinite, "must belong to both" sides between which he mediates, "it must be a part of the divine nature just as much as and in the same sense in which it is part of the finite" (RC 120; KGA I/2, 321). Christ confirmed this function, or even the office of Mediator (*Mittleramt*), by challenging the "old, corrupt religion" and accepting martyrdom on the cross.

Christ did not regard Himself as the only Mediator, for He was also the Holy Spirit, who became the creative force of the Christian religion. It may be said, then, that the essence of this faith is a living principle of spiritual mediation

---

[112] See RC 114, 116 et seq.; KGA I/2, 315 and 317 et seq.

which ensures a continuous link, a communication between the Infinite and the finite. This communication easily overcomes the differences of various "schools" or views, since it is centered on dynamic "intuitions and feelings." Christ perfectly showed its essence, appearing as a *translator*, aware of the infinity of the object he was communicating: "Never did he pass off the intuitions and the feelings he himself could communicate as the whole compass of religion that was to proceed from his basic intuition; he always pointed to the truth that would come after him" (RC 121; KGA I/2, 322). His disciples understood what that the transfer of faith was, recognizing its limitlessness and openness, made real by the Holy Spirit, whose unlimited action knows no limits (RC 121; KGA I/2, 323). Every attempt at a limited, definitive codification of the Christian faith was ultimately an attempt to imprison it in a closed code, to kill it off in a dead letter. All those, on the other hand, who understood the freedom of this Holy *Translator-Exegete of the Father and Son*, were not closing off but rather opening up the canon of faith. "By virtue of this unlimited freedom and this essential infinity, the fundamental idea of Christianity about divine mediating powers has developed in many ways, and all intuitions and feelings of the indwelling of the divine nature in finite nature have been brought to perfection within it," Schleiermacher's Speaker concludes, perfectly capturing the essence of the idea of mediation between finite subjective being and the infinite universe of the Deity (RC 121; KGA I/2, 323). As Christianity developed, so did the idea of mediation. Scripture, inspired by the Holy Spirit, was recognized as an intermediary whose task it was to put knowledge of the infinite, the divine, into the language of finite human reason. The Holy Spirit, on the other hand, has become an "ethical mediator," bringing it as close as possible to human daily life. The Christian spirit of freedom, however, allows for the existence of many mediators gifted with the charism of translation; some Christians also recognize as such people who can be for others "a connecting point to the Infinite" (RC 122; KGA I/2, 323).

This freedom and the related historical variability of Christianity, through which the "living spirit" of this religion is renewed from time to time, without letting it freeze up into a "dead husk of the letter" protects it from anachronism. A positive correlate of Christianity's recognition of the "transitoriness of its nature" is the eschatological promise that there will someday come a time "when there will be no more talk of a mediator, but the Father will be all in all" (RC 122; KGA I/2, 323–324). This is the promise of the union of the language of the infinite with the language of the finite, and moreover of the abolition of all strangeness, of all otherness, of all remoteness – the root cause of all mediation.

However, the abolition of mediation remains a utopia at this stage of history. "Times of corruption await everything earthly," Schleiermacher writes; they are times in which the force that draws people to the Infinite has been divided unevenly: in some it is present in excess, in others it has no effect at all (RC 123; KGA I/2, 324–325). This is why "new messengers of God" are needed – to bind together that which has dissolved and receded, to bring back that which has "withdrawn," to purify that which has become "corrupt" (RC 123; KGA I/2, 324–325). Such mediators herald the birth of a new Christian spirit. For communication with the Infinite, this religious communication, renews meaning, breaking apart the frozen husk of letters. Christianity avoids the trap of "uniformity" because, through mediators, that is, through interpreters of the Divine and of His infinite, it continually relativizes what constitutes its Letter and rejuvenates its Spirit by opening itself to "other intuitions and feelings" and allowing them to enter into the element of religious communication (RC 123, 122; KGA I/2, 324, 323). The mediators – of whom Christ was the most perfect – stimulate religious communication and thereby bring together a living, dynamic community based on intersubjectivity. The vision of such a community, constituting the transcendental plane within which the individual lays down his particularity through the bonds of religion, is outlined by Schleiermacher in his *Die Weihnachtsfeier – Ein Gespräch* (*The Christmas Dialog*, 1806),[113] emphasizing the special prerogatives of Christ as "God-man" (*Gottmensch*) and "the Light of men" transferring "self-cognition" and the idea of humanity (KGA I/5, 96).[114]

Schleiermacher's remarks are accompanied by the hope that soon there will be a rehabilitation of religious views, and with it a great return of religion, which will testify to a renaissance of spiritual life. At the end of his reflections, the Speaker heightens the pathos of the approaching new creation, proclaiming the imminent arrival of a new community of religious people, a "communion of saints" (RC 124; KGA I/2, 326). Those who become part of it will communicate using language in which the mystery of holiness is encoded. The "profane" will not penetrate the depths of this speech, since, remaining in the grip of the "cold, earthly sense of the age," they are unable to reach the universe with their sense and relate it to their own being (RC 124, 10; KGA I/2, 326, 196). Their understanding will remain superficial, since it will not be the self-understanding of a man viewing the infinite and seeking connection with it, striving for the synthesis of what is separated. Therefore, the mystery of mediation between the finite and the Infinite will not open itself up to them.

7 Concluding thoughts: how to express the inexpressible?

We have seen how important a role communication plays in Schleiermacher's understanding of religion. The general model of this transfer-based communication that emerges in the course of our analysis includes religious experience (with intuition of the Infinite as its basic exponent), as well as the figure of the mediator-translator (*Mittler-Dolmetscher*) and the language of religion breaking out of the realm of discourse. A very important question arises in this context, to which it is difficult to

---

[113] See Xavier Tilliette, *Le Christ de la philosophie* (Paris: CERF, 1990).
[114] Friedrich Schleiermacher, *Die Weihnachtsfeier – Ein Gespräch* (Halle: Schimmelpfennig, 1806); English version taken from: Friedrich Schleiermacher, *Christmas Eve: A Dialogue on the Celebration of Christmas*, trans. W. Hastie (Edinburgh: T. & T. Clark, 1890), 71; see also: Kurt Nowak, *Schleiermacher: Leben, Werk und Wirkung* (Göttingen: Vandenhoeck & Ruprecht, 2001), 172.

find a clear answer in the speeches *On Religion*: namely, what is the essence of this extra-discursive language, which is the medium of individual experience, direct "intuition," intimate communion with the Infinite, with "the God that is within you"?[115] From certain hints that Schleiermacher scattered through the particular speeches (which I have drawn attention to), it may seem that he allowed for a plurality of such languages, although it seems that they share a common essence – which I would be inclined to associate with a particular mode of representation. Let me try, in summing up these considerations, to illuminate the issue in a broader context, so that all its important aspects may resound as clearly as possible.

One of the most significant philosophers of religion contemporary to Schleiermacher was Benjamin Constant. The author of *De la religion considérée dans sa source, ses formes et sos développements* (*On Religion*; 1824–1831) knew and valued Schleiermacher's speeches *On Religion*, as can be seen from his famous *Journal Intime*. He was at the same time fascinated and bewildered by the radicalism of the German theologian, whose ideas on religion he regarded as "the most peculiar system in the world."[116] Constant tried to pinpoint for himself Schleiermacher's key concept of religious feeling, agreeing with him that it has to do with intuiting things beyond the narrow confines of human existence, and that it does not necessarily have to do with an unshakeable faith in a personal God.[117] The Swiss-born philosopher preferred to speak of the "religious sentiment" inherent in man, independent of specific religious forms.[118] In his view, it is a movement, a multiform "élan toward the unknown" that "is born of the need that man experiences to put himself in communication with invisible powers."[119] The difficulty here lies in the elusiveness of this feeling, in fact inexpressible by means of discourse.

"All our intimate sentiments," writes Constant, "seem to mock the efforts of language. Words fail what they express by the very fact that they generalize, serving to designate and to distinguish rather than to define."[120] As words, the philosopher writes, are "an instrument of the mind, they render well only the notions of the mind."[121] In its "pure form" religious feeling remains an inexpressible stirring of the soul, but it is apprehensible in its many forms, in which it is already objectified and conventionalized in the form of symbolic languages.[122] To the enlightened, these

---

115 These are the final words of the speeches *On Religion*: RC 124; KGA I/2, 326. This problem is rarely discussed by researchers, yet it is very important.
116 Benjamin Constant, *Journal intime de Benjamin Constant et lettres à sa famille et à ses amis*, ed. Dora Melegari (Paris: Paul Ollendorff, 1895), 114, https://ebooks-bnr.com/ebooks/pdf4/constant_journal_intime.pdf. (accessed 20 May 2022).
117 See ibid. and also Benjamin Constant, *On Religion, Considered in Its Source, Its Forms, and Its Developments*, trans. Peter Paul Seaton (Carmel, Indiana: Liberty Fund, 2017), 31
118 Benjamin Constant, *On Religion*, 36–7.
119 Ibid., 36 and 38.
120 Ibid., 36.
121 Ibid.
122 Ibid., 36–37 and 38.

forms often seem primitive, anachronistic, and ridiculous, but they refer to a spiritual reality that is not translatable into a language based on the identification and differentiation of concepts – and Constant recognizes no other. The fundamental problem here concerns the experiential content related to religion, which undergoes transfer and – finally – is expressed in conceptual language. In Hegel's system this content is expressed in representations (*Vorstellungen*), in pictorial language, the transformation of which is performed by philosophy. For it is philosophy that "was to translate the pictorial language of the believer into concepts," because only these "are capable of adequately expressing the content of the cognition of the Spirit,"[123] identifying "the truth of being and essence."[124] Only philosophy can "express both itself and religion, because it is able to express in concepts the statements made symbolically by religion [...]," as the Polish philosopher Jan Andrzej Kłoczowski explains the Hegelian point of view.[125] However, this type of translation is not, from the perspective of Schleiermacher's Speaker, a positive point of reference, because it nullifies the animating power of religious feeling.[126]

But if the Hegelian way of reasoning does not lead to an explanation of the problem of the transfer of religious experience, what route is more adequate? It turns out that the philosophy of Immanuel Kant is able to bring us closer to the heart of this question. Rudolf Otto, the publisher and commentator of the speeches *On Religion*, who was himself a philosopher of religion inspired by Schleiermacher's thought, refers to Kant in his monograph *Das Heilige* (1917) (*The Idea of the Holy*), which can be seen as a productive critique of the ideas of the author of *Der christliche Glaube*. His point of departure, however, stands in opposition to Kant: Otto, as a disciple of Schleiermacher, considers the experience of holiness, while omitting the moral and rational element.[127] To emphasize this opposition, he defines it with the word *numinous*, coined from the Latin *numen*.[128] In this way, he invokes one of the funda-

---

[123] Jan Andrzej Kłoczowski, "Max Scheler – myśliciel poważny" [Max Scheler – A Serious Thinker], in Max Scheler, *Problemy religii* [Problems of Religion], trans. and introduction by Adam Węgrzecki, afterword by Jan Andrzej Kłoczowski (Kraków: Znak, 1995), 368.
[124] Georg Wilhelm Friedrich Hegel, *Hegel's Logic: Being Part One of the Encyclopedia of the Philosophical Sciences*, trans. William Wallace (New York, Clarendon Press, 1975), 189 (§ 159).
[125] Jan Andrzej Kłoczowski, *Między samotnością a wspólnotą – Wstęp do filozofii religii* [Between Loneliness and Community – An Introduction to a Philosophy of Religion] (Tarnów: BIBLOS 1994) 26.
[126] It is worth adding in this context that Schleiermacher's attitude towards the person and philosophy of Hegel was highly critical – see Richard Crouter, "Hegel and Schleiermacher at Berlin: A Many-Sided Debate," *Journal of the American Academy of Religion* 48, no. 1 (1980): 19–43. On the differences in Schleiermacher's and Hegel's treatment of religion, see Andreas Arndt, *Friedrich Schleiermacher als Philosoph* (Berlin: Walter de Gruyter, 2013), 240–247, and Kipton E. Jensen, "The Principle of Protestantism: On Hegel's (Mis)Reading of Schleiermacher's 'Speeches,'" *Journal of the American Academy of Religion* 71, no. 2 (2003): 405–422.
[127] Rudolf Otto, *The Idea of the Holy: An Inquiry into the Non-Rational Factor in The Idea of the Divine and Its Relation to the Rational*, trans. John W Harvey (Oxford: Oxford Univ. Press, 1936), 6–7.
[128] Ibid., 7.

mental notions of Kantian philosophy[129] and refers to its assumption that "we finite beings can have ideas but no knowledge of such supersensible matters, which are part of that noumenal realm of things-in-themselves inaccessible to human understanding (*Verstand*)."[130]

In Otto's opinion, Schleiermacher highlighted an essential element of the numinous experience, calling it the "feeling of absolute dependence."[131] Otto, however, accused his teacher, firstly, of using this notion in a peculiar, non-intuitive sense, and secondly, of wanting "to determine the real content of the religious emotion," he focused on "a first subjective concomitant and effect of another feeling-element,"[132] leaving aside the fundamental emotional element of "fear." And it is fear that directly attunes itself to the numinous object.[133]

Otto claims that, according to Schleiermacher, this feeling of dependence opens man to "impressions of the universe," experienced in the form of "intuitions" and "feelings."[134] They take shape, Rudolf Otto writes:

> in definite statements and propositions, capable of a certain groping formulation, which are not without analogy with theoretic proposition, but are to be clearly distinguished from them by their free and merely felt, not reasoned, character. In themselves they are groping intimations of meanings figuratively apprehended. They cannot be employed as 'statements of doctrine' in the strict sense, and can neither be built into a system nor used as premises for theoretical conclusions.[135]

Nevertheless, the author of *The Idea of the Holy* refers to them as "cognitions," which are "not the product of reflection but the intuitive outcome of feeling."[136] Otto places them in the domain of the aesthetic faculty of judgement, which Kant analyzes in his *Critique of Pure Reason*. An aesthetic judgement, Otto argues, "is not worked out in accordance with a clear intellectual scheme, but in conformity to obscure, dim principles which must be felt and cannot be stated explicitly as premises."[137] Indeed, since for Kant the domain of "feeling" (*Gefühl*) is subjective and thus as mysterious as the (aesthetic) judgment of taste, "concealed from us even as to its sources."[138] Following this interpretative suggestion of Rudolf Otto, we can conclude that there is a

---

[129] See the definition of *nuomena* in the context of sensual awareness and the limits of human cognition in: Immanuel Kant, *Critique of Pure Reason*, trans. Norman Kemp Smith, reissue edition (New York: Pallgrave Macmillan, 2007), 338 ff.
[130] Martin Jay, *Songs of Experience*, 128–129.
[131] Otto, *The Idea of the Holy*, 112. This, however, is his later account of this experience, see KGA I/12, 133.
[132] Otto, *The Idea of the Holy*, 12.
[133] Ibid., 13.
[134] Ibid., 150.
[135] Ibid., 150–51.
[136] Ibid., 151
[137] Ibid., 152.
[138] Kant, *Critique of Judgement*, 214.

realm of the language of feelings – an aesthetic realm, relating to "the supersensible in us" (E. Kant)[139] – the existence of which, as the author of *The Idea of the Holy* emphasizes, has long been guessed at by poets.[140] Is it possible, then, that poetic inspiration enables the creation of non-conceptual (or pre-conceptual)[141] languages that are "analogous" representations of feelings and intuitions? That is, by implication, did it make non-conceptual languages possible? These would then be the natural languages of religious mediators: visionaries, prophets, virtuosi.

Among contemporary philosophers of religion, much attention was paid to this issue by Charles Taylor. For him, and important starting point was William James's theory of religion, which is based on the assumption that its source lies in individual experience, remaining in the realm of sensation. The formulas by which people define and rationalize their religious feelings are, in James's view, secondary to "the world of living individualized feelings" – they are, in comparison, "without solidity or life."[142] James's theory shows many parallels with Schleiermacher's perspective of the Speaker[143] and thus faces similar questions. One of them concerns, as Taylor writes, the "conceptual" or "transcendental" question.[144] The question, of course, is whether it is possible to have "the very idea of an experience that is in no way formulated."[145] Taylor thinks that James could answer such a question by saying that the description of experience does not require the observance of some rigid rules of descriptiveness, characteristic of an objectifying language based on a conventional conceptual apparatus.[146] But is it not the case, he asks, that the description of experience does not require the observance of certain rigid rules of descriptiveness, characteristic of an objectifying language based on a conventional conceptual apparatus? And is it not the case, the Canadian philosopher further asks, that even the individual experiences "require some vocabulary, and these are inevitably in large part handed to us in the first place by our society, whatever transformations we may

---

139 Ibid.
140 Otto, *The Idea of the Holy*, 152–53.
141 See Peter Grove, *Deutungen des Subjekts: Schleiermachers Philosophie der Religion* (Berlin: Walter de Gruyter, 2004), 349. It seems that the philosophical basis for the "pre-conceptual" understanding of the Infinite that Grove writes about (referring here to Heidegger) can be found precisely in Kant.
142 Charles Taylor, *Varieties of Religion Today: William James Revisited* (Cambridge, MA: Harvard, 2002) 11. Cf. William James, *The Varieties of Religious Experience: A Study of Human Nature* (London: Longmans, Green and Co., 1902), 502
143 Cf. e.g. James's remarks in his *Varieties of Religious Experience*, 447, about how philosophical and theological speculations are "after-effects, secondary accretions upon those phenomena of vital conversation with the unseen divine."
144 Taylor, *Varieties of Religion Today*, 26.
145 Ibid.
146 Ibid., 27

ring on them later"?¹⁴⁷ Taylor is convinced that there are individual experiences that are "immensely enhanced by the sense that they are shared."¹⁴⁸

This pathway of reflection on religious experience leads directly to Romantic thought, and thus also to Schleiermacher. The Romantics – distrustful of analytical reason and the world of concepts and distinctions it yields – decided, Taylor writes, that

> what was needed was a subtler language that could make manifest the higher or the divine. But this language required for its force that it resonate with the writer or reader. Getting assent to some external formula was not the main thing; being able to generate the moving insight into higher reality was what was important.¹⁴⁹

Deep personal intuitions, such as Schleiermacher's sense of dependence upon something greater, therefore require a voice capable of stirring and opening the way to individual insights into the nature of the infinite. Thus Charles Taylor leads us to the origins of modern expressivism, to which he devoted much space in his scholarly work. "In an age that seems to be dominated by 'the learned despisers of religion'," he writes, referring to Schleiermacher's speeches," what is really viable is spiritual insight/feeling. This will inevitably draw on a language that resonates very much with the person who possesses it.¹⁵⁰

Modern expressivism, which became dominant in the Romantic era, gives such language the highest value because it articulates individual sensitivity, the subject's own, unique world.¹⁵¹ The view of the universe, the sense of infinity and connection with it are inscribed in this world and expressed along with it in poetic speech. This is because poets:

> make us aware of something in nature for which there are as yet no adequate words. The poems are finding the words for us. In this 'subtler language' – the term is borrowed from Shelley – something is defined and created as well as manifested.¹⁵²

In this way the Romantics define the very essence of poetry, treating it as an event related to with the sublime (evoked, for example, by the image of the immensity of the universe).¹⁵³ This sublimity is, in a way, the environment in which the poetic

---

147 Ibid., 27–28. Andreas Arndt accuses Schleiermacher in this vein that the "immediacy of religious consciousness" he invokes is "mediated by philosophy" (Andreas Arndt, *Friedrich Schleiermacher als Philosoph*, 241).
148 Taylor, *Varieties of Religion Today*, 28.
149 Ibid., 99–100.
150 Ibid., 100
151 Charles Taylor, *The Ethics of Authenticity* (Cambridge, MA: Harvard Univ. Press, 1991), 84.
152 Ibid., 85.
153 Cf. Kant, *Critique of Judgment*, 98.

language is born and the poetic event that is realized through this particular language.[154] It is a staging (a *performance*) of the inexpressible.

Taylor claims that the Romantic artist is in fact a mediator (the Canadian scholar is referring in specific to the notion of *Mittler* in Friedrich Schlegel's *Ideas*), because through his speech other people come to know spiritual reality.[155] In this context the philosopher recalls Schleiermacher's well-known words about the creative, artistic nature of intermediation, which inclines the "priests of the Most High" to transmit the Infinite in the "finite form" of an inspired translation into images and words.[156] What is also relevant here, albeit omitted by Taylor, is the purpose of this creative transfer: to "transform the common life into something higher," to show the *Transcendence*, which is the domain of freedom, to the "children of the earth" bound by rationalism and materialism (RC 8; KGA I/2, 194). Schleiermacher himself seems to have shaped the language of his speeches *On Religion* with the power of poetic transfer in mind – hence, as Martin Jay notes, the "wealth of metaphorical allusions rather than dry literalism," the "rhapsodic intensity of expression," and the "organic images of dynamic oppositions being overcome by higher mediations."[157] He undoubtedly adapts himself in this way to the language used by the recipients of the speeches *On Religion:* he prefers poetic style, argumentation sometimes bearing the traces of improvisation, and finally, as he himself once admitted, making music more than laying forth an argument.[158]

The role of music, which the Romantics saw as the most perfect of all sensitive languages, enabling direct, spiritual communication, cannot be overlooked in this context. In Kant's view, music is the "language of sensations that every human being can understand," expressing the aesthetic ideas of some ineffable "wealth of thought."[159] Schleiermacher linked this specificity of music and its influence with religious feeling and its expression. If, following Karl Barth, usually radical in his judgments, we assume that in the eyes of the author of the speeches *On Religion* "the divine is unspeakable," the ultimate truth "remains reserved for a silent, at best singing, and ultimately only inadequately expressive feeling [*inadäquat redenden Gefühl*]."[160] And although it seems that Barth's somewhat apophatic approach to the notion of feeling in Schleiermacher's theology distorts it, weakening its com-

---

[154] See Johnathan Culler, *Literary Theory: A Very Short Introduction* (Oxford: Oxford Univ. Press, 1997), 77.
[155] Charles Taylor, *Sources of the Self: The Making of the Modern Identity*, (Cambridge, MA: Harvard Univ. Press, 1989), 378.
[156] Ibid., 378; also RC 7; KGA I/2, 193.
[157] Jay, *Songs of Experience*, 94.
[158] Barth, *Die Protestantische Theologie*, 397.
[159] Kant, *Critique of Judgment*, 199.
[160] Barth, *Die Protestantische Theologie*, 406 and 407.

municative potential, it nevertheless sensitizes us to the role of music as a metaphor bringing this central notion closer in the theologian's religious discourse.[161]

In his speeches *On Religion* Schleiermacher several times takes up this "musical" theme: in the second speech, for example, we read that "religious feelings should accompany every human deed, like a holy music" (RC 30; KGA I/2, 219),[162] and at the beginning of the third, the Speaker describes the influence of religion, which, through the "natural expressions of its own life," emits, as it were, sounds that resonate in the ears of the listeners. This kind of direct communication was also used by him, counting – as he confesses – on the emotional stirring of his audience: "How often have I struck up the music of my religion in order to move my those present, beginning with soft individual tones and longingly progressing with youthful impetuosity to the fullest harmony of religious feelings" (RC 55–56; KGA I/2, 134). Finally, in the third *Speech*, when the theme of reflection is again the transfer of feeling, aimed at "implanting" in the souls of the listeners the "sacred feeling" of religion, we recall the idea of the Mediator's speech becoming music. It is symmetrical with the music of the sacred choirs: it is "speech without words, the most definite, the most comprehensible expression of the deepest interior" (RC 75; KGA I/2, 269). Schleiermacher develops this thought:

> The muse of harmony, whose intimate relation to religion still belongs to the mysteries, has from time immemorial offered the most splendid and most perfect works of her most dedicated pupils on the altars of region. In holy hymns and choruses, to which the words of the poet cling only loosely and lightly, that is exhaled which definite speech can no longer comprehend, and thus the sounds of thought and feeling support one another and alternate until everything is saturated and full of the holy and infinite (RC 75; KGA I/2, 270).

This religious-aesthetic bond is constituted by music, which makes it possible "for religious people to influence one other" (RC 75; KGA I/2, 270). However, the condition for such interaction is always the musical hearing of the potential participants in the communication; when this condition is not fulfilled, the result can be disappointing; in such a case the Speaker complains: "yet nothing stirred or responded in them!" (RC 56; KGA I/2, 134).[163]

---

[161] It is worth remembering that emotion retains a central position in all of Schleiermacher's important religious writings, from the speeches *On Religion* (*Ueber die Religion*) through his *Monologues* (*Monologen*) and *Christmas Dialog* (*Weihnachtsfeier*) to the *Christian Faith* (*Der christliche Glaube*) and the *Sermons* (*Predigten*), and that he continued preaching until his final days. See on this Karl Barth, *Die Protestantische Theologie*, 409 (Barth writes of Schleiermacher's "dogmatics of emotional states" and "theology based on feeling").
[162] Cf. the reference to "music of sublime feelings," RC 92; KGA I/2, 289.
[163] Schleiermacher returned to the musical theme and musical metaphor in his later writings. In his talk *Die Weihnachtsfeier*, published seven years after the Speeches *On Religion*, he argues that the perfect representation of religious feeling is not the word but sound, music: "For every beautiful feeling is only fully revealed when we find the right tone for it; not the word, it is always a mediated expression, a plastic element, if we may say so, but precisely the tone, in its true sense. And it is with reli-

A subtler language, rooted in individual sensitivity, is thus comprehensible only to those who are endowed with a sensitivity that "resonates."[164] This makes "sensitive" communication possible – it is how the transfer of feelings and perceptions occurs. This also applies to the religious Transcendence – that is to say, to "what-is-not-put-in-words," impossible to adequately express, and what is expressed by more sensitive artistic languages.[165] The languages of art open up to us the imaginative space of religious communication.[166] They make us aware of how many things we cannot grasp in this field, how many things we cannot understand, how many things we cannot translate into concepts. The resulting amazement and openness to the suggestive power of more sensitive languages and the phenomenon of mediation lead us to hermeneutics.[167] In this sense, perhaps not without exaggeration, Schleiermacher's speeches *On Religion* can be called an introduction to the wide range of issues of hermeneutics. "All the problems of assimilation and understanding are thus brought together in the speeches," writes Hans-Joachim Rothert in the introduction to the German edition of this work.[168] These key problems for hermeneutics concern, *inter alia*, the understanding of the infinite from the point of view of a finite, historically determined present, the cultural mediation of religious experience, and constituting the understanding of Revelation as human self-understanding. These issues are relevant not only to Protestant hermeneutical theology but also to general hermeneutics, which combines the former with the rhetorical and philological traditions.[169]

It is no coincidence that after writing his *Speeches on Religion* and the *Christmas Dialog*, Schleiermacher turned his attention to hermeneutics – or indeed, that he

---

gious feeling that music is most closely allied" (KGA I/5, 63), English version from F. Schleiermacher, *Christmas Eve: dialogue on the celebration of Christmas*, 25. For more on this, especially in the context of *Aesthetics*, see Gunter Scholtz, *Schleiermachers Musikphilosophie* (Göttingen: Vandenhoeck & Ruprecht, 1981).

164 Taylor, *The Ethics of Authenticity*, 8/.
165 See Karol Tarnowski, *Usłyszeć niewidzialne – Zarys filozofii wiary* [To Hear the Invisible: Outline of a Philosophy of Faith] (Kraków: Instytut Myśli Józefa Tischnera, 2005) 181–182.
166 On the role of imagination in the context of the mutual relationship between religion and art in Schleiermacher's *Speeches*, see Thomas Lehnerer, *Die Kunsttheorie Friedrich Schleiermachers* (Stuttgart, Klett-Cotta, 1987), 340–341.
167 Tarnowski, *Usłyszeć niewidzialne*, 186; Funke, "Glaubensbewußsein: Hermeneutik als Sprachlehre des Glaubens," 361.
168 Hans-Joachim Rothert, *Einleitung*, in Friedrich Schleiermacher, *Über die Religion – Reden an die Gebildeten unter ihren Verächtern* (Hamburg: Felix Meiner 1970), XI. Rothert stresses that the reader of the speeches is inclined to adopt a hermeneutical stance: he must "distance himself from the immediacy of the thing" and "taking the thing, as it were, with him, do the work of critical examination and assimilation" (X).
169 See Kurt Mueller-Vollmer, "Foundations: General Theory and Art of Interpretation – Friedrich D.E. Schleiermacher," in *The Hermeneutics Reader: Texts of the German Tradition from the Enlightenment to the Present*, ed. Kurt Mueller-Vollmer (Oxford: Basil Blackwell, 1986), 72.

soon precipitated an important turning-point in the field, bringing to bear all his expertise in rhetoric, philology, as well as philosophy.[170]

---

[170] Schleiermacher's considerations on the transfer of feeling and the understanding of works of art, which are important in the context of hermeneutics, also owe much to the speeches *On Religion,* as the notes to the *Ethics* for the semester 1805/1806 clearly testify. See Friedrich Schleiermacher, *Aus: Broullion zur Ethik,* in idem, *Hermeneutik und Kritik,* ed. Manfred Frank (Frankfurt am Main: Suhrkamp, 1977), 361–370.

V Modelling Translation Criticism: Schlegel and Schleiermacher

1 Preliminary historical remarks on translation criticism

In this chapter, I will examine Schleiermacher's translation criticism, juxtaposing it with analogous work by his Berlin-based friend and collaborator, Friedrich Schlegel. The topic is highly relevant here in that translation criticism always presupposes a certain underlying theory of translation; moreover, translation critique figured particularly prominently within the Romantic translation-studies discourse.

Criticism levelled against literal or non-literal approaches to translation, as has been discussed at various places in this book, has throughout history often played a *theory-constitutive* role. For example, Jerome, the translator of the Vulgate Bible, was provoked to write his famous letter to Pammachius (known as *De optimo genere interpretandi*, dating to the year 395) in which he summarizes his principles for translating the Bible, invoking the authority of Cicero and Horace, after he read a criticism of one of his translations – an unjust and foolish critique, in his view. Rufinus of Aquileia had accused Jerome of having made embarrassing errors in his Greek-to-Latin translation of a letter written by Bishop Epiphanius to Bishop John of Jerusalem.[1] This compelled Jerome, today recognized as the patron saint of all translators, to write a letter, pouring out his views on the subject of translation. In it, he advocates a kind equivalence that might nowadays be described as dynamic, because it favors meaning over literalness.[2] Even the omission or addition of a few words from or to a religious text does not, the learned translator argues, pose any threat to the faith or to the Church.[3] However, this dynamism (variability) at the level of re-expression does not exempt the translator, as St Jerome stresses, from the hermeneutical effort of penetrating the text, "where even the syntax contains a mystery."[4]

More than 1,100 years later, Martin Luther was similarly provoked – by some harsh criticism against his own translation of Paul's letters into German – to write his *Circular Letter on Translation* (*Sendbrief vom Dolmetschen*, 1530), addressed to his friend, a clergyman from Nuremberg. Luther was here continuing a debate he had been waging with Hieronymus Emser, his antagonist and a translator of the New Testament.[5] Luther explains in his letter that the accusation that he had distort-

---

[1] Jerome, "On The Best Kind of Translator," trans. H.M. Hubbell, in *Western Translation Theory: From Herodotus to Nietzsche*, ed. Douglas Robinson (Manchester: St. Jerome, 1997), 23–30.
[2] Ibid., 26. Jerome writes here that when he translated the biography of St. Anthony of Egypt, as elsewhere, he "always attempted to translate the substance, not the literal words"
[3] Ibid., 29.
[4] Ibid., 25.
[5] See Hans-Wolfgang Schneiders, "Luthers Sendbrief vom Dolmetschen – Ein Beitrag zur Entmythologisierung," *trans-kom* 5, no. 2 (2012): 256.

ed the sense of St. Paul's message in his translation by adding an unnecessary word (*allein*) was completely misguided.⁶ The accusation was a serious one, as the "papists" (including Esmer) were, as Luther writes, "getting themselves all worked up over the fact that Paul never wrote the word *sola* (*allein* or "alone/only"), and who am I to be adding things to the word of God?"⁷ And indeed, there is no such word to be found in the original (or in the Vulgate): λογιζόμεθα γὰρ δικαιοῦσθαι πίστει ἄνθρωπον χωρὶς ἔργων νόμου – we read in Romans (3:28).⁸ The father of the Reformation nevertheless argues in his own defense that this addition is essentially an explication, which "fits the meaning of the text,"⁹ thus expressing its spirit, rather than its letter. Developing this argument further, Luther posits a theory of translation appropriate to his endeavor that might today be called functionalism, including a requirement of fidelity to the original.¹⁰ This meant an obligation to piously consider the literal sense and to adhere to it anywhere "a lot seemed to be riding on a passage" in the Bible.¹¹ But such fidelity is only possible if the translator is able to grasp the *truth* of the inspired text, which in fact presupposes a gift of grace. This is why, Luther argues, no "false" Christian "will ever be a good translator"¹²; for fidelity comes from sharing in the *spirit* of the word of God. Otherwise, the Jewish cult of the letter would have remained normative, the cult against which St. Paul turned, knowing that it limited the communicability (and therefore the translatability) of the word, posing an obstacle of strangeness and untranslatability.¹³

---

6 Schneiders ("Luthers Sendbrief vom Dolmetschen," 263) compares two versions of the relevant passage: from the New Testament translation and from the *Sendebrief*: "*Wir halten, das der mensch gerecht werde on des gesetzes werck, allein durch den glauben*" (*Sendbrief* 1530) and "*So halten wyrs nu/das der mensch gerechtfertiget werde/On zuthun der werck des gesetzs/alleyn durch den glawben*" (NT 1522). In the NT version Luther clearly places emphasis on the (multiple) deeds of the Law.
7 Martin Luther, "Circular Letter on Translation (*Sendbrief vom Dolmetschen*)," trans. by Douglas Robinson, in Robinson, *Western Translation Theory*, 84. Emser translates "*Dann wir halten dafür das der mensch gerechtfertiget werde/durch den glauben/on die werck des gesetzes.*" In the margin of his translation of the New Testament (the second version; the first appeared in 1527) Esmer notes Martin Luther's solution and the meaning of his gloss. Emser's gloss provides an interpretation of Rom 3:28, while the annotation that follows dissects Luther's argument, not without a certain dose of malice. Hieronymus Esmer, *Das gantz neü testament: So durch den hochgelerrten Hieronymum Emser verteütsch* [...] (Tübingen: Morhart, 1532), CX.; see an earlier version of the annotation in: Hieronymus Emser, *Auß was gründ vnnd vrsach Luthers dolmatschung, vber das nawe testament, dem gemeine[n] man billich vorbotten worden sey* [...] (Leipzig: Wolfgang Stöckel, 1523), LXVII–LXVIII.
8 Cited: https://biblehub.com/interlinear/romans/3.htm (accessed 7 September 2019).
9 Luther, "Circular Letter on Translation," 86.
10 Ibid., 87.
11 Ibid.
12 Ibid., 88.
13 It is therefore hardly surprising that in translating the psalms, for example, Luther adopts a Christological exegesis and translates the Hebrew words and phrases in accordance with it. See Karl-Heinz Göttert, *Luthers Bibel – Geschichte einer feindlichen Übernahme* (Frankfurt am Main: S. Fischer, 2017), 355.

These two famous examples make it evident to what extent translation criticism contributes to the formulation of an agenda that stretches well beyond even translation theory itself, becoming a coherent cultural discourse that bears the hallmarks of a cultural paradigm. Jerome's and Luther's responses to translation critique have had a fundamental impact on how fidelity and loyalty in communication have been understood in Christian Europe.

Another, very important, moment when translation criticism demonstrated its theoretical and cultural power came at the turn of the eighteenth and nineteenth centuries, especially the Romantic period. A significant aspect in this context is highlighted by Maria Krysztofiak in her remarks on the cultural circumstances of translation criticism, namely "the closeness of translation criticism to literary criticism."[14] An awareness that the literary status of the original needs to be balanced by the artistry of translation was present from the very beginning of translation studies. The value and prestige of original works was largely judged by experts – literary critics, guided by certain aesthetic norms. The translation critic, knowing these evaluations – according to Krysztofiak – then decides "whether the translated work satisfies the requirements for a work of art as expected by literary critics."[15] Thus, he or she judges whether the form that a foreign-language work of literary art takes on in the domestic literature merits to be regarded as a valuable work.

As expressivist aesthetics gradually gained the status of a recognized model, more and more importance came to be attached to the originality of literary works of art (though not only literary), and thus also to the analogous impact being exerted by their translations, which were expected to defend themselves in their own literary context, within the axiological framework of native criticism. As a result, fidelity to the original (considered on various levels, of course) became one of the most important criteria of evaluation, often even less prominent than, for example, linguistic innovation.

In this paradigm, the ideal case can be regarded as one in which the critic combines expert competence in the foreign literature with a broad grasp of the domestic literature, including a profound awareness of its historical development and current "spiritual condition," including in comparative terms. Such a critic is, therefore, an insightful philologist, skilled at hermeneutics and criticism, and at the same time an excellent expert on native culture and the national literature, with his or her own vision of their distinctiveness and developmental trajectory. Certain critics meeting these ideal-case conditions were indeed to be found in German culture at the turn of the eighteenth and nineteenth centuries: they undoubtedly included Herder, the Schlegel brothers, and – to a more modest extent – also Schleiermacher.

---

14 Maria Krysztofiak, *Translatologiczna teoria i pragmatyka przekładu artystycznego* [Translatological Theory and Pragmatics of Artistic Translation] (Poznań: Wydawnictwo Naukowe UAM, 2011), 143.
15 Ibid.

The significance of Friedrich Schlegel's critical literary reflection for the new "modern" translation criticism has been clearly emphasized by Maria Krysztofiak. She points to Schlegel's observations formulated in his essay *Über Lessing* (1804), which, in her view, "can be successfully transferred to the context of contemporary translation criticism, as has been done, inter alia, by Katharina Reiß in her book on the possibilities and limitations of translation criticism."[16] Reiß has drawn attention to such important Romantic postulates as the endeavor "to enter into the thought processes of another person and be able to rebuild his whole perspective in all its particularity" and to "reconstruct the framework and how it operates in all its parts"[17] These, however, are only two of many elements of Schlegel's concept of modern criticism, which was to remain in close relation with philology as a synthesis of science (grammar) and art (criticism).[18] At the same time is worth bearing in mind how high Friedrich Schlegel set the bar for critics: he demanded artistic equivalence between the reviewed work and the review itself, because "poetry can only be criticized by way of poetry."[19]

One should remember that Romantic art criticism (*Kunstkritik*) was quite distinctive. As Walter Benjamin brilliantly argued, dogmatic judgment was alien to it, because it is based on reflection about the relationship of the described work to other works of art, and to the idea of art itself.[20] Schlegel emphasized, however, that as a critic he was guided by the ambition to "understand and explain."[21] Romantic criticism goes beyond evaluative commentary, becoming (at least intentionally) the domain of "culminating, completing, systematizing a work," all the way to its "dissociation in the absolute."[22] Note that construing criticism in this way, as a kind of prolongation of the original creative act, means that a perfect medium for it can be found in artistic translation, which – including because of its historicity

---

16 Ibid., 146.
17 Ibid. The words of Schlegel, quoted from: Katharina Reiß, *Möglichkeiten und Grenzen der Übersetzungskritik – Kategorien und Kriterien für eine sachgerechte Beurteilung von Übersetzungen* (Munich: Max Hueber, 1971), 17, English version *Translation Criticism – The Potentials and Limitations: Categories and Criteria for Translation Quality Assessment*, trans. Erroll F. Rhodes (London: Routledge, 2000), 9. Reiß notes that Schlegel's reflection implies a postulate, crucial for translation criticism, of confronting the translation with an "adequately" understood original. Ibid., 60.
18 Dorit Messlin, *Antike und Moderne: Friedrich Schlegels Poetik, Philosophie und Lebenskunst* (Berlin: Walter de Gruyter, 2011), 84.
19 In the same passage from "Lyceum" Schlegel continues: "A critical judgment of an artistic production has no civil rights in the realm of art if it isn't itself a work of art, either in its substance, as a representation of a necessary impression in the state of becoming, or in the beauty of its form and open tone, like that of the old Roman satires." Friedrich Schlegel, Fragment 117, in idem, *Friedrich Schlegel's Lucinde and the Fragments*, trans. Peter Firchow (Minneapolis: Univ. of Minnesota Press, 1971), 157.
20 Walter Benjamin, *Der Begriff der Kunstkritik in der deutschen Romantik* (Frankfurt am Main: Suhrkamp, 1973), 72.
21 Quoted in ibid.
22 Ibid.

– finds its fulfilment precisely in the critical dimension. Benjamin also stresses the importance of the very fact of engaging in criticism, as the act of subjecting a particular work to critique is itself tantamount to acknowledging its value.[23]

Antoine Berman, an expert in Romantic aesthetics and translation studies, considers this positive, constructive aspect of post-Enlightenment criticism of translation to be extremely important. In this paradigm, critics draw attention not only to the defects of a particular translation, but also to its communicative value and its contribution to the target language and culture:

> But since this positive discourse could never, prior to Goethe, Humboldt and Schleiermacher, move beyond the stage of a – just – apology for the collateral benefits of translation, without at all focusing on the ontological link between the original and its translations, it was easily dominated by the negative discourse which is the omission (or negation) of this link.[24]

The French scholar is referring here to the historical circumstances of translation criticism, but also suggesting wherein lies the weakness of contemporary criticism, suffering from a lack of memory.[25]

Berman points out another important aspect of Romantic translation criticism. It very often turns out to be second-order criticism, that is, criticism of "a text that is itself the outcome of critical activity."[26] This does not have to be a translation in the strict sense, but in cases that do involve a translation which is the next in a series of translations (as will be true for the cases we will be analyzing in this chapter), the result is usually a linguistic and literary critique, both descriptively and prescriptively oriented, not just of this one translation but also of the earlier one(s) at the same time.[27]

Having situated my considerations within this historical and discursive context, I will now analyze two reviews of important translations of works from the canon of European culture published at the end of the eighteenth century: I will start with Schlegel's text about the then-new German translation of *Don Quixote,* and then move on to an extensive discussion of Schiller's then-recent German translation of *Macbeth.* It is worth noting from the outset that, seen from the Romantic perspective, we are dealing here with translations that not only deserve, but even demand criticism, as these are versions of works by major authors who, at the end of the eighteenth century, were making spectacular inroads into the system of German literature, coming to be viewed as exemplary "modern" writers.

---

23 Ibid., 73.
24 Antoine Berman, *Pour une critique des traductions: John Donne* (Paris: Gallimard, 1995), 42.
25 Ibid. On the interdependence of Romantic literary criticism and translation criticism see Antoine Berman, *The Experience of the Foreign: Culture and Translation in Romantic Germany,* trans. S[tefan] Heyvaert, Albany: State Univ. of New York Press, 1992), 121–128.
26 Antoine Berman, *Pour une critique des traductions,* 40.
27 Ibid., 59–60.

2 The poet of prose in translation: Friedrich Schlegel on Tieck's Cervantes

In describing the context of Schlegel and Schleiermacher's joint plans for a translation of Plato, Wilhelm Dilthey wrote about the true translation "boom" that was evident in Germany in the last decade of the eighteenth century – pointing in specific to Voß's Homer (1793), August Wilhelm Schlegel's first volume of translations of Shakespeare (1797) and the first part of *Don Quixote* translated by Ludwig Tieck (1799).[28] It is therefore possible to speak of a major juncture in this sense, and there can be no exaggeration in claiming that, without the intellectual and organizational commitment of the Schlegel brothers, this boom would certainly not have happened. As Friedrich Schlegel wrote in a letter to his older brother, August Wilhelm, dated 26 August 1791:

> In the art of translation, the Germans have achieved the most of any nation, and you yourself have achieved the most of any German. On another occasion, I recently speculated a great deal about the art of translation, admiring this side of your work, which I had not yet looked at in detail.[29]

Thus, while the elder Schlegel was enriching his native literature with philologically meticulous and literarily sophisticated translations of Shakespeare[30] and Calderon, the younger of the two brothers was laying out the theoretical groundwork for the translational activity of the German Romantics, infecting not only August Wilhelm, but also Ludwig Tieck and – as we have already noted – Friedrich Schleiermacher with his ideas.[31]

Friedrich Schlegel also formulated poetological assumptions for how Miguel Cervantes' major work should be translated. He paid a lot of attention to this text, which fascinated him because of its modernity and even experimental character. In this sense, the author of *Lucinde* regarded *Don Quixote* as a fulfilment of the Romantic

---

28 Wilhelm Dilthey, *Leben Schleiermachers*, vol. I/2: *1803–1807*, 3rd ed., ed. Martin Redeker (Berlin: Walter de Gruyter, 1970), 43.
29 Friedrich Schlegel, KFSA XXIV: *Die Periode des Athenäums (25. Juli 1797 – Ende August 1799)*, ed. Raymond Immerwahr, Abt. 3: Briefe (Paderborn: Schöningh, 1986), 8. Cf. Héctor Canal, *Romantische Universalphilologie – Studien zu August Wilhelm Schlegel* (Heidelberg: Universitätsverlag Winter, 2017), 193 ff.
30 A huge and at the same time very creative contribution to this translation of Shakespeare's works must be attributed, as we know today, to August Wilhelm's wife Caroline. See Brigitte Roßbeck, *Zum Trotz glücklich – Caroline Schlegel-Schelling* (Munich: Siedler, 2008), 235 et seq.
31 It was in this context that the translation work of August Wilhelm served as a positive point of reference for Friedrich, while the translations of Johann Heinrich Voß, whom the younger of the Schlegel brothers regarded as a translator who ignored the historical dynamics of the original and the translation, and thus its critical essence, represented a negative one. See Friedmar Apel, *Sprachbewegung – Eine historisch-poetologische Untersuchung zum Problem des Übersetzens* (Heidelberg: Winter, 1982), 95.

ideal of the novel,³² "dominated by fantastic wit [*Witz*], along with a true variety of bold innovations."³³ A key role in Schlegel's interpretation of the Spanish masterpiece was played by the notion of parody, which he regarded as a hallmark of "Romantic poetry."³⁴

In Friedrich Schlegel's conception, *Don Quixote* exemplifies the kind of mechanism of parody that in fact draws it closer to translation. In one of his "literary notes" the critic wrote: "One can also translate whole genres; the restoration of old forms is a p[oetic] translation. (Parody is a witty translation")."³⁵ One of the "wittiest" translations in the history of literature was given to us by Cervantes: a parodic transformation of chivalric novels (*libros de caballerías*) and Socratic dialogues.³⁶ The Spanish author appears here as a patron and precursor of the Romantic poet, who escapes from the present on the wings of the past.³⁷ The parody makes the original present, but by the very same gesture goes beyond it, in order to show something new to contemporaneity. Thus, Laurie Maguire is not wrong to see "[t]his complex interrelationship, of repetition and novelty, homage and critique, debt and independence" as decisive.³⁸ This also illuminates the paradoxical nature of translation itself. The task of the translator of *Don Quixote*, according to this line of thought, would be to produce a translation of one of the "wittiest" literary translations of all time. Of course, it would also be the translator's task to express what is the object of the parody, i.e. the original (or rather, the *originals of the original*), because: "true parody has within it the material that is being parodied."³⁹ The progressive spirit of this kind of literature should also shine through such a translation. With such high expectations being made of translation, it seems a truly "impossible task." How can one create a translation that is at once a heightened "masterpiece of wit" and a philological "study"?⁴⁰

---

32 "D[on] Q[uixote] – still the only fully romantic novel," he wrote in his notes *Zur Poesie* – Friedrich Schlegel, *Literarische Notizen 1797–1801*, ed. Hans Eichner (Frankfurt am Main: Universitätsverlag Winter, 1980), 121. Cf. Rachel Schmidt, *Forms of Modernity: Don Quixote and Modern Theories of the Novel* (Toronto: Univ. of Toronto Press, 2011), 64.
33 Friedrich Schlegel, *Gespräch über die Poesie*, in KFSA II: *Charakteristiken und Kritiken I. 1796–1801*, ed. Hans Eichner (Paderborn: Schöningh, 1967), 299.
34 Friedrich Schlegel, *Literarische Notizen 1797–1801*, 90.
35 Ibid., 122.
36 See Rachel Schmidt, *Forms of Modernity*, 71. See in this context Nabokov's impressive list of *Don Quixote*'s errors and absurdities, which are in fact parodic elements; Vladimir Nabokov, *Lectures on Don Quixote* (San Diego: Harcourt, 1983), 110–111.
37 See Rachel Schmidt, *Forms of Modernity*, 71.
38 Laurie Maguire, *Helen of Troy: From Homer to Hollywood* (Chichester: Wiley-Blackwell, 2009), 164.
39 Friedrich Schlegel, *Literarische Notizen 1797–1801*, 114.
40 Friedrich Schlegel, *Philosophische Fragmente – Zweite Epoche*, in KFSA XVIII: *Philosophische Lehrjahre: 1796–1806; nebst philosophischen Manuskripten aus den Jahren 1796–1828*, T. 1, ed. Ernst Behler, Paderborn: Schöningh, 1963), 288: "Translation is a masterpiece of wit. [...] All translations should at least be studies."

Since neither Friedrich nor August Wilhelm Schlegel wanted to take on such a challenge themselves (for various reasons),[41] the brothers unanimously proposed the translation task to Ludwig Tieck, who was already known to the literary public as a witty parodist. In the face of the danger that the young and inexperienced Friedrich August Eschen, encouraged by the publisher, might resolve to undertake a translation of *Don Quixote*, the well-known and respected Tieck seemed to be an ideal candidate.[42] He was approached without delay and quickly accepted what must have been quite a challenge for him, given that his knowledge of Spanish was not particularly good.[43] But this was just the beginning of the interesting story of the German *Don Quixote*, as a race to publication soon ensued between Tieck and Dietrich W. Soltau – in 1799 the latter unexpectedly published an announcement that he was working on his own new translation of Cervantes' work, at the same time hinting at his rival Tieck's alleged lack of linguistic and intercultural competence. August Wilhelm Schlegel did not hesitate to react, responding to the criticism in a separate remark in the press where he vouched for the great literary competence of the author of *William Lovell* – which ultimately resulted in a quarrel between the Romantic camp on the one hand vs. the "classicists" supporting Soltau on the other.[44] This context is important, as it explains why, after the publication of first Tieck's and then Soltau's translations, the Schlegel brothers attached so much importance to reviewing these works.

When the first part of the translation of *Don Quixote* prepared by Tieck appeared in Berlin in 1799, Friedrich Schlegel welcomed it with great satisfaction and published an anonymous review of it in the second part of the second volume of his journal *Athenaeum*.[45] The review appeared under the rubric "*Notizen*," which provided "very brief reports about novelties in the arts and sciences, in poetry and prose."[46] Shortly afterwards, August Wilhelm Schlegel discussed the work in detail in the pages of *Jenaische Allgemeine Literatur-Zeitung*.[47]

Interestingly enough, this "news report" (*Nachricht*) about *Tieck's* translation of *Don Quixote* was announced in *Athenaeum* by a distinctive prolepsis, because on the preceding page, containing a translation of a fragment of Ariosto's *Orlando furioso*

---

[41] For Friedrich Schlegel, see KFSA XXIV: *Die Periode des Athenäums*, 33 and 54.
[42] Marek Zybura, *Ludwig Tieck als Übersetzer und Herausgeber – Zur frühromantischen Idee einer "deutschen Weltliteratur"* (Heidelberg, Universitätsverlag Winter, 1994), 40–43.
[43] Gabrielle Bersier, *A Metamorphic Mode of Literary Reflexivity: Parody in Early German Romanticism*, in *Parody: Dimensions and Perspectives*, ed. Beate Müller (Amsterdam: Rodopi, 1997), 36.
[44] More on this topic: Zybura, *Ludwig Tieck als Übersetzer und Herausgeber*, 43–46.
[45] "Notizen," *Athenaeum* 2, no. 2 (1799): 324–327 (KFSA II, 281–283).
[46] Publisher's comment in Friedrich Schlegel, *Werke in Zwei Bänden*, vol. 1 (Berlin: Aufbau, 1980), 352.
[47] August Wilhelm Schlegel, *Leben und Thaten des scharfsinnigen Edlen Don Quixote von La Mancha, von Miguel de Cervantes Saavedra, übersetzt von Ludwig Tieck. Erster Band. Berlin 1799*, in idem, *Vermischte und kritische Schriften*, part 5: *Recensionen*, ed. Eduard Böcking, Leipzig 1847 (*Sämmtliche Werke*, vol. 11), 408–426.

(the eleventh song), the reader could find a note entitled *Nachschrift des Übersetzers an Ludwig Tieck*, in which joy is expressed at the publication of a German translation of Cervantes' work. "Please accept, Dear Friend, our warmest embraces on the occasion of your joining our order of poetic translators" – August Wilhelm Schlegel emphatically begins this message, even though he himself was the author of both the *Nachschrift* and the translation of Ariosto's stanzas.[48] This is then followed by enthusiastic comments on the translation of *Don Quixote*, in which the critic perceives "the rich subtlety and the beautifully sounding and refined intricacy of Castilian prose."[49] Moreover, he also makes remarks about the failure to translate great works of literature into other languages, not without irony quoting Cervantes himself, who is alleged to have said that even "with all the diligence and skill" of translators "the poet will never appear to the reader in his original form." The work of the translator can be compared, the Spanish author allegedly asserts, "to the reverse side of Brussels tapestries: the shapes are still recognizable, but they are greatly disfigured by the threads that run together."[50]

Schlegel stresses, however, that these criticisms are currently aimed primarily at the French model of interpreting and translating *Don Quixote*, which obliterates the poetic and parodic qualities of that masterpiece. Here we can see, as repeatedly on other previous occasions, a polemic blade pointed at the French philosophy of translation, in which the German Romantics saw as the overt negation of their own translational ethics based on the postulate of "foreign resemblance" (*fremde Ähnlichkeit*).[51] And here, if not sooner, it becomes clear why the Schlegel brothers welcomed Ludwig Tieck as a new comrade-in-arms among the group of "poetic translators": this was a group fighting for the fundamental principles of the art of translation, fighting a battle that promised to precipitate a paradigm shift in the history of (literary) translation. One of the most important principles of this new philosophy of translation is summed up in the words of August Wilhelm Schlegel himself: "Only a manifold receptivity to foreign national poetry, which may ripen and give rise to universality, makes progress in the faithful reproduction of poetic works possi-

---

[48] August Wilhelm Schlegel, "Nachschrift des Uebersetzers an Ludwig Tieck," *Athenaeum* 2, no. 2 (1799): 277.
[49] Ibid.
[50] Ibid., 280. This image has gone down in history as one of the most evocative metaphors of translation – cf. e.g. André Lefevere, *Translating Literature: The German Tradition from Luther to Rosenzweig* (Assen/Amsterdam: Van Gorcum, 1977), 53.
[51] "How long have the Germans translated in a lame and mannered way, as the French have always done!" – exclaims August Wilhelm Schlegel a little further on in the same text (ibid., 282). See also his characterization of the French philosophy of translation in the 1798 dialogue *Der Wettstreit der Sprachen*, in August Wilhelm Schlegel, *Kritische Schriften und Briefe,* vol. 1: *Sprache und Poetik*, ed. Edgar Lohner, Stuttgart 1962), 252; originally printed in *Athenaeum* 1, no. 1 (1798). On August Wilhelm Schlegel's "anti-classical" and "anti-French" attitude, see Kyoung-Jin Lee, *Die deutsche Romantik und das Ethische der Übersetzung – Die literarischen Übersetzungsdiskurse Herders, Goethes, Schleiermachers, Novalis', der Brüder Schlegel und Benjamins* (Würzburg: Königshausen & Neumann, 2013), 124.

ble."⁵² And it is precisely this hermeneutical path, which was to lead to a new literature of translation, that Ludwig Tieck, in the eyes of the Schlegel brothers, followed as the translator of *Don Quixote*. And it is an arduous road, because the German language is "obstinate" (*halsstarrig*), "hard and rough"; the amused flexibility, the gentle musicality of the Romance languages is alien to the German language.⁵³ However, August Wilhelm Schlegel emphasizes, this trail leads toward legitimate national pride: "I believe," he writes (referring to Friedrich's ideas), "we are on the way to inventing a true art of poetic translation; this fame will fall to the Germans."⁵⁴

And so, such is the quite unusual way in which the discussion of Ludwig Tieck's *Don Quixote* that was published in *Athenaeum* by Friedrich Schlegel was introduced. As with everything in this ambitious journal, its *Notizen* section also has a solid theoretical foundation. The introductory sentences (by A.W. Schlegel) explain to the reader that this section is meant to provide more than just brief information about recommended works: "Not only the information that something exists, but also a determination of what it actually is; and all this taking into account [the reader] himself, his education, and possible foreseeable misunderstandings [...]."⁵⁵ The goals formulated are hermeneutical and critical in nature – an aim that Schleiermacher, in his lectures on hermeneutics, put above all as the "more strict practice" (*strengere Praxis*) of the art of interpretation, namely, "that misunderstanding [*Mißverstehen*]) results as a matter of course and that understanding must be desired and sought at every point."⁵⁶ The labor of understanding also implies the labor of translation: the fact that valuable literary and philosophical works speak their own language should prompt reviewers to make an effort "to translate the sense of the works into a generally intelligible language, and to present it in a new way."⁵⁷ It is worth pointing out, therefore, that a literary note, even a brief one, can represent a hermeneutical and translational achievement on the part of the author. This is the case with Friedrich Schlegel's longer discussion of Schleiermacher's speeches *On Religion*, which opens this section, as well as his review of the translation of *Don Quixote*, which closes it.⁵⁸ Schlegel understands a review as a "critical experiment" (*kritisches Experiment*), an experimental translation, but for him it is also a "tactically calculated" statement, because, as Willy Michel emphasizes in his work, "it has to take into

---

52 "Nachschrift des Uebersetzers an Ludwig Tieck," 280–281.
53 Ibid., 283. On the notion of Germany as the "country of translators" and related national translatological concepts, see Kyoung-Jin Lee, *Die deutsche Romantik und das Ethische der Übersetzung*, 129–141.
54 "Nachschrift des Uebersetzers an Ludwig Tieck," 281.
55 "Notizen," *Athenaeum* 2, no. 2 (1799): 286.
56 Friedrich Schleiermacher, *Hermeneutics and Criticism*, edited by Andrew Bowie (Cambridge: Cambridge Univ. Press, 1997), 22.
57 "Notizen," *Athenaeum* 2, no. 2 (1799): 286.
58 The journal immediately follows Friedrich Schlegel's review of the speeches *On Religion* with Schleiermacher's published critique of Kant's *Anthropologie in pragmatischer Hinsicht*.

account the contemporary realities, conditions, and tendencies."[59] In this context, the text of interest in *Athenaeum* can be seen as a clever move in the game against Tieck's competitor, Soltau, and the critics of the Romantic *Don Quixote* backing him.[60]

"The existing popular German translation of *Don Quixote* read pleasantly; what it lacked was poetry [...]," the review begins.[61] Schlegel is referring here to the second German translation of Cervantes' work (after Joachim Caesar's first translation of 1648), which had been prepared and printed in the years 1775–1777 by the Weimar-based publisher Friedrich Justin Bertuch.[62] It was considered complete, but, as Martin Ebel notes, "by today's standards it was not complete: Bertuch simply left out interpolated novellas, added and deleted as he saw fit [...]."[63]

Textual completeness, however, was not a decisive criterion for Friedrich Schlegel as a translation critic. As is evident from the assumptions of his criticism presented in the introduction, the translation invariant he sought in the target text was "poetry." In Schlegel's view, poetry was what was missing from the previous German translation of *Don Quixote*. And without this poetry the work loses its "coherence," that is to say, its "inner form,"[64] which the author of *Lucinde* ascribed to literary works, including Plato's dialogues.[65] The old translation was said to be dominated by a strategy of domestication, implemented, in the critic's view, using unsophisticated and inadequate means.[66] The new translator, Ludwig Tieck, familiar with "old Romantic poetry," recognized in Schlegel's opinion the "inner form" of *Don Quixote* and focused on "conveying and recreating the impression and spirit of the whole in Ger-

---

59 Willy Michel, *Ästhetische Hermeneutik und frühromantische Kritik. Friedrich Schlegels fragmentarische Entwürfe, Rezensionen, Charakteristiken und Kritiken (1795–1801)* (Göttingen: Vandenhoeck & Ruprecht, 1982), 72.
60 Friedrich Schlegel's short review of Stolberg's translation of Plato, published in 1797, also served a similar function. It was most likely a "tactical" move, as Schlegel was already thinking of his own edition of Plato. But of course the arguments against Stolberg's translation cited in the review are serious and philosophical in nature; see Friedrich Schlegel, *Rezension der Auserlesenen Gespräche des Platon, übersetzt von Friedrich Leopold Grafen zu Stolberg*, in KFSA VIII: *Studien zur Philosophie und Theologie*, ed. Ernst Behler, Ursula Struc-Oppenberg (Paderborn: Schöningh, 1975), 38–40.
61 "Notizen," *Athenaeum* 2, no. 2 (1799): 324.
62 Friedrich Justin Bertuch, *Leben und Thaten des weisen Junkers Don Quijote von Mancha*, Neue Ausgabe. Aus der Urschrift des Cervantes nebst Fortsetzung des Avellaneda (Weimar: Fritsch, 1775–1777).
63 Martin Ebel, "Ein 'Don Quijote' für unsere Zeit," *Die Welt* 11.03.2009, https://www.welt.de/welt_print/article3355226/Ein-Don-Quijote-fuer-unsere-Zeit.html (accessed 10 October 2019). On German translations of *Don Quijote* before *Tieck*, see Marek Zybura, *Ludwig Tieck als Übersetzer und Herausgeber*, 37–40
64 "Notizen," *Athenaeum* 2, no. 2 (1799): 324.
65 Dilthey, *Leben Schleiermachers*, vol. I/2, 43.
66 This is true, for Bertuch "placed the emphasis on blunt comedy on the plot level" (Martin Ebel, "Ein 'Don Quijote' für unsere Zeit").

man."⁶⁷ Tieck thus succeeded in "imitating the tone and color of the original," albeit without "timid fidelity."⁶⁸ The reviewer emphasizes that the translator achieves the effect of a "Spanish" style in an unforced and prudent manner, and where he imitates a foreign form (for example in the poems), he does not strive at all costs for "accuracy of meaning," because such a strategy would destroy – as one might think – the poetic aura of the work (that is, its *Kunsterscheinung* in R.-R. Wuthenow's hermeneutical theory⁶⁹). And the work appears as a truly synaesthetic creation, which of course makes the translator's task much more difficult: "In no other prose," writes Schlegel, "is the order of words so symmetrical and musical; no other prose makes use of different styles as if they were patches of color and light [...]."⁷⁰

Note that Schlegel describes the original from an intermedial perspective – the text has its own proper tone, characteristic color, operates with musical harmonies and painterly effects, which create and convey the impression of a complex, synthetically interacting whole. The unity so achieved is by no means "natural," as the musical metaphor might suggest, but on the contrary, it is the result of a productive, shaping force, and manifests itself in its artistic "artificiality."⁷¹ The aura (*Kunsterscheinung*) mentioned is nothing other than the revelation of the work as a complex, intentionally⁷² structured original artifact of art,⁷³ which stimulates our attention by various means of artistic impact. Such poetics lie, according to Schlegel, at the heart of the masterpiece under review: "Cervantes achieves the characterization of Don Quixote and Sanchez in a musical and ludic manner," we read in *Literarische Notizen*.⁷⁴ Finally, these poetic games of colors and sounds serve to evoke the intertexts parodied in the novel. *Don Quixote* thus embodies the ideal of the genre, because the novel is, from Schlegel's point of view, essentially intertextual, even intermedial.⁷⁵

To cope with such an aesthetically complex work, a truly poetic translation should cross the threshold of "exactness of meaning," for its aim is, as Wuthenow explains in the spirit of the early Romantics, "to render the proper color and form,

---

67 "Notizen," *Athenaeum* 2, no. 2 (1799): 324.
68 Ibid.
69 Ralph-Rainer Wuthenow, *Das fremde Kunstwerk – Aspekte der literarischen Übersetzung* (Göttingen: Vandenhoeck & Ruprecht, 1969), 18.
70 "Notizen," Athenaeum 2, no. 2 (1799), 327.
71 Eberhard Huge, *Poesie und Reflexion in der Ästhetik des frühen Friedrich Schlegel* (Stuttgart: J.B. Metzlersche Verlagsbuchhandlung, 1971), 84. In his *Kritische Fragmente* Schlegel speaks – tellingly – of a "grammatical sound art" (KFSA II: *Charakteristiken und Kritiken I*, 155).
72 See "Notizen," *Athenaeum* 2, no. 2 (1799), 327.
73 See Eberhard Huge, *Poesie und Reflexion*, 86.
74 Friedrich Schlegel, *Literarische Notizen 1797–1801*, 148.
75 Cf. the definition from his *Poesie und Literatur*: "The novel is a mixture of the various arts and sciences to which poetry is related; [it is] at once history and philosophy, and then even art," quoted by Marike Finlay, *The Romantic Irony of Semiotics: Friedrich Schlegel and the Crisis of Representation* (Berlin: Mouton de Gruyter, 1988), 206.

[...] renewing the original aesthetic in another language."⁷⁶ As a work of art, the translation is "foreign" because instead of "obliterating" the original, it "communicates" it,⁷⁷ making it appear in a foreign language as an expression of an internal poetic form.

Friedrich Schlegel now poses an important question: "will the reader [...] want to adopt the translator's perspective"?⁷⁸ Would Tieck's Romantic ideal of a poetic translation of prose be noticed at all by German readers, and thus would Cervantes finally be recognized as a prose poet, not merely a conveyor of stories (or even a "witty taleteller"⁷⁹)? Both Schlegel and Schleiermacher saw translations as elements of a national educational project in which both original and translated literature, hand-in-hand with science and art, interact and influence one another through a productive synergy. In this context, *Don Quixote* takes on even more importance because, according to Schlegel, Cervantes succeeded in creating the only prose capable of representing "modernity" vis-à-vis the immortal Greek prose of Tacitus and Plato. If we believe that the modern novel "should imagine for us the music of life," then this Spanish masterpiece of prose is "by all means worthy" of being included in that genre – just as the prose of antiquity is included in the genre of "rhetorical and historical works."⁸⁰ In contrast to the "popular writing of the French and English," Cervantes' works, alongside Shakespeare's dramas, are in Schlegel's view a model of what is modern and should serve as a model for contemporary authors.⁸¹

We should note that Schlegel, in recommending the author of *Don Quixote* to the attention of German readers, points to his entire literary output, believing that only in the light of the whole can the parts be properly understood. Therefore, the same hermeneutical principle can be applied to Cervantes as to all the classics: "one should translate and read everything that this immortal author created – or nothing at all."⁸²

3 Schiller's "astonishing" Macbeth

In a letter to Henrietta Herz of 17 May 1801, Schleiermacher enumerated the new publications which, in his opinion, merited close reading and criticism: firstly, Fichte's *Nikolai*, secondly *Maria Stuart*, and thirdly Schiller's *Macbeth*, "about which Schlegel

---

76 Ralph-Rainer Wuthenow, *Das fremde Kunstwerk*, 10.
77 Ibid.
78 "Notizen," *Athenaeum 2*, no. 2 (1799): 325.
79 Ibid., 326.
80 Ibid., 327.
81 Ibid.
82 Ibid., 326.

says such astonishing things that my fingers itch terribly to review it."[83] And so he did, earning, as the first reviewer of this important work, an honorable place in the history of the reception of Friedrich Schiller's work.[84]

With his review of *Macbeth*, published anonymously in the *Erlanger Literatur-Zeitung* on 30 and 31 July 1801,[85] Schleiermacher proved that he was not afraid of ambitious challenges, because here he took on an even more difficult task than Friedrich Schlegel had in his scrutiny of *Don Quixote*. This is because Schleiermacher had to insert his review into the formidable discourse of Shakespeare's reception in Germany, which decisively influenced the national literary history and the construction of the German literary canon in the eighteenth and nineteenth centuries. The "German Shakespeare" was polemical in nature – conceived as a kind of rebuttal to the French elaborations of his works, in which omissions, adaptations, and censorship interventions were the norm rather than the exception.[86] He was meant to represent an alternative to the image projected by the French classicists, afflicted as they were by "an addiction to embellishments" (Ch. Wieland).[87] And this Shakespeare became a monument. Hailed by authors of the *Sturm und Drang* period as a modern "genius of nature" (*Natur-Genie*), and later exalted in August Wilhelm Schlegel's monumental translation project as *Übershakespeare*,[88] he ultimately became an object of veneration and crowned as "a German classic." An important role in this was played by a deep conviction that for ethical and historical reasons, the Germans are particularly capable of properly understanding and faithfully translating the English playwright. It is in this context that Schleiermacher's critique of the translation of the famous *Macbeth* accrues particular significance.

Schleiermacher was encouraged to review this Schillerian translation (or adaptation) by the most famous translator of Shakespeare in German history, namely August Wilhelm Schlegel, who must have been even more tempted to write a review as

---

[83] KGA V/ 5, 122. Schleiermacher also mentions the second part of F. Schlegel's *Charakteristiken und Kritiken* at the end.
[84] See Heinz Gerd Ingenkamp, "Kommentar," to Friedrich Schiller, *Übersetzungen und Bearbeitungen*, ed. Heinz Gerd Ingenkamp (Frankfurt am Main: Deutscher Klassiker Verlag, 1995) (*Werke und Briefe*, vol. 9), 881.
[85] *Rezension von William Shakespeare: Macbeth. Ein Trauerspiel zur Vorstellung auf dem Hoftheater zu Weimar eingerichtet von Friedrich Schiller*, KGA I/3, 377–398.
[86] See Paul Steck, *Schiller und Shakespeare. Idee und Wirklichkeit* (Frankfurt am Main: Peter Lang, 1977), 9–19.
[87] Christoph Martin Wieland, *Der Geist Shakespears*, in *Shakespeare-Rezeption – Die Diskussion um Shakespeare in Deutschland. I. Ausgewählte Texte von 1741 bis 1788*, ed. Hansjürgen Blinn (Berlin: Erich Schmidt, 1982), 121.
[88] "Every *Übersetzung* is a movement in which the *Über* is a potentiating going-beyond: Thus one may say that A.W.Schlegel's Shakespeare is an Übershakespeare. The original is inferior to its translation in the same way 'Nature' is inferior to 'Fracture'" (Antoine Berman, *The Experience of the Foreign*, 107–108). Berman points out that according to the Romantics every translation is an aesthetic intensification of the original, while criticism is an intensification of translation.

soon as he saw that the translation had appeared.[89] This would hardly have been surprising, as it seemed obvious that this was a highly notable project by an eminent poet, and the new translation could in some ways be seen as representing a certain attempt at a "hostile takeover" of Schlegel's Shakespeare. After all, Schlegel's Shakespearean translation project had already been underway since 1797, and among the early Romantics – Schleiermacher of course being one of them – it was considered a model to emulate.[90]

Schiller's *Macbeth* is undoubtedly an important part of the literary oeuvre of the author of *The Robbers*, alongside numerous alongside other translations and stage adaptations – including include tragedies by Euripides (*Iphigenia in Aulis*, scenes from *The Phoenicians*) and Racine (*Britannica, Phaedra*), but also Goethe's *Egmont*, Lessing's *Nathan the Wise*, and Carlo Gozzi's *Turandot*. Schiller's ambition was to provide the German theatre with a selection of valuable dramatic texts that would stand up well on stage, which he wanted to convey in a form that would be "on the one hand suitable for the stage, and on the other hand in keeping with the spirit of the times" (J.W. Goethe).[91] Schiller employed a range of types of translation (adaptation) techniques, depending on how he approached the particular original work itself. It seems that he applied freer forms of translation when he considered the original to be particularly valuable and important. This attitude on the part of the poet did not, however, result from a "carefree subjectivism," but, as the publishers of Schiller's *Sämtliche Werke* emphasize, "from a desire to cross the divide between lan-

---

89 Here it is worth pointing out that in my analysis I treat adaptation (*Bearbeitung*) as a form of translation. Some translation scholars oppose such an approach and instead – citing norms of equivalence – draw a distinction between the reproduction and production of text (and therefore between *translation* and *adaptation*), but in the light of more recent, descriptively oriented translatological research such schematic distinctions ultimately seem unworkable. Every translation is, after all, both "reproductive" and "productive" (creative), in part depending on the perspective from which we view it. Every translation requires certain adaptive procedures correlated with the intended context of its reception, which include such interventions as omissions, additions, modulations or stylistic transformations. A boundary between an "acceptable" and "unacceptable" degree of intervention in the text can only be set arbitrarily. The specific case of drama translation highlights the problematic nature of any normative, ahistorical approach to the problem of adaptation. On this issue see especially Horst Zander, *Shakespeare "bearbeitet": Eine Untersuchung am Beispiel der Historien-Inszenierungen 1945–1975 in der Bundesrepublik Deutschland* (Tübingen: Gunter Narr, 1983), 30–31. In the context of the dispute outlined here – on the one hand the position of Werner Koller, advocating a normative notion of equivalence, and on the other the views of Katharina Reiß and Hans Vermeer, opting instead for the notion of adequacy – cf. Werner Koller, *Einführung in die Übersetzungswissenschaft*, 4th ed. (Heidelberg: Quelle & Meyer, 1992), 199–205; Katharina Reiß, Hans J. Vermeer, *Grundlegung einer allgemeinen Translationstheorie* (Tübingen: Max Niemeyer, 1984), 136–140.
90 See *Historische Einführung*, KGA I/3, CVIII.
91 So writes Goethe in *Über das deutsche Theater*, after Ingenkamp, "Kommentar," 763.

guages and times, and a wish to naturalize a foreign work for its own sake."[92] The program of assimilating foreign literature pursued by Schiller was situated within the broader paradigm of classicism[93] – it consisted in transforming a source text into a contemporary (dramatic) form, which in practice meant being adapted to the "Weimar style" and the expectations of the Weimar theatre audience.[94] And although Schiller was by no means an advocate of the characteristic style of classicist French tragedy,[95] he was often inclined towards analogous stylistic transformations – for example in his *Macbeth,* the subject of Schleiermacher's review.[96]

The German version of *Macbeth* produced by Schiller was not the first translation, as the play had already been performed in Germany since the 1770s in various stage adaptations.[97] In this context Schiller's work can be regarded as representative of a tendency, clearly noticeable in the German reception of Shakespeare at the time, to favour "dramaturgical" translation, oriented towards the needs of the theatre, over philological translation, oriented towards readers. When Schiller began thinking about producing a translation of *Macbeth,* the two trends were still on equal footing, although in the writings of the early Romantics one could already discern the early signs of a paradigm shift. This is well illustrated in August Wilhelm Schlegel's famous essay *Etwas über William Shakespeare bey Gelegenheit Wilhelm Meister* (1796) by August Wilhelm Schlegel, a text that can be read as a programmatic sketch preparing for Schlegel's own translations of Shakespeare.[98] The author sent it to

---

[92] [Gerhard Fricke and Herbert G. Göpfert], "Kommentar," to: Friedrich Schiller, *Übersetzungen und Bearbeitungen,* in idem, *Sämtliche Werke,* vol. 3: *Dramatische Fragmente, Übersetzungen, Bühnenbearbeitungen,* [ed. Gerhard Fricke, Herbert G. Göpfert] (Munich: Carl Hanser, 1980), 958.
[93] Rolf Kloepfer, *Die Theorie der literarischen Übersetzung – Romanisch-deutscher Sprachbereich* (Munich: Wilhelm Fink, 1967), 26–27.
[94] [Fricke and Göpfert] "Kommentar," 964, see also Heinz Gerd Ingenkamp, *Bearbeitungen und Übersetzungen,* in *Schiller-Handbuch: Leben – Werk – Wirkung,* ed. Matthias Luserke-Jaqui (Stuttgart-Weimar: J.B. Metzler, 2005), 530. In this context one can indeed speak of a translation "into the Weimar language" (ibid., 534). However, the commentary on Schiller's *Werke und Briefe* also refers to non-classical elements in some of his adaptations (e.g. in *Egmont* and *The Parasite* based on the play by Louis-Benoît Picard); see Ingenkamp, "Kommentar," 780.
[95] [Fricke and Göpfert], "Kommentar," 964.
[96] Ingenkamp, *Bearbeitungen und Übersetzungen,* 531. See also Eckhard Heftrich, *Shakespeare in Weimar,* in *Das Shakespeare-Bild in Europa zwischen Aufklärung und Romantik,* ed. Roger Bauer in collaboration with Michael de Graat and Jürgen Wertheimer (Bern: Peter Lang, 1988), 190. It is sometimes the case that the source texts used by Schiller quite visibly draw the translator into the classicist paradigm. *Iphigenia,* for example, is based on the French translation by Brumoy, a translator who strove to make "the persons in the translated dramas speak in French [...] as they would have originally spoken, presenting their thoughts in French" (quoted from: Ingenkamp, "Kommentar," 766). It is not difficult to see that in this case we are dealing with the method that Schleiermacher described in in his lecture on translation to the Prussian Academy as "naturalizing," and which he criticized.
[97] [Fricke and Göpfert], "Kommentar," 875 ff.
[98] "Shakespeare," wrote August Wilhelm Schlegel, "was certainly guided in many external matters by the needs of his theatre; but would he have done less for ours were he alive today? He did not spare the deep and subtle beauty which, with the rapid pace and inevitable moments of distraction

Schiller in March 1796, attaching to it several "translation attempts" of individual scenes from *Romeo and Juliet*. The addressee promptly submitted both the essay and the translation for publication in the journal he published, *Die Horen*.[99]

Schiller thought carefully about Schlegel's tenets and studied his translation attempts, above all because he himself had been thinking about translating Shakespeare for the theatre since at least 1784 (specifically about *Timon of Athens* and *Macbeth*).[100] On 11 March 1796, Schiller wrote back to the young poet and translator as follows:

> The whole business of translating Shakespeare is something we should probably discuss in person. This is a very happy thought, and may God reward You for wanting to free us from that sad Eschenburg. You dealt with him more gently than he deserved [...]. In my opinion you also treated Bürger's *Macbeth* and his translation of the Witches' songs too coolly and cautiously. I regard the latter as a true Bürgerian piece of work, unmatched by any previous one [...].[101]

Friedrich Schiller was clearly very critical of both Gottfried August Bürger's adaptation of *Macbeth* and Johann Joachim Eschenburg's translation.[102] However, as a possible translator of Shakespeare, he himself was exposed to criticism because of his relatively poor command of English – so poor that later, when working on his *Macbeth*, he had to make use of German translations, among them the prose translation by Christoph Martin Wieland published as part of the multi-volume edition of Shakespeare's *Theatralische Werke* (*Das Trauerspiel von Macbeth*, 1765), and indeed Eschenburg's translation – in the edition edited by Gabriel Eckert (*Schauspiele*, 1779). However, this does not mean that the poet did not make any use of the English text; as he wrote to Goethe on 2 February 1800:

> Since I received the original Shakespeare from F. v. Stein, I am convinced that I should have stuck to the original from the beginning, even with my poor knowledge of English, for the spirit of thought acts much more directly here, whereas I have toiled often unnecessarily to get at the true sense through the clumsy medium of both my predecessors.[103]

---

in public performances, is so easily obliterated, requiring the quiet concentration of the solitary reader. That is why stubborn people (among whom I count myself), who wish to have the author as he really is [...] content themselves with the fact that the original text should not and cannot be taken away from them" – August Wilhelm Schlegel, "Etwas über William Shakespeare bey Gelegenheit Wilhelm Meisters, *Die Horen – Eine Monatsschrift herausgegeben von F. Schiller* 6, no. 4 (1796): 72–73.
99 Cf. Richard Baum, *Die Entstehung eines Klassikers: Der deutsche Shakespeare*, in *Shakespeare und kein Ende? Beiträge zu Shakespeare-Rezeption in Deutschland und in Frankreich vom 18. bis 20. Jahrhundert*, ed. Béatrice Dumiche (Bonn: Romanistischer Verlag, 2012), 137.
100 See Hansjürgen Blinn, Einführung, in *Shakespeare-Rezeption: Die Diskussion um Shakespeare in Deutschland. II. Ausgewählte Texte von 1793 bis 1827*, ed. Hansjürgen Blinn (Berlin: Erich Schmidt, 1988), 17, and Paul Steck, *Schiller und Shakespeare*, 147.
101 Friedrich Schiller, *Briefe II: 1795–1805*, ed. Norbert Oellers (Frankfurt am Main: Deutscher Klassiker Verlag 2002) (*Werke und Briefe*, vol. 12), 155–156.
102 Ingenkamp, "Kommentar," 876.
103 Schiller, *Briefe II: 1795–1805*, 503–504.

It is not known to what extent Schiller consulted the English original, nor which edition he used, but he most likely had at his disposal Samuel Johnson's edition of *The Plays of William Shakespeare*.¹⁰⁴ However, it is known that he worked on the translation for almost four months. It was in January 1800 that he resolved to follow through on his plan to publish a new German edition of *Macbeth*, thus interrupting work on *Maria Stuart*. Schiller's letters to Johann Friedrich Cotta and Goethe testify to the fact that he wanted to complete the planned project quickly. However, he did not send the promised manuscript for a long time, as he was distracted from his work by a serious illness, and it was not until late March 1800 that he was able to complete his translation.¹⁰⁵

Shakespeare's "tragic drama" *Macbeth* – "prepared by Schiller for performance at the Weimar Hoftheater" (*zur Vorstellung auf dem Hoftheater zu Weimer eingerichtet von Schiller*), as the title page stated ¹⁰⁶ – had its premiere on 14 May 1800, staged under the direction of Goethe and with music by Johann Friedrich Reichardt. And it was an immediate success, soon becoming a true classic of the stage of the Goethe era.¹⁰⁷ Criticism on the part of the Romantics did not pose a threat to Schiller's *Macbeth*, which long dominated German theatres. It was not until the 1840s that another translation, by Dorothea Tieck (daughter of Ludwig), dethroned that of Schiller in theatrical repertories.¹⁰⁸ Schiller's *Macbeth* appeared in print, published by Cotta, in April 1801.

In order to properly understand the translation strategy Schiller adopted, it is crucial to recognize that it had a clearly defined goal, or *skopos* – this goal was to realize "the stage potential [*Spielbarkeit*] of *Macbeth*, understood in accordance with the guidelines based on the current [...] reception of Shakespeare and the theatrical habits of his [Schiller's] audience."¹⁰⁹ The adaptation thus corresponded to

---

104 For detailed discussion of this subject, see Ingenkamp, "Kommentar," 877–879; see also: [Fricke and Göpfert], "Kommentar," 993.
105 See "Kommentar" to: Friedrich Schiller, *Übersetzungen und Bearbeitungen* (*Werke und Briefe*, vol. 9), 876–877.
106 Friedrich Schiller, *Macbeth – Ein Trauerspiel von Shakespeare*, in idem, *Sämtliche Werke*, vol. 3, 735.
107 Ingenkamp, "Kommentar," 880; [Fricke and Göpfert], "Kommentar," 993.
108 Ingenkamp, "Kommentar," 880. Dorothea Tieck's "literary" translation, which, as Horst Turk notes, "when juxtaposed with Schiller's and Bürger's translations presents a greater theatrical challenge, was to become the most frequently performed German *Macbeth*" – Horst Turk, *Konventionen und Traditionen, Zum Bedingungsrahmen der Übersetzung für das Theater oder die Literatur*, in *Literatur und Theater – Traditionen und Konventionen als Problem der Dramenübersetzung*, ed. Brigitte Schultze et al. (Tübingen: Gunter Narr, 1990), 71.
109 Gordon Sebastian Gamlin, *Synergetische Sinnkonstruktion und das Bild des Macbeth in Friedrich von Schillers Einrichtung der gleichnamigen Tragödie von William Shakespeare am Weimarer Hoftheater am 14. Mai 1800 unter der Leitung von Johann Wolfgang von Goethe* (Konstanz: Hartung-Gorre, 1995), 45.

Weimar aesthetics and theatrical practice,[110] but this compatibility was achieved at the expense of often drastic interventions in the original text: omissions, mutations at the level of content, transpositions, stylistic transformations.[111] Additions of an interpretative nature also seemed necessary to the poet, "because the mass public cannot keep up with their attention and thoughts must be suggested to them" (in a letter to Körner, 3 July 1800).[112] In his translation, Schiller emphasized what he felt to be the classical elements of Shakespeare's drama (in the Greek sense of the term) – he streamlined the plot, shortened the already concise play, simplified the sequence of scenes, dropped some of the side characters and standardized the style.[113] The protagonist of the drama himself was also "ennobled" in the German version, and as a result he may be associated with the classical hero type.[114] Although Schiller sought to find a unity of character and destiny (*Charakter und Schicksal*) in *Macbeth*, in his translation he strengthened the role of destiny; the witches, "The Weyward Sisters," were thus rendered as *Schicksalsschwestern* ("Sisters of Destiny/Fate"), while he translated the word *chance* unequivocally as *Schicksal* ("destiny/fate").[115] The poet also unified the versification of the work in the classical fashion: following Goethe's advice, he translated consistently into iambic verses – even where Shakespeare had used prose.[116]

The outcome of Schiller's choice of translation strategy was evocatively described by Ralph-Rainer Wuthenow, characterizing above all the impact of the target text: "Even at first glance, this translation is cooler, more reflective, more subdued and logical. Already in this way, it does not conceal its clear distance from the original."[117] Thus, the classicism of this translation would (in sum) be expressed in gestures of lofty distance from the original *Macbeth*. In Wuthenow's view, Schiller disarms, as it were, Shakespeare's "power of expression," while the "Romantic version" in the Schlegel/Tieck edition captures it with understanding and empathy.[118]

---

110 The pragmatic repertory choices of Goethe and Schiller are discussed by Roger Paulin in his book *The Critical Reception of Shakespeare in Germany 1682–1914: Native Literature and Foreign Genius* (Hildesheim: Georg Olms, 2003), 244–245.
111 See [Fricke and Göpfert], "Kommentar," 993; Steck, *Schiller und Shakespeare*, 150; Paulin, *The Critical Reception of Shakespeare in Germany*, 247.
112 F. Schiller, *Briefe II: 1795–1805*, 515; cf. Steck, *Schiller und Shakespeare*, 148.
113 Blinn, "Einführung", in *Shakespeare-Rezeption. II*, 24–25.
114 Ernst Leopold Stahl, *Shakespeare und das deutsche Theater* (Stuttgart: Kohlhammer, 1947), 189.
115 Gamlin, *Synergetische Sinnkonstruktion*, 67. It is worth noting that in this oft-discussed case of the Witches, Schiller's term "*Schicksalsschwestern*" does not evoke the meaning of the original "The *Weyward/Weird* Sisters," but rather semantically profiles or amplifies it, since the English adjectives *weyward/weird* connote something "strange," "peculiar," "odd," but also closely related to fate (*fateful*). See William Shakespeare, *Macbeth*, ed. Cedric Watts (Hertfordshire: Wordsworth, 2005), 105; also William Shakespeare, *The Tragedy of Macbeth*, ed. Nicholas Brooke (Oxford: Oxford Univ. Press, 1990), 95 and 102.
116 Gamlin, *Synergetische Sinnkonstruktion*, 70.
117 Wuthenow, *Das fremde Kunstwerk*, 84.
118 Ibid., 86.

Moreover, the "Weimar *Macbeth*" subjugates what is "demonic" in Shakespeare. Dorothea Tieck, on the other hand, is not afraid of these demons and does not try to squeeze the "vicissitudes of misfortunate fate" into the logic of a "higher order of the world," as Schiller does.[119] This characterization is very telling, as it shows the power and durable influence of the Romantic paradigm in translation criticism. The ethics of authenticity, originality, source-orientation, and expressivity are key here, as criteria of evaluation. Taken as a point of reference, they depreciate not only the "classicist" translation, but also the entire culture of cool, intellectual distance from which it sprang. At the same time, this paradigm did not facilitate the perception of nuances and ambiguities, such as the aforementioned role of "destiny" and the "sisters of destiny" (i.e. the Witches).[120] In writing about Schiller's *Macbeth*, however, Schleiermacher opted for a different path, maintaining a scholarly distance towards aesthetic ideologies – including those originating within the very scholarly circle to which he himself belonged.

4 Schleiermacher's analysis

Already in the first sentences of his review Schleiermacher lays out his general stance on Schiller's work: in his opinion, it remains so close to the original that it automatically "exiles" from the stage all previous "maimed" German *Macbeths*. Nevertheless, he adds, the adaptation should be seen as a kind of "preparation for completely faithful representations" (KGA I/3, 379). Later, in his lecture *On the Different Methods of Translating*, Schleiermacher would speak in a similar context about "free imitations" that "should first arouse and enhance a desire for the foreign," in order to later "open doors for future translations" (DR 230; KGA I/11, 76). In line with this idea, the reviewer could see Schiller's work as paving the way for a faithful translation by August Wilhelm Schlegel (or rather, by Schlegel and Tieck). At the same time, Schleiermacher problematizes the notion of fidelity (in translation) that was crucial for August Wilhelm Schlegel.[121] *Macbeth*, he claims, must be consciously adapted to the requirements of the contemporary theatre stage, otherwise the drama will give the impression of a work "bursting at the seams," which will only serve to confirm

---

119 Ibid.
120 They are related to a certain ambivalence in Schiller's own attitude, as was very aptly identified by George Steiner. In his view, the author of *The Robbers* manifested "the characteristic romantic passion for Shakespeare," although at the same time he believed that Romanticism was alien to the Hellenistic spirit of tragedy. "Where Schiller is at his best the pressure of romantic sentiment against the ideal of dramatic objectivity and a tragic world view produces a characteristic tension," Steiner concludes – George Steiner, *The Death of Tragedy* (New York: Oxford Univ. Press, 1980), 173–174.
121 On August Wilhelm Schlegel's notion of "faithful translation" see Peter Gebhardt, *A.W. Schlegels Shakespeare-Übersetzung – Untersuchungen zu seinem Übersetzungsverfahren am Beispiel des Hamlet* (Göttingen: Vandenhoeck & Ruprecht, 1970), 87–91.

the "old conviction" that "Shakespeare's plays cannot be staged in their original form" (KGA I/3, 379). So, too, a "faithful" translation for the theatre must obey the aesthetic convention that defines the framework of the drama's "stageability." A poet like Schiller, who "through long practice is well acquainted with the mechanical side of dramatic art," understands what "sacrifices" the stage requires, and also knows how to limit their number (KGA I/3, 380). Note that we are dealing here with a very modern way of problematizing the translation of drama, emphasizing the difference between the text of a drama and a stage text.[122]

Schleiermacher, however, immediately makes us aware of the fundamental flaw in such translations, claiming that "every change, made – for whatever reason – supposedly only in the details [am Einzelnen], always affects the work as a whole, and in Shakespeare's case we are dealing with a truly inviolable unity and totality [Einheit und Ganzheit]" (KGA I/3, 380). This conviction is presented by the reviewer as a "conclusion" reached by "careful study and close comparison" of the texts (KGA I/3, 380). It is worth noting here that Schleiermacher juxtaposes what from today's perspective are two different models of translation – the functional *skopos* model and the hermeneutic model. Changes, adaptations are necessary to preserve the value that is the "stageability" of a work,[123] but at the same time they violate its unity and coherence, and there are no unimportant "details" in a valuable literary work. Only in its integral form does a masterpiece retain its full meaning – standing on this hermeneutical ground, Schleiermacher and the Schlegel brothers speak with one voice. A translation may even intensify this sense of the work, by shedding critical light on the original. However, this situation is a fortunate exception – more often, as Schleiermacher admits, translating requires "sacrifices" (*Aufopferungen*).

The critic of a translation may, of course, discuss the particular strategy chosen by the translator in adapting a work, assessing whether the outcome is satisfactory or not – but it seems that Schleiermacher, well versed in philological sciences, sets himself a different goal as a critic. Instead, he delves into details and shows us their significance in relation to the whole, which is the original presented as a unified totality.

In this way he manages to formulate a maximally objective evaluation of any particular departure from the original text: its essence, legitimacy, as well as consequences. Such an analytical and critical practice requires philological precision and broad hermeneutical horizons, so that a review also cannot be truncated or superficial.[124] The one written by Schleiermacher runs the length of a serious scholarly study, with the reviewer informing us at the very end that there remains at least "one important point" that he "failed to address," by which he means the versifica-

---

122 See, for example, Anne Ubersfeld, *Reading Theatre*, trans. Frank Collins (Toronto: Univ. of Toronto Press, 1999).
123 August Wilhelm Schlegel also allowed (very limited) changes from the original; see Peter Gebhardt, *A.W. Schlegels Shakespeare-Übersetzung*, 91–93.
124 On Schleiermacher's use of primary texts and other translations, see *Historische Einführung*, KGA I/3, CVII-CVIII. Of the English editions, he preferred those of Edmond Malone (1741–1812).

tion (KGA I/3, 398). The same holds true for other philologically oriented reviews written in the *Athenaeum* circle, another example being the extremely extensive review of Soltau's translation of *Don Quixote* published by August Wilhelm Schlegel.

Schleiermacher begins his analysis with the problem of the large (in the opinion of many, excessively large) *dramatis personae* in Shakespeare's original *Macbeth*. For the reasons we have already discussed, Schiller slims down this number in his translation (even deleting important characters, such as Lady Macduff and Macduff's son), but – as the reviewer notes – this comes at the price of losing cultural context (the "contrast between England and Scotland" fades), as well as Shakespeare's multi-perspective dramatic technique (as a consequence of "economizing" on the characters of Caithness and Menteith) (KGA I/3, 380–381). Apart from the fact that those reductions were not, Schleiermacher points out, carried out consistently enough, they make the dramatic art of the author of *Macbeth* lose the momentum and dynamic that contribute to its overall meaning. In this context, however, the reviewer notes, it is worth reflecting on the objective of such a translation: namely, whether "our viewers will actually be able to perceive this meaning" (KGA I/3, 382). The hermeneutic perspective gives way here to a functional one; for, according to Schleiermacher, the time is still far off when the theatre audience, confronted with the all-embracing artistry and the "foreign resemblance" of the art on display, will be able to recognize this quality and savor it properly.

The reviewer shows in a very precise way that every intervention in the organic totality of the drama (especially omissions), generates hermeneutical problems, which demand that the author of a translation for the stage, aware of its purpose and the artistic sense of the original, should show careful consideration and strategic balance.

As the translator engages with this text, Schleiermacher writes, "fragments of incomprehensibility and minor contradictions often arise" (KGA I/3, 382), effectively making the work difficult to access. Obvious "incomprehensibility" (*Unverständlichkeit*) arises, for instance, when Schiller mixes up the retorts of Malcolm and Macduff (KGA I/3, 383); no less problematic in this respect is the "change in the order of scenes" in *Macbeth's* fifth act, and "confusion" is also introduced by other manipulations of the drama's scenes (in Schiller's text they merge and flow into one another).[125] Note that Schleiermacher's method of translation criticism leads his review to cast a shadow on many contemporary analyses, primarily because it formulates important questions in the context of the aesthetics of reception, whereas today's scholars often unthinkingly praise Schiller's "interventions" as changes that bring "clarity, order, and unambiguity."[126]

Schleiermacher also writes about transformations that were made "for the sake of the audience and decency," and thus not directly related to the technical circum-

---

[125] KGA I/3, 385. On this problem of adaptation, cf. Ingenkamp, "Kommentar," 885–888.
[126] Gamlin, *Synergetische Sinnkonstruktion*, 71.

stances of the Weimar stage.[127] Everything violent, uncouth and low was seen as alien to the classical style, which is probably why Schiller spared his audience the head of the vanquished Macbeth, Macduff's insulting words to the Scottish women, and the coarseness of the Porter (KGA I/3, 386–387). The question that arises here, however, is whether such changes make sense in the case of a horrifying tragedy, the theme of which, after all, is violence and obsession. Why does Schiller delete "the murder of Macduff's family," representing "the pinnacle of Macbeth's tyranny," while leaving "the murder of Banquo" in all its (original) cruelty? (KGA I/3, 378) Schleiermacher thinks that many of the interventions undertaken by the poet stem not from a desire to preserve a certain kind of "morality" (*Sittlichkeit*) and its associated theatrical conventions, but rather from the translator's own individual poetics (KGA I/3, 390).

The reviewer makes an important distinction here from the point of view of translation analysis. He writes about two kinds of changes that appear in translations for the theatre: those that are functionally determined, related to the circumstances of a particular stage, and those that result solely from the "imagination of the artist" who "gives back to a foreign work what he has drawn from his own resources, thus influencing its nature" (KGA I/3, 387).

In the latter case what is foreign is transformed into one's own, or vice versa: the original is supplemented with "foreign material" – as in the case of Schiller, when he transforms Shakespeare's Witches internally and externally in his translation. Schleiermacher emphasizes that in Schiller's work the Witches are not as "plebian" or "clumsy in speech" as the original suggests, because "they are all excellent speakers, indeed – one even sings in almost regular stanzas, which are very reminiscent of a Schillerian ballad" (KGA I/3, 388). "The strangest thing, however," adds the reviewer, "is that they moralize and have a guilty conscience," so that "in short, they are not Witches, but rather 'Sisters of Destiny' [*Schicksalsschwestern*], priestesses of a newly established, supreme dramatic deity" (KGA I/3, 388). They are thus creations of Schiller the dramatist, but also at the same time they are characters of Shakespeare, in whose text "they are ultimately called Witches." And so these mythical characters, so deeply rooted in Elizabethan fantasy, assimilated by the brilliant German poet, paradoxically become alien elements in the drama. For "Witches like those of Schiller's [...] cannot be ascribed to any time" (KGA I/3, 388). In this respect, the text adapted by the poet-translator breaks away from the original in order to float in ahistorical space, far from the history-entangled audience. As in so many other cases, here, too, Schleiermacher stands out for his particular sensitivity to aporia and paradox in translation; indeed, he is not a systematist but an unsurpassed analyst of comprehension and translation.

---

[127] KGA I/3, 386. Changes dictated by "propriety" were acceptable even in the mind of August Wilhelm Schlegel, cf. Gebhardt, *A.W. Schlegels Shakespeare-Übersetzung*, 92.

As a reviewer well acquainted with the arcana of philological textual criticism, he also recognizes another important and difficult aspect of Schiller's translation of *Macbeth* – its dependence on Eschenburg's earlier translation (KGA I/3, 391). This question of the translation's originality, of the author's own contribution, is posed sharply by Schleiermacher. It turns out that Schiller remains in Eschenburg's debt not only in the scenes involving the Witches, but also elsewhere; the reviewer enumerates these fragments precisely, adding, however, in fairness, that the iambic meter and characteristic imagery do constrain the field of translation options. He notes at the same time the translator's significant "improvements" to and "deviations" from the original – both favorable and unfavorable (KGA I/3, 391–392).

Schleiermacher's critical analysis of three German translations of *Macbeth* in the light of the original (those by Schiller and Eschenburg, and also making reference to that by G.A. Bürger) is an example of an advanced *philology of translation*, which might be seen as resembling his own translation of Plato, based as it is on philological engagement with different editions of the original, existing translations and interpretations. In this case, however, the independence and originality of the final work (*Platons Werke*) seems indisputable. The situation is different in the case of Schiller and his text, which undoubtedly owes a great deal to the translations by Eschenburg and Bürger. With a certain dose of irony, Schleiermacher concludes by pointing out the often-dubious originality of Schiller's solutions. The critic was certainly aware, however, that the work he was reviewing had at its core a philosophy of translation that was not based on the Romantic ethic of originality, nor did it seek to chime with Friedrich Schlegel's bold maxims for the study of translation.

The fact that Schleiermacher's critical discourse cuts off rather abruptly shows that he found it difficult to adapt it to the requirements of a press publication. After all, he could have easily given his review the form of an extensive dissertation on translation, in which, among other things, he would have had the opportunity to address more precisely the problem of the metrical translation of Shakespeare's dramas (KGA I/3, 398). But in the remarks he did present, he managed to fulfil the general aim of his philological critique of Schiller's translation, which he summed up succinctly as follows: "to give readers a proper idea of what it means to adapt or translate *Macbeth*" (KGA I/3, 398).

One of the readers of Schleiermacher's review was August Wilhelm Schlegel, probably the person most interested in seeing such ruthless criticism of an undertaking largely competitive with respect to his own work. He presented his opinion about the review in *Erlanger Literatur-Zeitung*, in a letter to its author dated 7 September 1801:

> Your critique of Schiller's *Macbeth* gave us much joy; it is truly an admirable test of your philology. I should like to say [...] that it is even too meticulous and too philological; I do not think this is what you were aiming at, expressing the harshest judgments in such a way that only Schiller

himself and experts on the subject can understand them [...]. I will gladly consent to have you evaluate my Shakespeare as well, even if the review should contain many accusations.[128]

One can thus see that August Wilhelm Schlegel correctly recognized the (philological) profile of the review by the author of the speeches *On Religion* – but also the degree of difficulty and the "scope" of this ambitious criticism.[129] Schleiermacher – an insightful, scholarly analyst of the text at hand – is not a reviewer for everyone; he writes for the intellectual elite. He engages with the translation in a systematic, scholarly manner – offering a scholarly, philological critique of it. His objective seems to be prototypically understood science, rather than "scientific art" (*Wissenschaftskunst*), which according to Friedrich Schlegel was to be the domain of modern criticism.[130]

5 Academic criticism of translation and hermeneutics

It seems that the two translation critiques discussed in this chapter, Schlegel's and Schleiermacher's, illustrate very well the similarities and differences between the thinking of their authors – who, at that time, were close friends. While their texts are based on slightly different assumptions and project different model readers, the content expressed in them was nevertheless representative of the model of translation studies proposed by the early Romantics.

Both critics confronted very demanding material – two masterpieces of world literature that already had a history of translation into German and already significant-

---

[128] KGA V/5, 192–193 (see also Schleiermacher's reply, 206). A.W. Schlegel complains about the unsatisfactory quality of the reviews of his edition of Shakespeare's works (published since 1797) in the *Erlanger Literatur-Zeitung* in his article *Abfertigung eines unwißenden Recensenten der Schlegelschen Übersetzung des Shakespeare* (1800). At the end of his remarks, the author formulates the tenets of a fair and productive translation criticism: "If criticism is to be useful to the poetic art of translation, it is necessary, I think, to adhere to a principle which does not apply to other works of the human spirit: that if the critic reproves something, he should at the same time demonstrate by his own deed that it can be done better" – August Wilhelm Schlegel, *Abfertigung eines unwißenden Recensenten der Schlegelschen Übersetzung des Shakespeare*, in idem, *Vermischte und kritische Schriften*, ed. Eduard Böcking (*Sämtliche Werke*, vol. 12) (Hildesheim: Georg Olms, 1971), 140. The model of translation criticism that Schleiermacher seems to pursue does not respect this principle, as it is guided by premises common to scientific research within the humanities.
[129] If only even in light of this very statement by Schlegel, it is difficult to understand why some scholars claim that Schleiermacher published a malicious, devastating critique of Schiller and his *Macbeth* – see Astrid Dröse, *Schillers Kampf um den "brittischen Aeschylus": die Macbeth-Bearbeitung*, in *Schillers Europa*, ed. Peter-André Alt, Marcel Lepper (Berlin: Walter de Gruyter, 2017), 171. An unbiased reading of this review provides no argument for such a radical assessment.
[130] KFSA XVI, 137; cf. Messlin, *Antike und Moderne*, 370.

ly influenced the history of German culture.[131] As such, they had also affected the history of the German language, because – as Friedrich Schlegel aptly put it – translations, including adaptations, appear to be "the most comprehensive formation" of the target language (*Bildung der Sprache*).[132] The object of criticism in both cases thus required not only responsible and literary-supported opinions, but also a hermeneutic approach. In both reviews, the original work is thus seen as a "truly inviolable unity and totality" (Schleiermacher), as an organic whole that constitutes a natural, higher synthesis of heterogeneous, sometimes paradoxically juxtaposed elements.

In his hermeneutic reading of Cervantes, Schlegel favors synthesis: he is particularly sensitive to the whole, the inner form, the overall relationship of the constituent elements.[133] He advocates a balance between alienation and naturalization and emphasizes the historical-literary and pedagogical aspects of translation. In the latter respect, Schlegel and Schleiermacher are of one mind: they pay attention to the reception horizon of the recipients of the translated literature, asking both about "the translator's point of view" and about the perspective of the recipient, for both see translations as part of a national educational project. In his later lecture on translation methods, Schleiermacher mentions two important components of this project: the all-important synthesis of native and foreign sciences and arts, realized "at the focal point and heart of Europe," and the stylistic awareness heightened by translation (KGA I/11, 92–93).

Schleiermacher, on the other hand, shows himself to be a master of detailed, philological and translatological analysis, which leads him to the most important problems of modern translation studies: to technical and ethical issues, as well as to the great aporias and controversial questions in this field of study. Schleiermacher's review of *Macbeth* – juxtaposed against both August Wilhelm Schlegel's philological and poetic criticism and his own texts published in the pages of *Athenaeum* – may indeed seem to be "a retreat from the early Romantic form of criticism" (M. Bauer).[134] But even if this is the case, it is worth noting that it is not accidental that this shift is documented precisely in an analysis of translation. For translation is working in the medium of language itself, which – according to Schleiermacher –

---

[131] The durability of this influence is attested, for instance, by an international conference recently organized by the Alexander von Humboldt Foundation in Bonn, devoted, among other things, to the contexts of the cultural influence of Cervantes and Shakespeare. See *Networking Guide – 6. Bonner Humboldt-Preisträger Forum "Weltliteraturen – Meisterwerke: Shakespeare und Cervantes 2016,"* (Bonn: Alexander von Humboldt-Stiftung, 2016).
[132] Friedrich Schlegel, *Zur Poesie und Literatur – 1808*, in KFSA XVII: *Fragmente zur Poesie und Literatur II*, ed. Ernst Behler (Paderborn: Schöningh, 1991), 143.
[133] In this hermeneutical context, cf. Friedrich Schlegel's review of *Wilhelm Meister* in *Athenaeum* 1, no. 2 (1798): 147–178.
[134] Manuel Bauer, "Hermeneutische 'Teufeleyen'? Schleiermacher und die frühromantische Kritik," in *Der Begriff der Kritik in der Romantik*, ed. Ulrich Breuer, Ana-Stanca Tabarasi-Hoffmann (Paderborn: Schöningh, 2015), 189.

should be properly understood and illuminated by a rational *analysis*, not a poetic *synthesis*. Nevertheless, to situate his review outside the context of Romantic hermeneutics – as Bauer suggests – would be to commit the sin of one-sidedness.

The distinctiveness of Schleiermacher's review of Schiller's *Macbeth* is also apparent in comparison with August Wilhelm Schlegel's exhaustive discussion of Ludwig Tieck's *Don Quixote*, which also constitute an attempt at an analytical translation criticism. The latter, however, conspicuously lacks not only scholarly objectivity and a compositional structure tailored to the essence of the problem, but also – and very importantly – any interest shown in the theoretical aspects of translation (e. g. functionally determined transformations of the original text). Thus, what is missing in Schlegel's discourse is what distinguishes Schleiermacher's and inscribes it into the Romantic paradigm of thinking about translation. His discourse bears testimony to a quest to grasp and comprehend the construction of the work under review.[135] The aim of this endeavor is "thorough understanding" (*das gründliche Verstehen*), which, after all, according to Friedrich Schlegel himself, constitutes "the inner essence of criticism."[136]

This brings us back around to hermeneutics. Irrespective of the differences we have mentioned, Schleiermacher and Friedrich Schlegel, as critics of translation, are united by the hermeneutical basis of their reflections, the clear expression of which is their special respect for the original and for the translator's creative work.

---

135 See KGA I/3, 380.
136 Friedrich Schlegel, *Lessings Gedanken und Meinungen*, in KFSA III: *Charakteristiken und Kritiken II. 1802–1829*, ed. Hans Eichner (Paderborn: Schöningh, 1975), 60.

VI Philology and the Question of "the Original": Schleiermacher Translates Plato

1 The problem of the original – an introduction

In this chapter I scrutinize the concept of "the original," using this as a springboard for a critical analysis of Schleiermacher's choices and strategies as a translator of Plato's works (based in particular on several passages from his translation of the *Phaedrus*).

The notion of the original, in its modern sense, stretches back to the very beginnings of philology, whose task was "to reconstruct and make accessible ancient texts on the basis of various testimonies and comparisons."[1] The ideal in this context was to reach the source, i.e. the original text, or at least to get as close as possible to it. Here, however, scholars engaged in philological criticism come up against a fundamental difficulty: "The notion of the original, in the sense of an authentic text expressing the author's will, is one of the most elusive and ambiguous concepts in textual criticism," D'Arco Silvio Avalle writes in his *Principi di critica testuale*.[2]

The concept seems to involve both a technical and an ethical dimension, with the relation of *fidelity*, crucial in this context, illustrating this duality most clearly. It reveals itself, for instance, when the philologist is forced to make improvements. With each improvement, however, "there is confusion between what is 'given' in written form by the author or copyist, and what is later 'added' by the philologist as a result of his interpretation of the text as a consequence of the process of inference."[3] The observation so succinctly made here can also be found in the late Schleiermacher's influential lecture entitled *Über Begriff und Einteilung der philologischen Kritik* ("On the Concept and Classification of Philological Criticism" 1830; KGA I/11, 643–656), which is at the same time closely linked to his earlier work on hermeneutics and translation theory. In the latter case, after all, it is a fundamental question how the original relates to a representation of itself that emerges from reproductive and productive efforts, guided by various technical and ethical considerations.

From its beginnings, translatological reflection has been closely linked to (proto)philological thought. In the context of texts that have special authority, but which are often difficult to reconstruct and transmit to contemporaries, there has been much discussion of the question of the source text and the principles of remaining faithful

---

[1] Kai Bremer and Uwe Wirth, "Die philologische Frage – Kulturwissenschaftliche Perspektiven auf die Theoriegeschichte der Philologie," in *Texte zur modernen Philologie*, eds. Kai Bremer, Uwe Wirth (Stuttgart: Reclam, 2010), 31.
[2] D'Arco Silvio Avalle, *Principi di critica testuale* (Roma-Padova: Antenore, 1978), 33 et seq. (chapter on *Phenomenologia dell'originale*).
[3] Bremer and Wirth, "Die philologische Frage," 12.

to it. Sacred texts were obviously of particular importance here, among which the Bible has played the most important role in the process of shaping the awareness of what a "translation from the original" should be understood to be. This process played out through the successive testimonials of translators of and commentators on the Scriptures. The earliest and most important of these were the *Prologue* to the Greek version of the Wisdom of Sirach (ca. 132 BC), written by the translator (who was the grandson of the book's author), and two texts that shed light on the creation of the Septuagint: the anonymous *Letter of Aristeas* (ca. 130 BC) and a fragment of *De vita Mosis* by Philo of Alexandria (ca. 20 BC).[4]

In the first of these, the translator of the work of Jesus, son of Sirach – a Jewish sage, contemporary with King Ptolemy II – introduced his translation, together with a certain confession:

> You are invited therefore to read it with goodwill and attention, to be indulgent in cases where, despite our diligent labor in translating, we may seem to have rendered some phrases imperfectly. For what was originally expressed in Hebrew does not have exactly the same sense when translated into another language. Not only this book, but even the Law itself, the Prophecies, and the rest of the books differ not a little when read in the original.[5]

One can see here respect for the divinely inspired original and an awareness of the incommensurability of linguistic systems, that is, of the phenomenon which Schleiermacher referred to as the "irrationality of languages."[6] This means that reading in the original and in translation is not the same thing, as a translation is marked by imperfection. In this situation, translators may have the assistance of God himself, as the Author/Inspirator of the original, which, as Philo of Alexandria reports, happened when seventy-two wise men were ordered by Ptolemy II to translate the Hebrew books into Greek:

> [T]aking the sacred books, [they] stretched them out towards heaven with the hands that held them, asking of God that they might not fail in their purpose. And He assented to their prayers [...]. [...] Sitting here in seclusion [...], they became as it were possessed, and, under inspiration,

---

4 See Aristeas, *Der König und die Bibel: Griechisch/Deutsch*, trans. and ed. Kai Brodersen (Stuttgart: Reclam, 2008) 43–165 and 167–177; also Aristeas, "The Work of the Seventy-Two – from *Aristeas to Philocrates*," trans. Moses Hadas, in *Western Translation Theory from Herodotus to Nietzsche*, ed. Douglas Robinson (London: Routledge, 2002), 4; Philo Judaeus, "The Creation of the Septuagint – from *The Life of Moses*," trans. F.H. Colson, in Robinson, *Western Translation Theory*, 12–13.
5 The Prologue to Ecclesiasticus, 15–27, quoted from Paul D. Wegner, *The Journey from Texts to Translations: The Origin and Development of the Bible* (Grand Rapids: Baker Academic, 2004), 109
6 The most precise definition of this phenomenon is given by Schleiermacher in the second edition of *Kurze Darstellung des theologischen Studiums:* "By the concept of irrationality it is meant, as is already known, that neither the material nor the formal element of one language corresponds completely to that in another language. Therefore a speech or a text in translation, and even the translation itself, can only be fully understood by someone who is able to relate it back to the source language" (KGA I/6, 373).

wrote, not each several scribe something different, but the same word for word, as though dictated to each by an invisible prompter.⁷

This story is not – contrary to what Theo Hermans claims in his interpretation of Philo's text – about a conviction that external intervention can eliminate the difference between the original and the translation.⁸ Rather, it is about a conviction that the original is more than a textual tissue, a material fact, but a profound intersubjective meaning, the "author's will" that can penetrate the hearts and minds of the audience. The learned men who translated the Hebrew books on the island of Pharos were able to grasp this sense and to convey it:

> The clearest proof of this is that, if Chaldeans have learned Greek, or Greeks Chaldean, and read both versions, the Chaldean and the translation, they regard them with awe and reverence as sisters, or rather one and the same, both in matter and words, and speak of the authors not as translators but as prophets and priests of the mysteries, whose sincerity and singleness of thought has enabled them to go hand in hand with the purest of spirits, the spirit of Moses.⁹

Since the text is the carrier of the inspired sense, unerringly and identically interpreted by translators who are "servants of the word,"¹⁰ the question of the authoritativeness of its source is not of primary importance.¹¹

It is in this spirit that Spinoza understands the original when he contrasts the imperfect text of Scripture, "erroneous, mutilated, corrupt and inconsistent," as if that were not enough – derived from the lost "original text of the covenant," with the true original, written in our hearts ("true religion and faith"). The philosopher writes:

> For both reason and the beliefs of the prophets and Apostles evidently proclaim that God's eternal word and covenant and true religion are divinely inscribed upon the hearts of men, that is, upon the human mind. This is God's true original text, which he himself has sealed with his own seal, that is with the idea of himself as the image of his divinity.¹²

This argument is noteworthy – not only because Spinoza here conveys a picture of religion that the author of the speeches *On Religion* would also later develop, but

---

7 Philo Judaeus, "The Creation of the Septuagint," 13–14.
8 Theo Hermans, *The Conference of the Tongues* (London: Routledge, 2007), 11.
9 Philo Judaeus, *The Creation of the Septuagint*, 14.
10 Cf. Lech Stachowiak, *Prorocy – słudzy słowa* [Prophets – Servants of the Word] (Katowice: Księgarnia św. Jacka, 1980).
11 This means that the discussion of the existence of a normative Hebrew "original" of the Septuagint is also of secondary importance in this context. On the status of the original and translations of the *Septuagint*, cf. Michael Tilly, *Einführung in die Septuaginta* (Darmstadt: Wissenschaftliche Buchgesellschaft, 2005), 62–65.
12 Benedict Spinoza, *Theological-Political Treatise*, ed. Jonathan Israel, trans. Michael Silverthorne and Jonathan Israel (Cambridge: Cambridge Univ. Press, 2007), 163–4, 158.

also because it encourages us to extend our discussion of the notion of the original, facilitating a shift from the textual to the emotional and mental level. In this way, it fits into the paradigm of modern individualism and expressivism.[13] The domain of the original not the letter, but rather the *spirit* and its associated *feelings*, as it manifests itself as a text that is *lived* (through the senses) and *expressed* by the individual.[14] Sentimental and Romantic expressivism, which is an expression of radical individualism, affirms originality as the supreme value that constitutes a supposedly authentic life, which is realized in creativity in the broadest sense of the term; it is the very antithesis of reproducing and copying what is not original.[15] "The original" and "originality" appear in this context as concepts of a transdisciplinary nature, which are of particular interest to cultural anthropology.

This line of reflection, which takes a dynamic view of the original, owes much to the rhetorical theory of translation. By this I mean by a theory of translation developed in the context of transferring persuasive texts, whose essence was first and most accurately formulated by Marcus Tullius Cicero. In writing *The Best Kind of Orator*, he admitted that when he rendered in Latin the texts of great Greek orators, he translated them not as documents but as living "models for our imitation," possessing a powerful influence, whose speech therefore "instructs, delights and moves the minds of his audience."[16] Cicero's concept was later taken up by St. Jerome, who in his *Letter to Pammachius* argued that what was most important in the original was the meaning, not the letter.[17] This sense, however, was not so much an emanation of the original as the result of the translator's intention. This is why Jerome wrote about Hilary the Confessor, that he "did not bind himself to the drowsiness of literal translation"; instead, "like some conqueror, he marched the original text, a captive, into his native language."[18] We find this image later in Friedrich Nietzsche, contrasting his contemporaries' "historical sense" with the spirit of the "great *imperium Romanum*." As he writes in excerpt 83 (on "Translations") from *The Gay Science* (1882/1887):

---

13 On expressivism see Taylor, *Sources of the Self*, 368–393.
14 I am referring here to the views of J.G. Herder and W. von Humboldt. See Johann Gottfried Herder, *Treatise on the Origin of Language*, in *Philosophical Writings*, trans. Michael N. Forster (Cambridge: Cambridge Univ. Press, 2002), Chapter 2, and Michael Losonsky, "Introduction," in Wilhelm von Humboldt, *On Language: On the Diversity of Human Language Construction and its Influence on the Mental Development of the Human Species*, trans. Peter Heath, ed. Michael Losonsky, 2nd ed. (Cambridge: Cambridge Univ. Press, 2000), xxiii.
15 See Taylor, *Ethics of Authenticity*, 25–29.
16 Marcus Tullius Cicero, "The Best Kind of Orator (*De optimo genere oratorum*)," trans. H.M. Hubbell, in Robinson, *Western Translation Theory*, 7 and 9.
17 Although, at the same time, he feared that by translating Scripture he would not unravel the mystery hidden in the order of words in the inspired texts, see Jerome, "On The Best Kind of Translator," trans. Paul Carroll, in Robinson, *Western Translation Theory*, 25.
18 Ibid., 26

> In the age of Corneille and even of the Revolution, the French took possession of Roman antiquity in a way for which we would no longer have courage enough – thanks to our more highly developed historical sense. And Roman antiquity itself: how forcibly and at the same time how naively it took hold of everything good and lofty of Greek antiquity, which was more ancient! How they translated things into the Roman present! How deliberately and recklessly they brushed the dust off the wings of the butterfly that is called moment! [19]

Reaching for the Greek originals, the Romans seemed to be asking: "Should we not make new for ourselves what is old and find ourselves in it? Should we not have the right to breathe our own soul into this dead body"[20] For the original is dead until the will of the present power breathes life into it by appropriating it. "What was past and alien was an embarrassment" for the Romans, "an incentive for a Roman conquest," for indeed, "translation was a form of conquest."[21]

The foreign original becomes here a building-block to be used in creating something that is our own. Its sense becomes fulfilled in the act of assimilation, which is an expression of the affirmative will of power. Thus we can speak of a kind of "dominant-power policy" towards foreign-language originals, which may be based on either a certain "stylistic regime" (French classicism) or a particular philosophy of the nation (German classicism and romanticism). Such policy can also be seen as part of a functional model of intercultural communication that places the target culture at its axiological center. It is essentially forward-looking, appearing to reverse the traditional – retrospective – historical-philological perspective according to which the source/original belongs to the past.[22] This context makes it easier for us to understand the Friedrich Schlegel's passage about the translator whose task is not so much to copy the ancient original, but restore it in a creative way (*wiederschaffen*).[23]

It was on this ground that an extremely interesting interdisciplinary discussion sprang up in the late eighteenth and early nineteenth centuries, concerning the status of the original as a text, concerning the "originality of the original" (H.-J. Frey)[24] as well as the authenticity/fidelity of its representation. This is, of course, an extension of the ongoing dispute between the "spirit" vs. "letter" approaches to the original.[25] It also echoes the Renaissance turn towards the proper (i.e. correctly reconstructed) original, which gave rise to modern biblical hermeneutics and philo-

---

[19] Friedrich Nietzsche, "Translation as Conquest – from *The Gay Science*," trans. Walter Kaufmann, in Robinson, *Western Translation Theory*, 262.
[20] Ibid.
[21] Ibid.
[22] See Edward W. Said, "On Originality," in idem, *The World, the Text, and the Critic* (London: Faber & Faber, 1984), 138–139.
[23] Friedrich Schlegel, *Fragmente*, in idem, *Werke in zwei Bänden*, vol. 1 (Berlin: Aufbau, 1980), 244.
[24] Hans-Jost Frey, *Der unendliche Text* (Frankfurt am Main: Suhrkamp, 1990), 24.
[25] For more on these two tendencies of understanding, reading, and interpreting source texts, see David R. Olson, *The World on Paper: The Conceptual and Cognitive Implications of Writing and Reading* (Cambridge: Cambridge Univ. Press, 1999), 143–159.

logical textual criticism, resulting in such influential works as Lorenzo Valla's *Adnotationes in Novum Testamentum* (1505) and Erasmus of Rotterdam's *Novum Instrumentum omne* (1516).[26]

Schleiermacher – as a theologian, but also as a philologist, an expert in hermeneutics, an outstanding philosopher and, lastly, as a translator – was directly and indirectly involved in this discussion. Hans-Jost Frey claims in this context that recognition of the "originality of the original" goes hand in hand with an "anxiety about the original," and he attributes this anxiety also to Schleiermacher, referring to his "rejection of the bilingual translator, bordering on moral condemnation," which he expresses in his lecture *On the Different Methods of Translating*.[27] Is the German expert on Romantic philosophy right? In my opinion, Schleiermacher's views on this matter are best reflected in the extraordinary undertaking that Friedrich Schlegel – as we already know – urged him to undertake and prepared him for, namely, his translation of Plato's dialogues. It is precisely this enormous work on the textual basis (corpus) for his translation and the target text, when analyzed, that can bring us closer to answering the question of Schleiermacher's relation to the original. This question is of fundamental importance not only in the context of the hermeneutics[28] he was constructing almost at the same time, but also because of the role that philology together with hermeneutics and the art of translation play in his theology, and especially in his exegetics.[29] However, before attempting to answer this question, we should first take a closer look at the historical background – the aforementioned discussion in which philologists and translators problematized the status of the original, which has exerted a significant impact on contemporary philology, translation studies, and philosophy.

---

26 See Józef Kudasiewicz, *Biblia – historia – nauka: Rozważania i dyskusje biblijne* [Bible – History – Science: Biblical Considerations and Discussions] (Kraków: Znak, 1977), 113. The emphasis that Protestants placed on approaching the original Scriptures competently, based on philological knowledge (especially Matthias Flacius, author of *Clavis scripturae sacrae* of 1567), was also significant in this context.
27 Hans-Jost Frey, *Der unendliche Text*, 24.
28 The first version of Schleiermacher's translation of the *Phaedrus* was written in early 1801, and his earliest notes for a course on hermeneutics at the University of Halle date from 1805. The correlation between Plato's conception of philosophical understanding in this dialogue and Schleiermacher's hermeneutics from Halle has been pointed out by Lutz Käppel. In his view, this hermeneutics owes a lot to close reading of the *Phaedrus*, in connection with the translation project *Platons Werke*. See Lutz Käppel, *Schleiermachers Hermeneutik zwischen zeitgenössischer Philologie und "Phaidros"-Lektüre*, in *Schleiermacher-Tag 2005: Eine Vortragsreihe*, ed. Günter Meckenstock (Göttingen: Vandenhoeck & Ruprecht, 2006), 72–74.
29 See here especially the first chapter of Schleiermacher's *Kurze Darstellung des theologischen Studiums* (KGA I/6, 365–379).

2 Enlightenment, Romanticism, and the rediscovery of the original

In a very inspiring sketch on Friedrich Hölderlin's translations (especially of Sophocles' tragedies), Klaus Nickau distinguished between three ways of conceiving of what "the original" is – "what Hölderlin had in before him," "what Hölderlin translated," and "what Sophocles wrote."[30] Nickau sees last of these three notions as an ideal to which we today have come much closer, it seems, than Schiller's and Schleiermacher's contemporaries did. Nevertheless, this ideal remains an enigma for the classical philologist: "translations – both his own and those of others," Nickau writes, "often remind him how foreign are those ancient works that he thought he had already managed, to some extent, to come to know and understand."[31] There much to suggest that this kind of experience of foreignness also influenced Schleiermacher as a translator of Plato. In my analysis, however, I fill focus on the *textual* reality, especially the stance adopted by the translator (and philologist) to the original that was the subject of his translational efforts. I will examine this issue based on the example of the first of Schleiermacher's translations of Plato's dialogues, namely the *Phaedrus*, in the form published by the translator as the second edition (of 1817). However, when writing about this particular original/translation relationship, we cannot forget about its cultural background – Schleiermacher's translations were not, of course, produced in a historical vacuum.

It seems that already in the first half of the eighteenth-century German scholars had begun to rediscover the original – to "rediscover" it, because the initial discovery of the original in modern culture had come during the Italian Renaissance, in connection with the demand for faithful translations of Greek fiction into Latin (e. g. Homer and Euripides) and the already mentioned development of biblical hermeneutics and textual criticism. Three hundred years after Leonardo Bruni's death, the champions of reason in Germany postulated a "translation directly from the original language" (J.Ch. Gottsched),[32] and critics took the trouble to compare the translator's work to the original text.[33] Also emphasized was the importance of translation for the field of philological research that involves reconstructing the original source, or *Urtext*. The essence of the original lies in its meaning, which is related to the "mind and intention" of the author, or, more directly, to his "thoughts."[34] These thoughts, how-

---

[30] Klaus Nickau, *Die Frage nach dem Original*, in *Die literarische Übersetzung – Fallstudien zu ihrer Geschichte*, ed. Brigitte Schultze (Berlin: Erich Schmidt, 1987), p 86.
[31] Ibid., 86–87.
[32] Johann Christoph Gottsched demanded this, criticizing the idea of translating from English via a French translation – *Beyträge zur critischen Historie der deutschen Sprache, Poesie und Beredsamkeit*, vol. 7 (Leipzig: Breitkopf, 1741), 167–168.
[33] Anneliese Senger, *Deutsche Übersetzungstheorie im 18. Jahrhundert (1734–1746)* (Bonn: Bouvier, 1971), 55.
[34] Ibid., 56–57.

ever, are formulated in the original language, so the translator must be aware that, as Gottsched aptly observes, what is expressed in foreign words cannot be accurately rendered in the target language.³⁵

This surge in interest in the original in the German-speaking translation culture that emerged the second half of the eighteenth century, and reached its culmination at the beginning of the nineteenth, is even described by Andreas Poltermann as the "invention of the original," stressing that this came at a the time when the "culture of understanding foreignness" (*Kultur des Fremdverstehens*)³⁶ began to develop. Poltermann argues that the basis for this was a new cosmopolitan discourse that was gaining in importance, emphasizing the benefits of opening up to the foreign, which also means encouraging the reader of literature to, as it were, come out to meet the foreign original.³⁷ Poltermann notes that during the period in question, a translation in conformity with the original was understood as a translation "faithful in style," as it was believed that the translator, representing the author of the work, should respect the latter's individuality.³⁸ The Enlightenment, as we know, strengthened the position of the author, who was now most often seen as an independent intellectual, while at the same time augmenting the authoritativeness of the author's text. In this context it is also important to note that the increasingly common perception of a literary text as a coherent, integral whole, an expression of the author's personality and creative invention (his original style) also started to gain a legal dimension – thanks to the emergence of copyrights, which also applied to translations.³⁹ Note that already at the end of the eighteenth century, translations written by famous writers were treated on a par with their original works.⁴⁰

With these circumstances in mind, Poltermann argues that as a result of the shifts within (German) cultural discourse, the author's work was "discovered" and the original itself was "invented" by means of "deep reading" (*verstehende Lektüre*) and a translation formulated on its basis.⁴¹ In line with the perspective outlined in the previous section of this chapter, this idea should be relativized, to speak instead

---

35 Ibid., 57.
36 Andreas Poltermann, "Die Erfindung des Originals – Zur Geschichte der Übersetzungskonzeptionen in Deutschland im 18. Jahrhundert," in *Die literarische Übersetzung – Fallstudien zu ihrer Kulturgeschichte*, ed. Brigitte Schultze (Berlin: Erich Schmidt, 1987), 14.
37 Ibid., 14–15. Already in 1797, Novalis wrote: "Germanness is cosmopolitanism combined with the strongest individuality" – letter to A.W. Schlegel, Jena, 30 November 1797; Novalis, *Schriften*, vol. 4, ed. Richard Samuel (Stuttgart: W. Kohlhammer, 1975), 237.
38 Poltermann, "Die Erfindung des Originals," 16.
39 Ibid., 36 and 39.
40 In the above-cited letter, Novalis complains that although "there is hardly any respectable German writer left who does not translate, valuing translations no less than his original works, it seems that there is nothing more marked by ignorance than translation" (Novalis, *Schriften*, 237).
41 Poltermann, "Die Erfindung des Originals," 16.

of a certain re-evaluation of the approach to the source text within the framework of the "dialectics of the original" that had functioned for centuries.[42]

Another noteworthy turning point in thinking about the original came at the end of the eighteenth century, in connection with the dynamic development of philology (textual criticism), hermeneutics, and literary theory. With the advancement of the humanities and the rise of interdisciplinary thought, the notion of the original garnered increasing attention, which also meant increasing consideration of theoretical assumptions and practical aspects of translation itself – already functioning as a model of interpretation and criticism. The protagonists of this turn included Herder, Hölderlin, the Schlegel brothers, Novalis, Wilhelm von Humboldt, and Schleiermacher, some of whom became famous for their extraordinary, even ground-breaking translations.[43]

Common to them all was a shared conviction that was once formulated by Herder in his *Fragments:* "The best translator should be the best explainer," being "at the same time a philosopher, a poet, and a philologist," who appears as "the morning star of a new era in German literature."[44] This was an epoch in which translations were to be venerated on the same level as original works.[45] This growing awareness of the special mission of translators corresponded with the gradually rising prestige of German philology in the nineteenth century. The views of Ulrich von Wilamowitz-Moellendorff are characteristic in this context: ancient Greek poetry, he argued, should be translated only by philologists, because only they had a calling to show the way to the ideal to those who are searching for it.[46] These scholars rescue and recreate the original, because, as August Boeckh noted, "ancient writings have been preserved only in a small part in the original" and are usually the last link in a

---

[42] Perhaps it would be appropriate here, taking a cue from H.-J. Frey, to emphasize the special respect for the original evident in almost all German-language pronouncements on translation during the period of our interest. This is well elucidated by Marcia Sá Cavalcante Schuback, showing the idealization of the original shared by the theoretically divergent commentaries of Goethe and Wilhelm von Humboldt – see Marcia Sá Cavalcante Schuback, "Hermeneutics of Tradition," in *Rethinking Time: Essays on History, Memory and Representation.* eds. Hans Ruin & Andrus Ers (Södertörn: Södertörns högskola, 2011), 63–74. This respect, however, does not mean that the original was not problematized.
[43] Cf. Friedrich Hölderlin's translations of Sophocles' tragedies, Wilhelm von Humboldt's translation of Aeschylus' *Agamemnon*, August Wilhelm Schlegel's translations of Shakespeare's plays and works of Spanish literature, and of course Schleiermacher's Plato.
[44] Johann Gottfried von Herder, *Ueber die neuere Deutsche Litteratur – Zwote Sammlung von Fragmenten*, vol. 2 (Riga: Hartknoch, 1767), 237 and 238–239. Cf. Ralph-Rainer Wuthenow, *Das fremde Kunstwerk – Aspekte der literarischen Übersetzung* (Göttingen: Vandenhoeck & Ruprecht, 1969), 18–19. On Herder's theory of translation and its linguistic principles see: Michael N. Forster, "Herder's Philosophy of Language, Interpretation, and Translation: Three Fundamental Principles," *The Review of Metaphysics* 56, no. 2 (Dec., 2002), 341.
[45] Herder, *Ueber die neuere Deutsche Litteratur*, 237.
[46] Wuthenow, *Das fremde Kunstwerk*, 65.

long chain of copies.⁴⁷ Hence the task of the philologist is to reconstruct an ideal original, based on what is generally a corrupted transmission, while the task of the translator is to translate this reconstructed original into another language, the language of another world.

In the ideal case, then, there is close cooperation between the expert philologist and the translator. The former presents, or describes, the original, on the basis of which the latter, often making use of the privilege of personal consultation, prepares an interpretation of the text in another language, i.e. a translation. Wilhelm von Humboldt describes this kind of cooperation in the introduction to his metrical translation of *Agamemnon:* "In correcting and interpreting the text I had the assistance of Mr. Professor Herrmann [*sic!*]. Busy with the new edition of Aeschylus, he was kind enough to give me from his study of Agamemnon all that could be useful for the translation."⁴⁸ Humboldt emphasizes that philological rigor is also obligatory for translators, who should not approach their sources with complete freedom. This is why he writes about "his" original:

> I stayed as close to this text as I could. For I have always been unable to stand the eclectic manner of those translators who, having sometimes sifted through hundreds of manuscript variants and critics' corrections, choose at random, often guided by misleading intuition. To publish an old author means to reduce a document, if not to its true and original form, then at least to a source that appears to us as the last available one. Such an edition should therefore be carried out with the precision and conscientiousness of a historian, with underlying knowledge, and especially with consistency; and it should be bound together by a single spirit⁴⁹.

Striving to maintain philological meticulousness and respect for the original led Humboldt to work on his manuscript of Aeschylus' drama for twenty years, consulting many learned men, not only the eminent classical philologist Gottfried Hermann, whom he mentioned above.⁵⁰ Friedrich Schleiermacher worked on his Plato more efficiently than Humboldt, albeit certainly no less meticulously. He too benefited from the assistance of a philologist: Ludwig Friedrich Heindorf, the author of *Specimen Coniecturarum in Platonem*⁵¹ (KGA IV/3, XVII–XVIII) – and tried to avoid arbitrary interpretations that contradicted scholarly research of the source. However, as we shall see, the author of the speeches *On Religion*, unlike Humboldt, had not only lit-

---

47 August Boeckh, *Encyclopädie und Methodologie der philologischen Wissenschaften* (Leipzig: Tuebner, 1877), 188.
48 Wilhelm von Humboldt, *Aeschylos Agamemnon metrisch übersetzt (Einleitung)*, in idem, *Gesammelte Schriften*, Abt. 1, vol. 8: *Übersetzungen* (Berlin: B. Behr's Verlag, 1968, reprint of 1909 edition), 134.
49 Ibid., 134–135.
50 See Ernst Howald, "Wilhelm von Humboldts Agamemnon," *Museum Helveticum: schweizerische Zeitschrift für klassische Altertumswissenschaft* 16, no. 4 (1959): 292–301.
51 See Ludovicus Fridericus Heindorf, *Specimen Coniecturarum in Platonem* (Berlin: Halis Saxonum Grunert, 1798), and KGA IV/3, XVII-XVIII.

erary talent and the flexibility characteristic of outstanding translators, but above all also great consideration for his readers.[52]

3 Schleiermacher's Dialogues of Plato

Initiated as a joint project together with Friedrich Schlegel, Schleiermacher's translation of Plato's works was undoubtedly, alongside August Wilhelm Schlegel's Shakespeare, the most important translation project undertaken by the German Romantics. The genesis and theoretical background of this project were already discussed in Chapter III of this book. However, it is worth mentioning here that Schleiermacher's translation of Plato, being, as Andreas Arndt writes, "a systematic and genetic reconstruction of a certain whole," appears as "a programme of the hermeneutical turn in the late eighteenth and early nineteenth centuries, thanks to which the detailed hermeneutics of the Enlightenment was inscribed into a broad model of explaining the whole on the basis of its integral parts."[53] As we remember, Friedrich Schlegel had a great influence on the shape of the theoretical foundation of the project. This influence can be seen above all on the philological level, most clearly through the influence of Schlegel's concept of "higher philological criticism," which inspired Schleiermacher.[54]

German readers were meant to receive not only the complete Plato, in chronological order, but also the "real" Plato. Schleiermacher presents his hermeneutics of the original in his introduction (*Einleitung*) to the dialogues, in which he tries to familiarize readers with the "true Platonic form [*ächt platonische Form*]," that is, with what is original in the original (KGA IV/3, 58).[55] He posits a definition of what is Platonic, which then serves a certain regulative function: for the more the extant texts deviate from this formula, the more their authenticity is in doubt – as works that are insufficiently "Platonic." Wherein lies the essence of a truly Platonic work? For Schleiermacher, it lies to a large extent in such aesthetic values as unity (of form, content, etc.), spirit (genius), mimetic art (*mimische Kunst*), strength, beauty, tone, color, form, composition. These were the original values that were meant to become invariant aspects of his translation.[56] It is worth noting at this point, however, that

---

[52] Humboldt's translation is difficult to read, not least because of its deficiencies on the literary level.
[53] Andreas Arndt, *Friedrich Schleiermacher als Philosoph* (Berlin: Walter de Gruyter, 2013), 267.
[54] Cf. especially Wilhelm Dilthey, *Leben Schleiermachers*, vol. I/2: *1803–1807*, 3rd ed., ed. Martin Redeker (Berlin: Walter de Gruyter, 1970), 37–75. On Schlegel's influence on Schleiermacher, see "Friedrich Schlegels 'Philosophie der Philologie' und Schleiermachers frühe Entwürfe zur Hermeneutik," *Zeitschrift für Theologie und Kirche* 63, no. 4 (1966): 434–472.
[55] On basic interpretive principles in Schleiermacher's "General Introduction" see Julia A. Lamm, *Schleiermacher's Plato* (Berlin: Walter de Gruyter, 2021), 89–91.
[56] A thorough account of Platonic "invariants" is presented by Thomas Alexander Szlezák in: "Friedrich Schleiermacher und das Platonbild des 19. und 20. Jahrhunderts," *Plato Journal* 2 (2002): 4,

Schleiermacher "reads" this Platonic core into the incomplete, often incoherent and ambiguous texture from which its original emerges. Schleiermacher's aesthetic reading, complemented by an unusually suggestive philosophical concept of the interrelation of the realm of desire and the realm of thought in Plato's dialogues (seen most clearly in the *Phaedrus*), is impressive in its coherence and clarity. With time, this concept matured; later, in his lectures on the history of philosophy, Schleiermacher emphasizes the role of dialectics, meant to give to Plato's discourse coherence, forging a unity of essence despite the multiplicity of relations manifesting themselves in the world.[57]

In his Preface (*Vorerinnerung*), to the first volume of the dialogues, Schleiermacher writes about the special challenge faced by the translator of Plato's complete works, as he has to keep in mind the "unity, or uniform approach" that is "necessary for such a whole" (KGA IV/3, 7). Plato's dialogues, in all their diversity, constitute in his opinion a single (written) text by a single author. In the footnotes to *Des Socrates Vertheidigung* Schleiermacher mentions Johann Heinrich Voß's translation as his most important point of reference, but stresses that "the translator of the whole Plato sometimes has to avoid what the translator of the individual dialogues is perfectly entitled to employ."[58] The strategy of translation constituted as a coherent whole of the corpus of Platonic texts also necessitates a different attitude in terms of "reading and interpretation" (*Lesart und Auslegung*).[59] The translator may follow here, as Schleiermacher writes, a trail of "certain suppositions" which as an editor he would certainly not have chosen to use in the text (*Vorerinnerung*, KGA IV/3, 8). In this respect he proceeds differently from the philologist – for the translator often pursues his own purposes and needs, which may not coincide with the aims of philological criticism. His "suppositions" are the result of divinations, oriented towards the translator's comprehension, characterized by a particular intentionality (*Verstehensinteresse*).[60] The essence of this endeavor is not so much to make the preserved text legible, but rather, while aiming for the ideal of "foreign semblance" (*fremde Ähnlichkeit*), to make the translation legible.[61]

---

https://digitalis-dsp.uc.pt/bitstream/10316.2/42272/3/Friedrich_Schleiermacher_und_das_Platonbild.pdf (accessed 15 November 2019).

57 See Hans-Georg Gadamer, "Schleiermacher als Platoniker," in idem, *Kleine Schriften III: Idee und Sprache: Plato, Husserl, Heidegger* (Tübingen: J. C. B. Mohr, 1972), 146–147.

58 Friedrich Schleiermacher, *Platons Werke. Ersten Theiles zweiter Band*, 3rd ed., Berlin 1855, 298–299. Schleiermacher is referring to the *Defense of Socrates* (*Vertheidigung des Sokrates*) with footnotes by Johann Heinrich Voß. Cf. Georg Ludwig Spalding's letter to Schleiermacher of 5 January 1803, KGA V/7, 185. On Schleiermacher's ambivalent attitude towards Voß see Hermann Patsch, *Alle Menschen sind Künstler – Friedrich Schleiermachers poetische Versuche* (Berlin: Walter de Gruyter, 1986), 70–71.

59 See Schleiermacher, *Platons Werke – Ersten Theiles zweiter Band*, 299.

60 See Bremer and Wirth, "Die philologische Frage," 17.

61 On the concept of "foreign semblance" (*fremde Ähnlichkeit*), cf. *On the Different Methods of Translating*, DR 232; KGA I/11, 81.

Schleiermacher interpreted Plato's philosophy "organologically," claiming that it "develops genetically from a seed-like beginning – the *Phaedrus* – in order to reach the perfect maturity of the *Republic* and the *Timaeus*";[62] he assumed "that Plato already had a robust philosophical theory at a young age, and implemented it throughout his life in various stages."[63] Thus, the first was the *Phaedrus*, from which other dialogues started to grow, forming "three trilogies": elementary dialogues (*Phaedrus, Protagoras, Parmenides*), indirectly dialectical dialogues (*Theaetetus, Sophist/Statesman/Symposium, Phaedo/Philebus*) and constructive dialogues (the *Republic, Timaeus, Critias*).[64] As Julia A. Lamm explains, the "basic structure of three trilogies (…) is the armature around which Schleiermacher's Plato was formed."[65] This order reflected the chronology, but it also had a didactic dimension, making it easier for contemporary viewers to orient themselves in Plato's work and, thanks to that, to "symphilosophize" together with the thinker.[66] The latter aspect is worth remembering, as it is related to Schleiermacher's translation strategy.

Schleiermacher's conception was coherent and well thought out, yet oppositional classifications emerged quite quickly, for example that of Karl F. Hermann, who took greater account of the unsystematic nature of Plato's works and their dependence on other thinkers.[67] This is because he was skeptical of the aspiration shared by Friedrich Schlegel and Schleiermacher, to develop a system that was not disturbed by any "non-Platonic" elements.[68] Finally, the *Phaedrus* being ascribed to the

---

[62] Christoph Asmuth, *Interpretation – Transformation: Das Platonbild bei Fichte, Schelling, Hegel, Schleiermacher und Schopenhauer und das Legitimationsproblem der Philosophiegeschichte* (Göttingen: Vandenhoeck & Ruprecht, 2006), 202. This evolution can be seen as a path from debatable knowledge to knowledge that is grounded and presented discursively; see Jörg Jantzen, "'…daß ich nämlich sterben will, wenn der Platon vollendet ist' – Schleiermachers Übersetzung des Platon," in *Übersetzung antiker Literatur – Funktionen und Konzeptionen im 19. und 20. Jahrhundert*, eds. Martin S. Harbsmeier et al. (Berlin: Walter de Gruyter, 2008), 39.
[63] Kazimierz Leśniak, *Platon*, 2nd ed. (Warsaw: Wiedza Powszechna, 1993), 20. On possible precursors to Schleiermacher's conception see Björn Pecina, "Gerettetes Vergehen – Ethos und Kontext zweier Platonübersetzungen" in *Reformation und Moderne: Pluralität – Subjektivität – Kritik. Akten des Internationalen Kongresses der Schleiermacher-Gesellschaft in Halle (Saale), März 2017*, ed. Jörg Dierken, Arnulf von Scheliha, Sarah Schmidt (Berlin / Boston: De Gruyter, 2018), 80.
[64] Ibid., 21 and KGA I/3, 373 (*Zum Platon*). See also Lamm, *Schleiermacher's Plato*, 44.
[65] Lamm, *Schleiermacher's Plato*, 44–45. See also Lamm's table in which she lays out Schleiermacher's ordering of the Platonic Dialogues alongside the volumes of *Platons Werke* and the structure of the "three trilogies" (45–46).
[66] Lutz Käppel, "Schleiermachers Platon-Übersetzungen," in *Schleiermacher Handbuch*, ed. Martin Ohst, Tübingen: Mohr Siebeck, 2017), 161.
[67] See Leśniak, *Platon*, 21.
[68] See Karl Friedrich Hermann, *Geschichte und System der Platonischen Philosophie*, pt. 1 (Heidelberg: C.F. Winter, 1839), 363. On this polemic in the context of disputes over *Plato's* interpretation, see E[ugène] N[apoleon] Tigerstedt, *Interpreting Plato* (Stockholm: Almqvist & Wiksell International, 1977), 25.

early Platonic dialogues (which today are referred to as the Socratic dialogues) was questioned.[69]

Hegel, generally quite critical of Schleiermacher, even questioned not so much the very concept of Plato's legacy, as the value of this type of philological and philosophical research in general. As he wrote in his lecture on Plato in the history of philosophy:

> it is quite superfluous for Philosophy, and belongs to the hypercriticism [*Hyperkritik*] of our times, to treat Plato from a literary point of view, as Schleiermacher does, critically examining whether one or another of the minor dialogues is genuine or not. Regarding the more important of the dialogues, we may mention that the testimony of the ancients leaves not the slightest doubt.[70]

The author of the *Phenomenology of Spirit* believed that by properly understanding philosophy as such, he was able to perceive the essence and value of Platonic thinking – in the context of speculative philosophy, of course.

Schleiermacher's stance towards the so-called *esoteric* teaching of Plato – i.e. the (largely hypothetical) unwritten transmission, which is held by a long interpretative tradition to be primary in relation to the preserved writings, has become a separate, controversial and still debated problem. This is a very important question, because the way it is resolved provides an indication of what the proper *original* of Plato's philosophy is: the oral transmission or the written text. Schleiermacher believed that only the extant (authentic) dialogues contain Plato's teachings; thus he worked within the tradition of exoteric interpretation.[71] His argument in favor of such a marginalization of esotericism was much more subtle and scientifically persuasive than it might seem judging by the polemics of his critics[72] – he argues that Plato's dialogues exhibit a kind of coexistence of speech and writing, which actually makes it unnecessary to look for any unspoken truths outside the domain of the text.[73]

Thus, as the translator of *Plato's Werke* argues, the question of esotericism vs. exotericism becomes primarily a function of how the text is understood by the reader, who is always likely to become "a true hearer of what is internal" (*Hörer des In-*

---

[69] See Käppel, "Schleiermachers Platon-Übersetzungen," 162.
[70] Georg Wilhelm Friedrich Hegel, *Vorlesungen über die Geschichte der Philosophie*, vol. 2 (Leipzig: Reclam, 1971), 15. English version cited: *Hegel's Lectures on the History of Philosophy*, trans. E.S. Haldane, Francis H. Simson, vol 2. (London: Kegan Paul, Trench, Trübner, 1894), 10. Hegel lectured on the history of philosophy from 1805 to 1831 (with interruptions and at various universities).
[71] See Jantzen, "...daß ich nämlich sterben will, wenn der Platon vollendet ist," 42.
[72] Cf. *Einleitung*, KGA IV/3, 24–33. Justice is done to his argument, however, by Thomas Alexander Szlezák, who critiques Schleiermacher's "theory of dialogue" in his article *Friedrich Schleiermacher und das Platonbild des 19 und 20 Jahrhunderts*.
[73] See Thomas Alexander Szlezák, "Platon und die neuzeitliche Theorie des platonischen Dialogs" in *Dialog Schule – Wissenschaft, Klassische Sprachen und Literaturen*. Vol. 23: *Neue Perspektiven*, ed. Peter Neukam (München: Bayrischer Schulbuch-Verlag 1989), 174.

neren; KGA IV/3, 32).[74] Consequently, the content of the work appears as *communicative* and *translatable* – hence the "communicative opening" of Plato that is attributed to Schleiermacher and his disciples.[75] Nevertheless, Schleiermacher's conviction of the autonomy of Plato's writings led his work to be criticized by those who supported an esoteric interpretation of Plato. Such critique centered around the question of what purpose writings/texts are actually meant to serve: as a reminder of knowledge to those who have already been given it, or as a way of imparting knowledge to those who do not have it.[76]

This is how Friedrich Nietzsche formulated the question in his early lectures on ancient philosophy, accusing Schleiermacher of turning Plato into a "literary teacher" (*den literarischen Lehrer*), creating works with his readers in mind, ideal recipients whom he wants to "educate methodically," much like the Speaker from the speeches *On Religion*.[77] Thus, in Nietzsche's eyes, the author of the *Phaedrus* is naturalized, becomes *translated* into the discourse of contemporary literary culture. Yet the objective of a true philologist should be "to translate Plato the writer into Plato the man" (*den Schriftsteller Plato in den Menschen Plato zu übersetzen*).[78] I will return to this issue in the context of the passage of the *Phaedrus* concerning the shortcomings of writing, which, together with the *Seventh Letter*, is the crowning argument of the "esotericists" in their dispute against the "exotericists."

Schleiermacher began translating the *Phaedrus* at the beginning of 1801, at the urging of the impatient Friedrich Schlegel. The basis for his translation – that is to say, the "original he had before him" – was, as the editors of the critical edition of the dialogue, Lutz Käppel and Johanna Loehr, report, "a manuscript draft of an

---

74 Schleiermacher is referring here to the Platonic term τα ἔσω.
75 Thomas Alexander Szlezák, *Plato und die Schriftlichkeit der Philosophie – Interpretationen zu den frühen und mittleren Dialogen* (Berlin: De Gruyter, 1985), 369.
76 Giovanni Reale, *A History of Ancient Philosophy II: Plato and Aristotle*, trans. John R. Catan (Albany, State Univ. of New York Press), 17. Tigerstedt notes, however, that at the level of interpreting the coherence and continuity of Plato's philosophy, the proponents of "esoteric doctrine" do not differ much from Schleiermacher's discourse (see Tigerstedt, *Interpreting Plato*, 85).
77 Friedrich Nietzsche, *Werke – Kritische Gesamtausgabe*, Abt. 2, vol. 4: *Vorlesungsaufzeichnungen (WS 1871/72–WS 1874/75)*, ed. Fritz Bornmann (Berlin: Walter de Gruyter, 1995), 13.
78 Ibid., 8. Nietzsche is echoed today by the most innovative interpreters of *Plato*, who stress that for the author of the *Phaedrus*; "philosophy is essentially a form of life, not a set of doctrines" – claims Charles H. Kahn in idem, *Plato and the Socratic Dialogue: The Philosophical Use of a Literary Form* (Cambridge: Cambridge Univ. Press, 1997), 383. Seen in this context, Plato's theory of knowledge seems to be based on the assumption that knowledge cannot be objectified (and transferred in this form to others) because it has a subjective character, being a property of the *knower*, who can *express* his knowledge, but not *transfer* it – Wolfgang Wieland, "Platons Schriftkritik und die Grenzen der Mitteilbarkeit," in *Romantik – Literatur und Philosophie*, ed. Volker Bohn (Frankfurt am Main: Suhrkamp, 1987), 32–33. While this theory differs from Schleiermacher's view of dialectics and knowledge transfer, it is at the same time related to his strategy of translating Plato, as the author of the lecture *On the Different Methods of Translating* took this point of view into account.

annotated edition prepared by his friend Ludwig Friedrich Heindorf."[79] But Schleiermacher also had other source texts at his disposal: these included the great Bipontina edition and separate editions by Friedrich August Wolf and Johann Christoph Gottleber, earlier works by Heindorf, and later also a critical edition by Immanuel Bekker (*Platonis Dialogi Graece et Latine*, 1816–1818).[80] In his commentaries he also referred to Marsilio Ficino's translation and Henricus Stephanus' edition.

After Schlegel had reviewed the *Phaedrus* manuscript sent to him by Schleiermacher in mid-March 1801, the text was sent to the publisher Friedrich Frommann for typesetting (KGA IV/3, XXII–XXIII and XCII). But further work on revisions to the translation began to be delayed, so Schleiermacher, having already terminated the planned collaboration with Friedrich Schlegel, entrusted the publication of his translations to the publishing house of Georg Andreas Reimer. The first volume of *Platons Werke*, containing the dialogues *Phaedrus*, *Lysis*, *Protagoras*, and *Laches*, was published in May 1804 (KGA IV/3, XXV–XXVII und XXXV).[81]

The early reception of this landmark edition was quite unexpected for Schleiermacher; as a result, in his introduction to the second edition the translator complained about the scarcity of serious reviews.[82] However, while the reviews were indeed not numerous, at least two reviewers were quite serious and contributed much to the discussion of the canon of Platonic writings and the strategy of their translation into German[83] – these were the eminent experts in philological criticism and hermeneutics, Friedrich Ast and August Boeckh, who published reviews in 1808.

Ast's review in the *Zeitschrift für Wissenschaft und Kunst* was critical (as had been Schleiermacher's own review of Ast's *De Platonis Phaedro* published six years earlier, see KGA I/3, 469–481). Although Ast praises the philological accuracy and philosophical competence of the translator and commentator, he points out certain shortcomings. First of all, he disagrees with the translator's concept of the corpus of Plato's works (he questions the authenticity of the *Laches* and *Lysis*), but he

---

[79] Lutz Käppel, Johanna Loehr, *Einleitung der Bandherausgeber*, KGA IV/3, XIX. This refers to Heindorf's four-volume work *Platonis Dialogi selecti*, published between 1802 and 1810.
[80] See Kurt Nowak, *Schleiermacher – Leben, Werk und Wirkung* (Göttingen: Vandenhoeck & Ruprecht, 2001 2001) 134–137; cf. KGA IV/3, 1044–1046, and also *Schleiermachers Bibliothek*, Bearbeitung des facsimilierten Rauchschen Auktionskatalogs und der Hauptbücher des Verlages G. Reimer, besorgt von Günter Meckenstock (Berlin: De Gruyter, 1993), 80, 88 and passim.
[81] Further volumes of *Platons Werke* appeared in the following order: 1804: *Ersten Theiles erster Band*, 1805: *Ersten Theiles zweiter Band*, 1805: *Zweiten Theiles erster Band*, 1807: *Zweiten Theiles zweiter Band*, 1809: *Zweiten Theiles dritter Band*. A second, revised edition was published in 1817, and in 1828 a third volume of *Platons Werke* was published, containing a translation of the *Republic*. Schleiermacher did not manage to include all of Plato's works in his edition (which is missing the *Laws* and *Timaeus*, among other dialogs).
[82] Lutz Käppel, *Die frühe Rezeption der Platon-Übersetzung Friedrich Schleiermachers am Beispiel der Arbeiten Friedrich Asts*, in *Geist und Buchstabe. Interpretationen und Transformationsprozesse innerhalb des Christentums – Festschrift für Günter Meckenstock zum 65. Geburtstag*, ed. Michael Pietsch, Dirk Schmid (Berlin: Walter de Gruyter, 2013), 45.
[83] A full list of reviews is given by Lutz Käppel – ibid., 50 f. (1804–1817) and 53 (1819–1830).

also criticizes the translation itself for its lack of domestication, which is claimed to be an appropriate solution if the German language used in the translation is to retain its "purity and Doric harmony."[84]

August Boeckh, in turn, who had been a student of Schleiermacher's and later became a professor of classical philology at the University of Berlin, published his review of the first part of *Platons Werke* in the journal *Heidelbergische Jahrbücher der Literatur für Theologie, Philosophie und Pädagogik*. This review can be described as exemplary in terms of its philosophical, linguistic and translational insight; one can perceive the considerable engagement of a critic who appreciates the translator, recognizes the novelty of his undertaking, and places it in a wider context. As such, it is worth presenting this review in more detail. Schleiermacher actually appreciated it – some of the ideas Boeckh expressed in the review would later resurface in the Berlin lecture on translation.

Boeckh argues that previous translations of Plato into German had been characterized by an ignorance of Platonic teaching and its presentation, but also of the language and character of Hellenistic antiquity, thereby attesting to the insufficient competence of their translators.[85] And the task facing such a translator is a difficult one: for a translation to be successful, it must achieve a synthesis of philology and philosophy, which in tandem should produce something qualitatively new – reflecting the synthetic character of Plato's work. Readers should come to see Plato as an artist, at the same time perceiving the unity of form and content in his works.[86] In Boeckh's opinion, Plato found an ideal translator in Schleiermacher, because apart from his philosophical knowledge and literary talent, he was competent in Greek (despite not being a philologist!), was familiar with the culture of antiquity, and collaborated closely with eminent experts on Plato (such as Spalding and Heindorf).[87]

Boeckh praises Schleiermacher's analysis of Plato's language, the form and composition of the dialogues. In his opinion, *Platons Werke* provides its readers with the key to Plato's thought and art – a thoroughly dramatic art, because by precisely arranging the individual scenes of his drama, he allows the discussants to arrive at a common idea.[88]

The reviewer then turns to the translation itself. He states that there is a consensus of opinion that a translation should convey not only the content, but also the form, the way the content is presented, as well as what is individual about the lan-

---

84 Quoted after: ibid., 58. Ast also points out a number of errors made by the translator at the syntactic, semantic, and historical level.
85 August Boeckh, "Kritik der Uebersetzung des Platon von Schleiermacher", *Heidelbergische Jahrbücher der Literatur für Theologie, Philosophie und Pädagogik* 1808, H. 1; cited after the reprint in idem, *Gesammelte Kleine Schriften*, vol. 7: *Kritiken*, eds. Ferdinand Aschersohn, Paul Eichholz (Leipzig: Tuebner, 1872), 1.
86 Ibid., 2.
87 Ibid., 3.
88 Ibid., 12.

guage. What is in dispute, however, is whether that which is purely national in the language should be translated/transferred to our own land (*zu uns übergetragen*), or whether it should be transformed in such a way as to give the impression that the author has become one of us and himself speaks our language. But, asks Boeckh, what sort of idea is this: to separate the author's spirit from that of his nation, to wrest it away from the environment in which it developed? How can the link between thought and word be severed? After all, a brilliant representation, in which the spirit shines through the language and the sign melts into what it signifies, is a delicate shell. If an ancient Greek appeared among us, the reviewer argues, he would, after all, speak in his own language, and if he switched language, his perception of reality would also change.[89] Therefore, one should not reject Plato faithfully rendered in German, in a language that, while hosting an ancient Greek philosopher, retains its inner essence. Boeckh thus welcomes a Plato who, while wearing his Hellenistic garb, treads with dignity among contemporary German audiences.[90]

In Boeckh's opinion, the impression that one has when reading Schleiermacher's rendering of the whole and larger parts of the dialogues is almost the same as that of interacting with the original. Of course, to the extent that this is possible, since each ancient original retains something of its own, indescribable, which no translation can convey.[91] On the other hand, the style of the translation imitates, in Boeckh's opinion, not so much the Hellenic as the Platonic idiom – the characteristic briefness and conciseness was achieved by Schleiermacher through the use of ellipses and a specific syntax, drawing out the "dialectical clarity" of the original. He eliminated the repetitions that are typical of the German language, but alien to Plato's prose. The loose Greek syntax did not pose a problem for the translator, as he is not inclined to pedantry. Schleiermacher was to translate certain linguistic structures of the original from the original into German, without distorting the language.[92]

Boeckh stresses that the translation is very faithful to the original, which among other things is said to be evidenced by the fact that the rhythm of the prose is maintained, especially when poetic fragments are translated.[93] Similarly in the case of language games: Schleiermacher does not abandon them, but tries to render them faithfully or replace them with similar ones.[94] The minor errors and oversights of the volumes under discussion do not dampen Boeckh's joy at the fact that German readers would soon be receiving all of Plato. And what nation could better understand what is Hellenistic? – asks the reviewer, rhetorically.[95]

---

89 Ibid., 17. See in this context a similar passage by Schleiermacher in his lecture *On the Different Methods of Translating* (1813), DR 228, KGA I/11, 74 ff.
90 Ibid., 18.
91 Ibid.
92 Ibid., 19–20.
93 Ibid., 21.
94 Ibid., 22.
95 Ibid., 23.

In Schleiermacher's paratexts and notes to Plato, one finds very little information about the theoretical-translational foundations of his work. Nevertheless, important thoughts in this regard do appear in the Berlin lecture *On the Different Methods of Translating* (1813), where Schleiermacher presents a hermeneutical analysis of translation that focuses on the author rather than the original text. It is based on the notion that, on the one hand, every author remains in under the power of his own native language, which generates his thinking, while on the other hand, he has the possibility to shape language to his own liking (KGA I/11, 70–71). Therefore, every work of verbal art (*Wortkunstwerk*) is a product of language and at the same time an expression of the creative spirit of the individual. In Plato's texts, too, the spirit of language and the genius of the author together form a unity. The great challenge for the translator is to convey to his readers this foreign unity in its uniqueness. Essentially, he has two methods at his disposal here: to encourage the reader to move closer to what is foreign, or to bring the foreign into the world in which the reader resides (KGA I/11, 75).

It is very often claimed that in his translation of Plato, Schleiermacher consistently applied the first of the above-mentioned methods, namely that of *foreignization*. Evidence for this is sought at the stylistic level of translation. "The spirit of our language differs from that of the Greek language, which is distinguished by an abundance of participles and a periodic style," wrote Otto Apelt, the editor and translator of Plato, an advocate of *domestication* in translation, at the beginning of the twentieth century.[96] "And it is here," he continued his thought, "that Schleiermacher succeeded in achieving true virtuosity in his art of imitation."[97] But for Apelt, this did not at all mean a "triumph of the art of translation," since such a strategy can, he feels, impede the assimilation of content.[98] As we recall, such a problem was not perceived by Boeckh, but such critical opinions did appear during Schleiermacher's lifetime, and they continue to appear regularly today.[99] They are based on a far-from-true view that Plato's Greek is especially characterized by participles and particular syntactic structures,[100] or the unfounded claim that Schleiermacher (like medieval

---

[96] Otto Apelt, *Vorwort* [1919], in Plato, *Sämtliche Dialoge*, vol. 1, ed. Otto Apelt (Hamburg: Meiner, 2004), VII.
[97] Ibid.
[98] Ibid.
[99] From among the more recent works, cf. e.g. Lutz Käppel's article argues that Schleiermacher did indeed produce a philosophical discourse in German, but nevertheless "quite like the Greek original," which does not seem to agree with Schleiermacher's own views – Lutz Käppel (*Re-)Konstruktion von Antike als (Neu-)Konstruktion von Moderne. Schleiermachers Auseinandersetzung mit Platon und Heraklit*, in *Reformation und Moderne. Pluralität – Subjektivität – Kritik. Akten des Internationalen Kongresses der Schleiermacher-Gesellschaft in Halle (Saale), März 2017*, eds. Jörg Dierken, Arnulf von Scheliha, Sarah Schmidt (Berlin: Walter de Gruyter, 2018), 708.
[100] These phenomena (especially the participles denoting function and result) are related to the gradual scholarly understanding of everyday language in Greek philosophy – see Bruno Snell, *The Discovery of the Mind: The Greek Origins of European Thought*, trans. Thomas G. Rosenmeyer (Oxford:

translators of Greek) overzealously "imitated" Plato's idiom, without much concern for his readers. An objective assessment of this level of translation is also rendered difficult by the need to abstract away, in this context, from the "classicism" that prevailed in the theory of translation from ancient languages in the early nineteenth century, whose most prominent representative was Johann Heinrich Voß.[101] It is also significant that criticism of the language of Schleiermacher's Plato translation often goes hand in hand with a dislike for the linguistic aesthetics of the Romantics, especially the Schlegel brothers.[102]

Schleiermacher sees the translation of philosophical discourse as a difficult undertaking, for it is here that the differences between linguistic systems are most clearly revealed. As he states in his lecture on translation methods:

> Here more than anywhere else [...] every language embodies a single system of concepts whose contiguous, connective, and complementary relationships form a single whole, individual parts of which can never correspond to individual parts of other systems (DR 236; KGA I/11, 89).

This linguistic system is the "well of all wisdom" from which a philosopher "buckets out what can be reached by hand" [*schöpft aus dem Vorhandenen*]" to create something new – his wisdom finds expression within his language. According to Schleiermacher, the translator of a philosophical text is faced with a choice: he can "contort" the language of the translation in line with the language of the original, or he can simply paraphrase the philosopher's speech. Or, he can opt to "rebuild his author's entire wit and wisdom [*Weisheit und Wissenschaft*] within the target-language conceptual system," which can, however, end up lapsing into irresponsible arbitrariness (DR 236; KGA I/11, 90). Schleiermacher admits that he has Plato in mind here. However, it is not the text itself and its conceptuality, but the author and his concepts that are taken as the object of linguistic transfer. Thus it is not a philosopher's writing, but rather his speech that is presented as a problem for the theory of translation.

Basil Blackwell, 1953), Chapter XII. Cf. also in this respect the detailed philological description of *Plato's* style presented by Ulrich von Wilamowitz-Moellendorff, in which the author does not limit himself to just a few features – Ulrich von Wilamowitz-Moellendorff, *Platon – Beilagen und Textkritik*, 3rd ed. (Berlin: Weidmannsche Verlagsbuchhandlung, 1962), 412–429.

101 See Josefine Kitzbichler, Katja Lubitz and Nina Mindt, *Dokumente zur Theorie der Übersetzung antiker Literatur in Deutschland seit 1800* (Berlin: Walter de Gruyter, 2009), 18–24. Without addressing this or other historical issues, contemporary translation scholars usually present unconvincing analyses of Schleiermacher's Platonic translations. A case in point is Theo Hermans, who repeats the allegation of the supposedly Greek syntax of these translations. See Theo Hermans, "Schleiermacher and Plato, Hermeneutics and Translation," in *Friedrich Schleiermacher and the Question of Translation*, eds. Larisa Cercel and Adriana Şerban (Berlin: Walter de Gruyter, 2015), 84.

102 See, for example, Charlotte von Schiller's critique, quoted in: Lutz Käppel (*Re-)Konstruktion von Antike als (Neu-)Konstruktion von Moderne*, 708.

4 Schleiermacher's *Phaedrus* – selected aspects of the translator's strategy

Let us now examine what Schleiermacher's confrontation with the Platonic original looked like in practice. If we follow carefully his footnotes to individual dialogues in the second edition of *Platons Werke*, we will notice that he practices a translation-oriented philology.[103] The assumptions he makes and readings he adopts, as well as those of others,[104] help him to constitute an original text that functions as the basis of his translation. Sometimes, however, a conflict arises between the philological ethos and the pragmatics of translation, since the translator's understanding marked by intentionality (*Verstehensinteresse*) must also take into account the intended transfer of the original and thus its communicability. Phenomena such as ambiguity and foreignness, seen from this perspective, appear as obstacles to communication. This is also the case in the *Phaedrus*, in the passage with Socrates' Homeric invocation (237a). Schleiermacher translates it this way: "*Wohlan denn, o Musen! mögt ihr nun wegen einer Art des Gesanges die hochgekehlten heißen, oder nach dem langhalsigen Geschlecht der tonreichen Schwäne diesen Namen führen [...]*" (KGA IV/3, 141–143).[105] As Schleiermacher explains in the second edition of *Platons Werke*:

> In this difficult place, the correct sense of which will perhaps never be established with absolute certainty, I have opted for an altogether unlikely interpretation, guided rather by the appeal of easier translatability [*der Reiz der leichteren Uebertragbarkeit*] than by any firm conviction [...] (KGA IV/3, 143).

The passage is indeed difficult, since Socrates permits himself to play, depending on the accent, with different meanings of the epithet of the Muses (*epitheum ornans*) – *ligeiai* (λίγειαι) – also evoking the words *ligòs/λιγὺς* ("loud") and *ligos/λίγυς* ("Ligurian," "of the people of the land of Liguria"). Schleiermacher opts to resolve this difficulty by means of a highly suggestive literary reference to swans (*Schwäne*). Although the presence of swans in Schleiermacher's translation appears incidental at first glance, is actually based on Heindorf's commentary, which refers to Kyknos ("the Swan") as the ruler of the Ligurians.[106] In the interpretation formulated by the

---

103 Schleiermacher himself explains in the *Vorerinnerung* that the footnotes he added serve two functions: they are meant to support his interpretation of the dialogues in detail, but also to clarify what "might be less understandable for uninformed readers" (KGA IV/3, 9).
104 Primarily those of Heindorf and Bekker.
105 In the running text, I present passages of Schleiermacher's translation in the original German (as this is the only sensible way to make the points I wish to make), instead of attempting to gloss or re-translate them. When pertinent, however, at times I also compare Schleiermacher's German to a few of the numerous extant translations of the *Phaedrus* into other languages (English, Polish, Swedish).
106 See the editors' footnote in KGA IV/3, 143.

translator in the target text, the original image acquires a literary grace – the double (linguistic and cultural) foreignness of this invocation, reinforced by the etymological suggestion based on paronomasia, in Schleiermacher's explicative translation ends up hardly noticeable. We can compare this, for instance, to the very different tack taken in the English translation by Nehamas and Woodruff, which has Socrates saying in 237a: "Come to me, O you clear-voiced Muses, whether you are called so because of the quality of your song, or from the musical people of Liguria" – a significantly less reader-friendly version, which the translators try to rescue by attaching a quite technical footnote explaining the link Plato is presumably drawing between the "clear-voiced" Muses and the phonologically similar name of the Ligurians.[107]

Moving on to another example passage, in the same speech by Socrates (237d), we read in the Schleiermacher's German: "*Wir müssen demnach bemerken, daß es in einem Jeden von uns zwei herrschende und führende Triebe giebt, welchen wir folgen, wie sie eben führen, eine eingebohrne Begierde nach dem Angenehmen und eine erworbene Gesinnung, welche nach dem Besten strebt*" (KGA IV/3, 147–149). In the relevant footnote Schleiermacher admits that he dared to render the important concepts *idea/ἰδέα* and *doxa/δόξα* occurring here as *Trieb* ("drive") and *Gesinnung* ("sentiment"),[108] respectively. The freedom exercised by the translator here, however, requires, by his own admission, a certain "defense" (*einer Vertheidigung*). For why did he not opt for a "seemingly more literal translation"? First, because "it would be too unpleasant to our ears if desire [*die Begierde*] were to be called an idea [*eine Idee*], while the rational will [*das vernünftige Wollen*] is called an opinion [*eine Meinung*]" (KGA IV/3, 147).

---

107 Indeed, Nehamas and Woodruff even make note of their own philological evaluation that this purported etymological link is "far-fetched" – Plato, *Phaedrus*, trans. Alexander Nehamas, Paul Woodruff, in Plato, *Complete Works*, ed. John M. Cooper (Indianapolis: Hackett, 1997), 516. Hackforth's English translation takes a similar approach, maintaining the opaque reference to the Ligurians and explaining in a footnote that this is one of "those etymological jests" which Plato "sometimes rather pointlessly indulges" – *Plato's Phaedrus*, trans. Reginald Hackforth (Cambridge: Cambridge Univ. Press, 1952), 36. These versions – as well as Schleiermacher's – might be contrasted with, for instance, Edward Zwolski's starkly foreignizing Polish translation – Platon, *Phaidros*, trans. Edward Zwolski (Kraków: Aureus, 1996), 57. Cf. the Polish commentary on this translation problem by Leopold Regner in: Plato, *Faidros*, translation, introduction, commentary and index by Leopold Regner (Warsaw: PWN, 1993), 17 and also the German translation by Kurt Hildebrandt: Plato, *Phaidros oder Vom Schönen*, trans. Kurt Hildebrandt (Stuttgart: Reclam, 1957), 8, http://www.peter-matussek. de/Leh/V_06_Material/V_06_M_08/Phaidros_Dialog.pdf (accessed 20 September 2019).
108 KGA IV/3, 147. Nehamas & Woodruff's English translation has: "We must realize that each of us is ruled by two principles which we follow wherever they lead: one is our inborn desire for pleasures, the other is our acquired judgement that pursues what is best" (*Phaedrus,* trans. Alexander Nehamas, Paul Woodruff, 516); Hackforth's translation uses a similar opposition between "desire" and "judgement" (*Plato's Phaedrus*, trans. Reginald Hackforth, p 38). Władysław Witwicki's Polish version, in turn, opts instead for the opposition "*istota*" ("essence") vs. "*rozsądek*" ("reason") – Platon, *Fajdros*, trans. Władysław Witwicki (Warsaw: PWN, 1958), 56. Edward Zwolski, on the other hand, evokes a monumental effect of foreignness here by using poetic phrases and the Polish word "*mniemanie*" ("opinion") for *idea* (*Phaidros*, trans. Edward Zwolski, 58).

Such a juxtaposition of terms would therefore sound foreign, evoking a distinct dissonance in the reader. Secondly, this decision was motivated by the fact that a literal translation, passing over contextual references, would "falsify the Platonic sense to a much greater extent" by imparting a foreign emphasis to the original. Schleiermacher has in mind here an emphasis thus revealed in the language on the "fusion [*Verschmelzung*] of the theoretical with the practical," which, in his view, is absent in the original (KGA IV/3, 147). A less literal translation appears from this perspective not only more reader-friendly, but also closer to what is considered to be the original sense. After all, the effect of strangeness ("desire" as an *idea*) could ultimately contribute to the transfer of a false image of the original, i.e. distorting the reception of its sense.

In his lectures on the history of philosophy, Schleiermacher argues that the concept of *idea* has a real and an ideal aspect, representing "a higher combination between Heraclitus and Anaxagoras" (between phenomenon and reason).[109] The essence of the science of ideas, he argues, is that the abstract "unity of the concept" (εἶδος) is at the same time a "real, actual entity" which has a dynamic character (ἰδέα).[110] The term εἶδος or ἰδέα is used depending on whether we are dealing with the former, or the latter kind, of relation (*Beziehung*) or *aspect* of being.[111] The *idea* appears here as a "productive force of nature," a kind of paradigm for becoming, which legitimizes the German equivalent *Trieb* proposed in Schleiermacher's *Phaedrus*.

The matter is not a simple one, however. As Gunter Scholtz aptly observes,[112] this differentiation of concepts seems rather dubious in the light of Schleiermacher's *Dialectics 1814/15*: "According to the ancient Platonic convention," we read in this work, "a distinction is not drawn between the words εἶδος, ἰδέα, γένος, which are used as terms for what is general, as constituted either in thought or in reality."[113] Although the linguistic "differentiation within the idea concept" (G. Scholtz)[114] is not easy to document, Schleiermacher nevertheless insisted on his own interpretation of Plato's science of ideas because it corresponded to an idealist philosophy of identity close to his own thinking (and to the spirit of Romanticism), which is based on a logic of differentiation and synthesis.[115] In the excerpt I have analyzed,

---

[109] Friedrich Schleiermacher, *Geschichte der Philosophie*, ed. Heinrich Ritter (*Sämmtliche Werke*, Abt. III, vol. 4/1) (Berlin: Reimer, 1839), 104.
[110] Ibid.
[111] See Gunter Scholtz, "Schleiermacher und die platonische Ideenlehre," in *Internationaler Schleiermacher-Kongreß Berlin 1984*, ed. Kurt-Victor Selge, vol. 2 (Berlin: Walter de Gruyter, 1985), 861.
[112] Gunter Scholtz, *Ethik und Hermeneutik – Schleiermachers Grundlegung der Geisteswissenschaften* (Frankfurt am Main: Suhrkamp, 1995), 273.
[113] *Ausarbeitung zur Dialektik (1814/15)*, KGA II/10,1, 118.
[114] Scholtz, *Ethik und Hermeneutik*, 273.
[115] See Scholtz, *Schleiermacher und die platonische Ideenlehre*, 862. On this Romantic paradigm of Plato interpretation in which Schleiermacher was part of, see Giovanni Reale, *Towards a New Inter-*

this differentiating philosophical interpretation organizes the ambiguity prevailing in the original speech. Note, however, that it is precisely this kind of speech – often resisting strangeness and ambiguity – that invites us, as it were, into a discussion about the philosophical meaning of the dialogue.

Noting how Plato's use of language often confounds us, Diogenes Laertius writes that he "used a variety of terms in order to make his system less intelligible to the ignorant." Plato also used – the ancient biographer and historian of philosophy adds – "the same words in a number of different senses."[116] This strategy might be linked to the hermetic aspect of Plato's science, but it seems that in confronting his audience with such a challenge, the philosopher wanted to invite them into a joint thinking exercise, to show knowledge to be something that arises within ourselves. We should also remember that he created his philosophical language by imparting metaphorical meanings to common words. By combining what belongs to the world of phenomena with what belongs to the inner world of the mind, Plato deliberately generates a tension between the primary (colloquial, sensual) and secondary contexts of the expression used. Therefore, as Hannah Arendt writes in analyzing this practice, his *idea* (εἶδος) is the "image or model perceived beforehand by the craftsman's eye," guiding the fabrication process, which "not only precedes it, but does not disappear with the finished product, which it survives intact, present, as it were, to lend itself to an infinite continuation of fabrication."[117] Metaphorical translation of concepts is thus intelligible and pedagogically effective, as long as we do not lose sight of the original.

But is this thoughtful, philosophical work with the concepts of *idea* and *doxa* possible on the basis of the Schleiermacher's translation? Does Plato's philosophically inspiring speech shine through the text of his translation? The German text embodies Schleiermacher's interpretation of Plato's philosophy, according to which the German notions of *Trieb* and *Gesinnung* may function as contextual (and thus *not* foreign-sounding) equivalents of the original Greek notions. In the case of the latter, however, the use of contextual lexical equivalents makes it impossible to render the semantic space in which they attain their meaning, and thus also the transformative dynamics of these concepts.[118] One may, therefore, get the impression that

---

pretation of Plato, trans. John R. Catan, Richard Davies (Washington, D.C.: Catholic Univ. of America Press, 1996).

116 Diogenes Laertius, *Lives of the Eminent Philosophers*, trans. Pamela Mensch, ed. James Miller (Oxford: Oxford Univ. Press, 2018), 160 (§ 63).
117 Hannah Arendt, *The Human Condition*, 2nd ed. (Chicago: Chicago Univ. Press, 1988), 141–142.
118 See the important comment in this regard by William K.C. Guthrie: "Even in contemporary languages, beyond a few words for material objects, it is practically impossible to translate a word so as to give exactly the same impression to a foreigner as is given by the original to those who hear it in their own country. With the Greeks, these difficulties are greatly increased by the lapse of time and difference of cultural environment [...]. When we have to rely on single-word English equivalents like 'justice' or 'virtue' without an acquaintance with the various usages of their Greek counterparts in different contexts, we not only lose a great deal of the content of the *Greek* words but import our

Schleiermacher's translation, as a product, embodies not so much a philological as a *pragmatic* model of the transfer of meaning, which focuses on an optimal representation of the original as read today. This model, as we recall, is related to the widely understood rhetorical paradigm in translation theory.

This tendency can be illustrated by another example passage. "*Denn wenn der Anfang aus etwas entstände, so entstände nichts mehr aus dem Anfang*" – Schleiermacher's Socrates states in his second speech (245d), but it is not entirely clear what he means. The translator's self-commentary reads: "To translate the word ἀρχή by means of some unnatural equivalent would be dangerous if one has in mind a reader who is not at home in Hellenistic thought" (KGA IV/3, 201).[119] Schleiermacher thus abandons the translational equivalent he had initially opted for – *Urgrund* ("primordial ground") – in the first draft of his translation that has survived in manuscript form, which includes corrections and suggestions by Friedrich Schlegel.[120] This concern for the reader makes it clear that Schleiermacher takes a pragmatic approach, translating for audiences who are not "experts" (*Kenner*) in Greek. Therefore, the Platonic text is autonomous in his translation and can in no way be considered merely an "optimal reading aid" for those who wish to grapple with the original.[121]

---

own English associations which are often quite foreign to the intention of the Greek." – W[illiam] K[eith] C[hambers] Guthrie, *The Greek Philosophers: from Thales to Aristotle* (New York: Harper Torchbooks, 1975), 4.

119 Nehamas & Woodruff's translation opts for "source" ("[...] a source has no beginning. That is because anything that has a beginning comes from some source, but there is no source for this, since a source that got its start from something else would no longer be the source" – *Phaedrus*, trans. Alexander Nehamas, Paul Woodruff, 524), while Hackforth's uses "first principle" ("while anything that comes to be must come to be from a first principle, the latter itself cannot come to be from anything whatsoever: if it did, it would cease any longer to be a first principle" – *Plato's Phaedrus*, trans. Reginald Hackforth, p 63). Zwolski's Polish translation, on the other hand, takes a surprising turn towards foreignization: "*Początek zaś nierodem. Z konieczności bowiem wszystko co rodne z początku się rodzi, a początek z niczego się nie rodzi. Gdyby bowiem z czegokolwiek się rodził, nie rodziłby się jako początek*" (Platon, *Phaidros*, trans. Edward Zwolski, 77). Zwolski toys here with the meanings of Polish *rodzić* "give birth/rise to," *rodzić się z* "be born of," *ród* "origin from which something springs" – ultimately yielding an effect not so distant from that of *Ursprung, Urgrund*.

120 KGA IV/3, 201, editors' note. Cf. the effect of foreignness generated by Kurt Hildebrandt's translation in which ἀρχή is indeed translated as *Urgrund*: "*Urgrund ist ungeworden. Denn aus dem Urgrund muß notwendig alles Entstehende entstehen, dieser aber nicht aus irgend etwas. Denn wenn der Urgrund aus einem Etwas entstünde, entstünde er nicht aus dem Urgrund. Da er ungeworden ist, muß er notwendig auch unvergänglich sein. Denn wenn der Urgrund verlorenginge, würde weder der aus etwas, noch ein Anderes aus ihm entstehen, da doch aus dem Urgrunde alles entstehen muß*" (*Phaidros oder Vom Schönen*, trans. Kurt Hildebrandt, 14).

121 As is argued, for example, by Rainer Kohlmayer, "Das Ohr vernimmts gleich und hasst den hinkenden Boten (Herder). Kritische Anmerkungen zu Schleiermachers Übersetzungstheorie und -praxis", in *Friedrich Schleiermacher and the Question of Translation*, eds. Larisa Cercel and Adriana Şerban (Berlin: Walter de Gruyter, 2015), 111.

Even the earliest readers of Plato were fascinated by the philosopher's linguistic inventiveness, his artistic diction, which the early Friedrich Schlegel perceived as dithyrambic, or even musical.[122] Schleiermacher, too, paid heed to the word games that often appeared in Plato's dialogues, considering them an important element of the linguistic artistry of the author of the *Phaedrus*. Indeed, homonymy, polysemy or paronomasia are not ornaments of speech in Plato's works, but forms that makes it possible to achieve a poetic and philosophical *density of meaning*. Literary scholars stress that the role of language games is to draw the reader's attention to the "linguistic" nature of an utterance, and thus to the poetic function of language. Where this function predominates, the standard referentiality of the message is weakened, while the self-referentiality (and thus self-reflexivity) of the text is highlighted, thus taking on a far-reaching autonomy.[123] This is how texts reveal their own textuality, so to speak. This phenomenon shapes the discursive mechanisms of texts, at this level revealing irony, ambiguity and transversality. The original, revealing its poetics and textuality, is undoubtedly a real nuisance for the translator, who is forced to operate on the border of non-translatability.

Also worth stressing here is the philological significance of Plato's language games: these distinctions of style are often taken into account when the authenticity of individual dialogues is analyzed through textual criticism. For example, the clever wordplay in *Hipparchus* is cited as proof that the dialogue is authentic, rather than pseudo-Platonic.[124] Schleiermacher, for example, also regards the wordplay ἔρωτα/ Πτερωτα in the verse of the Homeric scholars (*Phaedrus*, 252c), which cannot be properly translated, to be "authentically Platonic [...] wordplay" (KGA IV/3, 247).[125]

Elsewhere in the dialogue under review, Socrates closes his speech (238b-c) as follows, in Schleiermacher's translation:

Nämlich die vernunftlose jene auf das Bessere bestrebte Gesinnung beherrschende Begierde, zur Lust an der Schönheit geführt, und wiederum von den ihr verwandten Begierden auf die Schönheit der Leiber hingeführt, wenn sie sich kräftig verstärkt und den Sieg errungen hat in der Leitung, erhält von ihrem Gegenstande, dem Leibe, den Namen, und wird Liebe genannt (KGA IV/3, 151–153).

In a relevant footnote, the translator explains the difficulties posed by the original: "In the source language the words ἔρως and ῥώμη, love and strength, comprise a language game [...]. Since it is impossible to render it, keeping a similar sense, but also

---

[122] See Friedrich Schlegel, KFSA II: *Charakteristiken und Kritiken I. 1796–1801*, ed. Hans Eichner (Paderborn: Schöningh, 1967), 156.
[123] See Volker Wiemann, *Funktion, ästhetische/poetische*, in *Metzler Lexikon Literatur und Kulturtheorie*, ed. Ansgar Nünning, 3rd ed. (Stuttgart: J.B. Metzler, 2004), 204.
[124] Cf. the translator's notes and footnotes to Regner's Polish translation of the dialogue *Hipparchus, or on greed* (*Hipparch czyli o zachłanności*, in Pseudo-Platon, *Zimorodek i inne dialogi* [Halcyon and Other Dialogues] trans. Leopold Regner, Warsaw: PWN, 1985).
[125] For the play on the words "Eros" and "Winged"/"Feathered," see *Faidros*, trans. Leopold Regner, 36.

impossible to leave this space empty, the best solution turned out to be to imitate one of our poets. See *Poems* A.W. Schlegel, p. 205" (KGA IV/3, 153).

The translator is faced here with the difficult task of translating etymological language-games that include the adjective ἐρρωμένως ('powerful').[126] This task was solved by various translators of Plato in different ways, with many of them attempting to transpose the conceptual sense of the etymological affinity of "power" and "love" thematized in the original, which often had a negative impact on the readability and intelligibility of the target text.[127] Schleiermacher opts to "imitate" and, inspired by the poem *Deutung* by August Wilhelm Schlegel, proposes the pair of *Leib – Liebe* ("body" – "love").[128] This solution is, one has to admit, quite elegant, but it does not really convey the foreign thought and speech contained in the original – on the contrary, it resounds with the poetic rhetoric of the Romantics, very familiar in the early nineteenth century. In comparison with, for example, Nehemas and Woodruff's English translation, in which the original encroaches into the target text with all the force of the Greek nouns *rhōmē* and *erōs*,[129] Schleiermacher's German translation successfully defends itself against the power and suggestiveness of the original (connotations connected with Eros!). Anachronism, which Schleiermacher usually tried to avoid as an interpreter, although was not always able to,[130] turns out in this case to be a reader-friendly strategy, allowing him to convey the poetic beauty of the "real" Plato.[131] It is doubtful, however, whether this strategy will open up the way for the reader to explore the transformative dynamics of the

---

[126] On the significance of this language game in the *Phaedrus*, cf. Tushar Irani, *Plato on the Value of Philosophy: The Art of Argument in the Gorgias and Phaedrus* (Cambridge: Cambridge Univ. Press, 2017) 118–119. Julia A. Lamm stresses the dynamic notion of *erōs* in Plato's dialectics: it "provides the movement, the impulse toward philosophical communication" (Lamm, *Schleiermacher's Plato*, 93).

[127] Witwicki's Polish version proposes a literarily sophisticated solution to this pseudo-dithyramb. In his commentary, the Polish translator points out that Socrates underlines his definition of love with "alliterations, assonations and jokes" (*Fajdros*, trans. Władysław Witwicki, 57 and 155).

[128] See the publishers' footnote, KGA IV/3, 153. Here are two tercets from the sonnet by August Wilhelm Schlegel: "*Doch unauflöslich Leib und Geist verweben / Ist das Geheimniß aller Lust und Liebe; / Leiblich und geistig wird sie Quell des Lebens. // Im Manne waltet die Gewalt des Strebens; / Des Weibes Füll' umhüllet stille Triebe: / Wo Liebe lebt und labt, ist lieb das Leben*" – August Wilhelm Schlegel, *Poetische Werke*, pt. 1: *Vermischte Gedichte, Lieder, Romanzen und Sonette*, ed. Eduard Böcking (*Sämmtliche Werke*, vol. 1) (Leipzig: Weidmann, 1846), 355.

[129] Nehamas & Woodruff's English version is: "The unreasoning desire that overpowers a person's considered impulse to do right and is driven to take pleasure in beauty, its force reinforced by its kindred desires for beauty in human bodies – this desire, all-conquering in its forceful drive, takes its name from the word for force (*rhōmē*) and is called *erōs*." (Plato, *Phaedrus*, trans. Alexander Nehamas, Paul Woodruff, 517). Hackforth's English version avoids the issue in the translation itself, but debates the etymological issues in a philological footnote (*Plato's Phaedrus*, trans. Reginald Hackforth, 39).

[130] See Gadamer, *Schleiermacher als Platoniker*, 148.

[131] Cf. Hermans, *Schleiermacher and Plato*, 88.

Greek concepts Plato used, and thus a way into the world of the ancient Greeks. For as Martin Heidegger wrote whilst striving to translate a passage from Parmenides, the point is "[t]hat we ourselves, instead of merely transposing the Greek terms into terms of our language, pass over into the Greek sphere [...]. This passage is hard – not in itself, only for us. But it is not impossible."[132] Besides, Schleiermacher himself noted in his early period: "Plato's playing with language [*Sprachspielerei*] is a genuinely dialogical element and should be properly imitated, especially where a concept is shown through it" (*Gedanken V*, KGA I/3, 294).

In the footnotes to the *Phaedrus* we find ample testimony to the fact that a translation-oriented philological analysis may prove inconclusive. They are important because they convey an interesting picture of the foreign original, which is not discernible from the perspective of the reader of the target text. As an example of this, consider the proverb used by Socrates: γλυκὺς ἀγκών [ὦ Φαῖδρε] λέληθέ(ν) σε (257d; literally: "sweet elbow/bend, pleasant curve"[133]). This phrase in the original was and still is difficult for most scholars to understand, despite Hermias' explications. Interpreters are not, as Schleiermacher complains, in consensus as to its "source and meaning" (KGA IV/3, 277). Since the meaning of the idiom is difficult to grasp and does not seem to correspond to the context of the conversation or the work as a whole, some commentators have surmised that a gloss, and therefore an inauthentic element, got subsequently inserted here into Socrates' statement.[134] If a translation is supposed to convey a meaning that underlies the coherence of the dialogue, this kind of uncertainty obviously has an impact on the translator's work. It is possible for the translator to take the risk of foreignness, ambiguity and inconsistency (as Stolberg and Georgii would do in their foreignizing translations

---

132 Martin Heidegger, *What Is Called Thinking?*, trans. Fred D. Wieck and J. Glenn Gray (New York: Harper & Row, 1968), 226.
133 See publishers' footnote (38), KGA IV/3, 277
134 This is especially true of the words following the phrase in question, ὅτι ἀπὸ τοῦ μακροῦ ἀγκῶνος τοῦ κατὰ (tone) Νεῖλον ἐκλήθη, which may be regarded as an explication an idiomatic phrase. Due to the "impossibility of an exact translation" of the proverb, Schleiermacher is, as he admits, unable to make a final decision about the words. "They do not give the impression of being Platonic despite the extant manuscripts," the translator concludes (KGA IV/3, 279). Citing Heindorf and Schleiermacher, the phrase is omitted by Regner (Plato, *Faidros*, 42). Hackforth, for example, takes a different view: "There is no justification in bracketing the words ὅτι... ἐκλήθη with Heindorf and Robin; indeed, γλυκὺς ἀγκών λέληθέ(ν) σε would be intolerably abrupt and obscure by itself" (*Plato's Phaedrus*, trans. with an introd. and comm. by Reginald Hackforth, Cambridge: Cambridge Univ. Press, 1952, 113). Nehamas and Woodruff's English translation has Socrates saying: "Phaedrus, you don't understand the expression 'Pleasant Bend' – it originally referred to the long bend of the Nile" – to which the translators attach a footnote: "Apparently this was a familiar example of something named by language that means the opposite – though called 'pleasant' it was really a long, nasty bend." (Plato, *Phaedrus*, trans. Alexander Nehamas, Paul Woodruff, 534). Witwicki's Polish version proceeds similarly, proposing a translation with almost no omissions, but at the same time with impressive literary inventiveness (Platon, *Fajdros*, 90).

into German),[135] or to retreat into the conviction that the basis of the translation should be the text that is understood, that is clear for the philologist and translator and taken as the authentic work of the author.

In the first version of his translation, preserved in the manuscript, Schleiermacher tried to render this difficult phrase with a German proverb: "*Du weißt noch nicht, Phaidros, wo die Glocken hängen* [...]" (KGA IV/3, 276). However, in the first and second editions of *Platons Werke*, he abandoned this solution, proposing as an equivalent "sense of this proverb" the neutral "*Du weißt nur nicht, wie dies zusammenhängt, Phädros* [...]" (KGA IV/3, 277).[136] In this edition, after a brief comment on this passage, Schleiermacher states: "the proverb has not been translated because it cannot be rendered literally, and the possible equivalents at our disposal in our language do not seem noble enough" (KGA IV/3, 277–279). Abandonment and neutralization thus make it possible to convey a meaningful argument to the German reader. What appears foreign, obscure, and (perhaps) inauthentic in the original is thus dealt with in the paratext.[137] With this, the fundamental problem of the *Phaedrus* – the question of its inconsistencies, ambiguities and vagueness (referred to in the dialogue as immanent features of *text*)[138] – is, at best, transferred to the footnotes at the end of the volume.

It seems that a certain preliminary conclusion can be drawn here regarding the problem of the original in Schleiermacher's translation of *Phaedrus*. In a footnote, Schleiermacher admits that he had read this fragment of the text "from several manuscripts at Bekker's" (KGA IV/3, 337), which means that, through reading of often uncertain sources, he integrated his own original (the meaning of the term *zusammenlesen* used by Schleiermacher in this context being key here) into a unified whole, which is supposed to represent an ideal, coherent source text (*Urtext*), possessing the property that it can be transformed into a target text fulfilling specific expectations. As an object of philological scrutiny, the original may reveal its foreignness and obscurity, but as a source text it generally turns out to be an information

---

135 Cf. "*Du weißt wohl nicht, o Phädros! daß das Sprüchwort süsser Ellebogen von jener grossen Krümmung des Nils seinen Ursprung habe*" in Stolberg's translation (Plato, *Auserlesene Gespräche*, pt. 1, 1796, after KGA IV/3, 277) and "*Ein Glykys Ankon, o Phaidros!*" in Georgii's translation (Plato, *Werke*, Gruppe 1: *Gespräche zur Verherrlichung des Sokrates*, 2: *Phaidros oder vom Schönen. Lysis oder von der Freundschaft*, trans. by Ludwig Georgii (Stuttgart: Metzler, 1853), 138). In both cases, the translations of the idiom have been explained in footnotes.
136 It is worth noting that Schleiermacher also altered the spelling of the dialogue hero's name from *Phaidros* in the manuscript to the more Germanized *Phädros* in the first edition.
137 This is also the strategy adopted, for example, by the Swedish translator of the new edition of Plato's works, published in a form friendly to modern readers. He paraphrases the proverb we are considering, whilst quoting the "original text" (in Swedish) in an endnote. See Plato, *Faidros*, in idem, *Skrifter. Bok 2*, trans. Jan Stolpe (Stockholm: Atlantis, 2001), 347 and 499.
138 See Kahn, *Plato and the Socratic Dialogue*, 372 and 377.

offer for the recipient, i.e. the German reader.[139] The foreign original is present in the paratextual domain (and is problematized there), while the target text enjoys autonomy and projects its own model reader, who is not so much a specialist, but rather a connoisseur of literary art, able to appreciate the artistry of the philosophical text presented to him. Hence the translator's exceptional care for the artistic unity and literary quality of the translated work. It is true that Schleiermacher also makes use of the effect of "foreign semblance" (*fremde Ähnlichkeit*), but always for the purpose of emphasizing what is characteristically Greek in the speech, rather than to generate cognitive confusion. For if indeed in Schleiermacher's hermeneutics "to understand means to learn the language of the Other" (G. Scholtz),[140] then the translator, guiding his reader towards understanding, expands the reader's native perspective by showing him, in a *comprehensible* way, the specific elements of that language and the foreign culture in which he is immersed.[141] The fact that Schleiermacher's translation of Plato is still reprinted and digitized in today's German-speaking world, usually without the accompanying philological paratexts, seems to confirm the effectiveness of the strategy described here.

To close this chapter, I will now turn to a final example, perhaps the most famous and most frequently commented-on passage of the *Phaedrus*, in which Socrates develops his critique of writing. This is a passage that, incidentally, makes clear the intertextual, palimpsest-like nature of Plato's original,[142] as its pre-text seems to be *On the Sophists* by Alcidamas.[143] It is perhaps surprising that Schleiermacher does not actually comment in the footnotes on this discourse, which was after all highly problematic in the context of his own exoteric interpretation of Plato, refraining from confronting his general statements, which he made in both introductions, with linguistic specifics. He refers only to the opening words of Socrates' discussion of writing (274b): "*Weißt du wohl, wie du eigentlich Gott wohlgefällig das Reden behandeln und davon sprechen mußt?*" (KGA IV/3, 383).[144] Schleiermacher proposes a correction: "What is meant here, one should conclude, is writing [*das Schreiben*], not speaking

---

[139] The term "information offer" (*Informationsangebot*) used here refers to the system of concepts in Skopos Theory; see Katharina Reiß, Hans J. Vermeer, *Grundlegung einer allgemeinen Translationstheorie* (Tübingen: Max Niemeyer, 1984), 19, 35 and passim.
[140] Scholtz, *Ethik und Hermeneutik*, 145.
[141] I refer here to Hans Vermeer's interpretation of Friedrich Schleiermacher's hermeneutics and translation theory. See Hans J. Vermeer, "Hermeneutik und Übersetzung(swissenschaft)," *TEXTconTEXT* 9 (1994): 173.
[142] See Walter Pater, *Plato and Platonism: A Series of Lectures* (New York: Macmillan, 1893), 3.
[143] See *Plato's Phaedrus*, 162. On intertextuality in Plato's dialogues, cf. Kahn, *Plato and the Socratic Dialogue*, 3–4.
[144] Cf. Hackforth's English translation: "Now do you know how we may best please God, in practice and in theory, in this matter of words" (*Plato's Phaedrus*, trans. Reginald Hackforth, 156), and Nehamas and Woodruff's English translation: "Well, do you know how best to please god when you either use words or discuss them in general" (Plato, *Phaedrus*, trans. Alexander Nehamas and Paul Woodruff, 551).

[*das Reden*]; it is all the stranger that no manuscript corrects this oversight" (KGA IV/ 3, 383). Such a correction is meant to be justified, it seems, in terms of the thematic coherence of the text. But can we truly speak here of an error or oversight? The discussion here revolves around the problem of recorded speech or, more generally, around the ways in which words are used to convey knowledge. From this theme emerges the motif of proper planting and sowing, so that words are not barren but bear fruit (277a, KGA IV/3, 399).[145] The crucial question then is: what does writing do in this very context? Is it a cure for memory or rather a poison, which through deceptive "foreign signs" destroys memory and makes us forget?

At this point in the discourse, a key (and highly ambivalent) concept emerges – that of *pharmakon*. The Greek noun occurring in the original (φάρμακον, 274e) encompasses multiple meanings: "drug," "poison," "medicine," "potion," "dye." In the Egyptian myth recounted by Socrates, therefore, a polysemy is evoked, by virtue of the meanings of "medicine" and "poison." For when the god Theuth, presenting and extolling his inventions to king Thamus, comes to writing, he declares that it is a *pharmakon*, a medicine that provides memory and wisdom. The king, however, replies that this invention may indeed bring the opposite, that this *pharmakon* is a poison that "will induce forgetfulness into the souls of those who learn it" – "they will put their trust in writing, which is external and depends on signs that belong to others, instead of trying to remember from the inside, completely on their own."[146]

In his famous analysis of this passage, Jacques Derrida showed how the French translation destroys the polysemous unity of the *pharmakon*, and with it also obliterating Plato's ambivalent textuality. The founder of grammatology writes:

> When a word inscribes itself as the citation of another sense of the same word, when the textual center-stage of the word *pharmakon*, even while it means *remedy*, cites, re-cites, and makes legible that which *in the same word* signifies, in another spot and on a different level of the stage, *poison* (for example, since that is not the only other thing *pharmakon* means), the choice of only one of these renditions by the translator has as its first effect the neutralization of the citational play, of the "anagram," and, in the end quite simply of the very textuality of the translated text.[147]

---

145 Nehmas and Woodruff's version reads: "But it is much nobler to be serious about these matters, and use the art of dialectic. The dialectician chooses a proper soul and plants and sows within it discourse accompanied by knowledge – discourse capable of helping itself, as well as the man who planted it, which is not barren but produces a seed from which more discourse grows in the character of others" (Plato, *Phaedrus*, trans. Alexander Nehamas and Paul Woodruff, 553). A detailed analysis of this difficult passage can be found in: Thomas Alexander Szlezák, *Plato und die Schriftlichkeit der Philosophie*, 12–15.
146 Given here in Nehamas and Woodruff's translation (Plato, *Phaedrus*, 555).
147 Jacques Derrida, "Plato's Pharmacy," in *Dissemination*, trans. Barbara Johnson, reissue edition (Chicago: Univ. of Chicago Press, 2017), 97. See also Jörg Lagemann, *Signifikantenpraxis – Eine Einklammerung des Signifikats im Werk von Jacques Derrida*, PhD dissertation (Oldenburg: Universität Oldenburg, 2001), 176.

Thus, the choice of a single equivalent here means nullifying not only the interplay of quotations, but also the entire *textual game* in the *Phaedrus*. This analytical "severing" of polysemy and resolution of ambiguity also occur in Schleiermacher's translation: here he chooses the equivalent *Mittel*,[148] while in other dialogues the same term *pharmakon* is rendered as *Arznei, Gift* and *Trank*.[149] This kind of neutralization is inevitable from the point of view of the pragmatics of translation, but it is connected with the fact that – as Derrida emphasizes – it is conditioned by the logic of identity-based thinking typical of modern Western metaphysics, a logic ingrained in modern languages.[150] The textual ambivalence and ambiguity is displaced in favor of a contradiction-free "paradigm of thinking and signifying."[151] Thus eliminated is the dangerous power of the *pharmakon*, which intoxicates and misleads – as does writing, i.e. speech (*logos*) that has been "deprived of its father – the speaking, present subject."[152] Note, however, that Plato is able to make use of this power, exposing the self-referential character of the discourse about writing, because, as Charles H. Kahn aptly remarks, "in reflecting upon writing the dialogue reflects upon itself," on its own status and mechanisms of influence.[153]

Plato's *Pharmakon* symbolizes the tension between homogenizing discourse and ambivalent textuality, but this symbolism is not revealed in Schleiermacher's translation. The "anagrammatics" of the original lose out when confronted with its "strong" hermeneutics, abolished by a translation practice that relies on hermeneutical and functional-pragmatic assumptions.

So what is revealed to us by this symbolic absence, which can also be seen as a synecdoche of the foreignness of the original, absent from the target text? Is it that, in the end, the Platonic *Urtext* speaking in peculiar language falls prey to the "rage of the understanding" (J. Hörisch)[154] and mediation? No, it seems instead that modern hermeneutics and the art of translation – which Schleiermacher represented and co-shaped – needed a politics of the original that did not allow the strangeness of the

---

148 "*Diese Kunst, o König, wird die Aegypter weiser machen und gedächtnißreicher, denn als ein Mittel für den Verstand und das Gedächtniß ist sie erfunden*" (KGA IV/3, 385). The term "means" (German: *Mittel*, Polish *środek*) is also used in Regner's Polish translation (Platon, *Faidros*, 74).
149 Lagemann, *Signifikantenpraxis*, 168. Lagemann rightly argues that the relevant "studies of Derrida" remain relevant even in the context of Schleiermacher's translation. Although the German equivalent (*das Mittel*) is less unambiguous than the French and English equivalents (*remède/remedy*), it connotes even more strongly the "transparent rationality of science, technique, and therapeutic causality" (Jacques Derrida, *Plato's Pharmacy*, 97).
150 See Derrida, *Plato's Pharmacy*, 99.
151 Lagemann, *Signifikantenpraxis*, 169.
152 Agnieszka Kijewska, "Francuska literatura naukowa wobec nowej interpretacji Platona," [French Scientific Literature in the Face of a New Interpretation of Plato] in *Platon: Nowa interpretacja* [Plato: New Interpretations], eds A[gnieszka] Kijewska, E[dward] I[wo] Zieliński (Lublin: Redakcja Wydawnictw KUL, 1993), 30.
153 Kahn, *Plato and the Socratic Dialogue*, 376.
154 Jochen Hörisch, *Die Wut des Verstehens – Zur Kritik der Hermeneutik* (Frankfurt am Main: Suhrkamp, 1988), 50–56.

foreign to cross established boundaries, confounding the sense of security with ambivalence, indeterminacy, ambiguity, and radical otherness. This fact can be interpreted in the context of the mechanisms of excluding ambivalence described by Zygmunt Bauman, which emerged in the era of modernity.[155] Interestingly, this discourse has, as Derrida argues, its roots in Platonism.[156]

---

[155] Zygmunt Bauman, *Modernity and Ambivalence* (Ithaca: Cornell Univ. Press, 1991).
[156] Cf. Michael Naas, *Earmarks: Derrida's Reinvention of Philosophical Writing in 'Plato's Pharmacy'*, in *Derrida and Antiquity*, ed. by Miriam Leonard (Oxford: Oxford Univ. Press, 2010), 54.

VII Conclusion: Translation and Dialectics

1 Rhetoric, hermeneutics, dialectics, and translation

In the various chapters of this book, I have analyzed a number of different segments of Schleiermacher's work in terms of translational issues. I began with his lectures on style, which served as an introduction to the problems of rhetoric. The overall point of reference has been the field in which Schleiermacher achieved perhaps the most, namely hermeneutics – viewed here from the standpoint of the question of rhetorical style, the question of translatability and comprehensibility. Ultimately, therefore, issues of rhetoric are intertwined with those of hermeneutics, which in turn – the reader will recall – is closely linked to dialectics.

This "dialectical nature" of Schleiermacher's elocutionary rhetoric noticed in the course of our analysis is nothing extraordinary, given that the link between rhetoric and dialectics was already stressed both by Plato and by Aristotle, who were both analyzed and translated by Schleiermacher. The latter called rhetoric the counterpart of dialectics, as both "have to do with matters that are in a manner within the cognizance of all men and not confined to any special science."[1] By partaking in society and communicating with others, every one of us has "a share of both."[2] Through the use of rhetoric and dialectics, we are able to argue for often contradictory theses, formulate contradictory arguments, and thus partake in different realities – as seems to be necessary in societal life dominated by *difference*.[3] This difference is revealed both at the level of thinking and in the domain of language.

Hans-Georg Gadamer, in his later years, related these two arts together by focusing on the dialectical rhetoric of Plato and Aristotle, whose roots he sought in the Heraclitan discourse on logos.[4] An outstanding interpreter of Schleiermacher, Gadamer argued that the time had come for us to return to the old, broad sense of the word rhetoric, as the art of constructing utterances that foster understanding (*synesis*) and agreement, i.e. authentic communication (*syngnome*).[5] Thus under-

---

[1] Aristotle, *Rhetoric*, translated by J. H. Freese, in *Aristotle in 23 Volumes*, vol. 22 (Cambridge, MA: Harvard Univ. Press, 1926), 3 (1354a), in Perseus Digital Library, ed. Gregory R. Crane. Tufts University. www.perseus.tufts.edu (accessed 20 May 2022). This last statement can be interpreted as saying that rhetoric and dialectic, not being sciences, belong to "the arts," or differently – that they are both sciences of a universal (rather than specific) character.
[2] Ibid.
[3] Ibid., 13–15 (1355b).
[4] Rafał Toczko, *Hermeneutyka a dziedzictwo retoryki – Hans-Georg Gadamer i jego interpretacje sztuki przekonywania* [Hermeneutics and the Heritage of Rhetoric: Hans-Georg Gadamer and his Interpretations of the Art of Persuasion] in *Retoryka klasyczna i retoryka współczesna – Pola i perspektywy badań* [Classical Rhetoric and Contemporary Rhetoric: Fields and Perspectives of Research], ed. Cyprian Mielczarski (Warsaw: Wydawnictwo Naukowe Sub Lupa, 2017), 138.
[5] Ibid., 138.

stood, *techne rhetorike* is related to *phronesis* – comprehension that leads us to consensus and mutual understanding.[6] The latter values are important in hermeneutics, and even crucial in dialectics, including in Schleiermacher's approach to the latter.

It is worth remembering here that dialectics was for Schleiermacher one of the most important, if not the most important field of inquiry (as the supreme science [*oberste Wissensschaft*], or as the basis of philosophical systematics), which he continued to study and teach from his youth to his old age.[7] He had high hopes for it, trying (especially in his late lectures) within his dialectics to synthesize and harmonize his views on language, hermeneutics, and the art of translation. In this final chapter, I will look at the extent to which his *Dialektik* (*Dialectics*) addresses issues related to the art of translation – as we have seen were considered by Schleiermacher in various contexts, and found concise expression in his 1813 lecture *Ueber die verschiedenen Methoden des Uebersetzens* (*On the Different Methods of Translating*).

2 Schleiermacher's dialectics in general

How did Schleiermacher understand dialectics? We can find a succinct answer to this question in his earliest Berlin lectures on dialectics (summer term 1811), a preserved in notes taken by one of his students, August Twesten. "By 'dialectic' we mean the principles of the art of doing philosophy," Schleiermacher explains in his second lecture. And he specifies: "The supreme and most general elements of knowing, therefore, and the principles for doing philosophy themselves are the same." In the next lecture he clarifies, referring to ancient philosophy: "The term refers to the art of pursuing a philosophical construct jointly with someone else" (KGA II/10,2, 6 and 7).[8] In this clarification and in the remainder of this section of the lecture, he relates to Plato's dialectics and its ethical dimension. This is very characteristic, since Schleiermacher pursued his own research under the influence of Platonism, in clear opposition to Immanuel Kant and Johann Gottlieb Fichte (even a direct rival in this respect).[9] At the same time, Schleiermacher's dialectics is, as Andreas Arndt points out, a consequence of Kant's program of transcendental logic, and

---

[6] Ibid.
[7] Schleiermacher taught dialectics at the University of Berlin from the summer semester of 1811 until the academic year 1832/1833, thus until the final years of his life (see [Andreas Arndt], *Einleitung des Bandherausgebers*, KGA II/10,1, VIII). Although the concept of dialectics appears in Schleiermacher's work in 1811, he formulated the postulate of a science of the foundations and internal systematics of science much earlier, in *Grundlinien einer Kritik der bisherigen Sittenlehre* (1803). See Andreas Arndt, *Friedrich Schleiermacher als Philosoph* (Berlin: Walter de Gruyter, 2013), 182.
[8] English version taken from *Dialectic, or the Art of Doing Philosophy*, A Study Edition of the 1811 Notes, trans. Terrence N. Tice (Atlanta: Scholars Press, 1996), 3 and 5.
[9] For a detailed discussion of the philosophical context and significance of Schleiermacher's theory of dialectics, see especially Ingolf Hübner, *Wissenschaftsbegriff und Theologieverständnis – Eine Untersuchung zu Schleiermachers Dialektik* (Berlin: Walter de Gruyter, 1997), 14–28.

thus an attempt to build a critical philosophy of "emerging knowledge" on the ruins of the old metaphysics, from which uncertain and contradictory claims remained.[10]

German historians of philosophy today agree that Schleiermacher's understanding of dialectics was greatly shaped by his contact with Friedrich Schlegel during his Berlin period. The strong influence of the younger of the Schlegel brothers on Schleiermacher's notion of translation was already extensively examined in Chapter III; however, the vast range of their common interests included not only hermeneutics, philology, philosophy (especially Plato's), aesthetics, and translation, but also dialectics. Andreas Arndt argues that Schleiermacher was most likely familiar with Schlegel's concept of dialectics, sketchily developed by him as early as 1796, which was distinctly polemical with respect to Kant's transcendental dialectics.[11] Under the latter's framework, it seems impossible for objective knowledge to be grounded, whereas such a possibility does exist in the dialectics of Schlegel and Schleiermacher.[12]

Their Platonic inspirations, Arndt feels, grant their concept of dialectics a special, metaphysical profile: "The concept of dialectics should therefore be understood not only in the context of communication, situating it within the framework of intersubjectivity, because it also refers to the metaphysical assumption of the presence/sharing [*Mit-Teilung*] of the absolute within the finite [...]."[13] One can, however, without losing sight of Plato, emphasize the art of understanding rather than the metaphysics – stressing, as Gunter Scholtz does, that the basis of productive thinking consists in (comprehendingly) adopting the thoughts of others, because, in a pragmatic view, science is precisely a process of communication that embraces many *objects* and *subjects* of knowledge.[14] The particular difficulty here lies in the necessity of establishing the foundation of knowledge by way of intersubjective communication via the medium of language – or rather, *languages* – that shape the representations of this transcendental foundation and are themselves shaped in acts of interpretation (with which hermeneutics is concerned).[15]

A careful reading of Schleiermacher's lectures leads to the conclusion that this communicative dimension is most often audible in his dialectics, that this is its

---

10 Arndt, *Friedrich Schleiermacher als Philosoph*, 26.
11 Arndt argues that we are dealing here with a "positive understanding of dialectics," directed against Kant's concept of transcendental dialectics. It is based on a "Platonizing notion of dialectics" and is closely related to Schlegel's interpretation of Plato. Andreas Arndt, "Kommentar," in Friedrich Schleiermacher, *Schriften*, ed. Andreas Arndt (Frankfurt am Main: Deutscher Klassiker Verlag, 1996) 1101–1102.
12 See ibid., 1103.
13 Ibid., 1104.
14 Gunter Scholtz, "Schleiermacher im Kontext der neuzeitlichen Hermeneutik-Entwicklung," in *Friedrich Schleiermachers Hermeneutik – Interpretationen und Perspektiven*, ed. Andreas Arndt, Jörg Dierken (Berlin: Walter de Gruyter, 2016), 6.
15 See Manfred Frank, *Die Unhintergehbarkeit von Individualität* (Frankfurt am Main: Suhrkamp, 1986), 118–119.

most valuable (most modern) element from today's point of view.[16] This can be seen, for instance, in the very formulation of dialectics as an "organ of philosophy," that is, a set of tools of cognition that are "adequate for the object of cognition" to the extent that they make this object "communicable" (A. Arndt).[17] This is, as it seems, a process somewhat similar to adequate translational transformation, in which foreign content is communicated to a target recipient in order to achieve mutual understanding between the participants of communication. Knowledge, however, as one of the outcomes of human cognition, which will always remain incomplete, is never perfect. Like understanding, it remains in the realm of plurality and difference. "Knowledge," Andreas Arndt very aptly states, "thus remains something always becoming, never completed, something that functions in the field of conflicting opposing views."[18] However, as the fruit of an effort made for the sake of dialogue and understanding, "what emerges is a relative identity, achieved each time in the order of progression, a neutralization of conflict, in which the tendency towards the culmination of knowledge, established as the goal of the process, comes to the fore."[19] In this light, dialectics, like translation, appears as a domain of progressivity, openness, preliminariness[20] – as a truly "endless task" (*unendliche Aufgabe*).[21]

This communicative dimension of dialectics is also revealed at the level of the most elementary mechanisms of translation realized in everyday life. By simultaneously availing ourselves of the language of the senses and the language of reason, Sarah Schmidt argues, we translate images into concepts and concepts into images.[22] For if we want to communicate something that we perceive – some image – we have to translate it into the language of concepts (see KGA II 10/2, 483).[23] Here arises the problem of the intersubjective realm, which Schleiermacher did not manage to resolve convincingly.[24] It seems, however, that both imagery-based and conceptual

---

16 Note that Arndt writes about *Mit-Teilung*, or sharing by communicating, conveying information.
17 Arndt, "Kommentar," 1104.
18 Ibid., 1104–1105. This is related to the approach of Schleiermacher's dialectics as a theory of conversation in a situation of conflict or dispute (*Streit*). Note that while the starting point of hermeneutics was for Schleiermacher a situation of non-understanding, the initial moment of dialectics is a dispute over some issue; the background to both is the phenomenon of historicity. See on this subject Sarah Schmidt, *Die Konstruktion des Endlichen – Schleiermachers Philosophie der Wechselwirkung* (Berlin: Walter de Gruyter, 2005), 110–111.
19 Arndt, "Kommentar," 1105.
20 Cf. Ralph-Rainer Wuthenow, *Das fremde Kunstwerk – Aspekte der literarischen Übersetzung* (Göttingen: Vandenhoeck & Ruprecht, 1969), 18.
21 Cf. Klaus Reichert, *Die unendliche Aufgabe – Zum Übersetzen* (Munich: Carl Hanser, 2003).
22 Schmidt, *Die Konstruktion des Endlichen*, 138–139.
23 The process of *schematization* underlying the formation of concepts in language is repeated here in many respects. See on this subject Hans-Georg Gadamer, "Das Problem der Sprache bei Schleiermacher," in idem, *Gesammelte Werke*, vol. 4: *Neuere Philosophie* II (Tübingen: Mohr Siebeck, 1987), 366–367.
24 Ibid., 140.

thinking have a certain, albeit difficult to describe, potential for "generality" that becomes active in everyday communication.

3 Lecture on translation at the Prussian Academy of Sciences

In April 1810, at the plenary session of the Royal Prussian Academy of Sciences in Berlin (*Königlich-Preußische Akademie der Wissenschaften zu Berlin*), Friedrich Schleiermacher was elected a full member of the Academy (KGA I/11, XII). He joined the philosophical section, which consisted of scholars less accomplished and talented than him.[25] From this point of view, his appearance among the Prussian scholars undoubtedly raised the caliber of the scientific activity of this newly reorganized institution. Schleiermacher regularly gave lectures at the Academy, participated in scientific projects, including the publication of Aristotle's works, and was also involved in statutory and administrative work (KGA I/11, XV). He was very keen for the Prussian Academy of Sciences to be an institution that promoted communication among scholars, fostered the transfer of knowledge, and helped nurture an intellectual community based on interpretation and intellectual exchange. These are, it is worth noting, goals that corresponded with his understanding of *dialectics*, which he refined and developed during his university lectures on the subject (cf. KGA I/11, XVII).[26]

Schleiermacher drew up many of the scientific lectures he delivered at Academy meetings for subsequent publication, with the printed versions naturally differing in certain respects from the oral presentation. This was the case, for instance, with the famous lecture *On the Different Methods of Translating* that interests us here. For instance, its printed version (of 1816) refers to Goethe's third volume of *Aus meinem Leben*, which, after all, had not yet been available on 24 June 1813 when Schleiermacher delivered the lecture (KGA I/11, XXII). The most important of his speeches appeared in print in the regularly published *Abhandlungen der Königlich-Preußischen Akademie der Wissenschaften*, in which he published thirteen papers beginning in 1815 (KGA I/11, XXIII). Most of them dealt with the problems of philosophical ethics, four concerned Greek philosophy, and a few texts were devoted to political questions. Against this background, the text *On the Different Methods of Translating* seems rather isolated.

Schleiermacher began work on the lecture on 21 June 1813, as he informed his wife in a letter of the same day: "Today I began writing a treatise on the various principles [employed] in translation, which I am to read on Thursday at the Academy" (KGA I/11, XXXII). Note that this letter still speaks of "principles" and not "methods" of translation, which is a significant difference, as the original term is more norma-

---

[25] From 1812 he was also a member of the historical-philological section. Cf. KGA I/11, XIII.
[26] Being a member of the philosophical section of the Academy, Schleiermacher was entitled as a theologian to lecture in philosophy at the Berlin University (KGA I/11, XX).

tive and in a sense dogmatic (*Grundsatz* = *feste Regel*). As one can see, Schleiermacher had little time to prepare his speech, but he clearly used this time well, because, as he later wrote to his wife, it was well received by the audience: "It is actually quite a trivial thing, but that is precisely why people found it brilliant and beautiful [...]" (KGA I/11, XXXIII). The irony and slight sarcasm that can be sensed here do not seem to be coquetry on Schleiermacher's part – for it was clear that he had taken up a topic which was not the main subject of his scientific inquiry and which did not pose intellectual difficulties commensurate with the ambitions of a scholar renowned as an eminent theologian and philosopher – polemicizing with Kant, rivalling Fichte and Hegel. The subsequent triumph of this particular text, which in the twentieth century rose to unprecedented fame, would probably have surprised its author even more than the positive reaction of his esteemed colleagues at the Academy did.[27]

There is much to suggest that when writing about the problems of translation, Schleiermacher drew not only on his own experiences and reflections as a translator of Aristotle, Blair, Fawcett, Mungo Park, and – above all – Plato, but also on the observations of Herder, and possibly those of Goethe as well.[28] The latter published at the same time an extensive eulogy to the memory of the late Christoph Martin Wieland, delivered in Weimar in February 1813, in which he not only underscored the value of Weiland's Shakespearean translations but also, summing up his attitude to the ancient world, painted a picture of a German sage who would gladly himself have moved into the world of Horace and Cicero in order to "give us an intelligible

---

[27] The study was first reprinted in *Sämmtliche Werke* (1838), and later in the influential anthology edited by Hans Joachim Störig, *Das Problem des Übersetzens* (Darmstadt: Wissenschaftliche Buchgesellschaft, 1963). As translation studies gained momentum as an academic discipline in the subsequent decades of the twentieth century, interest in the text grew and translations into foreign languages appeared, including Italian, English, and Swedish.

[28] In Herder's case, it is not unlikely that Schleiermacher was familiar at least with the thoughts on translating Homer that Herder had published in the first part of *Kritische Wälder* – Johann Gottfried von Herder, *Kritische Wälder oder Betrachtungen, die Wissenschaft und Kunst des Schönen betreffend*, vol. 1 (Riga: Hartknoch, 1769), 184–185. Herder's remarks sketch out, as Alessandro Costazza notes, two visions of assimilating foreign works – by entering their world, which is linguistically and culturally distant to us, or by transferring their world into our own contemporary linguistic and cultural reality. "The two possibilities suggested by Herder seem to anticipate the famous alternative before which Schleiermacher places the translator: 'The translator either disturbs the writer as little as possible and moves the reader in his direction' as Herder does, moving in spirit to the Greek agora, or he 'disturbs the reader as little as possible and moves the writer in his direction', here too like Herder, who delights in Homer in his own native language even when he reads it in the original," the Italian scholar writes – Alessandro Costazza, "Herders Übersetzungstheorie zwischen Linguistik, Ästhetik und Geschichtsauffassung," *Germanisch-Romanische Monatsschrift* 57, no. 1 (2007), 136. Cf. also Costazza's remarks on the convergence between Herder's and Schleiermacher's interpretations of the role of the translator (ibid., 147).

picture of that past."²⁹ Following through on this thought, Goethe formulates his famous remarks about two maxims for translation (*Uebersetzungsmaximen*), the first of which "requires that the foreign author be brought over to us so that we can look upon him as one of our own," while the second requires "that we cross over to the foreign and find ourselves inside its circumstances its modes of speech, its uniqueness."³⁰ He admits that Wieland had tried to reconcile the two maxims, although in difficult and doubtful cases, being "a man of feeling and taste," he followed the former. The convergence of Goethe's formulations and Schleiermacher's metaphors in terms of the principles/methods/maxims of translation is so clear that the editors of the eleventh volume of the KGA decided to point out the possible influence of the former on the latter, quoting the key passage of Goethe's text on Wieland in this regard (KGA I/11, XXXIV).

In any event, setting aside the question of whether there was direct influence, it seems to be no coincidence that a similar typology of translation methods appears in the reflections of Herder, Goethe, and Schleiermacher around the same time. This is closely related to the philological tradition, to the discussion of ways of understanding and assimilating ancient authors, which shaped reflection on translation in the late eighteenth and early nineteenth centuries. It is also related to rhetorical thinking about translation, in which foreignness is contrasted against the "language that conforms to our usage" (Cicero).³¹ This is certainly an important interpretative thread, one that I have already explored in this monograph. However, to follow it now would be to risk losing sight, amidst the web of similarities and parallels, of what is characteristic and distinctive in Schleiermacher's text on translation, against the background of other approaches from that epoch.³²

In the context of Schleiermacher's *Akademie-Rede*, it is also significant that he smuggled various thoughts and allusions of a *philological* nature into a text devoted to methods of translation, clearly making reference to the kinds of issues that were most important to him. Scholars of Schleiermacher's "academic" writings point out that he admitted to having hidden in the lecture "some critical references to Wolf's

---

29 Johann Wolfgang Goethe, *Wieland's Andenken in der Loge Amalia zu Weimar gefeiert den 18. Februar 1813*, Gedruckt als Manuscript (Weimar: Ms., 1813), 16. Wieland had translated into German the *Epistles* and *Satires* of Horace and the *Epistles* of Cicero.
30 Johann Wolfgang Goethe, "The Two Maxims, from *Oration in Memory of Wieland, Our Noble Poet, Brother, and Friend*," trans. Douglas Robinson, in *Western Translation Theory from Herodotus to Nietzsche*, ed. Douglas Robinson (London: Routledge, 2002), 222.
31 Marcus Tullius Cicero, "The Best Kind of Orator (*De optimo genere oratorum*)," trans. H.M. Hubbell, in Robinson, *Western Translation Theory*, 9.
32 This kind of "dissemination" of Schleiermacher's paper is usually performed by juxtaposing his theses with various more or less contemporary considerations on the issue of translation (e.g. with d'Alembert, as in Michael N. Forster, "Eine Revolution in der Philosophie der Sprache, der Linguistik, der Hermeneutik und der Übersetzungstheorie im späten 18. und frühen 19. Jahrhundert: deutsche und französische Beiträge," in *Friedrich Schleiermacher and the Question of Translation*, eds. Larisa Cercel and Adriana Şerban (Berlin, Walter de Gruyter, 2015) 36–39).

views" (KGA I/11, XXXIV). This, of course, is not all that the text conceals. Commentators of *On the Different Methods of Translating* often stress that it is closely related to Schleiermacher's hermeneutics, in which translation can be seen as a special case of interpretation.[33] It is true, however, that this is a rather simplistic approach; it should be remembered, after all, that Schleiermacher considered hermeneutics to be something more than the mere analysis of texts from the standpoint of their (possible) translation, and it extends beyond this scope when it deals with "presenting/ explaining ones' own understanding to others."[34] And in the process of translation, the translator, by preserving his understanding of the original in the language of the recipient, does indeed present/explain his own interpretation to the latter.[35] Thus, the relation of hermeneutics to the art of translation has a specific character that is not based on a simple relationship of one being subordinate to the other. This becomes visible from the perspective of dialectics – as a "common path" shared by the art of interpretation and the art of translation, jointly striving to realize the idea of knowledge by bringing forth the conceptual content of language (*Auflösung der Sprache in ein Denken*; *Dialektik, Kolleg 1818/19*, KGA II/10,2, 227). Dialectics embodies the same idea, but taking a different path – a path towards a common language, while remaining mindful of the difficulties involved in the correlation of language and thought. In turn, the space within which they all operate appears to be the space of communication, situated by Schleiermacher within the framework of a "theory of conversation" he sought to construct (W. Pleger).[36]

Taking this perspective as a starting point, I would like to extract from Schleiermacher's lecture on translation the elements that are closely linked to his dialectics. In my view, it is in this broader, philosophical context that his approach to translation becomes properly intelligible and understandable. His remarks on translation presented to the members of the Academy, in my opinion, stemmed from the very

---

[33] See for example Antoine Berman, *The Experience of the Foreign: Culture and Translation in Romantic Germany*, trans. by S[tefan] Heyvaert (Albany: State Univ. of New York Press, 1992); Christian Berner, "Das Übersetzen verstehen – Zu den philosophischen Grundlagen von Schleiermachers Vortrag 'Ueber die verschiedenen Methoden des Uebersetzens,'" in Cercel and Şerban, *Friedrich Schleiermacher and the Question of Translation*, 45.

[34] "[T]he exposition of one's understanding to others is once again a presentation, and so a speech, and not hermeneutics but rather the object of hermeneutics. [...] the usual view says too little in so far as it refers to foreign languages or to passages that in their own language call for a translation" (*Hermeneutik. Erster Entwurf* 1805, KGA II/4, 38, cited here in Clancy's translation – Friedrich Schleiermacher, *Schleiermacher's Early Lectures on Hermeneutics: The 1805 "First Draft" and the 1809 "General Hermeneutics*," trans. Timothy R. Clancy (Lewiston: Edwin Mellen, 2004).

[35] Contrary to what Theo Hermans suggests, a translation is always an interpretation, as is excellently reflected by the term *Darlegung* ("explanation, presentation") when applied to the work of a translator – see Theo Hermans, "Schleiermacher and Plato, Hermeneutics and Translation," in Cercel and Şerban, *Friedrich Schleiermacher and the Question of Translation*, 99.

[36] Wolfgang H. Pleger, *Schleiermachers Philosophie* (Berlin: Walter de Gruyter, 1988), 134–188.

same fundamental questions about the essence of human understanding that inspired the German scholar throughout his life.

4 Translation in the domain of difference

In Schleiermacher's approach, translation is a universal phenomenon – as universal as communication. Thanks to translation, that which is distant becomes near, and that which is silent can regain its voice, speaking from ancient times to contemporary audiences.

Translation is a kind of mediation (*Vermittlung*), aimed at enabling people to understand and communicate with each other, overcoming the distance separating them – the distance between nations, ethnic groups and social classes, between which there are conditional differences in speech and thought. Such differences may manifest themselves even on the level of character and temperament, which can be an obstacle in communication. In this context, there is the problem of difference at the level of word choice, of emphasis – that is, of individual style.

It then seems, Schleiermacher concludes his introductory considerations, that if we try to specify to ourselves more closely the emotional component of a message addressed to us, we translate it into thought, rationalizing it ("It will then come to us, as we bring this feeling into sharper focus, incorporate it into our thinking, that we are *translating*"). Even more: "Sometimes we even have to translate our own words, when they feel alien and we want to make them truly our own once again" (DR 226; KGA I/11, 67). This is because the message breaks away from the sender, especially when it becomes set down in written form. Writing – as Plato taught – generates distance, breaks the connection with the subject, and is therefore as much a blessing as it is a curse for communication.[37] This rupture creates alienation, which is magnified by the temporal distance between writing and reading – the resulting historical distance.

Translation may proceed on two levels: firstly, products of science and verbal art are translated so that they can be transferred to foreign lands and reach the widest possible audience. On the second level, everyday speech used in commercial and diplomatic communication is translated. Each of these fields corresponds to a different type of translator: an "interpreter" (*Dolmetscher*) is active "in the business world" (*in dem Gebiete des Geschäftslebens*), while the "translator proper" (*Uebersetzer*) works "in the fields of scholarship and art" (DR 226; KGA I/11, 68). It is no coincidence that the former term is typically used for translators who work orally, the latter for those who deal with writing. After all, Schleiermacher reminds us, works of scholarship and art are created in written form, whereas commerce, trade, business are

---

[37] Jacques Derrida, "Plato's Pharmacy," in *Dissemination*, trans. Barbara Johnson, reissue edition (Chicago: Univ. of Chicago Press, 2017), 61–171.

oral, domains of the living word. Writing appears in this context only as a "mechanical contrivance," and written translation is secondary to oral translation (DR 226; KGA I/11, 68). It is difficult to say how much these remarks are an outcome of Schleiermacher pondering the meaning of the critique of writing that is to be found in Plato's *Phaedrus* – but in any case, here, unlike in Plato, speech is given a lower rank than writing.

Because narrative prose also tends to focus on things and facts, translating it is akin to oral translation, interpreting, and in Schleiermacher's view it is not an art but a craft (KGA I/11, 69). The more the text is saturated with what is subjective, unique, individual, peculiar (*eigentümlich*), the greater the effort required of the translator, who must become comprehensively competent: perfectly familiar with the expressive capabilities of the author as well as with the "spirit" of the language the author uses.

The language used in the world of commerce and business is close to being unambiguous, because it describes a quantifiable reality, a calculable world of measures and weights (DR 227; KGA I/11, 70). The use of language in this case is predictable; if we have knowledge of a thing, we usually have no trouble understanding a message from someone referring to that thing – we can predict relatively easily where it is going. "Translating in this field is thus a merely mechanical task [*ein mechanisches Geschäft*] that can be performed by anyone with a modest proficiency in both languages [...]" concludes Schleiermacher (KGA I/11, 70). From the standpoint of modern scholarship on interpreting and translation, this conclusion appears well off the mark, but it should be borne in mind that the author of these words was primarily concerned with separating the *mechanical*, rationalized realm from the *organic* realm of creativity, creativity dominated by the subject interpreting reality through language.[38]

Translating works of art and scholarship is a difficult task, above all because languages differ at the level of words, concepts and their combinations, and so, metonymically speaking, we cannot expect that any "word in one [language] will correspond precisely to one in another" (KGA I/11, 70). And it is precisely this lack of precision that makes interlingual translation so challenging. Schleiermacher calls this phenomenon the "irrationality of languages." It makes itself felt, of course, on all levels of communication, but where communication deals with concrete actions and objects, most often subject to normalization, it does not usually inhibit understanding (KGA I/11, 70).

Schleiermacher draws a clear distinction between "thing" and "thought," regarding the latter as the domain of art and science, "and generally wherever thought, one

---

[38] See Gusdorf's juxtaposition of mechanism and organism in the Classical and Romantic paradigms; Georges Gusdorf, *Le romantisme I* (Paris: Payot, 1993), 283. On Schleiermacher's concept of *Dolmetschen*, see Miriam P. Leibbrand, "'Marktgespräche' – Beobachtungen zur Translation 'in dem Gebiete des Geschäftslebens' in der Romantik mit Bezug zur Leistungsfähigkeit eines hermeneutisches Ansatzes in der Translationswissenschaft heute," in *Friedrich Schleiermacher and the Question of Translation*, eds. Cercel and Şerban, 230–251.

with the world, reigns more securely than the thing of which the word is but an arbitrary and yet well-established sign" (D 227; KGA I/11, 71). The relation of the thing to the word is thus generally based on convention, and if we introduce a rational order into this domain of communication – as John Locke[39] wanted, for instance – there should not be any major problems in human communication, including communication mediated by translators. But wherever "thought reigns," the difficulties so often warned against by proponents of the struggle for the rationality of language become multiplied:

> For how infinitely difficult and intricate the business [*das Geschäft*] becomes here! What accurate knowledge, what command of both languages it then requires! And how often, with a similar sovereign command of the subject matter and the languages involved, and sharing the belief that no perfect equivalent can be found do two translators differ as to which rendering most closely approximates the original. This is equally true of the most vivid poetic images and of the most inward and universal scholarly terms (DR 227; KGA I/11, 71).

Here Schleiermacher touches upon what is perhaps the most important problem of dialectics: the fact that discrepancies exist between the words that are used to refer to mental entities existing in the space of thought. He develops this theme in the final part of his text:

> If one admits what we discussed above, that even in everyday usage there are very few words in one language that correspond fully to their counterparts in another, so that one might be employed to precisely the same effect in every context in which the other appears, it is difficult to avoid the conclusion that the same is even more true of concepts, especially of philosophically charged ones – indeed the bulk of philosophy proper (DR 236; KGA I/11, 89).

Each language develops its own system of concepts, which in its characteristic weave constitutes a coherent whole (*Ganzes*), where no individual part of one such system can ever correspond to the individual part of another: "not even, perhaps, God and To Be, the primordial noun and verb" [*Urhauptwort und Urzeitwort*] (DR 236; KGA I/11, 89).[40] From this linguistic basis emerges knowledge about the world, expressed in a specific natural language.

---

39 See the broader discussion of Locke in Chapter II.
40 Conclusions convergent with those presented here were also formulated by Wilhelm von Humboldt: "It has often been remarked, and both linguistic research and everyday experience bear this out, that with the exception of expressions denoting material objects, no word in one language is ever entirely like is counterpart in another. Different languages are in this sense only synonymous: each one puts a lightly different spin on a concept, charges it with this or that connotation, sets it one rung higher or lower on the ladder of affective response" (Wilhelm von Humboldt, "The More Faithful, The More Divergent – from the introduction to his translation of Aeschylus' Agamemnon," trans. Douglas Robinson, in Robinson, *Western Translation Theory*, 239). The concept that it is impossible to reach a concept unrelated to a word in a particular language and, what is more, not produced by that language, is the basis of Humboldt's theory of translation, emphasizing the difference and distance between original and translation. See Hans-Jost Frey, *Übersetzung und Sprachtheorie bei*

Therefore the translator, realizing the "componential dissimilarity of languages" (DR 236; KGA I/11, 90), can either bend his language to imitate the original, or he is left to paraphrase or transform the initial conceptual system so that it conforms to the target one (*Nachbildung*). Schleiermacher ascribes a special dialectical value to the latter kind of translation, which, in order to reveal it, needs to be reduced to "a detailed illustration of the interconnections between certain types of expressions and collocations in different languages, and in general to cast on the target language the light of a foreign author's unique spirit – but untied and cast adrift from his language (DR 260; KGA I/11, 91). So the point of such a translation would be to bring the different conceptual systems closer, to compare them on the basis of a concrete philosophical statement whose content would be separated from its linguistic form.

The German theologian draws attention to another aspect of the translation problem. When a speaker wants to express a thought (and not merely point to a thing or a state of affairs), his relation to language is twofold. On the one hand, language determines his thinking, proscribes it, as it were, by shaping concepts and ideas. On the other hand, every spiritually independent person puts his own stamp on language, using its semantic productivity to create new linguistic forms. In this way language reaches its perfection in the artistic and scientific realms (DR 227; KGA I/11, 71).

If it is the case that a language *thinks*, and *is thought*, one should keep this in mind when making an effort to understand linguistic utterances. One may focus on the "spirit of the language" as the main determinant of an utterance, or one may focus on the spirituality of the speaker, analyzing how he or she produces language (DR 228; KGA I/11, 72). The true art of understanding is to relate these two perspectives to each other, establishing their relationship, "so that one knows which of the two is ascendent in any given segment" of speech (DR 228; KGA I/11, 72). This is indeed the very essence of Schleiermacher's hermeneutics, which I have examined in previous chapters: posited as a synthesis of grammatical and technical/psychological reading, combining the analysis of linguistic forms and divination based on psychological intuitions.

The artistry of interpretation lies in recognizing the subtle interplay between the formative influence of language and the creative influence of personality, or personal style. Schleiermacher describes here two ways of looking at speech, which foreshadow the dichotomy of translation methods he lays out a little further on in the lecture. One can consider speech "through the spirit of the language from whose elements it was made, as a representation bound and conditioned by that spirit and then vividly reproduced by it in the speaker"; but also "though the speaker's felt sense of it as his act, something that could only have emerged out of, and can only be explained as a

---

Humboldt, in idem, *Die Autorität der Sprache* (Lana: Howeg, 1999), 122 and 145. Convergences between Schleiermacher's and Humboldt's approach to language and translation are visible in many places in the analysis presented herein, but I will not be addressing them separately.

product of, his essence." The former context implies in practice that we sense that "only a Greek could have thought and spoken like that, only this language could have had this particular impact on a human mind," while the latter context implies the impression "only this author could have thought and spoken in this particular Greek mode: only he could hold and mould the language in just this way." Establishing the interrelation of these two perspectives "requires a precise and profound penetration into the spirit of language and the author's unique character" (DR 228; KGA I/11, 72).

The understanding of foreign speech is the highest level of artistry, requiring numerous competences – linguistic, historical, and others. It is no less challenging to pass this understanding on to others through the mediation of translation. What, then, is a translator to do? Schleiermacher asks:

> Given two people as far apart as the author of the original and the potential reader of the translation – people who don't even speak each other's language! – is it really advisable to bring them into a relationship as intimate as that between the author and the source-language reader? Suppose on the other hand that the translator desires only to provide the target-language reader with some simulacrum of his own pleasure and understanding, fraught, to be sure, with traces of his labours and feel for the foreign; how does he achieve the latter, let alone the former, with the means at his disposal? (DR 228; KGA I/11, 72)

In doing so, the translator has at his disposal only his own language, often very distant from the language of the original, plus his own, often uncertain, divinations. "In this light, does translation not seem a foolish undertaking?" Schleiermacher asks rhetorically (DR 228; KGA I/11, 73). He then discusses two possible ways of dealing with this basic problem of translation – through *paraphrase* or through *imitation* (*Nachbildung*). The first is a way of overcoming the irrationality of languages, while the second entails succumbing to the inevitability of this irrationality (DR 228; KGA I/11, 73). Note, however, that the German theologian's hermeneutical discussions of understanding of foreign speech indicate that, in interpreting it, we can focus on making present either the language, or the speaker expressing himself through that language. Thus, the moment Schleiermacher makes his famous statement about the two methods of translation ("The translator either (1) disturbs the writer as little as possible and moves the reader in his direction, or (2) disturbs the reader as little as possible and moves the writer in his direction" (DR 229; KGA I/11, 74)), it is already clear that the alternatives include bringing the reader closer to the original language or bringing the (foreign) author himself closer to the reader, by introducing the author's individual style into the target linguistic community (DR 229; KGA I/11, 74–75).

In this context, Schleiermacher reveals the practical intention of his analysis: to "explore the most general aspects of both methods," paving the way "for an understanding not only of the strong points and impediments of each, but of how each best realizes the goals of translation and where each reaches the limits of its applicability" (DR 230; KGA I/11, 76). This lecture is thus intended as just a "mere introduction" to an extensive propaedeutics of translation, including indications as to the applicability of each method to "various types of utterance" and discussions of the "finest efforts of translators" made in line with either of these methods (DR 230; KGA I/11, 76). Schleiermacher never produced such a broader treatise on the issues of translation – which perhaps should come as no surprise, given that this was not really a topic at the center of his scholarly interests. And yet, even though the author of *On the Different Methods of Translating* did not return in later years to the larger project outlined in his lecture, the key linguistic and philosophical themes nevertheless did recur regularly in his lectures on hermeneutics and dialectics. Particularly in the context of the latter, his thoughts on the problem of communication in the face of the "irrationality of languages" proved important.

5 Communication, understanding, and translation

As I have noted, Schleiermacher began his lecture on the different methods of translation by analyzing the semantic scope of the term "translation" and distinguishing *Dolmetschen* from *Übersetzen*. Comparing these remarks with the basic distinctions he taught in the domain of dialectics turns up interesting parallels.

Let me begin, however, by noting that, in Schleiermacher's understanding, the need for dialectics stems from a certain imperfection: from the fact that existing systems of knowledge are incompatible with one another, much like as if they spoke different languages. Instead of seeking to establish a single, universal language for the science of knowledge (*Wissenschaft des Wissens*), Schleiermacher proposes instead to "establish an art of disagreeing, in the hope that in this way the common premises of knowledge can be reached" (*Vorarbeiten zur Einleitung in die Dialektik*; KGA II/10,1, 372). In essence this concerns an "art of conversation" that leads towards understanding – and in this context "conversation" is to be understood very broadly (just as "translation" was in the context of the *Akademie-Rede* mentioned above), to include both conversations between two people and the internal conversations one has with oneself – internal dialogues, in the course of which "two different and separated sequences of mental activities are alternately related to each other" (*Einleitung*; KGA II/10,1, 392). In this understanding, dialectics appears as "instructions, consistent with the rules of art, for conducting a conversation in the realm of pure thinking" (KGA II/10,1, 358).

What does "pure thinking" (*reines Denken*) mean here? Schleiermacher explains the meaning of this concept by contrasting it with thinking in the domain of economics, commerce, and business (*geschäftliches Denken*) and in the domain of art (*künstlerisches Denken*). The former focuses on the means necessary to realize a certain end, related to the realm of man's practical life (KGA II/10,1, 394), his interests.[41] Artistic thinking, on the other hand, is not directed towards a specific end, being connected with pleasure, satisfaction (*Wohlgefallen*), and thus with the realm of (Kantian) aesthetics, whose matter is language and imagery (KGA II/10,1, 361, 394).[42] "Pure thinking," too, is unbound by a practical purpose, but it is "knowledge-oriented thinking," whose point of reference is a being (*Sein*). That being may, in the course of a dispute, be the thought represented by the Other, a partner in dialogue ("For in the course of a dispute the being for me is the thinking Other," KGA II/10,1, 361), situated within a specific "linguistic circle" ("That which is thought is thus determined as a being, namely within a particular linguistic circle, as one from among a number of thinkers," KGA II/10,1, 361). The proper goal of "pure thinking," and thus of dialectics, is, as Pleger writes, "'to construct' a single, unquestionable, binding field of knowledge for all."[43] Just as "true" translation, *das Übersetzen*, appears where easy, rationalized and mechanical communication ends, so too "pure thinking" rises above the realm of everyday communicative practices, rising also above the subjectivity of aesthetic communication (cf. KGA II/10,1, 361). These concepts thus meet in the space where mediation (*Vermittlung*) is most difficult; in the case of the art of translation, because of the logic of universally individual expression (*das individuelle Allgemeine*), and in the case of the art of conversation, because of the regulative fiction of the immutability, the inconclusiveness, and the universality of knowledge (cf. KGA II/10,1, 395).

Commenting on the theoretical basis of Schleiermacher's dialectics, Pleger asks about the source of the incompatibility of our ideas (*Vorstellungen*). This incompatibility is closely related to non-comprehension (*das Nichtverstehen*), which is the starting point for hermeneutics – often serving as its cause. Note that both the incompatibility of imagery and misunderstanding (of foreign speech) are phenomena that explain the necessity of translation; I will return to this topic later. The source of this incompatibility is, as Pleger writes, the fact that each of us "arrives at our ideas by a different route and in a different context." "If we translate ideas into the linguistic plane, we find that different ideas correspond to different linguistic circles."[44] The notion of "linguistic circle" (*Sprachkreis*) is crucial here, for each of us belongs to such a circle, which greatly determines our ideas and thinking. And here arises an obstacle for dialectics, an obstacle of a communicative nature: how is it possible to achieve understanding at the meeting-point of different "linguistic circles"? In order to attain this understanding, the conversation must be initiated and continued in such a way that a "common language" of knowledge emerges from it.

---

[41] Therefore, as Sarah Schmidt rightly points out, conflicts in the realm of this kind of thinking are precisely about interests, not about the "thing" itself. Schmidt, *Die Konstruktion des Endlichen*, 130.
[42] Cf. Pleger, *Schleiermachers Philosophie*, 145.
[43] Ibid., 146.
[44] Ibid.

Schleiermacher suggests that we begin with what is close at hand. Sketching an introduction to his *Dialectic*, he notes that guidelines on how to achieve agreement on the level of thought must first be formulated in relation to a particular linguistic circle, recognizing its distinctiveness from others (KGA II/10,1, 373). For primordially, a conversation is held by the speakers of a single language (*Sprachgenossen*) "and within each language, the more it develops its system, the more the conflict referred to here arises" (KGA II/10,1, 373), that is, a clash in the domain of pure thinking. It is primarily associated with the problem of the "linguistic articulation of knowledge."[45]

But what happens if someone engages in the very same dispute, not just within their own linguistic circle, but in the domain of a foreign language, associated with a foreign linguistic circle? Such a situation took place, in Schleiermacher' view, for the first time in the history of culture, probably at the time of the transition from Greek to Roman philosophy, when the latter was not yet everywhere using its own, Latin language (KGA II/10,1, 373). Schleiermacher observes: "These difficulties faced by Cicero as a translator make it clear that a Roman who was unfamiliar with the value of the Greek expression he was translating, when drawing upon his Latin, could by no means have had the same thing in mind as someone who was at home in Greek" (KGA II/10,1, 373).

Considering the correlation between (adequacy of) thought and power postulated by Schleiermacher here, the difficulties faced by Cicero, rooted in a different – still emerging – linguistic circle, are obvious.[46] In this case, the issue of dialectics connects up with hermeneutics and the issue of translation, the exemplification of which becomes the work of Cicero, a mediator, and indeed a theorist of mediation, between Greek and Roman culture. Cicero, as a translator, showed a tendency for amplification and strove to ensure that the Greek text translated into Latin did not sound foreign. But was he deluding himself about the equivalence of Greek and Latin when he wrote that the translator should not "count out" words "to the reader like coins," but "to pay them by weight, as it were,"[47] deceiving himself as to the equivalence of the Greek and Latin concepts? When he recounts in *De optimo genere oratorum* how he tried to preserve the meanings of the words and the content of the sentences of the Greek speakers,[48] did he fail to take into account the fact that being a Roman, not a Greek, he himself does not have access to the *conceptual content* of the original formulations?

---

[45] Udo Kliebisch, *Transzendentalphilosophie als Kommunikationstheorie – Eine Interpretation der Dialektik Friedrich Schleiermachers vor dem Hintergrund der Erkenntnistheorie Karl-Otto Apels* (Bochum: Brockmeyer, 1981), 133.
[46] On the theoretical problems of Schleiermacher's correlation between language and thought, including especially communication between different linguistic circles, see ibid., 128–131.
[47] Marcus Tullius Cicero, "The Best Kind of Orator (*De optimo genere oratorum*)," trans. H.M. Hubbell, in Robinson, *Western Translation Theory*, 9.
[48] Ibid.

Schleiermacher does not claim that Cicero was unable to translate the speeches of Aeschines and Demosthenes; he only suggests that he could not translate them in any other way than in what we today call a functional fashion, because being outside the circle of native speakers (*Sprachgenossen*) he could not fully grasp their concepts – just as the Greeks could not (would not) understand the concepts used by the Roman rhetors who belonged to the Latin language circle. In this context, Cicero's statement about the opponents of his translation work acquires additional clarity – Cicero notes that some critics might say that the "Greeks are better," to which one might respond by asking "what can they [the Greeks] do better in Latin?"[49]

Here we see the significance of the differences between communities speaking different languages; this is where familiarity and foreignness arise – values fundamental both to the theory of conversation (dialectics) and to the theory of translation. Foreignness is, of course, intensified by the passage of time, which in the case of Greek texts posed a formidable obstacle to understanding for Schleiermacher's contemporaries, although it was allegedly counteracted by a certain structural affinity that the German Romantics felt ancient Greek shared with German.[50]

In Schleiermacher's view, every language has its own individuality, uniqueness, peculiarity (*Eigentümlichkeit*), which can be seen as its identity. This gets reflected differently in the mirror of other languages – hence the English or French "assimilate the scientific language of the ancients" quite differently from the Germans (KGA II/10,1, 374). This of course explains the differences between the French and German translations of Plato, but it also leads to important general conclusions: firstly, that "no element in one language can be accurately rendered in another, not even by combining several other elements from that language," and secondly: "that languages are irrational in relation to each other, so that no expression in one language corresponds to the same one in another, that is, to one that would have exactly the same value" (KGA II/10,1, 374). The "irrationality of languages" is the fundamental concept here; it also appears, as I have already mentioned, in *On the Different Methods of Translating*, in which Schleiermacher argues that, "the greater the distance between the two languages either chronologically or genealogically, the less true it is that any given word in one will correspond precisely to one in the other, or that

---

49 This is a modification of Douglas Robinson's above-cited translation of Cicero, with a different rendering of this passage of the original: *Huic labori nostro duo genera reprehensionum opponuntur. Unum hoc: 'Verum melius Graeci.' A quo quaeratur ecquid possint ipsi melius Latine?* In Robinson's version, the question being asked in response is whether *the critics themselves* can perform any better; the different interpretation presented here – that the question is being asked rhetorically of *the Greeks* – also chimes, for instance, with Józef Korpanty's translation of the same passage into Polish – Marcus Tullius Cicero, "O najlepszym rodzaju mówców," trans. Józef Korpanty in *Rzymska krytyka i teoria literatury* [Roman Literary Theory and Literary Criticism], Vol. II, ed. Stanisław Stabryła (Wrocław: Ossolineum, 2005), 205.

50 See for example Jochen A. Bär, *Sprachreflexion der deutschen Frühromantik – Konzepte zwischen Universalpoesie und Grammatischem Kosmopolitismus* (Berlin: Walter de Gruyter, 1999), 250 (referring to A.W. Schlegel).

an inflection [*Beugungsweise*] in one will unify the same complex of relationships as any conceivable counterpart in the other" (DR 227; KGA I/11, 70).[51] He adds that this irrationality permeates languages to the core, and its effects are visible at every level of social contact. In essence, translation, or rather its various methods, are ways of dealing with this irrationality: thus paraphrase "would prevail over the irrationality of languages," whereas imitation (*Nachbildung*) "gives in to the irrationality of language" (DR 228–29; KGA I/11, 73). But from what source, one may ask, does this negatively connoted concept of irrationality stem?

Its source lies in the observation that, within science, there is a tangible need for *universalization*, because time, place, and language often pose obstacles to understanding the content of what science communicates. Above all, natural language poses serious difficulties here, "because within any language it is not even possible to determine the exact value of words if we cannot place next to the sign what it represents, which makes the value always fluctuate and change [...]." These familiar-sounding words of Schleiermacher, which correspond to the thoughts already quoted here from *Dialectics* and from *On the Different Methods of Translating*, come from a late speech he gave at the Academy, dedicated to Gottfried Wilhelm Leibniz (KGA I/11, 711).[52] Natural languages are based on arbitrary relations, so that the "values" of individual words are not fixed and stable, but rather relative and pragmatically conditioned. Language is therefore a system distinct from mathematics, which, thanks to its unambiguity, precision, and stability, has become the universal language of the sciences, a *rational* language that organizes reality and is the "art of giving the same names to different things" (H. Poincaré).[53] The strength of mathematics is that it makes only limited use of imperfect, far-from-rational natural languages (KGA I/11, 712). Is the prescribed remedy, then, for the problems of the (inadequate) universality of the concepts of science meant to be its mathematization? This was

---

51 The original German is actually a bit stronger on this point than Douglas Robinson's translation would indicate: "*je weiter sie der Abstammung und der Zeit nach von einander entfernt sind, um desto mehr so, daß keinem einzigen Wort in einer Sprache eins in einer andern genau entspricht*," which would perhaps be better rendered as "the greater the distance between the two languages either chronologically or genealogically, the more so it is that no single word in one language will correspond precisely to one in the other."

52 *Zur Öffentlichen Sitzung am 7. Juli 1831 [Über Leibniz' unausgeführt gebliebenen Gedanken einer allgemeinen Philosophie]* (KGA I/11, 710–724). Schleiermacher had been concerned with Leibniz's philosophy since his youth. Manuscripts entitled "Leibniz I" and "Leibniz II," containing 74 aphoristic remarks on the philosopher's person and work, have survived from 1797–1798 (KGA I/2, 75–103). They were probably written under the influence of discussions with Friedrich Schlegel and do not reflect a systematic study of Leibniz's thought (see KGA I/2, XXV–XXVII). Dilthey claims that the strong criticism towards Leibniz's philosophy visible in *Schleiermacher's* notes is connected with the fact that he measured him by "the measure of Spinoza," the most important philosopher for him at that time – Wilhelm Dilthey, *Leben Schleiermacher*, vol. I/1: *1768–1802*, 3rd ed., ed. Martin Redeker (Berlin: Walter de Gruyter, 1970), 342.

53 Henri Poincaré, *Science and Method*, New York, trans. Francis Maitland (New York: Cosimo Classics, 1914/2007), 34.

precisely the remedy that Leibniz proposed, with his concept of a "general philosophical language," a mathematized system of "general terms, the elements of which are to be real numbers, representing all objects" (KGA I/11, 711). On the basis of Leibniz's project, therefore, there would be an opportunity to establish a "common language" of knowledge as a solution to the fundamental problem of dialectics.

As Józef Życiński, an expert in the philosophy of science, explains, in developing the Cartesian project of an integrated science, Leibniz "sought means that could be used to make the language of all scientific disciplines similar to arithmetic," freeing it up from the plague of ambiguity.[54] Życiński writes:

> In various scientific disciplines, Leibniz attempted to achieve certainty through the arithmetization of their language, which consisted in assigning to particular terms their numerical equivalents and in applying strict rules defining permissible operations on those numbers.[55]

Thus, the German philosopher had posited rules of equivalence between words and numbers and rules for formulating and transforming scientific claims into the domain of *calculus ratiocinator*.

However, the translation of concepts into numbers turned out to be much more difficult than Leibniz himself had expected.[56] And as Schleiermacher stresses, although the problem was posed correctly, the method for solving it was not.[57] He argues that task as it was then formulated, "to elevate philosophy above the errors which inevitably arise both from the mutual irrationality of languages and from the indeterminacy of their individual elements, with the result that no system achieves universal validity," remains valid (KGA I/11, 712). Simply speaking, one can reduce this problem to relativism and indeterminacy, which at the level of linguistic communication leads philosophical discourse astray. Note that in the twentieth century, a diagnosis similar to this one precipitated a "linguistic turn" in philosophy.[58] But what appears as an obstacle in the light of philosophical dialectics, in the context of translation becomes a challenge, as a confrontation with what is different, individual, evades universality. For, as Manfred Frank rightly states, the concept of the

---

54 Józef Życiński, *Świat matematyki i jej materialnych cieni* [The World of Mathematics and its Material Shadows], 3rd edition (Kraków: Copernicus Center Press, 2018), 106.
55 Ibid.
56 The project was taken up 200 years later by Gottlob Frege, seeking to develop a "formal language of pure thinking, modelled on arithmetic" (*Begriffsschrift*). The link between this research and the fundamental question of dialectics is readily apparent (ibid., 107).
57 Schleiermacher had already earlier been critical of the project of "making language more like mathematical calculation," in his *Brouillon zur Ethik*, noting that creative philosophers tend to develop their own philosophical language (Friedrich Daniel Ernst Schleiermacher, *Brouillon zur Ethik (1805/06)*, ed. Hans-Joachim Birkner (Hamburg: Felix Meiner, 1981), 89; see also Schmidt, *Die Konstruktion des Endlichen*, 258–259).
58 See Richard Rorty, "Introduction," in *The Linguistic Turn: Recent Essays in Philosophical Method*, ed. Richard Rorty (Chicago: Univ. of Chicago Press, 1967), 3.

"semantically indifferent translatability of an utterance" (*bedeutungsindifferente Übersetzbarkeit der Aussagen*) reduces the otherness of the Other to pure fiction.[59]

The problem of relativity and ambiguity also appears in the intralingual dimension, affecting each linguistic community separately. Is understanding possible within such a community, or has philosophy developed a multitude of incompatible lexicons and grammars? "How have we advanced this field so as to make our own philosophical language available to other language users as well, and to translate their language confidently into ours?" Schleiermacher asks (KGA I/11, 712). Or perhaps the language of German philosophy (if there is one) is untranslatable into everyday language, and vice versa? Such a situation would narrow the field of conversation and mutual understanding, depriving dialectics of an essential social function. This seems to be the opposite of the state of affairs that Leibniz considered desirable.

Schleiermacher, perhaps with his own lecture on translation in mind, speaks in this context of two historically grounded "methods" of constructing a German philosophical language: one by imitating the clear, scholastic Latin, following the example of the French, the other by over-complicating the language and saturating it with foreign elements (to which Kant contributed) (KGA I/11, 712–713). This criticism should not come as a surprise to anyone familiar with Schleiermacher's lecture on style: as one can see, he remained faithful to his purist views – *undeutsch* in his mouth means "incompatible with the spirit of Germanness, incomprehensible." The crisis of philosophical Germanness should make Leibniz's compatriots feel shame. "What a strange Fate has caused us to find ourselves at the absolute antipodes of that mathematical simplicity towards which Leibniz wanted to lead us," Schleiermacher notes (KGA I/11, 713). Thus, it can be seen that the shape of language, its translatability, and the scope of human understanding are very closely intertwined. Difficulties on the level of interlingual translation explain disagreements on the level of intralingual translation. The desire to produce a successful translation that leads to understanding implies working within the domain of language – work on language. This conclusion is, I believe, consistent with the concepts and creative practices of Schleiermacher that I have discussed earlier – for instance, in his stylistics and his translation of Plato's dialogues.

Schleiermacher's lecture on Leibniz, delivered at the Prussian Academy, is not only conceptually rich but, as I have sought to show, extremely important in that it links dialectical themes together with reflection on translation. Schleiermacher accurately diagnoses the spirit of the new times – the era of cultural hegemony of a single culture had come to an end, and "spiritual beauty" (different in its various forms) is being shared by many different communities around the world (KGA I/11, 713). Spirituality flourishes through conversation, the exchange of ideas and experiences. Knowledge of dialectics and translation fosters dialogue, the transfer of

---

[59] Manfred Frank, *Die Unhintergehbarkeit von Individualität*, 121.

knowledge and the spiritual basis of existence. Schleiermacher speaks in this context of the "translation/transfer of life": "we thus express the hope that on this path of translation/transfer of life [*Lebensübertragung*] will continue to expand the realm of spiritual development until it covers the whole earth" (KGA I/11, 713). No nation should confine itself within the circle of its own language, Schleiermacher argues, "but everyone should remain in community with everyone, in accordance with the existing possibilities" (KGA I/11, 714). But does this postulate imply the creation of a common language based on a common *ratio?* Or the establishment of a common dominant language? No, because opening up to communication does not necessarily imply unification. "For even if there is an end to seclusion, all peculiarities [*Eigenthümlichkeiten*] will after all be preserved" (KGA I/11, 714).

Schleiermacher's key notion of "singularity/individuality/peculiarity" (*Eigenthümlichkeit*) resurfaces here, referring in this context above all to poetic art. Poetry – in all its individuality – paradoxically abhors uniformization, but is fond of multilingualism:

> The noble hospitality of peoples, which is an all-embracing invitation to share in the pleasures of individual life, never experiences greater satisfaction than when each hears its own poems in their original language also from foreign lips; similarly, the loving wish to look into the foreign finds no better realization than, on the one hand [...], to speak in a foreign language, and on the other, to translate into one's own language that in which the foreign peculiarity [*fremde Eigenthümlichkeit*] is most fully expressed (KGA I/11, 714).

Schleiermacher contrasts this beautiful vision of the phenomenon of "foreign semblance," which allows people from different cultures to come together, against communication carried out by "the throng of people in a vibrant global marketplace," which exists in the domain of "commercial thinking" (*geschäftliches Denken*)[60] and *Dolmetschen*. It seems that the German theologian fears that human communication will be devalued by the peculiar *lingua franca* of the people of the business world, rather than by the *lingua mathematica* of Leibniz's disciples.

In this context, Schleiermacher attributes a special role to science. It seeks to be "one for all" and strives to attain "all-embracing importance" (KGA I/11, 715). In his notes for the lecture on Leibnitz, he formulated the ideal of a universal scientific language: "no spirit should be hampered by the barrier placed upon it by its own language, for every thought should be able to reach all men" (KGA I/11, 724). The price to pay for this universalism, however, should not be entering into the "world market" (*Weltmarkt*) of "applied" thinking. The question of the language of science is, of course, a question about dialectics in the domain of "pure thinking." It would seem, especially for the sciences, that Leibniz's project is promising, that the math-

---

[60] In writing about *Dolmetschen*, Schleiermacher cleverly plays upon the German word *Geschäft* ("transaction, business, activity") and its links to *geschäftig* ("active, bustling") and *geschäftlich* ("commercial, economic").

ematization of language is desirable and possible. And yet, as Schleiermacher notes, the objects that the sciences describe are referred to by different names in different linguistic circles, resulting in ambiguity and incommensurability of concepts (KGA I/11, 715). Nevertheless, the pragmatics that guide the multilingual scientific community make expedient and readily available terms part of the vocabulary commonly accepted and used in that community (KGA I/11, 715).

Many problems are also posed by the language of the "speculative" sciences (including philosophy), which often make use of foreign notions and expressions (such as those taken from Greek). Here Schleiermacher distinguishes two methods of assimilating what is foreign:

> Either we translate philosophical elements from other languages into our language as accurately as possible, using newly coined compounds that are not, after all, natural linguistic source-constructs, [...], or we seek to maintain the purity of the German language, acting like Plato and Aristotle; unable to invent linguistic elements for a given scientific use, we then select from the nearest areas of knowledge those that are least worn out and most readily suited for this particular use, through appropriate contextualization and natural fit in terms of form (KGA I/11, 716).

We should add that he considers the first of these methods incapable of producing as coherent a language of philosophy as was developed by Plato and Aristotle, because it generates an effect of alienation, breaking the impression of linguistic unity and harmony. And as we remember from Schleiermacher's analysis of translating the *Phaedrus*, he did not advocate excessive foreignization. Here, the German theologian comes out in favor of developing a philosophical terminology that is creative yet natural for literary German, emphasizing that since the time of Christian Wolff many fortuitous solutions have come into use in domestic philosophical discourse (KGA I/11, 716). But does this not give rise to a danger that this method of internal development of language may result in its partial untranslatability, as that language, losing its grounding in the general, becomes distinctly "peculiar"?

Schleiermacher is not afraid of this process, emphasizing its communicative advantages. It is, in his view, not incompatible with Leibniz's aims, although it follows a different path towards reaching them. For in the method currently being pursued:

> in developing a philosophical language, from all the philosophical languages situated in the historical circle, [the Germans] have appropriated those elements in which the speculative content is revealed in its purest form and which are most easily purged of what has accrued to them through foreign usage [...] (KGA I/11, 717).

Subjected to this kind of "speculative purification," selected elements of other "philosophical" languages become part of the German language. "This appropriation is achieved in two forms: by linguistic assimilation and by translation that does not seek to displace the foreign source" (KGA I/11, 717). Assimilation erases the foreignness, while translation does not; nevertheless, both methods serve to assimilate and even appropriate (*in Besitz nehmen*) what is foreign and to transform it into a language of "pure thinking" that contains, as it were, an "extract" of human thought. Schleiermacher writes:

> We should, in time, arrive at a language of science, through the use of which the difference between a scientific work in a given language and its translations into other languages will be as small as possible, and perhaps even gradually disappear, and this means – as Leibniz wanted – that there will be a system of terms that everyone can easily assimilate into his own language, as his own language (KGA I/11, 717).

The universalism of the language of science would thus be guaranteed by the analytical nature, intelligibility and (pragmatically conceived) translatability of the concepts pertaining to the system of knowledge, and the attendant eidetic convergence of vocabularies within the bounds of "pure thinking."[61] We should note that this universalism is the expected finishing line, the postulated endpoint of the process of linguistic transfer, proceeding in an oscillating rhythm between the individual and the general.[62] If we assume the aforementioned "presence/sharing [*Mit-Teilung*] of the absolute within the finite" (A. Arndt),[63] the hope that such an endpoint will one day be reached becomes justified.

In the context of this late lecture on Leibniz, delivered, after all, at the end of Schleiermacher's scientific career, translation is depicted, in its most general formulation, as working towards common understanding (cf. KGA I/11, 720; *allgemeine Verständigung*) – as a methodical endeavour to approach a certain ideal on the level of interpersonal communication. Here there are no timeless, final solutions – although optimal choices can be found in a given historical moment (of cultural development) and in a given environment (national, intellectual). Elements of the Romantic paradigm of thinking about translation clearly shaped Schleiermacher's reflections in many respects: the historicity and preliminariness of translation (while at the same time orienting it towards a speculatively established ideal), its creative nature.[64] But also, the conviction that translation plays a key role in the development of (national) cultures and the evolution of universal spirituality.

---

[61] In his notes for the lecture on Leibniz, Schleiermacher suggests that there are many words/concepts that are not so far apart in various languages, despite the phenomenon of linguistic relativity – a fact that of course facilitates the universalization of concepts: "For even if we proceed from the assumption that no word in one language corresponds completely to a word in another language, there are nevertheless words that are very close to each other and in a large number of cases one can take the place of the other" (KGA I/11, 720). One can see here a clear reference to the lecture on translation (cf. DR 227; KGA I/11, 70).

[62] In Andrew Bowie's view, this universalism is conditioned by the very "possibility of translation" and agreement about the truth. At its foundations lie ethics and the stability of the semiotic system; see Andrew Bowie, "Introduction," in Friedrich Schleiermacher, *Hermeneutics and Criticism, and Other Writings*, trans. and ed. Andrew Bowie (Cambridge: Cambridge Univ. Press, 1998), XXVIII–XXIX.

[63] Arndt, "Kommentar," 1104.

[64] On these distinctions, see Wuthenow, *Das fremde Kunstwerk*, 18.

6 Dialectics and the problem of translation

In conclusion, let us return to Schleiermacher's dialectics. In his lecture notes of 1822, he wrote that dialectics, as the art of conversation, presupposes a difference of ideas (*Differenz der Vorstellungen*). Every dialectic conversation therefore ends either in the overcoming of this difference and the achievement of an identity (*Identität*) of ideas, or in a conviction that it is impossible to achieve such identity as would enable the interlocutors to come to an understanding (KGA II/10,1, 219). The same is true of translation, if we view it from this perspective. The starting point of translation is also a difference that poses an obstacle to communication, while its goal is also a certain identity (of concepts, of images). This may be achieved, or the efforts may fall short of their mark, or the goal may even be abandoned out of a conviction that identity of ideas, and thus full understanding, is unattainable in a situation of non-translatability. This applies to both intralingual and interlingual translation.

Thus the connection between the problem of dialectics and the problem of translation thereby becomes apparent. Moreover, note that in the background there also remains the question of understanding: in order to converse and translate, we must understand the language and grasp the individuality of the sender of the message. This is not easy especially when we are dealing with an interlocutor distant in time, an interlocutor from a distant and foreign past. Here, the art of hermeneutics closely cooperates with the art of translation: understanding brings the written word and the speaking subject to life, while translation performs its transfer. Any theory of knowledge also needs to take into account a fact well known to hermeneuticians and translators: "that thoughts and expressions are inwardly and essentially identical" (DR 234: KGA I/11, 85).[65] This is why translation is such a difficult task, revolving around the aporia of the identity of thought in two different languages,[66] an aporia that has its origins in the differential "irrationality" of tongues and its consequences on the level of dialectics.

It is clear from the notes taken on Schleiermacher's lecture by his students how much attention he paid to the differences between language systems, to the incompatibilities that most often thwart human understanding. Rationality is conducive to understanding, it fosters identity of ideas, whereas the irrationality of languages, like

---

[65] Interpreting the *Dialectics* in the light of Schleiermacher's remarks on psychology, Wolfgang H. Pleger insists that these two "higher spiritual activities" are inextricably linked, for thinking must have its outlet in speaking, becoming "inner" speaking. Abstraction of content does not lead to pure, non-linguistic thinking – in essence, there is no extra-linguistic content. Thinking is always *about something*, which forces the use of language, as this *something* is named by means of language (Pleger, *Schleiermachers Philosophie*, 140–141).

[66] From Schleiermacher's lecture on translation: "The conviction that thoughts and expressions are inwardly and essentially identical is fundamental to the hermeneutics of all speech, and thus also to translation; how then can anyone who shares this conviction truly want to split a speaker off from the language to which he was born? Can he truly suppose that a person, or even a single chain of that person's thoughts, could ever be one and the same in two languages?" (DR 234; KGA I/11, 85).

any individualizing element, is an obstacle to achieving a commonality of thought. Understanding is of course most difficult when people speak different languages. But what does this diversity of languages stem from? From different "forms of thinking" (*Denkformen*),[67] Schleiermacher responds – which in turn are closely related to the corresponding "language forms" (*Sprachformen*; KGA II/10,2, 479, *Kolleg 1822*).[68] In this pre-cognitivist view, it is not possible to align two languages in such a way that a fusion of thoughts occurs: their full equivalence is only a regulative fiction, only an "approximation" can realistically be achieved. "The endeavor to abolish conflicting ideas will only succeed, therefore, if we become aware of the extent to which we can come to an understanding in language," the lecturer concludes, suggesting to his audience that dialectics must presuppose a close connection between thought and language, or the necessity of mediation and negotiation within the medium of language and its specific schematization of the world (KGA II/10,2, 480) – mediation between the general and the specific/individual.

At the same time, anyone who wants to undertake such mediation must be aware that there are no universal rules of procedure, no Cartesian method of reconciling languages and the discrepancies they generate, "because the task differs in each individual case, in accordance with the peculiar spirit [*nach dem eigenthümlichen Geiste*] of the languages being compared" (*Kolleg 1818/19*; KGA II/10,2, 337). Solving this task requires, as Schleiermacher argues, hermeneutical competence:

> To find the points where the differences begin is in each case a matter of divination, which is why translation from one language into another is an art whose rules cannot be of a general nature, since they always concern the relation of the languages concerned to one another (KGA II/10,2, 337).

Again, we see how dialectics, hermeneutics, and the art of translation are intertwined. The latter two support dialectics in the struggle against the irrationality of languages (for the sake of the idea of knowledge), while dialectics has a special role in this relationship: "it alone remains in constant interaction with the others, not in an empty but in a completely synthetic way, since thinking and speaking must be connected: for it seems that we do not think until we start to speak" (KGA II/10,2, 339). Dialectics teaches how thinking can culminate in knowledge, the idea of which is, Schleiermacher assumes, inherently inscribed in each of us. Here, however, is where the mediation of language, and the cooperation of dialectics with hermeneutics, becomes necessary. "The art of interpretation and the art of translation [*Auslegungs und Uebertragungskunst*] consist in the dissolution [*Auflösen*] of language in thinking," the theologian concludes. "Dialectics is such a dissolution

---

[67] Schleiermacher suggests that they are organically conditioned, cf. *Kolleg 1822*; KGA II/10, 630.
[68] On the complex "thinking–speaking" relation in Schleiermacher's *Dialectics* (including the hermeneutic aspect), see Falk Wagner, *Schleiermachers Dialektik – Eine kritische Interpretation* (Gütersloh: Gütersloher Verlagshaus Gerd Mohn, 1982), 57–58.

of thought in language that involves a full understanding and purpose, which is the idea of knowledge" (KGA II/10,2, 339).

But let us set aside dialectics, which has been dominating our discussion here, and return to the above-quoted passage from Schleiermacher's lecture – the passage that speaks of translation as an *art*. The definition of translation that emerges from those words is extremely important, and not just in the historical sense: it is an approximative transfer, based on the hermeneutical act of divining (here: conjecturing differences), which allows one to enter the spirit of the languages being confronted. Transfer is an art which each time establishes its rules in the interplay of the differences that divide languages and the similarities that connect them, and also – in a broader aspect – in the tension between the singular and the general (KGA II/10,2, 337). Dialectics, as a project of achieving understanding and agreement across linguistic differences, therefore urgently needs hermeneutics and translation; but translation, too, arises in confrontation with the phenomenon of the irrationality of languages and the difficulties of communication between different linguistic communities. Mutual understanding and communication require translation. Translation is also necessary for self-understanding, which cannot take place without the mediation between *feeling* and *expression*, transfer between the realms of (individual) non-translatability and (common) conversation.[69]

* * *

How can we interpret these multifaceted interconnections? What are we to conclude from the fact that the question of translation turns up in so many cognitive configurations, virtually everywhere we turn to seek knowledge? Translation, as *transfer*, is in Friedrich Schleiermacher's approach a transdisciplinary category, and as *art* it remains in (inter)disciplinary contact with many scientific disciplines – much like the art of understanding (hermeneutics) and the art of discussing what we know (dialectics). And so, was Schleiermacher, being so sensitive to what is nowadays seen as the key issue of transfer/translation, a scholar far ahead of his time?

It seems not. Rather, he had a good sense for what can be called the "spirit of the times," which was also so clearly visible in Friedrich Schlegel's work. The holistic view of the world – permeating us and penetrated by us – characteristic of German Romanticism leads one to the conclusion that this world is based on symmetries and transfers, the understanding of which, and the expression of which, is perhaps the greatest challenge faced by mankind. Thus, translation belongs to the essence of the world, it is also a basic tool of our cognition and the foundation of our existence, oriented towards self-understanding and communication with others.

For Schleiermacher, transfer, translation, and communication define our being in the world and our self-awareness, as the basic categories of the humanistic project aimed at drawing together, consolidating, and learning from that which is foreign and different.

---

69 Schleiermacher, *Brouillon zur Ethik (1805/06)*, 21–22.

VIII Summary

In this interdisciplinary study, I have introduced readers to Friedrich Schleiermacher's diverse pathways of philosophical reflection and creative practice that are related to the field of translation in the broad sense. These are avenues of thought and action on the part of a scholar who rightly deserves to be called a pioneer of the modern-day understanding of translational *transfer*. By drawing attention to Schleiermacher's various writings on a range of subjects (including philology, criticism, hermeneutics, dialectics, rhetoric and philosophy of religion), I have sought to show how broadly Schleiermacher's best-known ideas have been adopted and popularized within modern translation theory, and beyond. At the same time, I have also sought to make it clear that his lecture *Über die verschiedenen Methoden des Übersetzens* (*On the Different Methods of Translating*) – though it is admittedly one of the most frequently cited works on translation of all time – represents but a fraction of Schleiermacher's contributions to modern-day insights into translation, and that this famous lecture becomes more fully understandable only in the light of his other writings.

Chapter II began with a discussion of the rhetorical lectures *Ueber den Stil* (*On Style*) that Schleiermacher delivered in Schlobitten (1790–1791) and their significance in the context of translation theory. When discussing the standards of speech and writing, the young theologian declares his belief in the intersubjectivity of human thinking and experience. In his stylistics, rationality at the level of oratorical delivery (*elocutio*) acts as a guarantor of intersubjectivity by simplifying the complexities of language and clarifying its vagueness. In Schleiermacher's approach, the art of good style is the art of successful *transfer:* if we cannot organize and objectivize our thoughts in a way that makes them understandable and interesting to our audience, the transfer will be misguided and the message will not achieve its aim. Here, the key concept is therefore *Übertragung*, which means *transmission, transfer*, and simultaneously *translation* – which is related not only etymologically but also conceptually to the process of transmission, as a type of transfer that overcomes a difference.

In Chapter III, I focused on Schleiermacher's and Friedrich Schlegel's philosophical and literary collaboration (initiated in 1797), showing how these two thinkers jointly contributed to the early development of translation theory, while simultaneously stressing the important differences between how Schleiermacher and Schlegel understood translation. Schleiermacher tended towards approaches that focused on the process and the transfer, which should be deeply rooted in practice. Schlegel, in turn, preferred to approach translation in its potentiality, construing it as a tool of cognition, a modus of philological critique, a way to potentialize the original, and also as poetry – a process of creation in itself. Likewise, differences between the intentions of Schleiermacher and of Schlegel can be observed on the hermeneutic level of what started out as their collaborative venture: the translation of Plato's complete works into German. Both wanted to preserve their understanding of Plato's philosophy and promote it through translation, but also, conversely, they wished by means of their translation venture to themselves glean a more thorough understanding of this philosophy. Schlegel focused mainly on synthesizing methods, which revealed the "eccentric peculiarity" of the Greek philosopher's works, whereas Schleiermacher approached the materials analytically, simultaneously cultivating his hermeneutical skills.

In Chapter IV, I analyzed Schleiermacher's famous 1799 speeches *Ueber die Religion: Reden an die Gebildeten unter ihren Verächtern* (*On Religion: Speeches to its Cultured Despisers*) from the perspective of their discourse, built around the concept of translational transfer in reference to the problems of communication in the religious sphere. The general model of such transfer-based communication includes religious experience (with *intuition of the Infinite* as its fundamental confirmation), the figure of the mediator-interpreter (*Mittler-Dolmetscher*), and the "subtle language" of religion. This analysis results from my understanding of the speeches *On Religion* as an attempt, embedded in hermeneutics, to capture the essence of religious faith and to *translate* it into the language of post-Enlightenment modernity, understandable for the cultural community that has emerged on its basis.

In Chapter V, I compared Schleiermacher's translation criticism with similar work published by his Berlin-based friend and associate, Friedrich Schlegel. This issue is an important one, I argued, because translation criticism is always based, explicitly or implicitly, on some form of translation theory. Moreover, translation criticism played a very important role in the translation-studies discourse of German Romanticism. In this context, I compared and contrasted Friedrich Schlegel's review of Ludwig Tieck's translation of *Don Quixote* (1799) and Schleiermacher's extensive discussion of Friedrich Schiller's translation of *Macbeth* (1801). In his hermeneutic critique of the German Cervantes, Schlegel was particularly sensitive to the whole, to the internal form which shapes the connections between the component parts of the work. He also advocated maintaining a balance between foreignness and naturalness in translation and highlights the aspects of translation that are related to the history of literature and teaching. On the latter issue, Schlegel and Schleiermacher concurred. As I showed, they both were conscious of the receptive horizon of the intended readers of the translated literature, and both perceived translations into German as elements of a national education project. Schleiermacher, in particular, demonstrated himself to be a maestro of detailed philological translation analysis, which leads him to uncover and engage with some of the crucial problems of translation studies in the modern sense: from technical and ethical questions to the great aporias and controversies that continue to drive this discipline. He saw translation as a kind of work done with the medium of language, which we should understand properly and explain through rational analysis, as opposed to poetic synthesis.

In Chapter VI, I focused on the complexities inherent in the concept of "the original," which paved the way for a critical analysis of Schleiermacher's achievements as a translator of Plato (1804–1828). In his endnotes on the individual dialogues from the second issue of *Platons Werke*, Schleiermacher strikes the tone of a philologist whose main concern is translation. However, as I have sought to show, we can frequently observe situations in which a conflict emerges between the philological ethos of the original and the pragmatics of translation, because the philologist-translator's understanding must also account for the intended transfer of the original, which means its communicability. Seen from this perspective, such phenomena as ambiguity and foreignness are obstacles that hinder communication. As a subject of philology, "the original" may be foreign and ambiguous, but the target text produced by a translator as a rule turns out to be an offer of information for recipients – in Schleiermacher's case, German-speaking readers of Plato. In his translations, the foreign original is present in the paratextual sphere (and is problematized there), whereas the target text itself is autonomous and projects its own readers, who are not experts but are connoisseurs of literary art, able to appreciate the artistry of the philosophical texts presented to them. Such issues were examined in detail in my analysis of selected passages of Schleiermacher's translation of Plato's *Phaedrus* dialogue.

In the final Chapter VI, I explored to what extent Schleiermacher's *Dialektik* (*Dialectics*) raises issues related to the art of translation, including those that were concisely expressed in his famous lecture *On the Different Methods of Translating*. An analysis of the *Dialectics* led me to the conclusion that its most important aspect is that of *communication*. This can be seen, for example, in the interpretation of dialectics as an "organ of philosophy," or a set of cognitive tools that are "adequate with respect to the subject of cognition" in the sense that they make this subject "communicable" (A. Arndt). This process is in a sense similar to adequate translational transfer, in the course of which foreign content is communicated to target recipients to secure mutual understanding of the participants in communication. However, knowledge – like understanding itself – remains in the sphere of pluralism and difference. In this light, dialectics, just like translation, appears to be a domain of progressiveness, openness, and preliminariness – a truly "unending task" (*unendliche Aufgabe*). As a project of understanding above language differences, dialectics urgently needs both hermeneutics and translation. Mutual agreement is not possible without mutual understanding, and both require translation, as does self-understanding, which is impossible without reconciliation between feelings and words, without transfer between the realm of (individual) untranslatability and that of (mutual) conversation.

All in all, the analysis of Schleiermacher's various pathways of reflection on translation presented in this book leads to the conclusion that translation is part of the essence of the world, as it is a fundamental tool of our cognition and a foundation of our existence, focused on self-understanding and communication with others. In Schleiermacher's works, *transfer, translation, mediation,* and *communication* underpin our very existence in the world and our self-awareness. At the same time, they represent fundamental categories for a project (like that of the German Romantics) that focuses on the consolidation and assimilation – through translation – of that which is foreign, different, diverse.

Bibliography

1 Primary Sources

Friedrich Daniel Ernst Schleiermacher, *Kritische Gesamtausgabe* De Gryuter:

Part I Schriften und Entwürfe

[KGA I/1]
    1983. *Jugendschriften 1787–1796*, hg. v. Günter Meckenstock, Berlin / New York: De Gruyter.
[KGA I/2]
    1984. *Schriften aus der Berliner Zeit 1796–1799*, hg. v. Günter Meckenstock, Berlin / New York: De Gruyter.
[KGA I/3]
    1988. *Schriften aus der Berliner Zeit 1800–1802*, hg. v. Günter Meckenstock, Berlin / New York: De Gruyter.
[KGA I/4]
    2002. *Schriften aus der Stolper Zeit 1802–1804*, hg. v. Eilert Herms / Günter Meckenstock / Michael Pietsch, Berlin / New York: De Gruyter.
[KGA I/5]
    1995. *Schriften aus der Hallenser Zeit 1804–1807*, hg. v. Hermann Patsch, Berlin / New York: De Gruyter.
[KGA I/6]
    1998. *Universitätsschriften. Herakleitos. Kurze Darstellung des theologischen Studiums*, hg. v. Dirk Schmid, Berlin / New York: De Gruyter.
[KGA I/7.1]
    1980. *Der christliche Glaube nach den Grundsätzen der evangelischen Kirche im Zusammenhange dargestellt (1821/22)*, hg. v. Hermann Peiter, Teilband 1, Berlin / New York: De Gruyter.
[KGA I/7.2]
    1980. *Der christliche Glaube nach den Grundsätzen der evangelischen Kirche im Zusammenhange dargestellt (1821/22)*, hg. v. Hermann Peiter, Teilband 2, Berlin / New York: De Gruyter.
[KGA I/7.3]
    1983. *Marginalien und Anhang*, hg. v. Ulrich Barth unter Verwendung vorbereitender Arbeiten v. Hayo Gerdes / Hermann Peiter, Berlin / New York: De Gruyter.
[KGA I/8]
    2001. *Exegetische Schriften*, hg. v. Hermann Patsch / Dirk Schmid, Berlin / New York: De Gruyter.
[KGA I/9]
    2000. *Kirchenpolitische Schriften*, hg. v. Günter Meckenstock unter Mitwirkung v. Hans-Friedrich Traulsen, Berlin / New York: De Gruyter.
[KGA I/10]
    1990. *Theologisch-dogmatische Abhandlungen und Gelegenheitsschriften*, hg. v. Hans-Friedrich Traulsen unter Mitwirkung v. Martin Ohst, Berlin / New York: De Gruyter.

[KGA I/11]
2002. *Akademievorträge*, hg. v. Martin Rössler unter Mitwirkung v. Lars Emersleben, Berlin / New York: De Gruyter.

[KGA I/12]
1995. *Über die Religion (2.–)4. Aufl.; Monologen (2.–)4. Aufl.*, hg. v. Günter Meckenstock, Berlin / New York: De Gruyter.

[KGA I/13.1]
2003. *Der christliche Glaube nach den Grundsätzen der evangelischen Kirche im Zusammenhange dargestellt. Zweite Auflage (1830/31)*, hg. v. Rolf Schäfer, Teilband 1, Berlin / New York: De Gruyter.

[KGA I/13.2]
2003. *Der christliche Glaube nach den Grundsätzen der evangelischen Kirche im Zusammenhange dargestellt. Zweite Auflage (1830/31)*, hg. v. Rolf Schäfer, Teilband 2, Berlin / New York: De Gruyter.

[KGA I/14]
2003. *Kleine Schriften 1786–1833*, hg. v. Matthias Wolfes / Michael Pietsch, CD-ROM mit "Preußischer Correspondent" Juni bis September 1813, Berlin / New York: De Gruyter.

[KGA I/15]
2005. *Register zur I. Abteilung*, erstellt v. Lars Emersleben unter Mitwirkung v. Elisabeth Blumrich / Matthias Hoffmann / Stefan Mann / Wilko Teifke; Addenda und Corrigenda zur I. Abteilung; Anhang. Günter Meckenstock: Schleiermachers Bibliothek nach den Angaben des Rauchschen Auktionskatalogs und der Hauptbücher des Verlages G. Reimer (Zweite, erweiterte und verbesserte Aufl.), Berlin / New York: De Gruyter.

Part II Vorlesungen

[KGA II/2]
2019. *Vorlesungen über die Theologische Enzyklopädie*, hg. v. Martin Rössler / Dirk Schmid, Berlin / Boston: De Gruyter.

[KGA II/4]
2012. *Vorlesungen zur Hermeneutik und Kritik*, hg. v. Wolfgang Virmond unter Mitwirkung v. Hermann Patsch, Berlin / Boston: De Gruyter.

[KGA II/6]
2006. *Vorlesungen über die Kirchengeschichte,* hg. v. Simon Gerber, Berlin / New York: De Gruyter.

[KGA II/8]
1998. *Vorlesungen über die Lehre vom Staat*, hg. v. Walter Jaeschke, Berlin / New York: De Gruyter.

[KGA II/10.1]
2002. *Vorlesungen über die Dialektik*, hg. v. Andreas Arndt, Teilband 1, Berlin / New York: De Gruyter.

[KGA II/10.2]
2002. *Vorlesungen über die Dialektik*, hg. v. Andreas Arndt, Teilband 2, Berlin / New York: De Gruyter.

[KGA II/12]
2017. *Vorlesungen über die Pädagogik und amtliche Voten zum öffentlichen Unterricht*, hg. v. Jens Beljan / Christiane Ehrhardt / Dorothea Meier / Wolfgang Virmond / Michael Winkler, Berlin / Boston: De Gruyter.

[KGA II/13]
    2019. *Vorlesungen über die Psychologie*, hg. v. Dorothea Meier unter Mitwirkung von Jens Beljan, Berlin / Boston: De Gruyter.

[KGA II/14]
    2021. *Vorlesungen über die Ästhetik*, hg. v. Holden Kelm, Berlin / Boston: De Gruyter.

[KGA II/15]
    2018. *Vorlesungen über das Leben Jesu*, hg. v. Walter Jaeschke, Berlin / Boston: De Gruyter.

[KGA II/16]
    2005. *Vorlesungen über die kirchliche Geographie und Statistik*, hg. v. Simon Gerber, Berlin / New York: De Gruyter.

Part III Predigten

[KGA III/1]
    2012. Predigten. Erste bis Vierte Sammlung (1801–1820), hg. v. Günter Meckenstock; Anhang. Günter Meckenstock: Kalendarium der überlieferten Predigttermine Schleiermachers, Berlin / Boston: De Gruyter

[KGA III/2]
    2015. Predigten. Fünfte bis Siebente Sammlung (1826–1833), hg. v. Günter Meckenstock, Anhang: Gesangbuch zum gottesdienstlichen Gebrauch für evangelische Gemeinen (Berlin 1829), Berlin / Boston: De Gruyter.

[KGA III/3]
    2013. Predigten 1790–1808, hg. v. Günter Meckenstock, Berlin / Boston: De Gruyter.

[KGA III/4]
    2011. Predigten 1809–1815, hg. v. Patrick Weiland, Berlin / Boston: De Gruyter.

[KGA III/5]
    2014. Predigten 1816–1819, hg. v. Katja Kretschmar unter Mitwirkung v. Michael Pietsch, Berlin / Boston: De Gruyter.

[KGA III/6]
    2015. Predigten 1820–1821, hg. v. Elisabeth Blumich, Berlin / Boston: De Gruyter.

[KGA III/7]
    2012. Predigten 1822–1823, hg. v. Kirsten Maria Christine Kunz, Berlin / Boston: De Gruyter.

[KGA III/8]
    2013. Predigten 1824, hg. v. Kirsten Maria Christine Kunz, Berlin / Boston: De Gruyter.

[KGA III/9]
    2017. Predigten 1825, hg. v. Kirsten Maria Christine Kunz unter Mitwirkung von Brinja Bauer, Berlin / Boston: De Gruyter.

[KGA III/10]
    2016. Predigten 1826–1827, hg. v. Brinja Bauer / Ralph Brucker / Michael Pietsch / Dirk Schmid / Patrick Weiland, Berlin / Boston: De Gruyter.

[KGA III/11]
    2014. Predigten 1828–1829, hg. v. Patrick Weiland, Berlin / Boston: De Gruyter.

[KGA III/12]
    2013. Predigten 1830–1831, hg. v. Dirk Schmid, Berlin / Boston: De Gruyter.

[KGA III/13]
    2014. Predigten 1832, hg. v. Dirk Schmid, Berlin / Boston: De Gruyter.

[KGA III/14]
    2017. Predigten 1833–1834. Einzelstücke. Addenda und Corrigenda zur III. Abteilung, hg. v. Günter Meckenstock, Berlin / Boston: De Gruyter.

[KGA III/15]
    2018. Register zur III. Abteilung, erstellt v. Günter Meckenstock / Brinja Bauer / Ralph Brucker / Britta Kunz / Michael Pietsch / Dirk Schmid / Patrick Weiland, Berlin / Boston: De Gruyter.

Part IV Übersetzungen

[KGA IV/1]
    2019. *Hugo (Hugh) Blairs Predigten. Aus dem Englischen übersetzt.* Band 4 (1795), Band 5 (1802), hg. v. Günter Meckenstock / Anette Hagan, Berlin / Boston: De Gruyter.
[KGA IV/2]
    2020. *Joseph Fawcett, Predigten Mungo Park, Reisen im Innern von Afrika*, hg. v. Anette Hagan / Günter Meckenstock, Berlin / Boston: De Gruyter.
[KGA IV/3]
    2016. *Platon, Werke I,1 (1804. 1817)*, hg. v. Lutz Käppel / Johanna Loehr unter Mitwirkung von Male Günther, Berlin / Boston: De Gruyter.
[KGA IV/5]
    2020. *Platon, Werke II,1 (1805. 1818)*, hg. v. Lutz Käppel / Johanna Loehr, Berlin / Boston: De Gruyter.

Part V Briefwechsel und biographische Dokumente

[KGA V/1]
    1985. *Briefwechsel 1774–1796 (Briefe 1–326)*, hg. v. Andreas Arndt / Wolfgang Virmond, Berlin / New York: De Gruyter.
[KGA V/2]
    1988. *Briefwechsel 1796–1798 (Briefe 327–552)*, hg. v. Andreas Arndt / Wolfgang Virmond, Berlin / New York: De Gruyter.
[KGA V/3]
    1992. *Briefwechsel 1799–1800 (Briefe 553–849)*, hg. v. Andreas Arndt / Wolfgang Virmond, Berlin / New York: De Gruyter.
|KGA V/4|
    1994. *Briefwechsel 1800 (Briefe 850–1004)*, hg. v. Andreas Arndt / Wolfgang Virmond, Berlin / New York: De Gruyter.
[KGA V/5]
    1999. *Briefwechsel 1801–1802 (Briefe 1005–1245)*, hg. v. Andreas Arndt / Wolfgang Virmond, Berlin / New York: De Gruyter.
[KGA V/6]
    2005. *Briefwechsel 1802–1803 (Briefe 1246–1540)*, hg. v. Andreas Arndt / Wolfgang Virmond, Berlin / New York: De Gruyter.
[KGA V/7]
    2005. *Briefwechsel 1803–1804 (Briefe 1541–1830)*, hg. v. Andreas Arndt / Wolfgang Virmond, Berlin / New York: De Gruyter.
[KGA V/8]
    2008. *Briefwechsel 1804–1806 (Briefe 1831–2172)*, hg. v. Andreas Arndt / Simon Gerber, Berlin / New York: De Gruyter.

[KGA V/9]
    2011. *Briefwechsel 1806–1807 (Briefe 2173–2597)*, hg. v. Andreas Arndt / Simon Gerber, Berlin / Boston: De Gruyter.

[KGA V/10]
    2015. *Briefwechsel 1808 (Briefe 2598–3020)*, hg. v. Simon Gerber / Sarah Schmidt, Berlin / Boston: De Gruyter.

[KGA V/11]
    2015. *Briefwechsel 1809–1810 (Briefe 3021–3560)*, hg. v. Simon Gerber / Sarah Schmidt, Berlin / Boston: De Gruyter.

[KGA V/12]
    2020. *Briefwechsel 1811–1813 (Briefe 3561–3930)*, hg. v. Simon Gerber / Sarah Schmidt, Berlin / Boston: De Gruyter.

[KGA V/13]
    2020. *Briefwechsel 1813–1816 (Briefe 3931–4320)*, hg. v. Simon Gerber / Sarah Schmidt, Berlin / Boston: De Gruyter.

[KGA V/14]
    2022. *Briefwechsel 1817–1818 (Briefe 4321–4685)*, hg. Simon Gerber / Sarah Schmidt, Berlin / Boston: De Gruyter.

[KGA V/K1]
    2017. *Kommentarband zum Briefwechsel 1808–1810 (Briefe 2598–3560)*, erarbeitet v. Sarah Schmidt, Berlin / Boston: De Gruyter.

Other Works by Schleiermacher Cited Herein

Ästhetik (1819/1825) – Über den Begriff der Kunst (1831/1832). Edited by Thomas Lehnerer. Hamburg: Felix Meiner, 1984.

Aus Schleiermacher's Leben – In Briefen. Edited by Wilhelm Dilthey, vol. 1. Berlin: Georg Reimer, 1860; vol. 4. Berlin: Georg Reimer, 1863.

Brouillon zur Ethik (1805/06). Edited by Hans-Joachim Birkner. Hamburg: Felix Meiner, 1981.

Dialektik (1811). Edited by Andreas Arndt. Hamburg: Felix Meiner, 1986.

Geschichte der Philosophie. Edited by Heinrich Ritter. *Sämmtliche Werke*, Abt. III, vol. 4/1. Berlin: Georg Reimer, 1839.

Hermeneutik und Kritik. Edited and introduction by Manfred Frank. Frankfurt am Main: Suhrkamp, 1977.

Hermeneutik. Edited by Heinz Kimmerle, 2nd ed. Heidelberg: Heidelberger Akademie der Wissenschaften, 1974.

Platons Werke – Ersten Theiles erster Band, 3rd ed. Berlin: Georg Reimer, 1855.

Platons Werke – Ersten Theiles zweiter Band, 3rd ed. Berlin: Georg Reimer, 1855.

Platons Werke – Zweiten Theiles zweiter Band, 3rd ed. Berlin: Gerog Reimer, 1857.

Schriften. Edited by Andreas Arndt. Frankfurt am Main: Deutscher Klassiker Verlag, 1996.

Über die Philosophie Platons. Edited by Peter M. Steiner with contributions from Andreas Arndt, Jörg Jantzen. Hamburg: Felix Meiner, 1996.

Über die Religion – Reden an die Gebildeten unter ihren Verächtern. Hamburg: Felix Meiner, 1970.

1 Primary Sources

Translations of Works by Schleiermacher Cited Herein

Translation:

"From *On the Different Methods of Translating*." Translated by Waltraud Bartscht. In *Theories of Translation: An Anthology of Essays from Dryden to Derrida*, edited by Rainer Schulte, John Biguenet, 36–56. Chicago: Chicago Univ. Press, 1992.

"On the Different Methods of Translating." Translated by Douglas Robinson. In *Western Translation Theory: From Herodotus to Nietzsche*, edited by Douglas Robinson, 225–238. Manchester: St. Jerome, 1997.

"On the Different Methods of Translating." Translated by Susan Bernofsky. In *The Translation Studies Reader,* edited by Laurence Venuti, 3rd edition, 43–63. London: Routledge, 2012.

"On the Different Methods of Translation." Translated by André Lefevere. In *Translating Literature: The German Tradition from Luther to Rosenzweig*. Assen: Van Gorcum, 1977, 67–89, also published in *German Romantic Criticism,* edited by A. Leslie Wilson, 1–30. New York: Continuum, 1982.

Hermeneutics:

Hermeneutics and Criticism and Other Writings. Edited by Karl Ameriks and Desmond M. Clarke. Translated by Andrew Bowie. Cambridge: Cambridge Univ. Press, 1998.

Hermeneutics: The Handwritten Manuscripts. Translated by James Duke and Jack Forstman. Oxford: Oxford Univ. Press, 1978; Atlanta: Scholars Press, 1986.

"Outline of the 1819 Lectures." Translated by Jan Wojcik and Roland Haas. *New Literary History* 10, no. 1, Literary Hermeneutics (Autumn 1978): 1–16.

Schleiermacher's Early Lectures on Hermeneutics: The 1805 "First Draft" and the 1809 "General Hermeneutics." Translated by Timothy R. Clancy. Lewiston: Edwin Mellen, 2004.

Religion:

On Religion: Speeches to its Cultured Despisers. Translated by John Oman. London: Paul, Trench, Trubner & Co., 1893.

On Religion: Speeches to its Cultured Despisers. Translated by Richard Crouter. Cambridge: Cambridge Univ. Press, 1988.

"The Second Speech." In idem, *Christmas Dialogue, The Second Speech, and Other Selections*, translated by Julia A. Lamm, 101–151. Mahwah, NJ: Paulist Press, 2014.

Other:

Christmas Eve: A Dialogue on the Celebration of Christmas. Translated by W. Hastie. Edinburgh: T. & T. Clark, 1890.

Dialectic, or the Art of Doing Philosophy, A Study Edition of the 1811 Notes. Translated by Terrence N. Tice. Atlanta: Scholars Press, 1996.

Introductions to the Dialogues of Plato. Translated by William Dobson. Cambridge and London: 1836; reprint, New York: Arno Press, 1973.

2 Secondary Sources

Adelung, Johann Christoph. *Über den deutschen Styl*, 2nd ed. Berlin: Vossische Buchhandlung, 1807.
Adorno, Theodor W. *Negative Dialectics*. Translated by E.B. Ashton. London: Routledge, 2004.
Al-Taie, Yvonne. *Tropus und Erkenntnis – Sprach und Bildtheorie der deutschen Frühromantik*. Göttingen: V&R Unipress, 2015.
Albrecht, Jörn. *Übersetzung und Linguistik*. Tübingen: Gunter Narr, 2015.
Apel, Friedmar. *Sprachbewegung – Eine historisch-poetologische Untersuchung zum Problem des Übersetzens*. Heidelberg: Universitätsverlag Winter, 1982.
Apel, Friedmar. "Virtuose in der historischen Form – Philologie und Übersetzung bei Friedrich Schlegel." In *Übersetzung antiker Literatur. Funktionen und Konzeptionen im 19. und 20 Jahrhundert*, edited by Martin S. Harbsmeier et al., 17–27. Berlin: Walter de Gruyter, 2008.
Apelt, Otto. "Vorwort [1919]." In Plato, *Sämtliche Dialoge*, vol. 1, edited by Otto Apelt, III–VIII. Hamburg: Meiner, 2004.
Arend, Stefanie. "Rhetorik, Stil und Verstehen: Theoriegeschichte der 'Angemessenheit' (aptum) von der Antike über Goethe und Kayser bis zur linguistischen Pragmatik." In *Gutes Übersetzen – Neue Perspektiven für Theorie und Praxis des Literaturübersetzens*, edited by Albrecht Buschmann, 119–135. Berlin: Walter de Gruyter, 2015.
Arendt, Hannah. *The Human Condition*, 2nd ed. Chicago: Chicago Univ. Press, 1988.
Aristeas. *Der König und die Bibel: Griechisch/Deutsch*. Translated and edited by Kai Brodersen. Stuttgart: Reclam, 2008.
Aristeas. "The Work of the Seventy-Two – from *Aristeas to Philocrates*." Translated by Moses Hadas. In *Western Translation Theory from Herodotus to Nietzsche*, edited by Douglas Robinson, 4–6. London: Routledge, 2002.
Aristotle. *On Interpretation*. Translated by E. M. Edghill. Adelaide: Univ. of Adelaide, 2015.
Aristotle. *Rhetoric*. Translated by J. H. Freese. In *Aristotle in 23 Volumes*, vol. 22. Cambridge, MA: Harvard Univ. Press, 1926). In *Perseus Digital Library*, edited by Gregory R. Crane, Tufts University. www.perseus.tufts.edu (accessed 20 May 2022).
Aristotle. *Rhetoric for Alexander*. Translated by E.S. Forster. In *The Works of Aristotle*, edited by W.D. Ross. Oxford: Oxford Univ. Press, 1924.
Arndt, Andreas. *Die Reformation der Revolution – Friedrich Schleiermacher in seiner Zeit*. Berlin: Matthes & Seitz, 2019.
Arndt, Andreas. *Friedrich Schleiermacher als Philosoph*. Berlin: Walter de Gruyter, 2013.
Arndt, Andreas. "Kommentar." In Friedrich Schleiermacher, *Schriften*, edited by Andreas Arndt, 996–1388. Frankfurt am Main: Deutscher Klassiker Verlag, 1996.
Asmuth, Christoph. *Interpretation – Transformation: Das Platonbild bei Fichte, Schelling, Hegel, Schleiermacher und Schopenhauer und das Legitimationsproblem in der Philosophiegeschichte*. Göttingen: Vandenhoeck & Ruprecht, 2006.
Assmann, Jan. *Moses der Ägypter – Entzifferung einer Gedächtnisspur*. Munich: Carl Hanser, 1998.
Athenaeum. Eine Zeitschrift von August Wilhelm Schlegel und Friedrich Schlegel. 1798, Bd. 1, Stück 2.
Athenaeum. Eine Zeitschrift von August Wilhelm Schlegel und Friedrich Schlegel. 1799, Bd. 2, Stück 2.
Augustine. *On Christian Doctrine: In Four Books*. Grand Rapids, MO: Christian Classics Ethereal Library. 25. http://www.ntslibrary.com/PDF%20Books/Augustine%20doctrine.pdf (accessed 1 April 2022).
Avalle, D'Arco Silvio. *Principi di critica testuale*. Roma-Padova: Antenore, 1978.

Bader, Günter "Spirit and Letter – Letter and Spirit in Schleiermacher's Speeches 'On Religion.'" In *The Spirit and the Letter: A Tradition and a Reversal*, edited by Paul S. Fiddes and Günter Bader, 131–153. London: T&T Clark, 2013.

Bakhtin, Mikhail M. "Aus der Vorgeschichte des Romanwortes." In *Die Ästhetik des Wortes*, edited by Rainer Grübel. Translated by Rainer Grübel and Sabine Reese, 301–337. Frankfurt am Main: Suhrkamp, 1979.

Bär, Jochen A. *Sprachreflexion der deutschen Frühromantik – Konzepte zwischen Universalpoesie und Grammatischem Kosmopolitismus*. Berlin: Walter de Gruyter, 1999.

Barth, Karl. *Die protestantische Theologie im 19. Jahrhundert – Ihre Vorgeschichte und ihre Geschichte*, 5th ed. Zürich: Theologischer Verlag Zürich, 1985.

Barth, Karl. *Die Theologie Schleiermachers*. Edited by Dietrich Ritschl. Zürich: Theologischer Verlag Zurich, 1978. *Gesamtausgabe*, II.11.

Barthes, Roland. "Erté: oder an den Buchstaben." In idem, *Der entgegenkommende und der stumpfe Sinn – Kritische Essays III*. Translated by Dieter Hornig, 110–135. Frankfurt am Main: Suhrkamp, 1990.

Bauer, Manuel. "Hermeneutische 'Teufeleyen'? Schleiermacher und die frühromantische Kritik." In *Der Begriff der Kritik in der Romantik*, edited by Ulrich Breuer, Ana-Stanca Tabarasi-Hoffmann, 173–198. Paderborn: Schöningh, 2015.

Bauer, Manuel. *Schlegel und Schleiermacher – Frühromantische Kunstkritik und Hermeneutik*. Paderborn: Schöningh, 2011.

Baum, Richard. "Die Entstehung eines Klassikers: Der deutsche Shakespeare." In *Shakespeare und kein Ende? Beiträge zu Shakespeare-Rezeption in Deutschland und in Frankreich vom 18. bis 20. Jahrhundert*, edited by Béatrice Dumiche, 123–172. Bonn: Romanistischer Verlag, 2012.

Bauman, Zygmunt. *Modernity and Ambivalence*. Ithaca: Cornell Univ. Press, 1991.

Bénichou, Paul. *Le Sacre de l'écrivain (1750–1830)*. Paris: Joseph Corti, 1973.

Benjamin, Walter. *Der Begriff der Kunstkritik in der deutschen Romantik*. Frankfurt am Main: Suhrkamp 1973.

Berman, Antoine. *The Experience of the Foreign: Culture and Translation in Romantic Germany*. Translated by Stefan Heyvaert. Albany: State Univ. of New York Press, 1992.

Berman, Antoine. *Pour une critique des traductions: John Donne*, Paris: Gallimard, 1995.

Berner, Christian. "Das Übersetzen verstehen – Zu den philosophischen Grundlagen von Schleiermachers Vortrag 'Ueber die verschiedenen Methoden des Uebersetzens.'" In *Friedrich Schleiermacher and the Question of Translation*, edited by Larisa Cercel and Adriana Șerban, 43–58. Berlin: Walter de Gruyter, 2015.

Bersier, Gabrielle. *A Metamorphic Mode of Literary Reflexivity: Parody in Early German Romanticism*. In *Parody: Dimensions and Perspectives*, edited by Beate Müller. Amsterdam: Rodopi, 1997.

Bertuch, Friedrich Justin. *Leben und Thaten des weisen Junkers Don Quijote von Mancha*, Neue Ausgabe. Aus der Urschrift des Cervantes nebst Fortsetzung des Avellaneda. Weimar: Fritsch, 1775–1777.

Birus, Hendrik. *Die Aufgaben der Interpretation – nach Schleiermacher*. In *Friedrich Schleiermachers Hermeneutik – Interpretationen und Perspektiven*, edited by Andreas Arndt and Jörg Dierken, 57–83. Berlin: Walter de Gruyter, 2016.

Black, Max. *The Labyrinth of Language*. New York: Mentor, 1968.

Blinn, Hansjürgen. "Einführung." In *Shakespeare-Rezeption – Die Diskussion um Shakespeare in Deutschland. II. Ausgewählte Texte von 1793 bis 1827*, edited by Hansjürgen Blinn, 9–66. Berlin: Erich Schmidt, 1988. 17.

Blum, Matthias. *"Ich wäre ein Judenfeind?" Zum Antijudaismus in Friedrich Schleiermachers Theologie und Pädagogik*. Köln: Böhlau, 2010.

Boeckh, August. *Encyclopädie und Methodologie der philologischen Wissenschaften*. Leipzig: Tuebner, 1877.
Boeckh, August. "Kritik der Uebersetzung des Platon von Schleiermacher," *Heidelbergische Jahrbücher der Literatur für Theologie, Philosophie und Pädagogik* 1 (1808); cited after the reprint in idem, *Gesammelte Kleine Schriften*, vol. 7: *Kritiken*, edited by Ferdinand Aschersohn, Paul Eichholz, 1–38. Leipzig: Tuebner, 1872.
Boehm, Gottfried. "Zu einer Hermeneutik des Bildes." In *Seminar: Hermeneutik und die Wissenschaften*, edited by Hans-Georg Gadamer, Gottfried Boehm, 444–471. Frankfurt am Main: Suhrkamp, 1978.
Bolz, Norbert W. *Friedrich D.E. Schleiermacher: Der Geist der Konversation und der Geist des Geldes*. In *Klassiker der Hermeneutik*, edited by Ulrich Nassen, 108–130. Paderborn: Schöningh, 1982.
Bończa Bukowski, Piotr de. "Schleiermacher und die Frage nach dem Original. Zu einem philologischen und übersetzungswissenschaftlichen Problem." In *Reformation und Moderne: Pluralität – Subjektivität – Kritik. Akten des Internationalen Kongresses der Schleiermacher-Gesellschaft in Halle (Saale), März 2017*, edited by Jörg Dierken, Arnulf von Scheliha, Sarah Schmidt, 719–732. Berlin: Walter de Gruyter, 2018.
Bończa Bukowski, Piotr de. "Słowo w retorycznej teorii przekładu" [The Word in the Rhetorical Theory of Translation]. In *Słowo – kontekst – przekład* [Word – Context – Translation], edited by Joanna Dybiec-Gajer and Anna Tereszkiewicz, 15–26. Kraków: Tertium, 2014.
Bończa Bukowski, Piotr de. "Zur Übersetzungstheorie bei Friedrich Daniel Ernst Schleiermacher und Friedrich Schlegel in der Zeit ihrer Zusammenarbeit." In *Wissenschaft, Kirche, Staat und Politik: Schleiermacher im preußischen Reformprozess*, edited by Andreas Arndt, Simon Gerber and Sarah Schmidt, 119–143. Berlin: Walter de Gruyter, 2019.
Bończa Bukowski, Piotr de. "Zwischen Platon und christlicher Kunst: Zu Friedrich Schleiermachers Verständnis der Übersetzung in seinen frühen Jahren." In *Odysseen des Humanen: Antike, Judentum und Christentum in der deutschsprachigen Literatur – Festschrift für Prof. Dr. Maria Kłańska zum 65. Geburtstag*, edited by Katarzyna Jaśtal, Paweł Zarychta, and Anna Dąbrowska, 195–204. Frankfurt am Main: Peter Lang, 2016.
Bowie, Andrew. "Introduction." In Friedrich Schleiermacher, *Hermeneutics and Criticism, and Other Writings*. Translated and edited by Andrew Bowie. VII–XXXI. Cambridge: Cambridge Univ. Press, 1998.
Braun, Herbert. *Jesus – der Mann aus Nazareth und seine Zeit*. Stuttgart: Kreuz, 1984.
Bremer, Kai. Uwe Wirth, "Die philologische Frage – Kulturwissenschaftliche Perspektiven auf die Theoriegeschichte der Philologie." In *Texte zur modernen Philologie*, edited by Kai Bremer and Uwe Wirth, 7–48. Stuttgart: Reclam, 2010.
Bunyan, John, *The Pilgrim's Progress*. Edited by Roger Sharrock and James Blanton Wharey. Oxford: Oxford Univ. Press, 1975.
Canal, Héctor. *Romantische Universalphilologie – Studien zu August Wilhelm Schlegel*. Heidelberg: Universitätsverlag Winter, 2017.
Cassirer, Ernst. *Philosophy of the Enlightenment*. Translated by Fritz C. A. Koelln and James Pettegrove. Princeton: Princeton Univ. Press, 1951.
Cavalcante Schuback, Marcia Sá. "Hermeneutics of Tradition." In *Rethinking Time: Essays on History, Memory and Representation*, edited by Hans Ruin and Andrus Ers, 63–74. Södertörn: Södertörns Högskola, 2011.
Cercel, Larisa and Adriana Şerban, eds., *Friedrich Schleiermacher and the Question of Translation*. Berlin: Walter de Gruyter, 2015.
Chudy, Wojciech. "Dialektyka" [Dialectics]. In *Powszechna encyklopedia filozofii* [General Encyclopedia of Philosophy], edited by Andrzej Maryniarczyk et al., vol. 2., 562. Lublin: Katolicki Uniwersytet Lubelski, 2001.

Cicero, Marcus Tullius. "The Best Kind of Orator (*De optimo genere oratorum*)." Translated by H.M. Hubbell. In *Western Translation Theory from Herodotus to Nietzsche*, edited by Douglas Robinson, 7–10. London: Routledge, 2002.

Cicero, Marcus Tullius [Marek Tulliusz Cyceron]. "O najlepszym rodzaju mówców [De optimo genere oratorum]." Translated by Józef Korpanty. In *Rzymska krytyka i teoria literatury* [Roman Literary Theory and Literary Criticism], Vol. II, edited by Stanisław Stabryła, 92–109. Wrocław: Ossolineum, 2005.

Clements, Keith W. "Introduction." In *Friedrich Schleiermacher: Pioneer of Modern Theology*, edited by Keith W. Clements, 7–65. London: Collins, 1987.

Constant, Benjamin. *Journal intime de Benjamin Constant et lettres à sa famille et à ses amis*. Edited by D. Melegari. Paris: Paul Ollendorff, 1895. https://ebooks-bnr.com/ebooks/pdf4/constant_journal_intime.pdf (accessed 20 May 2022).

Constant, Benjamin. *On Religion, Considered in Its Source, Its Forms, and Its Developments*. Translated by Peter Paul Seaton. Carmel, Indiana: Liberty Fund, 2017.

Costazza, Alessandro. "Herders Übersetzungstheorie zwischen Linguistik, Ästhetik und Geschichtsauffassung," *Germanisch-Romanische Monatsschrift* 57, no. 1 (2007): 135–149.

Cramer, Konrad. "'Anschauung des Universums' – Schleiermacher und Spinoza." In *200 Jahre "Reden über die Religion: Akten des 1. Internationalen Kongresses der Schleiermacher-Gesellschaft, Halle, 14.–17. März 1999*, edited by Ulrich Barth, Claus-Dieter Osthövener, 118–141. Berlin: Walter de Gruyter, 2000.

Crouter, Richard. "Hegel and Schleiermacher at Berlin: A Many-Sided Debate," *Journal of the American Academy of Religion* 48, no. 1 (1980): 19–43.

Culler, Johnathan. *Literary Theory: A Very Short Introduction*. Oxford: Oxford Univ. Press, 1997.

Derrida, Jacques. "Plato's Pharmacy." In *Dissemination*. Translated by Barbara Johnson, reissue edition, 61–171. Chicago: Univ. of Chicago Press, 2017.

Diderot, Denis. *Diderot's early philosophical works*. Translated by M. Jourdain. Chicago: Open Court, 1916.

Die Bibel – Mit Apokryphen, nach der Übersetzung Martin Luthers (revidierter Text 1975). Stuttgart: Deutsche Bibelstiftung, 1978.

Dilthey, Wilhelm. "Die Entstehung der Hermeneutik." In *Materialien zur Ideologiegeschichte der deutschen Literaturwissenschaft*, vol 1, edited by Gunter Reiß, 55–68. Tübingen: Max Niemeyer-Verlag, 1973.

Dilthey, Wilhelm. *Leben Schleiermachers*, vol. 1: *Denkmale der inneren Entwicklung Schleiermachers, erläutert durch kritische Untersuchungen*. Berlin: Georg Reimer, 1870.

Dilthey, Wilhelm. *Leben Schleiermachers*, vol. I/1: 1768–1802, and vol. I/2 1803–1807, 3rd ed. Edited by Martin Redeker. Berlin: Walter de Gruyter, 1970;

Dilthey, Wilhelm. *Leben Schleiermachers*, vol. II/2: *Schleiermachers System als Theologie*. Edited by Martin Redeker. Göttingen: Vandenhoeck & Ruprecht, 1966.

Diogenes Laertius, *Lives of the Eminent Philosophers*. Translated by Pamela Mensch. Edited by James Miller. Oxford: Oxford Univ. Press, 2018.

Dröse, Astrid. *Schillers Kampf um den "brittischen Aeschylus": die Macbeth-Bearbeitung*. In *Schillers Europa*. Edited by Peter-André Alt, Marcel Lepper. Berlin: Walter de Gruyter, 2017.

du Toit, Andrie. "Galatians and the περὶ ἰδεῶν λόγου of Hermogenes: A Rhetoric of Severity in Galatians 1–4." *HTS Theologiese Studies* 70, no. 1. 2014. http://www.scielo.org.za/scielo.php?script=sci_arttext&pid=S0259-94222014000100049 (accessed 7 December 2018).

Ebel, Martin. "Ein 'Don Quijote' für unsere Zeit." *Die Welt* 11.03.2009, https://www.welt.de/welt_print/article3355226/Ein-Don-Quijote-fuer-unsere-Zeit.html (accessed 10 October 2019).

Eco, Umberto. *Lector in fabula*. Milan: Bompiani, 1979.

Emser, Hieronymus. *Auß was gründ vnnd vrsach Luthers dolmatschung, vber das nawe testament, dem gemeine[n] man billich vorbotten worden sey […]*. Leipzig: Wolfgang Stöckel, 1523.

Emser, Hieronymus. *Das gantz neü testament: So durch den hochgelerrten Hieronymum Emser verteütsch* [...]. Tübingen: Morhart, 1532.
Enkvist, Nils Erik. *Stilforskning och stilteori*. Lund: CWK Gleerup Bokförlag, 1973.
Evans, Vyvyan. *A Glossary of Cognitive Linguistics*. Edinburgh: Edinburgh Univ. Press, 2007.
Fichte, Johann Gottlieb. "Ueber Geist und Buchstab in der Philosophie." In idem, *Gesamtausgabe der Bayerischen Akademie der Wissenschaften*, Series I: *Werke*, vol. 6: *1799–1800*, edited by Reinhard Lauth and Hans Gliwitzky, 313–362. Stuttgart: Frommann-Holzboog, 1981.
Finlay, Marike. *The Romantic Irony of Semiotics: Friedrich Schlegel and the Crisis of Representation*. Berlin: Mouton de Gruyter, 1988.
Fischer, Hermann. *Schleiermacher, Friedrich Daniel Ernst (1768–1834)*. In *Theologische Realenzyklopädie*, vol. 30, edited by Gerhard Müller et al., 143–189. Berlin: Walter de Gruyter, 1999.
Fischer, Hermann. *Friedrich Daniel Ernst Schleiermacher*. Munich: C.H. Beck, 2001.
Follak, Andrea. *Der "Ausblick zur Idee" – Eine vergleichende Studie zur Platonischen Pädagogik bei Friedrich Schleiermacher, Paul Natorp und Werner Jaeger*. Göttingen: Vandenhoeck & Ruprecht, 2005.
Forster, Michael N. "Eine Revolution in der Philosophie der Sprache, der Linguistik, der Hermeneutik und der Übersetzungstheorie im späten 18. und frühen 19. Jahrhundert: deutsche und französische Beiträge." In *Friedrich Schleiermacher and the Question of Translation*, edited by Larisa Cercel and Adriana Şerban, 23–40. Berlin: Walter de Gruyter, 2015.
Forster, Michael N. *German Philosophy of Language: From Schlegel to Hegel and Beyond*. Oxford: Oxford Univ. Press, 2011
Forster, Michael N. "Herder's Philosophy of Language, Interpretation, and Translation: Three Fundamental Principles," *The Review of Metaphysics* 56, no. 2 (Dec. 2002): 323–356.
Forstman, H. Jackson. "The Understanding of Language by Friedrich Schlegel and Schleiermacher." *Soundings: An Interdisciplinary Journal* 51, no. 2 (1968): 146–165.
Frank, Manfred. *Das individuelle Allgemeine – Textstrukturierung und Textinterpretation nach Schleiermacher*. Frankfurt am Main 1977.
Frank, Manfred. *Die Unhintergehbarkeit von Individualität*. Frankfurt am Main: Suhrkamp,1986.
Frank, Manfred. *Stil in der Philosophie*. Stuttgart: Reclam, 1992.
Frank, Manfred. "The Text and Its Style: Schleiermacher's Hermeneutic Theory of Language." Translated by Richard Hannah, and Michael Hays, *Boundary 2* 11, no. 3 (1983): 11–28.
Frey, Hans-Jost. *Der unendliche Text*. Frankfurt am Main: Suhrkamp, 1990.
Frey, Hans-Jost. "Übersetzung und Sprachtheorie bei Humboldt." In idem, *Die Autorität der Sprache*, 121–146. Lana: Howeg, 1999.
Fricke, Gerhard and Herbert G. Göpfert. "Kommentar." In Friedrich Schiller, *Übersetzungen und Bearbeitungen*, in idem, *Sämtliche Werke*, vol. 3: *Dramatische Fragmente, Übersetzungen, Bühnenbearbeitungen*, edited by Gerhard Fricke and Herbert G. Göpfert, 958–998. Munich: Carl Hanser, 1980.
Frischmann, Bärbel. "Friedrich Schlegels Platonrezeption und das hermeneutische Paradigma." *Athenäum – Jahrbuch für Romantik* 11 (2001): 71–92.
Funke, Gerhard. "Auslegen, Deuten, Verstehen." *Sprachforum* 3/4 (1959/60): 236–248.
Funke, Gerhard. "Glaubensbewußsein. Hermeneutik als Sprachlehre des Glaubens." In idem *Zur Signatur der Gegenwart*, 236–248. Bonn: Bouvier 1990.
Gadamer, Hans-Georg. "Das Problem der Sprache bei Schleiermacher." In idem, *Gesammelte Werke*, vol. 4: *Neuere Philosophie* II, 361–373. Tübingen: Mohr Siebeck, 1987. 361–373.
Gadamer, Hans-Georg. "Lesen ist wie Übersetzen." In idem, *Gesammelte Werke*, vol. 8, Ästhetik und Poetik I. 279–285. Tübingen: Mohr Siebeck, 1999.

Gadamer, Hans-Georg. *Rhetorik und Hermeneutik.* In idem, *Gesammelte Werke*, vol. 2: *Hermeneutik II*, 276–291. Tübingen: Mohr Siebeck, 1986.

Gadamer, Hans-Georg. "Schleiermacher als Platoniker." In idem, *Kleine Schriften* III: *Idee und Sprache: Plato, Husserl, Heidegger*, 146–147. Tübingen: J. C. B. Mohr, 1972. 146–147.

Gadamer, Hans-Georg. "Text and interpretation." In *Dialogue and Deconstruction: The Gadamer-Derrida Debate*, edited by Diane P. Michelfelder and Richard E. Palmer. Translated by Dennis J. Schmidt and Richard E. Palmer, 21–51. Albany, NY: State Univ. of New York Press, 1989.

Gadamer, Hans-Georg. *Truth and Method.* Translation revised by Joel Weinsheimer and Donald G. Marshall, 2nd revised edition. London: Continuum, 2004.

Gamlin, Gordon Sebastian. *Synergetische Sinnkonstruktion und das Bild des Macbeth in Friedrich von Schillers Einrichtung der gleichnamigen Tragödie von William Shakespeare am Weimarer Hoftheater am 14. Mai 1800 unter der Leitung von Johann Wolfgang von Goethe.* Konstanz: Hartung-Gorre, 1995.

Gebhardt, Peter. *A.W. Schlegels Shakespeare-Übersetzung – Untersuchungen zu seinem Übersetzungsverfahren am Beispiel des Hamlet.* Göttingen: Vandenhoeck & Ruprecht, 1970.

Gerber, Simon. "Geist, Buchstabe und Buchstäblichkeit – Schleiermacher und seine Vorgänger." In *Geist und Buchstabe. Interpretations- und Transformationsprozesse innerhalb des Christentums. Festschrift für Günter Meckenstock zum 65. Geburtstag*. Edited by Michael Pietsch and Dirk Schmid, 105–129. Berlin: Walter de Gruyter, 2013.

Gil, Alberto. "Hermeneutik der Angemessenheit – Translatorische Dimensionen des Rhetorikbegriffs *decorum*." In *Übersetzung und Hermeneutik / Traduction et herméneutique*, edited by Larisa Cercel, 317–330. Bucharest: Zeta Books, 2009.

Gloege, Gerhard. *Mythologie und Luthertum – Recht und Grenze der Entmythologisierung.* Göttingen: Vandenhoeck & Ruprecht, 1963.

Goethe, Johann Wolfgang. "The Two Maxims, from *Oration in Memory of Wieland, Our Noble Poet, Brother, and Friend*." Translated by Douglas Robinson. In *Western Translation Theory from Herodotus to Nietzsche*, edited by Douglas Robinson, 222–224. London: Routledge, 2002.

Goethe, Johann Wolfgang. *Wieland's Andenken in der Loge Amalia zu Weimar gefeiert den 18. Februar 1813*, Gedruckt als Manuscript. Weimar: Ms., 1813.

Goozé, Marjanne E. "Der 'verlorene' Briefwechsel zwischen Henriette Herz und Friedrich Schleiermacher: Freundschaft, Religion und Nachruf." In *"…nur Frauen können Briefe schreiben" – Facetten weiblicher Briefkultur nach 1750*, vol. 1, edited by Renata Dampc-Jarosz and Paweł Zarychta, 177–190. Berlin: Peter Lang, 2019.

Göttert, Karl-Heinz. *Luthers Bibel – Geschichte einer feindlichen Übernahme.* Frankfurt am Main: S. Fischer, 2017.

Gottsched, Johann Christoph. *Beyträge zur critischen Historie der deutschen Sprache, Poesie und Beredsamkeit*, vol. 7. Leipzig: Breitkopf, 1741.

Gräb, Wilhelm. "Der kulturelle Umbruch zur Moderne und Schleiermachers Neubestimmung des Begriffs der christlichen Religion." In *200 Jahre "Reden über die Religion": Akten des 1. Internationalen Kongresses der Schleiermacher-Gesellschaft, Halle, 14.–17. März 1999*, edited by Ulrich Barth, Claus-Dieter Osthövener, 167–177. Berlin: Walter de Gruyter, 2000.

Grimal, Pierre. *Dictionary of Classical Mythology.* Translated by A. R. Maxwell-Hyslop. Oxford: Blackwell, 1996.

Grondin, Jean. "Hermeneutics." In *New Dictionary of the History of Ideas*, vol. 3, edited by Maryanne Cline Horowitz, 982–987. New York: Thomson Gale, 2005.

Grondin, Jean. *Hermeneutik.* Translated by Ulrike Blech. Göttingen: Vandenhoeck & Ruprecht, 2009.

Grondin, Jean. *Introduction to Philosophical Hermeneutics.* Translated by Joel Weinsheimer. New Haven: Yale Univ. Press, 1994.

Gross, Alexander. *Hermes – God of Translators and Interpreters: The Antiquity of Interpreting: Distinguishing Fact from Speculation*, https://www.translationdirectory.com/article340.htm (accessed 1 April 2022).

Grove, Peter. *Deutungen des Subjekts: Schleiermachers Philosophie der Religion*. Berlin: Walter de Gruyter, 2004.

Gusdorf, Georges. *Le romantisme I*. Paris: Payot, 1993.

Guthrie, W[illiam] K[eith] C[hambers]. *The Greek Philosophers: from Thales to Aristotle*. New York: Harper Torchbooks, 1975.

Heftrich, Eckhard. *Shakespeare in Weimar*. In *Das Shakespeare-Bild in Europa zwischen Aufklärung und Romantik*, edited by Roger Bauer in collaboration with Michael de Graat and Jürgen Wertheimer. Bern: Peter Lang, 1988.

Hegel, Georg Wilhelm Friedrich. *Hegel's Lectures on the History of Philosophy*. Translated by E.S. Haldane and Francis H. Simson, vol 2. London: Kegan Paul, Trench, Trübner, 1894.

Hegel, Georg Wilhelm Friedrich. *Hegel's Logic: Being Part One of the Encyclopedia of the Philosophical Sciences*. Translated by William Wallace. New York, Clarendon Press, 1975.

Hegel, Georg Wilhelm Friedrich. *Vorlesungen über die Geschichte der Philosophie*, vol. 2. Leipzig: Reclam, 1971.

Heidegger, Martin. *What Is Called Thinking?* Translated by Fred D. Wieck and J. Glenn Gray. New York: Harper & Row, 1968.

Heindorf, Ludovicus Fridericus. *Specimen Coniecturarum in Platonem*. Berlin: Halis Saxonum Grunert, 1798.

Heine, Heinrich. *Zur Geschichte der Religion und Philosophie in Deutschland*. In *Heines Werke in fünf Bänden*, vol. 5, edited by Helmut Holtzhauer, 167–308. Berlin: Aufbau, 1981.

Herder, Johann Gottfried von. *Fragmente zur deutschen Literatur – Zweite Sammlung, Sämmtliche Werke*, pt. 2. Tübingen: Cotta, 1805.

Herder, Johann Gottfried von. *Kritische Wälder oder Betrachtungen, die Wissenschaft und Kunst des Schönen betreffend*, vol. 1. Riga: Hartknoch, 1769.

Herder, Johann Gottfried von. "Treatise on the Origin of Language." In *Philosophical Writings*. Translated by Michael N. Forster, 65–164. Cambridge: Cambridge Univ. Press, 2002.

Herder, Johann Gottfried von. *Ueber die neuere Deutsche Litteratur – Zwote Sammlung von Fragmenten*, vol. 2. Riga: Hartknoch, 1767.

Hermann, Karl Friedrich. *Geschichte und System der Platonischen Philosophie*, part 1. Heidelberg: C.F. Winter, 1839.

Hermans, Theo. "Schleiermacher and Plato, Hermeneutics and Translation." In *Friedrich Schleiermacher and the Question of Translation*, edited by Larisa Cercel and Adriana Şerban, 77–106. Berlin: Walter de Gruyter, 2015.

Hermans, Theo. *The Conference of the Tongues*. London: Routledge, 2007.

Hermans, Theo. ed., *The Manipulation of Literature: Studies in Literary Translation*. London: Croom Helm, 1985.

Hermogenes of Tarsus, *Hermogenes' On Types of Style*. Translated by Cecil W. Wooten III. Chapel Hill: UNC Press, 1997.

Hörisch, Jochen. *Die Wut des Verstehens – Zur Kritik der Hermeneutik*. Frankfurt am Main: Suhrkamp, 1988.

Howald, Ernst. "Wilhelm von Humboldts Agamemnon." *Museum Helveticum: schweizerische Zeitschrift für klassische Altertumswissenschaft* 16, no. 4 (1959): 292–301.

Hübner, Ingolf. *Wissenschaftsbegriff und Theologieverständnis – Eine Untersuchung zu Schleiermachers Dialektik*. Berlin: Walter de Gruyter, 1997.

Huge, Eberhard. *Poesie und Reflexion in der Ästhetik des frühen Friedrich Schlegel*. Stuttgart: J.B. Metzlersche Verlagsbuchhandlung, 1971.

Humboldt, Wilhelm von. *Aeschylos Agamemnon metrisch übersetzt (Einleitung)*. In idem, *Gesammelte Schriften*, Abt. 1, vol. 8: *Übersetzungen*. Berlin: B. Behr's Verlag, 1968, reprint of 1909 edition.

Humboldt, Wilhelm von. "The More Faithful, The More Divergent – from the introduction to his translation of Aeschylus' Agamemnon." Translated by Douglas Robinson. In *Western Translation Theory: From Herodotus to Nietzsche*, edited by Douglas Robinson, 239–240. London: Routledge, 2002.

Humboldt, Wilhelm von. *On Language: On the Diversity of Human Language Construction and its Influence on the Mental Development of the Human Species*. Translated by Peter Heath. Edited by Michael Losonsky, 2nd ed. Cambridge: Cambridge Univ. Press, 2000.

Huyssen, Andreas. *Die frühromantische Konzeption von Übersetzung und Aneignung – Studien zur frühromantischen Utopie einer deutschen Weltliteratur*. Zürich: Atlantis Verlag, 1969.

Ingenkamp, Heinz Gerd. "Bearbeitungen und Übersetzungen." In *Schiller-Handbuch: Leben – Werk – Wirkung*, edited by Matthias Luserke-Jaqui, 529–535. Stuttgart: J.B. Metzler, 2005.529

Ingenkamp, Heinz Gerd. "Kommentar." In Friedrich Schiller, *Übersetzungen und Bearbeitungen*, ed. Heinz Gerd Ingenkamp, *Werke und Briefe*, vol. 9. Frankfurt am Main: Deutscher Klassiker Verlag, 1995.

Irani, Tushar. *Plato on the Value of Philosophy: The Art of Argument in the Gorgias and Phaedrus*. Cambridge: Cambridge Univ. Press, 2017.

Jakobson, Roman. "On Linguistic Aspects of Translation." In *On Translation*, edited by Reuben A. Brower, 232–239. Cambridge, Mass.: Harvard Univ. Press, 1959.

James, William. *The Varieties of Religious Experience: A Study of Human Nature*. London: Longmans, Green, and Co, 1902.

Jantzen, Jörg. "'...daß ich nämlich sterben will, wenn der Platon vollendet ist' – Schleiermachers Übersetzung des Platon." In *Übersetzung antiker Literatur – Funktionen und Konzeptionen im 19. und 20. Jahrhundert*, edited by Martin S. Harbsmeier et al., 29–48. Berlin: Walter de Gruyter, 2008.

Jantzen, Jörg. "Zu Schleiermachers Platon-Übersetzung und seinen Anmerkungen dazu." In Friedrich Schleiermacher, *Über die Philosophie Platons*, edited by Peter M. Steiner with contributions from Andreas Arndt, Jörg Jantzen, XLV–LVIII. Hamburg: Felix Meiner, 1996.

Jaroszyński, Czesław and Piotr Jaroszyński, *Podstawy retoryki klasycznej* [Foundations of Classical Rhetoric]. Warsaw: Wydawnictwo Sióstr Loretanek, 1998.

Jauss, Hans Robert. *Ästhetische Erfahrung und literarische Hermeneutik*. Frankfurt am Main: Suhrkamp, 1991.

Jauss, Hans Robert. *Wege des Verstehens*. Munich: Wilhelm Fink, 1994.

Jay, Martin. *Songs of Experience: Modern American and European Variations on a Universal Theme*. Berkeley: Univ. of California Press, 2005.

Jensen, Kipton E. "The Principle of Protestantism: On Hegel's (Mis)Reading of Schleiermacher's 'Speeches'," *Journal of the American Academy of Religion* 71, no. 2 (2003): 405–422.

Jerome, "On The Best Kind of Translator." Translated by Paul Carroll. In *Western Translation Theory from Herodotus to Nietzsche*, edited by Douglas Robinson, 23–30. London: Routledge, 2002.

Kahn, Charles H. *Plato and the Socratic Dialogue: The Philosophical Use of a Literary Form*. Cambridge: Cambridge Univ. Press, 1997.

Kaiser, Bernhard. *Die Scheidung von Geist und Buchstabe in der Heiligen Schrift – ihr geistiger Hintergrund und ihre praktischen Folgen*, Institut für Reformatorische Theologie, http://www.irt-ggmbh.de/downloads/scheidunggeistwort.pdf%20 (accessed 6 June 2019). originally printed in *Bibel und Gemeinde* 94, (1994): 34–51.

Kant, Immanuel. *Critique of Judgement*. Translated by Werner S. Pluhar. Indianapolis, Hackett, 1987.

Kant, Immanuel. *Critique of Pure Reason*. Translated by Norman Kemp Smith, reissue edition. New York: Pallgrave Macmillan, 2007.
Kantzenbach, Friedrich Wilhelm. *Friedrich Daniel Ernst Schleiermacher in Selbstzeugnissen und Dokumenten*. Reinbek bei Hamburg: Rowohlt, 1967.
Kapp, Volker. "Zum Verhältnis von Übersetzen und Rhetorik." In *Übersetzung – Ursprung und Zukunft der Philologie?*, edited by Christoph Strosetzki, 15–29. Tübingen: Gunter Narr, 2008.
Käppel, Lutz. "Die frühe Rezeption der Platon-Übersetzung Friedrich Schleiermachers am Beispiel der Arbeiten Friedrich Asts." In *Geist und Buchstabe: Interpretations- und Transformationsprozesse innerhalb des Christentums – Festschrift für Günter Meckenstock zum 65. Geburtstag*, edited by Michael Pietsch and Dirk Schmid, 45–62. Berlin: Walter de Gruyter, 2013.
Käppel, Lutz. "(Re-)Konstruktion von Antike als (Neu-)Konstruktion von Moderne. Schleiermachers Auseinandersetzung mit Platon und Heraklit." In *Reformation und Moderne. Pluralität – Subjektivität – Kritik. Akten des Internationalen Kongresses der Schleiermacher-Gesellschaft in Halle (Saale). März 2017*, edited by Jörg Dierken, Arnulf von Scheliha, Sarah Schmidt, 45–62. Berlin: Walter de Gruyter, 2018.
Käppel, Lutz. "Schleiermachers Hermeneutik zwischen zeitgenössischer Philologie und 'Phaidros'-Lektüre." In *Schleiermacher-Tag 2005: Eine Vortragsreihe*, edited by Günter Meckenstock, 72–74. Göttingen: Vandenhoeck & Ruprecht, 2006.
Käppel, Lutz. "Schleiermachers Platon-Übersetzungen." In *Schleiermacher Handbuch*, edited by Martin Ohst, Tübingen: Mohr Siebeck, 2017.
Karski, Karol. "Friedrich Daniel Ernst Schleiermacher – życie i dzieło" [Friedrich Daniel Ernst Schleiermacher: Life and Work]. In *Europa – Slavia – Germania: Hermeneutyka pogranicza* [Europa – Slavia – Germania: Hermeneutics of the Borderland], edited by Maciej J. Dudziak, 96–107. Gorzów Wielkopolski: Wydawnictwo Państwowej Wyższej Szkoły Zawodowej, 2010.
Kierkegaard, Søren. *The Concept of Anxiety*. Translated by Reidar Thomte. Princeton: Princeton Univ. Press, 1980.
Kijewska, Agnieszka. *Francuska literatura naukowa wobec nowej interpretacji Platon* [French Scientific Literature in the Face of a New Interpretation of Plato]. In *Platon. Nowa interpretacja* [Plato. New Interpretations], edited by A[gniezska] Kijewska and E[dward] I[wo] Zieliński, 27–33. Lublin: Redakcja Wydawnictw KUL, 1993.
Kimmerle, Heinz. "Einleitung." In Fr[iedrich] D.E. Schleiermacher, *Hermeneutik*, edited by Heinz Kimmerle, 9–24. Heidelberg: Carl Winter Universitätsverlag, 1974.
Kittel, Harald. Andreas Poltermann, "The German Tradition." In *Routledge Encyclopedia of Translation Studies*, edited by Mona Baker, 418–428. London: Routledge, 2001.
Kitzbichler, Josefine, Katja Lubitz, and Nina Mindt. *Dokumente zur Theorie der Übersetzung antiker Literatur in Deutschland seit 1800*. Berlin: Walter de Gruyter, 2009.
Klemm, David E. "Culture, Arts, and Religion." In *The Cambridge Companion to Friedrich Schleiermacher*, edited by Jacqueline Mariña, 251–268. Cambridge: Cambridge Univ. Press, 2005.
Kliebisch, Udo. *Transzendentalphilosophie als Kommunikationstheorie – Eine Interpretation der Dialektik Friedrich Schleiermachers vor dem Hintergrund der Erkenntnistheorie Karl-Otto Apels*. Bochum: Brockmeyer, 1981.
Kłoczowski, Jan Andrzej. "Max Scheler – myśliciel poważny" [Max Scheler – A Serious Thinker]. In Max Scheler, *Problemy religii* [Problems of Religion]. Translated and introduction by Adam Węgrzecki, afterword by Jan Andrzej Kłoczowski, 367–372. Kraków: Znak, 1995.
Kłoczowski, Jan Andrzej. *Między samotnością a wspólnotą – Wstęp do filozofii religii* [Between Loneliness and Community – An Introduction to a Philosophy of Religion]. Tarnów: BIBLOS, 1994.

Kloepfer, Rolf. *Die Theorie der literarischen Übersetzung – Romanisch-deutscher Sprachbereich.* Munich: Wilhelm Fink, 1967.

Knape, Joachim. *Was ist Rhetorik?.* Stuttgart: Reclam, 2000.

Kohlmayer, Rainer. "'Das Ohr vernimmts gleich und hasst den hinkenden Boten' (Herder). Kritische Anmerkungen zu Schleiermachers Übersetzungstheorie und -praxis." In *Friedrich Schleiermacher and the Question of Translation*, edited by Larisa Cercel and Adriana Șerban, 107–126. Berlin: Walter de Gruyter, 2015.

Kohlmayer, Rainer. "Rhetorik und Theorie der Literaturübersetzung – Überlappungen und Differenzen." In *Unterwegs zu einer hermeneutischen Übersetzungswissenschaft – Radegundis Stolze zu ihrem 60. Geburtstag*, edited by Larisa Cercel and John Stanley, 131–152. Tübingen: Narr, 2012.

Koller, Werner. *Einführung in die Übersetzungswissenschaft*, 4th ed. Heidelberg: Quelle & Meyer 1992.

König, Christian. *Unendlich gebildet – Schleiermachers kritischer Religionsbegriff und seine inklusivistische Religionstheologie anhand der Erstauflage der Reden.* Tübingen: Mohr Siebeck, 2016.

Korolko, Mirosław. *Sztuka retoryki: Przewodnik encyklopedyczny* [The Art of Rhetoric: An Encyclopedic Guide]. Warsaw: Wiedza Powszechna, 1990.

Krämer, Hans-Joachim. "Fichte, Schlegel und der Infinitismus in der Platondeutung," *Deutsche Vierteljahrsschrift für Literaturwissenschaft und Geistesgeschichte* 62, no. 4 (1988): 583–621.

Kristeva, Julia. "Word, Dialogue and Novel." In idem, *The Kristeva Reader*, edited by Toril Moi, 34–61. New York: Columbia Univ. Press, 1986.

Krysztofiak, Maria. *Translatologiczna teoria i pragmatyka przekładu artystycznego* [Translatological Theory and Pragmatics of Artistic Translation]. Poznań: Wydawnictwo Naukowe UAM, 2011.

Kudasiewicz, Józef. *Biblia – historia – nauka: Rozważania i dyskusje biblijne* [Bible – History – Science: Biblical Considerations and Discussions]. Kraków: Znak, 1977.

Kuhn, Irène. *Antoine Bermans "produktive" Übersetzungskritik – Entwurf und Erprobung einer Methode.* Tübingen: Gunter Narr, 2007.

Lagemann, Jörg. *Signifikantenpraxis – Eine Einklammerung des Signifikats im Werk von Jacques Derrida*, PhD dissertation. Oldenburg: Universität Oldenburg, 2001.

Lamm, Julia A. "The Art of Interpreting Plato." In *The Cambridge Companion to Friedrich Schleiermacher*, edited by Jacqueline Mariña, 91–108. Cambridge: Cambridge Univ. Press, 2005.

Lamm, Julia A. *Schleiermacher's Plato.* Berlin: Walter de Gruyter, 2021.

Lange, Dietz, ed., *Friedrich Schleiermacher 1768 1834: Theologe – Philosoph – Pädagoge.* Göttingen: Vandenhoeck & Ruprecht, 1985.

Laurentin, René. *L'Esprit Saint – 1. Cet Inconnu, découvrir son expérience et sa personne.* Paris: Fayard, 1997.

Lausberg, Heinrich. *Handbuch der literarischen Rhetorik – Eine Grundlegung der Literaturwissenschaft*, 3rd ed. Stuttgart: Franz Steiner, 1990.

Lee, Kyoung-Jin. *Die deutsche Romantik und das Ethische der Übersetzung – Die literarischen Übersetzungsdiskurse Herders, Goethes, Schleiermachers, Novalis', der Brüder Schlegel und Benjamins.* Würzburg: Königshausen & Neumann, 2013.

Leeuw, Gerardus van der. *Religion in Essence and Manifestation: A Study in Phenomenology.* Translated by John Evan Turner. London: George Allen & Unwin, 1938.

Lefevere, André. *Translating Literature: The German Tradition.* Assen: Van Gorcum, 1977.

Lehnerer, Thomas. *Die Kunsttheorie Friedrich Schleiermachers.* Stuttgart, Klett-Cotta, 1987.

Leibbrand, Miriam P. "'Marktgespräche' – Beobachtungen zur Translation 'in dem Gebiete des Geschäftslebens' in der Romantik mit Bezug zur Leistungsfähigkeit eines hermeneutisches Ansatzes in der Translationswissenschaft heute." In *Friedrich Schleiermacher and the*

Question of Translation, edited by Larisa Cercel and Adriana Şerban, 231–251. Berlin: Walter de Gruyter, 2015.

Leibniz, Gottfried Wilhelm. *New Essays Concerning Human Understanding*. Translated by A. G. Langley. London: Macmillan, 1896.

Leśniak, Kazimierz. *Platon*, 2nd edition. Warsaw: Wiedza Powszechna, 1993.

Leśniak, Kazimierz. "Wstęp tłumacza" [Translator's Introduction]. In Aristotle, *Hermeneutyka. Dzieła wszystkie* [Collected Works] vol. 1, 66–67. Warsaw, PWN, 1990.

Levý, Jiří. *The Art of Translation*. Translated by Patrick Corness. Edited by with a critical foreword by Zuzana Jettmarová. Amsterdam: John Benjamins, 2011 (first edition in Czech, 1963).

Lichański, Jakub. *Co to jest retoryka?* [What Is Rhetoric?]. Kraków: Wydawnictwo Oddziału PAN, 1996.

Lindblom, Johannes. *Prophecy in Ancient Israel*. Oxford: Blackwell, 1963.

Lipiński, Krzysztof. *Übungstexte zur Methodologie der literarischen Übersetzung*. Kraków: Wydawnictwo UJ, 1986.

Locke, John. *An Essay Concerning Human Understanding*. Edited by Peter H. Nidditch, The Clarendon Edition of the Works of John Locke. Oxford: Oxford Univ. Press, 1975.

Luther, Martin. "Circular Letter on Translation (*Sendbrief vom Dolmetschen*)." Translated by Douglas Robinson. In *Western Translation Theory from Herodotus to Nietzsche*, edited by Douglas Robinson, 84–89. London: Routledge, 2002.

Luther, Martin. *Werke – Kritische Gesamtausgabe*, vol. 30, part 2. Weimar: Hermann Böhlau, 1909.

Mädler, Inken. "Friedrich Schleiermacher: Sinn und Geschmack fürs Unendliche." In *Kompendium Religionstheorie*, edited by Volker Drehsen, Wilhelm Gräb, Brigit Weyel, 11–18. Göttingen: Vandenhoeck & Ruprecht, 2005.

Maguire, Laurie. *Helen of Troy: From Homer to Hollywood*. Chichester: Wiley-Blackwell, 2009.

Man, Paul de. *The Rhetoric of Romanticism*. New York: Columbia Univ. Press, 1984.

Margolis, Joseph. "Schleiermacher among the Theorists of Language and Interpretation." *Journal of Aesthetics and Art Criticism* 45, no. 4 (1987): 361–368.

Markowski, Michał Paweł. *Efekt inskrypcji: Jacques Derrida i literatura* [The Inscription Effect: Jacques Derrida and Literature]. Bydgoszcz: Homini, 1997.

Mauthner, Fritz. "Einleitung." In *Jacobis Spinoza-Büchlein nebst Replik und Duplik*, edited by Fritz Mauthner, XVIII-XIX. Munich: Georg Müller Verlag, 1912.

Meier-Dörken, Christoph. *Die Theologie der frühen Predigten Schleiermachers*. Berlin: Walter de Gruyter, 1988.

Messlin, Dorit. *Antike und Moderne: Friedrich Schlegels Poetik, Philosophie und Lebenskunst*. Berlin: Walter de Gruyter, 2011.

Michel, Willy. *Ästhetische Hermeneutik und frühromantische Kritik. Friedrich Schlegels fragmentarische Entwürfe, Rezensionen, Charakteristiken und Kritiken (1795–1801)*. Göttingen, Vandenhoeck & Ruprecht, 1982.

Moretto, Giovanni. "Schleiermachers 'Reden' und die Mystik." In *200 Jahre "Reden über die Religion": Akten des 1. Internationalen Kongresses der Schleiermacher-Gesellschaft, Halle, 14.–17. März 1999*, edited by Ulrich Barth, Claus-Dieter Osthövener, 364–380. Berlin: Walter de Gruyter, 2000.

Mounin, Georges. *Problèmes théoriques de la traduction*. Paris: Gallimard, 1963.

Moxter, Michael. "Arbeit am Unübertragbaren: Schleiermachers Bestimmung des Ästhetischen." In *Schleiermacher und Kierkegaard – Subjektivität und Wahrheit*, edited by Niels Jørgen Cappelørn et al., 53–72. Berlin: Walter de Gruyter, 2006.

Mueller-Vollmer, Kurt. "Foundations: General Theory and Art of Interpretation – Friedrich D.E. Schleiermacher." In *The Hermeneutics Reader: Texts of the German Tradition from the Enlightenment to the Present*, edited by Kurt Mueller-Vollmer, 72. Oxford: Basil Blackwell, 1986.

Müller, Lothar. "Nachwort." In August Wilhelm Schlegel, *Die Gemählde – Gespräch*, edited by Lothar Müller, 165–196. Amsterdam-Dresden: Verlag der Kunst, 1996.

Müller, Siegfried. "Die Erfahrung des jungen Schleiermacher als Grundlage seines philosophisch-theologischen Denkens." In *Internationaler Schleiermacher-Kongreß Berlin 1984*, edited by Kurt-Victor Selge, sub-vol. 1., 153–161. Berlin: De Gruyter, 1985.

Naas, Michael. *Earmarks: Derrida's Reinvention of Philosophical Writing in 'Plato's Pharmacy'*. In *Derrida and Antiquity*, ed by Miriam Leonard, 43–72. Oxford: Oxford Univ. Press, 2010.

Nabokov, Vladimir. *Lectures on Don Quixote*. San Diego: Harcourt, 1983.

Nassar, Dalia T. "Immediacy and Mediation in Schleiermacher's 'Reden über die Religion'." *The Review of Metaphysics* 59, no. 4 (2006): 807–840.

Networking Guide – 6. Bonner Humboldt-Preisträger Forum "Weltliteraturen – Meisterwerke: Shakespeare und Cervantes 2016". Bonn: Alexander von Humboldt-Stiftung, 2016.

Nickau, Klaus. "Die Frage nach dem Original." In *Die literarische Übersetzung – Fallstudien zu ihrer Geschichte*, edited by Brigitte Schultze. Berlin: Erich Schmidt, 1987.

Nietzsche, Friedrich. "Translation as Conquest – from *The Gay Science*." Translated by Walter Kaufmann. In *Western Translation Theory from Herodotus to Nietzsche*, edited by Douglas Robinson, 262. London: Routledge, 2002.

Nietzsche, Friedrich. *Werke – Kritische Gesamtausgabe*, Abt. 2, vol. 4: *Vorlesungsaufzeichnungen. WS 1871/72–WS 1874/75)*. Edited by Fritz Bornmann. Berlin: Walter de Gruyter, 1995.

Novalis, *Fragmente I*. In *Gesammelte Werke*, vol. 2, edited by Carl Seelig. Herrliberg-Zürich: Bühl, 1945.

Novalis, *Schriften*, vol. 4. Edited by Richard Samuel. Stuttgart: W. Kohlhammer, 1975.

Nowak, Kurt. *Schleiermacher – Leben, Werk, Wirkung*. Göttingen: Vandenhoeck & Ruprecht, 2001.

Nowak, Kurt. *Schleiermacher und die Frühromantik – Eine literaturgeschichtliche Studie zum romantischen Religionsverständnis und Menschenbild am Ende des 18. Jahrhunderts in Deutschland*. Berlin: Walter De Gruyter, 1986.

Nuzzo, Angelica. "Theorie." In *Enzyklopädie Philosophie*, vol. 2, edited by Hans Jörg Sandkühler, 1621. Hamburg: Felix Meiner, 1999.

Oesterreich, Peter L. *Spielarten der Selbsterfindung – Die Kunst des romantischen Philosophierens bei Fichte, F. Schlegel und Schelling*. Berlin: Walter de Gruyter, 2011.

Olson, David R. *The World on Paper: The Conceptual and Cognitive Implications of Writing and Reading*. Cambridge: Cambridge Univ. Press, 1999.

Otto, Rudolf. *The Idea of the Holy: An Inquiry into the Non-Rational Factor in The Idea of the Divine and Its Relation to the Rational*. Translated by John W Harvey. Oxford: Oxford Univ. Press, 1936.

Paepcke, Fritz. "Übersetzen zwischen Regel und Spiel." In *Im Übersetzen leben – Übersetzen und Textvergleich*, edited by Klaus Berger, Hans-Michael Speier, 121–134. Tübingen: Gunter Narr, 1986.

Palmer, Richard E. *Hermeneutics: Interpretation Theory in Schleiermacher, Dilthey, Heidegger, and Gadamer*. Evanston: Northwestern Univ. Press, 1969.

Pankiewicz, Ryszard. *Sztuka rozmawiania z Bogiem – Modlitwa a teoria komunikacji* [The Art of Talking to God – Prayer and the Theory of Communication]. Kraków: Wydawnictwo WAM, 2009.

Park, Mungo. *Reisen in Innern von Afrika [...], aus dem Englischen*. [Translated by F Schleiermacher and H. Herz]. Berlin: Haude und Spener, 1799.

Park, Mungo. *Travels in the Interior Districts of Africa [...]*. London: W. Bulmer, 1799.

Pater, Walter. *Plato and Platonism: A Series of Lectures*. New York: Macmillan, 1893.

Patsch, Hermann. *Alle Menschen sind Künstler – Friedrich Schleiermachers poetische Versuche*. Berlin: Walter de Gruyter, 1986.

Patsch, Hermann. "Friedrich Asts Eutyphrion-Übersetzung im Nachlass Friedrich Schlegels. Ein Beitrag zur Platon-Rezeption in der Frühromantik." *Jahrbuch des Freien Deutschen Hochstifts* (1988): 112–127.

Patsch, Hermann. "Friedrich Schlegels 'Philosophie der Philologie' und Schleiermachers frühe Entwürfe zur Hermeneutik." *Zeitschrift für Theologie und Kirche* 63, no. 4 (1966): 434–472.

Patsch, Hermann. "Schleiermacher und die philologische Bibelübersetzung." In *Übersetzung – Translation – Traduction: Ein internationales Handbuch zur Übersetzungsforschung*, vol. 3, edited by Harald Kittel et al., 2400–2405. Berlin: Walter de Gruyter, 2011.

Paulin, Roger. *The Critical Reception of Shakespeare in Germany 1682–1914: Native Literature and Foreign Genius*. Hildesheim: Georg Olms, 2003.

Pecina, Björn. "Gerettetes Vergehen – Ethos und Kontext zweier Platonübersetzungen." In *Reformation und Moderne. Pluralität – Subjektivität – Kritik. Akten des Internationalen Kongresses der Schleiermacher-Gesellschaft in Halle (Saale), März 2017*, edited by Jörg Dierken, Arnulf von Scheliha, Sarah Schmidt, 59–86. Berlin: Martin de Gruyter, 2018.

Perelman, Chaïm. *L'empire Rhetorique : Rhetorique et Argumentation*. Paris: Vrin, 1977.

Perelman, Chaïm. *Logik und Argumentation*. Edited by and translated by Freyr Roland Varwig. Weinheim: Beltz Anthenaum, 1994.

Peters, John D. "John Locke, the Individual and the Origin of Communication." *Quarterly Journal of Speech* 75, no. 4 (1989): 387–399.

Pfau, Thomas. "Immediacy and the Text: Friedrich Schleiermacher's Theory of Style and Interpretation." *Journal of the History of Ideas* 51, no. 1 (1990): 51–73.

Philo Judaeus, "The Creation of the Septuagint – from *The Life of Moses*." Translated by F.H. Colson. In *Western Translation Theory from Herodotus to Nietzsche*, edited by Douglas Robinson, 12–14. London: Routledge, 2002.

Pickle, Joseph W. Schleiermacher on Judaism, *The Journal of Religion* 60, no. 2. (1980): 115–137.

Plato. *Cratylus*, trans. Benjamin Jowett. In *The Dialogs of Plato*. New York: Macmillan, 1892.

Plato. *Faidros*. Translation, introduction, commentary and index by Leopold Regner. Warsaw: PWN, 1993)

Plato. *Faidros*. In idem, *Skrifter. Bok 2*. Translated by Jan Stolpe. Stockholm: Atlantis, 2001.

Plato. *Phaedrus*. Translated by Alexander Nehamas, Paul Woodruff. In Plato, *Complete Works*, edited by John M. Cooper. Indianapolis: Hackett, 1997.

Plato. *Phaidros oder Vom Schönen*. Translated by Kurt Hildebrandt. Stuttgart: Reclam, 1957. http://www.peter-matussek.de/Leh/V_06_Material/V_06_M_08/Phaidros_Dialog.pdf (accessed 20 September 2019).

Plato. *Plato's Phaedrus*. Translated by Reginald Hackforth. Cambridge: Cambridge Univ. Press, 1952.

Plato. *Werke*, Gruppe 1: *Gespräche zur Verherrlichung des Sokrates*, 2: *Phaidros oder vom Schönen. Lysis oder von der Freundschaft*. Translated by Ludwig Georgii. Stuttgart: Metzler, 1853.

Plato. [Platon]. *Fajdros*. Translated by Władysław Witwicki. Warsaw: PWN, 1958.

Plato. [Platon]. *Phaidros*. Translated by Edward Zwolski. Kraków: Aureus, 1996.

Pleger, Wolfgang H. *Schleiermachers Philosophie*. Berlin: Walter de Gruyter, 1988.

Poincaré, Henri. *Science and Method*, New York. Translated by Francis Maitland. New York: Cosimo Classics, 1914/2007.

Polledri, Elena. "'Übersetzungen sind φλ [philologische] Mimen' – Friedrich Schlegels Philologie und die Übersetzungen von Johann Diedrich Gries." In *Friedrich Schlegel und die Philologie*, edited by Ulrich Breuer, Remigius Bunia, and Armin Erlinghagen, 165–187. Paderborn: Schöningh, 2013.

Poltermann, Andreas. "Die Erfindung des Originals – Zur Geschichte der Übersetzungskonzeptionen in Deutschland im 18. Jahrhundert." In *Die literarische*

Übersetzung – Fallstudien zu ihrer Kulturgeschichte, edited by Brigitte Schultze, 14–52. Berlin: Erich Schmidt, 1987.

Pseudo-Platon, *Zimorodek i inne dialogi* [Halcyon and Other Dialogues]. Translated by Leopold Regner. Warsaw: PWN, 1985.

Pym, Anthony. *On Translator Ethics*. Translated by Heike Walker, revised and updated by the author. Amsterdam: John Benjamins: 2012.

Pym, Anthony. "Schleiermacher and the Problem of *Blendlinge*." *Translation and Literature* 4, no. 1 (1995): 8, http://usuaris.tinet.cat/apym/on-line/intercultures/blendlinge.pdf (accessed 30 September 2019).

Quintilian, *Institutio Oratoria*, Loeb Classical Library edition, vol. III, 1920. https://penelope.uchicago.edu/Thayer/E/Roman/Texts/Quintilian/Institutio_Oratoria/8A*.html (accessed 20 May 2022).

Reale, Giovanni. *A History of Ancient Philosophy II: Plato and Aristotle*. Translated by John R. Catan. Albany, State Univ. of New York Press, 1990.

Reale, Giovanni. *Towards a New Interpretation of Plato*. Translated by John R. Catan and Richard Davies. Washington, D.C.: Catholic Univ. of America Press, 1996.

Reichert, Klaus. *Die unendliche Aufgabe – Zum Übersetzen*. Munich: Carl Hanser, 2003.

Reiß, Katharina. *Möglichkeiten und Grenzen der Übersetzungskritik – Kategorien und Kriterien für eine sachgerechte Beurteilung von Übersetzungen*. Munich: Max Hueber, 1971.

Reiß, Katharina. *Translation Criticism – The Potentials and Limitations: Categories and Criteria for Translation Quality Assessment*. Translated by Erroll F. Rhodes. London: Routledge, 2000.

Reiß, Katharina and Hans J. Vermeer, *Grundlegung einer allgemeinen Translationstheorie*. Tübingen: Max Niemeyer, 1984.

Ricoeur, Paul. "Schleiermacher's Hermeneutics," *The Monist* 60, no. 2 (1977): 181–197.

Rieger, Reinhold. *Interpretation und Wissen – Zur philosophischen Begründung der Hermeneutik bei Friedrich Schleiermacher und ihrem geschichtlichen Hintergrund*. Berlin: Walter de Gruyter, 1988.

Ritter, Joachim, ed., *Historisches Wörterbuch der Philosophie*, vol. 1. Basel: Schwabe, 1971. vol. 2. Basel: Schwabe, 1972.

Robinson, Douglas. *Schleiermacher's Icoses: Social Ecologies of the Different Methods of Translating*. Bucharest: Zeta Books, 2013.

Rohls, Jan. "Schleiermachers Platon." In *Schleiermacher und Kierkegaard – Subjektivität und Wahrheit*, edited by Niels Jørgen Cappelørn et al. Berlin: Walter de Gruyter, 2006. 709–732.

Rorty, Richard, ed., *The Linguistic Turn: Recent Essays in Philosophical Method*. Chicago: Univ. of Chicago Press, 1967.

Roßbeck, Brigitte. *Zum Trotz glücklich – Caroline Schlegel-Schelling*. Munich: Siedler, 2008.

Rothert, Hans-Joachim. "Einleitung." In Friedrich Schleiermacher, *Über die Religion – Reden an die Gebildeten unter ihren Verächtern*. Hamburg: Felix Meiner, 1970.

Said, Edward W. "On Originality." In idem, *The World, the Text, and the Critic*. London: Faber & Faber, 1984.

Salevsky, Heidemarie. "Schleiermacher-Kolloquium 1993." *TEXTconTEXT* 9, (1994): 159–162.

Schanze, Helmut. "Rhetorik und Stilistik der deutschsprachigen Länder von der Romantik bis zum Ende des 19. Jahrhunderts." In *Rhetorik und Stilistik – Ein internationales Handbuch historischer und systematischer Forschung*, edited by Ulla Fix, Andreas Gardt, and Joachim Knape, vol. 1, 31–146. Berlin: Walter de Gruyter, 2008. (Handbücher zur Sprach und Kommunikationswissenschaft [HSK], 31/1).

Scheliha, Arnulf von. "Schleiermacher als Denker von Pluralität." In *Reformation und Moderne: Pluralität – Subjektivität – Kritik. Akten des Internationalen Kongresses der Schleiermacher-Gesellschaft in Halle (Saale), März 2017*, ed. Jörg Dierken, Arnulf von Scheliha, Sarah Schmidt, 25–44. Berlin: Walter de Gruyter 2018.

Schiller, Friedrich. *Briefe II: 1795–1805.* Edited by Norbert Oellers. Frankfurt am Main: Deutscher Klassiker Verlag, 2002. (*Werke und Briefe*, vol. 12).

Schiller, Friedrich. *Die Götter Griechenlands.* 1788. http://www.friedrich-schiller-archiv.de/ge dichte-schillers/highlights/die-goetter-griechenlands/ (accessed 18 July 2019).

Schiller, Friedrich. *Macbeth: Ein Trauerspiel von Shakespeare.* In idem, *Sämtliche Werke*, vol. 3: *Dramatische Fragmente, Übersetzungen, Bühnenbearbeitungen*, edited by Gerhard Fricke and Herbert G. Göpfert. Munich: Carl Hanser, 1980.

Schiller, Friedrich. *Übersetzungen und Bearbeitungen.* In idem, *Sämtliche Werke*, vol. 3: *Dramatische Fragmente, Übersetzungen, Bühnenbearbeitungen*, edited by Gerhard Fricke and Herbert G. Göpfert. Munich: Carl Hanser, 1980.

Schiller, Friedrich. *Übersetzungen und Bearbeitungen.* In idem, *Werke und Briefe*, vol. 9, edited by Heinz Gerd Ingenkamp. Frankfurt am Main: Deutscher Klassiker Verlag, 1995.

Schlegel, August Wilhelm. "Abfertigung eines unwißenden Recensenten der Schlegelschen Übersetzung des Shakespeare." In idem, *Vermischte und kritische Schriften*, edited by Eduard Böcking, 133–140. *Sämtliche Werke*, vol. 12. Hildesheim: Georg Olms, 1971.

Schlegel, August Wilhelm. *Die Gemähide – Gespräch.* Edited and introduction by Lothar Müller. Amsterdam-Dresden: Verlag der Kunst, 1996.

Schlegel, August Wilhelm. "Etwas über William Shakespeare bey Gelegenheit Wilhelm Meisters," *Die Horen – Eine Monatsschrift herausgegeben von F. Schiller* 6, no. 4 (1796): 72–73.

Schlegel, August Wilhelm. "Fragment (177)." *Athenaeum* 1, no. 2 (1798): 46.

Schlegel, August Wilhelm. "Homers Werke, von Johann Heinrich Voss." In *Dokumente zur Theorie der Übersetzung antiker Literatur in Deutschland seit 1800*, edited by Josefine Kitzbichler, Katja Lubitz, Nina Mindt, 3–38. Berlin: Walter de Gruyter, 2009.

Schlegel, August Wilhelm. *Kritische Schriften und Briefe*, vol. 1: *Sprache und Poetik*. Edited by Edgar Lohner, Stuttgart 1962.

Schlegel, August Wilhelm. *Leben und Thaten des scharfsinnigen Edlen Don Quixote von La Mancha, von Miguel de Cervantes Saavedra, übersetzt von Ludwig Tieck. Erster Band. Berlin 1799.* In idem, *Vermischte und kritische Schriften*, part 5: *Recensionen*, edited by Eduard Böcking, 408–426. Leipzig: Weidmann, 1847. *Sämmtliche Werke*, vol. 11.

Schlegel, August Wilhelm. *Poetische Werke*, pt. 1: *Vermischte Gedichte, Lieder, Romanzen und Sonette*. Edited by Eduard Böcking. *Sämmtliche Werke*, vol. 1. Leipzig: Weidmann, 1846.

Schlegel, August Wilhelm. "Nachschrift des Uebersetzers an Ludwig Tieck." *Athenaeum* 2, no. 2. (1799): 277.

Schlegel, August Wilhelm. "Über Zeichnungen zu Gedichten und John Flaxman's Umrisse." *Athenaeum* 2, no. 2 (1799): 203

Schlegel, Friedrich. *Kritische Friedrich Schlegel Ausgabe* [KFSA]. Paderborn: Schöningh, 1958–. Volumes cited:

KFSA II: *Charakteristiken und Kritiken I.* 1796–1801. Edited by Hans Eichner. Paderborn: Schöningh, 1967.

KFSA III: *Charakteristiken und Kritiken II.* 1802–1829. Edited by Hans Eichner. Paderborn: Schöningh, 1975.

KFSA IV: *Ansichten und Ideen von der christlichen Kunst.* Edited by Hans Eichner. Paderborn: Schöningh, 1959.

KFSA VIII: *Studien zur Philosophie und Theologie.* Edited by Ernst Behler and Ursula Struc-Oppenberg. Paderborn: Schöningh, 1975.

KFSA XI: *Wissenschaft der europäischen Literatur: Vorlesungen, Aufsätze und Fragmente aus der Zeit von 1795–1804.* Edited by Ernst Behler. Paderborn: Schöningh, 1958.

KFSA XVI: *Fragmente zur Poesie und Literatur I.* Edited by Hans Eichner, Paderborn: Schöningh, 1981.

KFSA XVII: *Fragmente zur Poesie und Literatur II*. Edited by Ernst Behler, Paderborn: Schöningh, 1991.
KFSA XVIII: *Philosophische Lehrjahre: 1796–1806; nebst philosophischen Manuskripten aus den Jahren 1796–1828*, sub-vol. 1. Edited by Ernst Behler. Paderborn: Schöningh, 1963.
KFSA XXIV: *Die Periode des Athenäums (25. Juli 1797 – Ende August 1799)*. Edited by Raymond Immerwahr. Paderborn: Schöningh, 1986.
Schlegel, Friedrich. *Friedrich Schlegel's Lucinde and the Fragments*. Translated by Peter Firchow. Minneapolis: Univ. of Minnesota Press, 1971.
Schlegel, Friedrich. *Hefte "Zur Philologie."* Edited by Samuel Müller. Paderborn: Schöningh, 2015.
Schlegel, Friedrich. *Literarische Notizen 1797–1801*. Edited by Hans Eichner. Frankfurt am Main: Universitätsverlag Winter, 1980.
Schlegel, Friedrich. Review of *Wilhelm Meister*, *Athenaeum* 1, no. 2 (1798): 147–178.
Schlegel, Friedrich. *Schriften zur Kritischen Philosophie 1795–1805*. Edited by Andreas Arndt, Jure Zovko. Hamburg: Felix Meiner, 2007.
Schlegel, Friedrich. *Werke in zwei Bänden*, vol. 1. Berlin: Aufbau, 1980.
Schmidt, Lawrence K. *Understanding Hermeneutics*. Stocksfield: Acumen Publishing Limited: 2006.
Schmidt, Rachel. *Forms of Modernity: Don Quixote and Modern Theories of the Novel*. Toronto: Univ. of Toronto Press, 2011.
Schmidt, Sarah. *Die Konstruktion des Endlichen – Schleiermachers Philosophie der Wechselwirkung*. Berlin: Walter de Gruyter, 2005.
Schmidt, Sarah. "Wahrnehmung und Schema: Zur zentralen Bedeutung des bildlichen Denkens in Schleiermachers Dialektik." In *Schleiermacher und Kierkegaard – Subjektivität und Wahrheit*, edited by Niels Jørgen Cappelørn et al., 73–91. Berlin: Walter de Gruyter, 2006.
Schneiders, Hans-Wolfgang. "Luthers Sendbrief vom Dolmetschen – Ein Beitrag zur Entmythologisierung." *trans-kom* 5, no. 2 (2012): 254–273.
Schnitzer, Adam. "A History in Translation: Schleiermacher, Plato, and the University of Berlin." *The Germanic Review: Literature, Culture, Theory* 75, no. 1 (2000): 53–71.
Schnur, Harald. *Schleiermachers Hermeneutik und ihre Vorgeschichte im 18. Jahrhundert – Studien zur Bibelauslegung, zu Hamann, Herder und F. Schlegel*. Stuttgart-Weimar: Metzler, 1994.
Scholtz, Gunter. *Ethik und Hermeneutik – Schleiermachers Grundlegung der Geisteswissenschaften*. Frankfurt am Main: Suhrkamp, 1995.
Scholtz, Gunter. "Schleiermacher im Kontext der neuzeitlichen Hermeneutik-Entwicklung." In *Friedrich Schleiermachers Hermeneutik – Interpretationen und Perspektiven*, edited by Andreas Arndt and Jörg Dierken, 1–26. Berlin: Walter de Gruyter, 2016.
Scholtz, Gunter. "Schleiermacher und die platonische Ideenlehre." In *Internationaler Schleiermacher-Kongreß Berlin 1984*, edited by Kurt-Victor Selge, vol. 2., 849–871. Berlin: Walter de Gruyter, 1985.
Scholtz, Gunter. *Schleiermachers Musikphilosophie*. Göttingen: Vandenhoeck & Ruprecht, 1981)
Scholz, Heinrich. *Christentum und Wissenschaft in Schleiermachers Glaubenslehre – Ein Beitrag zum Verständnis der Schleiermacherschen Theologie*. Berlin: Arthur Glaue, 1909.
Schön, Karl. *Über Klopstocks Epos Messias*, after: https://de.wikipedia.org/wiki/Messias_(Klopstock) (accessed 1 October 2019).
Schubert, Klaus. "'So gewiß muß es auch eine Uebersetzungswissenschaft geben' – Erweiterte Recherchen zur ersten Forderung nach einer wissenschaftlichen Beschäftigung mit dem Übersetzen." *trans-kom* 2015, 8, no. 2: 560–617.
Seifert, Paul. *Die Theologie des jungen Schleiermacher*. Gütersloh: Gütersloher Verlagshaus Gerd Mohn, 1960.
Senger, Anneliese. *Deutsche Übersetzungstheorie im 18. Jahrhundert (1734–1746)*. Bonn: Bouvier, 1971.

Seruya, Teresa and José Miranda Justo, eds., *Rereading Schleiermacher: Translation, Cognition and Culture*. Berlin: Springer, 2016.
Shakespeare, William. *Macbeth*. Edited by Cedric Watts. Hertfordshire, Wordsworth, 2005.
Shakespeare, William. *The Tragedy of Macbeth*. Edited by Nicholas Brooke. Oxford: Oxford Univ. Press, 1990.
Shuttleworth, Mark and Moira Cowie, *Dictionary of Translation Studies*. London and New York: Routledge 1997.
Snell, Bruno. The *Discovery of the Mind: The Greek Origins of European Thought*. Translated by Thomas G. Rosenmeyer. Oxford: Basil Blackwell, 1953.
Snell-Hornby, Mary. "Venutis 'foreignization': Das Erbe von Friedrich Schleiermacher in der Translationswissenschaft?" In *Und sie bewegt sich doch… Translationswissenschaft in Ost und West – Festschrift für Heidemarie Salevsky zum 60. Geburtstag*, edited by Ina Müller, 333–344. Frankfurt am Main: Peter Lang, 2004.
Sophocles, *Oedipus rex*. Edited by Roger D. Dawe. Cambridge: Cambridge Univ. Press, 2006.
Spinoza, Benedict. *Theological-Political Treatise*. Edited by Jonathan Israel. Translated by Michael Silverthorne and Jonathan Israel. Cambridge: Cambridge Univ. Press, 2007.
Springer, Bernd. *Die antiken Grundlagen der neuzeitlichen Hermeneutik*. Frankfurt am Main: Peter Lang, 2000.
Stachowiak, Lech. *Prorocy – słudzy słowa* [Prophets – Servants of the Word]. Katowice: Księgarnia św. Jacka, 1980.
Stahl, Ernst Leopold. *Shakespeare und das deutsche Theater*. Stuttgart: Kohlhammer, 1947.
Starobinski, Jean. "Jalons pour une histoire du concept d'imagination." In idem, *L'oeil vivant II*. Paris, 173–195: Gallimard, 1970.
Steck, Paul. *Schiller und Shakespeare. Idee und Wirklichkeit*. Frankfurt am Main: Peter Lang, 1977.
Steiner, George. *After Babel: Aspects of Language and Translation*. New York and London: Oxford Univ. Press, 1975.
Steiner, George. *The Death of Tragedy*. New York: Oxford Univ. Press, 1980.
Sterne, Laurence. *The Life and Opinions of Tristram Shandy, Gentleman*. London: Methuen, 1894.
Sterne, Laurence. *Podróż sentymentalna przez Francję i Włochy* [A Sentimental Journey through France and Italy]. Translated by Agnieszka Glinczanka. Edited and introduction by Zofia Sinko, 2nd ed. Wrocław: Zakład Narodowy im. Ossolińskich, 2009.
Sterne, Laurence. *A Sentimental Journey through France and Italy*. London: Becket and De Hondt, 1769.
Stolze, Radegundis. "Die Wurzeln der hermeneutischen Übersetzungswissenschaft bei Schleiermacher." In *Friedrich Schleiermacher and the Question of Translation*, edited by Larisa Cercel and Adriana Şerban, 129–151. Berlin: Walter de Gruyter, 2015.
Stolze, Radegundis. *Übersetzungstheorien – Eine Einführung*, 5th ed. Tübingen: Narr, 2008.
Störig, Hans Joachim, ed. *Das Problem des Übersetzens*. Darmstadt: Wissenschaftliche Buchgesellschaft, 1963.
Szlezák, Thomas Alexander. "Friedrich Schleiermacher und das Platonbild des 19. und 20. Jahrhunderts," *Plato Journal* 2 (2002): 4, https://digitalis-dsp.uc.pt/bitstream/10316.2/42272/3/Friedrich_Schleiermacher_und_das_Platonbild.pdf (accessed: 15 November 2019).
Szlezák, Thomas Alexander. "Platon und die neuzeitliche Theorie des platonischen Dialogs." In *Dialog Schule – Wissenschaft, Klassische Sprachen und Literaturen*. Vol. 23: *Neue Perspektiven*, edited by Peter Neukam, 161–176. München: Bayrischer Schulbuch-Verlag 1989.
Szlezák, Thomas Alexander. *Plato und die Schriftlichkeit der Philosophie – Interpretationen zu den frühen und mittleren Dialogen*. Berlin: De Gruyter, 1985.
Szulakiewicz, Marek. *Filozofia jako hermeneutyka* [Philosophy as Hermeneutics]. Toruń: Wydawnictwo Naukowe UMK, 2004.

Tarnowski, Karol. *Usłyszeć niewidzialne – Zarys filozofii wiary* [To Hear the Invisible: Outline of a Philosophy of Faith]. Kraków: Instytut Myśli Józefa Tischnera, 2005.
Taylor, Charles. *The Ethics of Authenticity.* Cambridge, MA: Harvard Univ. Press, 1991.
Taylor, Charles. *Sources of the Self: The Making of the Modern Identity.* Cambridge. MA: Harvard Univ. Press, 1989.
Taylor, Charles. *Varieties of Religion Today: William James Revisited.* Cambridge. MA: Harvard Univ. Press, 2002.
Thouard, Denis. "Die Sprachphilosophie der Hermeneutik." In *Friedrich Schleiermachers Hermeneutik – Interpretationen und Perspektiven*, edited by Andreas Arndt and Jörg Dierken, 85–99. Berlin: Walter de Gruyter, 2016.
Tigerstedt, E[ugène] N[apoleon]. *Interpreting Plato.* Stockholm: Almqvist & Wiksell International, 1977.
Till, Dietmar. "Rhetorik und Stilistik der deutschsprachigen Länder in der Zeit der Aufklärung." In *Rhetorik und Stilistik, Ein internationales Handbuch historischer und systematischer Forschung,* ed. Ulla Fix, Andreas Gardt, Joachim Knape, sub-volume 1, 112–130. Berlin–New York 2008 (Handbücher zur Sprach- und Kommunikationswissenschaft [HSK], 31/1SK 31/1.)
Tilliette, Xavier. *Le Christ de la philosophie.* Paris: CERF, 1990.
Tilly, Michael. *Einführung in die Septuaginta.* Darmstadt: Wissenschaftliche Buchgesellschaft, 2005.
Toczko, Rafał. *Hermeneutyka a dziedzictwo retoryki – Hans-Georg Gadamer i jego interpretacje sztuki przekonywania* [Hermeneutics and the Heritage of Rhetoric: Hans-Georg Gadamer and his Interpretations of the Art of Persuasion]. In *Retoryka klasyczna i retoryka współczesna – Pola i perspektywy badań* [Classical Rhetoric and Contemporary Rhetoric: Fields and Perspectives of Research], edited Cyprian Mielczarski, 129–141. Warsaw: Wydawnictwo Naukowe Sub Lupa, 2017.
Toit, Andrie du. "Galatians and the περὶ ἰδεῶν λόγου of Hermogenes: A Rhetoric of Severity in Galatians 1–4." *HTS Theologiese Studies* 70, no. 1. 2014. http://www.scielo.org.za/scielo.php?script=sci_arttext&pid=S0259-94222014000100049 (accessed 7 December 2018).
Turk, Horst. "Konventionen und Traditionen, Zum Bedingungsrahmen der Übersetzung für das Theater oder die Literatur." In *Literatur und Theater – Traditionen und Konventionen als Problem der Dramenübersetzung*, edited by Brigitte Schultze et al., 63–93. Tübingen: Gunter Narr, 1990.
Ubersfeld, Anne. *Reading Theatre.* Translated by Frank Collins. Toronto: Univ. of Toronto Press, 1999.
Ueding, Gert and Bernd Steinbrink. *Grundriß der Rhetorik, Geschichte, Technik, Methode,* 4th ed. Stuttgart: J.B. Metzler, 2005.
Venuti, Lawrence. "Ekphrasis, Translation, Critique." *Art in Translation* 2, no. 2 (2010): 131–152.
Venuti, Lawrence. "Genealogies of Translation Theory: Schleiermacher." *Traduire la théorie* 4, no. 2 (1991): 125–150.
Venuti, Lawrence. "Genealogies of Translation Theory: Schleiermacher and the Hermeneutic Model." In *Un/Translatables: New Maps for Germanic Literatures*, edited by Bethany Wiggin, Catriona MacLeod, 45–62. Evanston: Northwestern Univ. Press, 2016.
Venuti, Lawrence. *Translation Changes Everything: Theory and Practice.* London: Routledge, 2013.
Venuti, Lawrence. *The Translator's Invisibility: A History of Translation,* 2nd ed. London: Routledge, 2008.
Vermeer, Hans J. "Hermeneutik und Übersetzung(swissenschaft)." *TEXTconTEXT* 9 (1994): 163–182.
Virmond, Wolfgang. "Bemerkungen zu Schleiermachers Schlobittener Stil-Vorträgen von 1/91." In *200 Jahre "Reden über die Religion": Akten des 1. Internationalen Kongresses der Schleiermacher-Gesellschaft, Halle, 14.–17. März 1999*, edited by Ulrich Barth and Claus-Dieter Osthövener, 247–261. Berlin: Walter de Gruyter, 2000.

Virmond, Wolfgang. "Neue Textgrundlagen zu Schleiermachers früher Hermeneutik." In *Internationaler Schleiermacher Kongreß, Berlin, 1984*, edited by Kurt-Viktor Selge, vol. 1, 576–590. Berlin: Walter De Gruyter, 1985.

Wackenroder, Wilhelm Heinrich. "Herzensergießungen eines kunstliebenden Klosterbruders: Zwey Gemähldeschilderungen." In idem, *Sämtliche Werke und Briefe*, vol. 1, edited by Silvio Vietta and Richard Littlejohns, 82–83. Heidelberg: Carl Winter Universitätsverlag, 1991.

Wagner, Falk. *Schleiermachers Dialektik – Eine kritische Interpretation*. Gütersloh: Gütersloher Verlagshaus Gerd Mohn, 1982.

Wanning, Berbeli. *Friedrich Schlegel – Eine Einführung*. Wiesbaden: Panorama, 2000.

Weber, Max. "Science as a Vocation." Translated by Rodney Livingstone. In *The Vocation Lectures*, 1–31. Hackett: Indianapolis, 2004.

Wegner, Paul D. *The Journey from Texts to Translations: The Origin and Development of the Bible*. Grand Rapids: Baker Academic, 2004.

Wieland, Christoph Martin. "Der Geist Shakespeares." In *Shakespeare-Rezeption – Die Diskussion um Shakespeare in Deutschland. I. Ausgewählte Texte von 1741 bis 1788*, edited by Hansjürgen Blinn, 119–122. Berlin: Erich Schmidt, 1982.

Wieland, Wolfgang. "Platons Schriftkritik und die Grenzen der Mitteilbarkeit." In *Romantik – Literatur und Philosophie*, edited by Volker Bohn, 22–44. Frankfurt am Main: Suhrkamp, 1987.

Wiemann, Volker. "Funktion, ästhetische/poetische." In *Metzler Lexikon Literatur und Kulturtheorie*, edited by Ansgar Nünning, 3rd ed, 204. Stuttgart: J.B. Metzler, 2004.

Wilamowitz-Moellendorff, Ulrich von. *Platon – Beilagen und Textkritik*, 3rd ed., Berlin: Weidmannsche Verlagsbuchhandlung, 1962.

Wittekind, Folkart. "Die Vision der Gesellschaft und die Bedeutung religiöser Kommunikation: Schleiermachers Kritik am Atheismusstreit als Leitmotiv der 'Reden.'" In *200 Jahre "Reden über die Religion": Akten des 1. Internationalen Kongresses der Schleiermacher-Gesellschaft, Halle, 14.–17. März 1999*, edited by Ulrich Barth, Claus-Dieter Osthövener, 397–415. Berlin: Walter de Gruyter, 2000.

Woroniecka, Grażyna. *Interakcja symboliczna a hermeneutyczna kategoria przed-rozumienia* [Symbolic Interaction and the Hermeneutic Category of Pre-Understanding]. Warsaw: Oficyna Naukowa, 2003.

Wuthenow, Ralph-Rainer. *Das fremde Kunstwerk – Aspekte der literarischen Übersetzung*. Göttingen: Vandenhoeck & Ruprecht, 1969.

Wysłouch, Seweryna. "Ekfraza czy przekład intersemiotyczny?" [Ekphrasis or Intersemiotic Translation?]. In *Ruchome granice literatury – W kręgu teorii kulturowej* [Moving Boundaries of Literature – In the Circle of Cultural Theory], edited by Seweryna Wysłouch and Beata Przymuszała, 48–64. Warsaw: PWN, 2009.

Zander, Horst. *Shakespeare "bearbeitet": Eine Untersuchung am Beispiel der Historien-Inszenierungen 1945–1975 in der Bundesrepublik Deutschland*. Tübingen: Gunter Narr, 1983.

Zarychta, Paweł. "Tod oder Wiedergeburt? Zur Rhetorik zwischen 1720 und 1760 in Deutschland." *Studia Litteraria Universitatis Iagellonicae Cracoviensis* 1 (2006): 137–147.

Zdunkiewicz-Jedynak, Dorota. *Wykłady ze stylistyki* [Lectures on Stylistics]. Warsaw: PWN, 2008.

Zima, Peter V. *Literarische Ästhetik – Methoden und Modelle der Literaturwissenschaft*. Tübingen-Basel: Francke, 1995.

Ziomek, Jerzy. *Retoryka opisowa* [Descriptive Rhetoric]. Wrocław: Zakład Narodowy im. Ossolińskich, 1990.

Zovko, Jure. *Verstehen und Nichtverstehen bei Friedrich Schlegel – Zur Entstehung und Bedeutung seiner hermeneutischen Kritik*. Stuttgart: Frommann-Holzboog, 1990.

Zybura, Marek. *Ludwig Tieck als Übersetzer und Herausgeber – Zur frühromantischen Idee einer "deutschen Weltliteratur."* Heidelberg: Universitätsverlag Winter, 1994.

Życiński, Józef. *Świat matematyki i jej materialnych cieni* [The World of Mathematics and its Material Shadows], 3rd edition. Kraków: Copernicus Center Press, 2018.

Index

Adelung, Johann Christoph   27–30, 35f., 50, 53, 64
Adorno, Theodor W.   21
Aeschylus   177, 188f., 223
Al-Taie, Yvonne   87, 89
Albrecht, Jörn   63
Alcidamas   209
Alembert, Jean Le Rond d'   219
Alt, Peter-Andre   177
Ameriks, Karl   2, 67
Anaxagoras   202
Antonio Allegri see Correggio
Apel, Friedmar   81, 158, 228
Apelt, Otto   198
Arend, Stefanie   63f., 69
Arendt, Hannah   203
Ariosto, Ludovico Giovanni   160f.
Aristeas   181
Aristotle   9, 11, 36, 41–43, 46f., 49f., 62, 194, 204, 213, 217f., 234
Arndt, Andreas   3, 8f., 12, 22f., 44, 67, 77f., 82, 89f., 92, 99, 102, 127, 145, 148, 190, 214–216, 235, 241
Aschersohn, Ferdinand   196
Ashton, E.B.   21
Asmuth, Christoph   89, 98, 192
Assman, Jan   123
Ast, Friedrich   92, 95, 195f.
Augustine St.   43–45
Avalle, D'Arco Silvio   180

Bader, Gunter   128, 130
Baker, Mona   14, 181
Bakhtin, Mikhail M.   94
Bär, Jochen A.   229
Barnabas   110
Barth, Karl   104f., 106, 108, 149f.
Barth, Ulrich   24, 101, 106, 149f.
Barthes, Roland   128
Bartscht, Waltraud   1
Bauer, Manuel   24, 30–32, 77, 78, 82, 84, 95, 107f., 131, 178f.
Bauer, Roger   30–32, 78, 82, 84, 95, 168, 178f.
Baum, Richard   169
Bauman, Zygmunt   212
Behler, Ernst   78, 91, 159, 163, 178

Bekker, Immanuel   195, 200, 208
Bénichou, Paul   109
Benjamin, Walter   14, 21, 110, 156f., 161
Berger, Klaus   41
Berman, Antoine   16–19, 81, 157, 166, 220
Berner, Christian   22, 220
Bernofsky, Susan   1
Bersier, Gabrielle   160
Bertuch, Friedrich Justin   163
Biguenet, John   1
Birkner, Hans-Joachim   86, 231
Birus, Hendrik   67
Black, Max   38
Blair, Hugh   10, 218
Blech, Ulrike   77
Blinn, Hansjurgen   166, 169, 171
Blum, Matthias   123, 140
Böcking, Eduard   160, 177, 206
Bode, Johann Joachim Christoph   54
Bodmer, Johann Jacob   21
Boeckh, August   21, 90, 188f., 195–198
Boehm, Gottfried   89
Bohn, Volker   194
Bolz, Norbert W.   33f.
Bonaparte, Napoleon I   116
Bończa Bukowski, Piotr de   3, 23, 49, 86
Bornmann, Fritz   194
Bowie, Andrew   2, 67, 83, 162, 235
Breitinger, Johann Jacob   21
Bremer, Kai   180, 191
Breuer, Ulrich   80, 178
Brittnacher, Hans Richard   23
Brodersen, Kai   181
Brooke, Nicholas   171
Brumoy, Pierre   168
Bruni, Leonardo   186
Bultmann, Rudolf   122
Bunia, Remigius   80
Bunyan, John   110f.
Bürger, Gottfried August   169f., 176
Buschmann, Albrecht   63

Caesar, Joachim   163
Calderon de la Barca Pedro   158
Canal, Hector   158
Cappelørn, Niels Jorgen   86
Cassirer, Ernst   129

Catan, John R.   62, 194, 203
Cavalcante Schuback, Marcia Sá   188
Cercel, Larisa   14, 22, 61, 64, 67, 199, 204, 219 f.
Cervantes Saavedra, Miguel de   160
Chamfort, de (Sebastien-Roch Nicolas)   79
Christian, Timotheus   8, 26, 32 f., 43 f., 57, 87, 102–104, 109, 111, 127, 131, 137, 140–143, 150, 154 f.
Chudy, Wojciech   46
Cicero, Marcus Tullius   34, 153, 183, 218 f., 228 f.
Clancy, Timothy R.   2, 220
Clarke, Desmond M.   2, 67
Clements, Keith W.   8
Colson, Francis Henry   181
Constant, Benjamin   144 f.
Cooper, John M.   201
Corneille, Pierre   184
Corness, Patrick   14
Correggio (Antonio Allegri)   85
Costazza, Alessandro   218
Cotta, Johann Friedrich   82, 88, 151, 170
Cowie, Moira   63
Cramer, Konrad   101
Crane, Gregory R.   41, 213
Crouter, Richard   2, 105, 145
Culler, Jonathan   149

Dąbrowska, Anna   86
Dampc-Jarosz, Renata   11
David (king)   11
Davies, Richard   203
Dawe, Roger D.   57
Derrida, Jacques   1, 22, 133, 210–212, 221
Diderot, Denis   129
Dierken, Jörg   22 f., 67, 140, 192, 198, 215
Dilthey, Wilhelm   9, 25–27, 39, 76 f., 79, 89, 92 f., 96, 100–102, 110, 158, 163, 190, 230
Diogenes, Laertius   203
Dobson, William   2, 97
Dohna-Schlobitten, Auguste zu   26
Dohna-Schlobitten, Caroline zu   26
Dohna-Schlobitten, Christiane zu   26
Dohna-Schlobitten, Fabian zu   26
Dohna-Schlobitten, Friederike zu   26
Dohna-Schlobitten, Friedrich Alexander zu   26
Dohna-Schlobitten, Friedrich zu   26
Dohna-Schlobitten, Ludwig (Louis) zu   26

Drehsen, Volker   106
Dröse, Astrid   177
Dryden, John   1
Dudziak, Maciej J.   8
Duke, James   2, 15
Dumiche, Beatrice   169
Dybiec-Gajer, Joanna   50

Ebel, Martin   163
Eberhard, Johann August   8 f.
Eckert, Gabriel   169
Eco, Umberto   40
Edghill, E.M.   36
Eichholz, Paul   196
Eichner, Hans   79, 87, 159, 179, 205
Emser, Hieronymus   153 f.
Enkvist, Nils Erik   46
Epiphanius of Salamis   153
Erasmus of Rotterdam   185
Erlinghagen, Armin   80
Ers, Andrus   188
Eschen, Friedrich August   160
Eschenburg, Johann Joachim   169, 176
Euripides   167, 186
Evans, Vyvyan   37
Ezekiel   112 f.

Fawcett, Joseph   10, 218
Fichte, Johann Gottlieb   53, 64, 80, 89, 91 f., 103, 121, 128, 165, 192, 214, 218
Ficino, Marsilio   195
Fiddes, Paul S.   128
Finlay, Marike   85, 164
Firchow, Peter   40, 80, 156
Fischer, Hermann   5, 8 f., 26, 100, 103, 154
Fix, Ulla   25
Flacius, Matthias   185
Flaxman, John   87
Follak, Andrea   95
Forberg, Friedrich Karl   103
Forster, E.S.   50, 77, 183, 188, 219
Forster, Michael M.   77, 183, 188, 219
Forstman, H. Jackson (Jack)   2, 15, 79
Foucault, Michel   17
Frank, Armin Paul   22, 72 f., 116, 173
Frank, Manfred   2, 22, 31, 71–73, 116, 152, 173, 215, 231 f.
Freese, J. H.   41, 213
Frege, Gottlob   231

Frey, Hans-Jost 184f., 188, 223
Fricke, Gerhard 168, 170f.

Gadamer, Hans-Georg 15, 22, 32, 73, 89, 110, 133, 191, 206, 213, 216
Gamlin, Gordon Sebastian 170f., 174
Gardt, Andrea 25
Gebhardt, Peter 172f., 175
Georgii, Ludwig 207f.
Gerber, Simon 23, 127f.
Gil, Alberto 64f.
Gliwitzky, Hans 128
Gloege, Gerhard 122
Goethe, Johann Wolfgang von 21, 33, 52, 54, 63, 76, 102, 130, 157, 161, 167, 169–171, 188, 217–219
Goozé, Marjanne E. 11
Göpfert, Herbert G. 168, 170f.
Göttert, Karl-Heinz 154
Gottleber, Johann Christoph 195
Gottsched, Johann Christoph 27f., 186f.
Gozzi, Carlo 167
Graat, Michael de 168
Gräb, Wilhelm 106, 135
Gray, J. Glenn 207
Grimal, Pierre 110
Grondin, Jean 77, 108
Gross, Alexander 110
Grove, Peter 147
Gusdorf, Georges 222
Guthrie, William Keith Chambers 203f.

Haas, Roland 2
Hackforth, Reginald 201, 204, 206f., 209
Hadas, Moses 181
Hannah, Richard 72
Harbsmeier, Martin S. 81, 192
Hardenberg Friedrich Leopold von, *see* Novalis

Harvey, John W 145
Hastie, William 3, 143
Hays, Michael 72
Heath, Peter 183
Hegel, Georg Wilhelm Friedrich 7, 21, 56, 77, 89, 102f., 106, 125, 145, 192f., 218
Heidegger, Martin 110, 147, 191, 207
Heindorf, Ludwig Friedrich (Ludovicus Fridericus) 67, 96, 189, 195f., 200, 207
Heine, Heinrich 127
Hemsterhuis, Frans (Francois) 100

Henricus, Stephanus 195
Heraclitus 202
Herder, Johann Gottfried von 21, 34, 52, 54, 76–78, 82, 155, 161, 183, 188, 204, 218f.
Hermann, Gottfried 124, 189
Hermann, Karl Friedrich 124, 192
Hermans, Theo 14, 182, 199, 206, 220
Hermogenes 43
Herodotus 1, 4, 124, 153, 181, 219
Herz, Henrietta 10f., 85, 101f., 165
Herz, Markus 10f.
Heyvaert, Stefan 16, 81, 157, 220
Hilary the Confessor 183
Hildebrandt, Kurt 201, 204
Hölderlin, Friedrich 16, 25, 85, 97, 186, 188
Holtzhauer, Helmut 127
Homer 42, 58, 108, 158f., 186, 218
Horace (Quintus Horatius Flaccus) 58, 153, 218f.
Hörisch, Jochen 112, 131, 211
Hornig, Dieter 128
Horowitz, Maryanne Cline 108
Howald, Ernst 189
Hubbell, H.M. 124, 153, 183, 219, 228
Hübner, Ingolf 78, 214
Huge, Eberhard 164
Humboldt, Wilhelm von 23, 75, 157, 178, 183, 188–190, 223f.
Huyssen, Andreas 95

Immerwahr, Raymond 101, 158
Ingenkamp, Heinz Gerd 166–170, 174
Irani, Tushar 206
Isaiah 112
Israel, Jonathan 109, 182

Jacobi, Friedrich Heinrich 100, 103f.
Jakobson, Roman 85
James, William 112, 147
Jantzen, Jorg 89, 93, 192f.
Jaroszyński, Czesław 37
Jaroszyński, Piotr 37
Jauß, (Jauss) Hans Robert 108
Jay, Martin 100, 146, 149
Jean Paul (Johann Paul Friedrich Richter) 102
Jenisch, Daniel 9
Jensen, Kipton E. 145
Jeremiah 112f.
Jerome, St. 1, 4, 34, 124, 153, 155, 183

Jesus, son of Sirach   87, 111–114, 127, 141, 181
Jettmarová, Zuzana   14
John II, bishop of Jerusalem   153
John the Evangelist   113, 127
Johnson, Barbara   210, 221
Johnson, Samuel   170
Jourdain, M.   129
Jowett, Benjamin   110
Justo, Jose Miranda   14

Kahn, Charles H.   194, 208f., 211
Kaiser, Bernhard   126f.
Kant, Immanuel   9f., 16, 40, 83, 103, 121, 131, 145–149, 162, 214f., 218, 232
Kantzenbach, Friedrich Wilhelm   10
Kapp, Volker   34f.
Käppel, Lutz   185, 192–195, 198f.
Karski, Karol   8
Kaufmann, Walter   184
Kierkegaard, Søren   4, 86, 89, 99
Kijewska, Agnieszka   211
Kimmerle, Heinz   2, 65
Kittel, Harald   14, 97
Kitzbichler, Josefine   58, 199
Klemm, David E.   130
Kliebisch, Udo   228
Kłoczowski, Jan Andrzej   145
Kloepfer, Rolf   15, 168
Klopstock, Friedrich Gottlieb   57
Knape, Joachim   25, 62
Koelln, Fritz C. A.   129
Kohlmayer, Rainer   61f., 64, 204
Koller, Werner   75, 167
König, Christian   117, 121, 181, 211
Körner, Theodor   171
Korolko, Mirosław   37, 41, 63f., 70
Kotzebue, August von   54
Krämer, Hans   91f.
Kristeva, Julia   94
Krysztofiak, Maria   155f.
Kudasiewicz, Józef   185
Kuhn, Irène   16f.

Lagemann, Jörg   210f.
Lamm, Julia A.   2, 89, 93, 96, 190, 192, 206
Lange, Dietz   6
Laurentin, Rene   110
Lausberg, Heinrich   70
Lauth, Reinhard   128

Lee, Kyoung-Jin   161f.
Leeuw, Gerardus van der   107
Lefevere, André   1, 98, 161
Lehnerer, Thomas   57, 88, 151
Leibbrand, Miriam P.   222
Leibniz, Gottfried Wilhelm   47f., 230–235
Leonard, Miriam   212
Lepper, Marcel   177
Leśniak, Kazimierz   47, 192
Lessing, Gotthold Ephraim   79, 86, 103, 127, 129, 156, 167, 179
Levý, Jiři   14, 20
Lichański, Jakub   36, 63
Lindblom, Johannes   109
Lipiński, Krzysztof   92
Littlejohns, Richard   87
Livingstone, Rodney   132
Locke, John   44–47, 50, 54–56, 223
Loehr, Johanna   194f.
Lohner, Edgar   161
Losonsky, Michael   183
Lubitz, Katja   58, 199
Luserke-Jaqui, Matthias   168
Luther, Martin   1, 13, 34, 75, 112f., 115, 124, 126, 128, 153–155, 161

MacLeod, Catriona   20
Mädler, Inken   126   106
Maguire, Laurie   159
Malone, Edmond   173
Man, Paul de   35, 111f.
Margolis, Joseph   22
Mariña, Jacqueline   93, 130
Markowski, Michał Paweł   22
Marshall, Donald G.   15
Maryniarczyk, Andrzej   46
Mauthner, Fritz   104
Maxwell-Hyslop, A.R.   110
Meckenstock, Günter   30, 92, 102, 127, 185, 195
Meier-Dörken, Christoph   10
Melegari, Dora   144
Mendelssohn, Moses   103
Mensch, Pamela   12, 58, 97, 99, 132, 191, 194, 203
Messlin, Dorit   156, 177
Michel, Willy   83, 91, 162f.
Michelfelder, Diane P.   133
Mielczarski, Cyprian   213
Miller, James   203

Mindt, Nina 58, 199
Moretto, Giovanni 134
Moritz, Karl Philipp 69
Moses 11, 109, 113, 123, 140, 181f.
Mounin, Georges 14
Moxter, Michael 86
Mueller-Vollmer, Kurt 151
Müller
– Beate 160
– Gerhard 100
– Ina 19
– Lothar 85
– Samuel 78
– Siegfried 101

Naas, Michael 212
Nabokov, Vladimir 159
Nassar, Dalia T. 118, 125
Nassen, Ulrich 34
Nehamas, Alexander 201, 204, 206f., 209f.
Nickau, Klaus 186
Nicolas, Sebastien-Roch see Chamfort, de
Nida, Eugene 75
Nidditch, Peter H. 44, 50
Nietzsche, Friedrich Wilhelm 1, 4, 17, 124, 153, 181, 183f., 194, 219
Novalis (Friedrich Leopold von Hardenberg) 25, 40f., 75f., 82, 101, 111, 161, 187f.
Nowak, Kurt 8–10, 26f., 81f., 89, 102, 104, 106f., 123, 143, 195
Nünning, Ansgar 205
Nuzzo, Angelica 76

Oellers, Norbert 169
Oesterreich, Peter L. 64, 80
Ohst, Martin 192
Olson, David R. 184
Oman, John 2
Osthövener, Claus-Dieter 24, 101
Otto, Rudolf 102, 145–147, 228

Paepcke, Fritz 41
Palmer, Richard E. 110, 133
Pankiewicz, Ryszard 43
Park, Mungo 11, 97, 218
Parmenides 95, 192, 207
Pater, Walter 209
Patsch, Hermann 12, 23, 58, 77f., 83, 95, 97, 99, 191
Paul the Apostle 110, 115, 154
Paulin, Roger 171
Perelman, Chaim 61
Peter the Apostle 70
Peters, John 44–46
Pettegrove, James 129
Pfau, Thomas 50, 69, 71, 73
Philo of Alexandria (Philo Judaeus) 109, 181
Picard, Louis-Benoît 168
Pickle, Joseph W. 140
Pietsch, Michael 127, 195
Pindar 86
Plato 2, 9, 12f., 16, 46, 49, 61f., 65, 67, 76, 79, 83, 86, 88–100, 105, 110, 134, 158, 163, 165, 176, 180, 185f., 188–199, 201–215, 218, 220–222, 229, 232, 234, 239–241
Pleger, Wolfgang H. 6f., 220, 227, 236
Pluhar, Werner S. 40, 131
Poincaré, Henri 230
Polledri, Ellena 80
Poltermann, Andreas 14, 187
Przymuszała, Beata 87
Pseudo-Plato 205
Ptolemy II 181
Pudor, Karl Heinrich 75
Pym, Anthony 20f.
Pythagoras 48

Quintilian 42

Racine, Jean Baptiste 167
Raphael, Santi 85, 86
Reale, Giovanni 62, 194, 202
Redeker, Martin 26, 77, 89, 100, 158, 190, 230
Regner, Leopold 201, 205, 207, 211
Reichardt, Johann Friedrich 170
Reichert, Klaus 216
Reimer, Georg Andreas 8f., 92, 96f., 99, 101f., 195, 202
Reiß (Reiss) Katharina 39, 156, 167, 209
Reni, Guido 88
Richter, Johann Paul Friedrich see Jean Paul
Ricoeur, Paul 73
Rieger, Reinhold 79
Ritschl, Dietrich 105
Ritter, Heinrich 202
Ritter, Joachim 43, 121
Robinson, Douglas 1, 4, 14, 124, 153f., 181, 183f., 219, 223, 228–230

Rohls, Jan 89, 92 f.
Rorty, Richard 231
Roßbeck, Brigitte 158
Ross, W.D. 50
Rothert, Hans-Joachim 151
Rufinus, of Aquileia 153
Ruin, Hans 188
Runge, Philipp Otto 87

Sack, Friedrich Samuel Gottfried 9 f., 26, 103 f.
Said, Edward W. 216 184
Salevsky, Heidemarie 19, 75
Samuel, Richard 220 78, 187
Sandkühler, Hans Jörg 76
Sax, Daniel J. 3
Schanze, Helmut 25
Scheler, Max 145
Scheliha, Arnulf von 23, 140, 192, 198
Schelling, Friedrich Wilhelm Joseph von 7, 64, 80, 89, 102 f., 106, 121 f., 125, 158, 192
Schiller, Charlotte von 40, 157, 165–177, 179, 186, 199
Schiller, Friedrich 40, 132, 157, 165–177, 179, 186, 240
Schlegel, August Wilhelm 12, 24 f., 30 f., 34, 57 f., 64, 75–95, 97–99, 102, 107 f., 122, 130 f., 153, 155–169, 171–173, 175, 177–179, 187 f., 190, 195, 199, 206, 215, 229, 239 f.
Schlegel, Caroline 12, 24 f., 30 f., 34, 58, 64, 75–95, 97–99, 102, 107 f., 122, 130 f., 153, 155–169, 171–173, 175, 177–179, 187 f., 190, 195, 199, 206, 215, 229, 239 f.
Schlegel, Friedrich 9–12, 23, 24 f., 30 f., 34, 40, 58, 61, 64, 75–95, 97–99, 102, 105, 107 f., 111, 122, 130 f., 149, 153, 155–169, 171–173, 175, 177–179, 184 f., 187 f., 190, 192, 195, 199, 204 f., 206, 215, 229, 239 f.
Schleiermacher, Charlotte 1–73, 75–86, 88–90, 92–153, 155, 157 f., 161–163, 165–168, 172–181, 185 f., 188–209, 211, 213–241, 246
Schleyermacher, Daniel 8
Schleyermacher, Gottlieb Adolph 8
Schmid, Dirk 127, 195
Schmidt, Dennis J. 133, 166, 169, 186 f., 216, 227, 231
Schmidt, Lawrence K. 5, 166, 169, 186 f., 216, 227, 231

Schmidt, Rachel 159, 166, 169, 186 f., 216, 227, 231
Schmidt, Sarah 23, 84, 99, 101, 140, 166, 169, 186 f., 192, 198, 216, 227, 231
Schneiders, Hans-Wolfgang 153 f.
Schnitzer, Adam 76
Schnur, Harald 78, 83 f.
Scholtz, Gunter 84, 151, 202, 209, 215
Scholz, Heinrich 32 f.
Schön, Karl 57, 201, 204, 208, 218
Schubert, Klaus 75
Schulte, Reiner 1
Schultze, Brigitte 170, 186 f.
Schumann, Johann Lorenz 9 f.
Seaton, Peter Paul 144
Seelig, Carl 41, 111
Seifert, Paul 107, 111
Selge, Kurt-Victor 2, 101, 202
Senger, Anneliese 186
Şerban, Adriana 14, 22, 67, 199, 204, 219
Seruya, Teresa 14
Shaftesbury, Anthony Ashley Cooper 100
Shakespeare, William 10, 158, 165–178, 188, 190
Sharrock, Roger 111
Shuttleworth, Mark 63
Silverthorne, Michael 109, 182
Sinko, Zofia 54 f.
Smith, Norman Kemp 146
Smollett, Tobias 55
Snell, Bruno 198
Snell-Hornby, Mary 19
Socrates 43, 91, 97, 110, 191, 200 f., 204–207, 209 f.
Solger, Karl Friedrich Ferdinand 58
Soltau, Dietrich W. 160, 163, 174
Sophocles 16, 57 f., 85 f., 186, 188
Spalding, Georg Ludwig 191, 196
Speier, Hans-Michael 41
Spinoza, Baruch 100 f., 103 f., 109, 128, 182, 230
Springer, Bernd 14, 112
Stabryła, Stanisław 229
Stachowiak, Lech 182
Stahl, Ernst Leopold 171
Stange, Theodor Friedrich 66
Stanley, John 61
Starobinski, Jean 40
Steck, Paul 166, 169, 171
Stein, Charlotte von 169

Steinbrink, Bernd   28 f., 32
Steiner, George   5, 15 f., 83, 70, 172
Steiner, Peter M.   5, 15 f., 70, 89, 172
Sterne, Laurence   54 f.
Stolberg, Christian zu   57 f., 91, 163, 207 f.
Stolberg, Friedrich Leopold zu   57 f., 91, 163, 207 f.
Stolpe, Jan   208
Stolze, Radegundis   61, 67, 75
Störig, Hans Joachim   218
Strosetzki, Christoph   34
Struc-Oppenberg, Ursula   91, 163
Stubenrauch, Elisabeth Maria Katharina   8
Stubenrauch, Samuel Ernst   8
Szlezák, Thomas Alexander   190, 193 f., 210
Szulakiewicz, Marek   105

Tabarasi-Hoffmann, Ana-Stanca   178
Tacitus (Publius Cornelius Tacitus Caecina)   165
Tarnowski, Karol   151
Taylor, Charles   147–149, 151, 183
Tereszkiewicz, Anna   50
Thomte, Reidar   4
Thouard, Denis   22
Tice, Terrence   3, 214
Tieck, Dorothea   57, 59, 86, 158, 160, 163–165, 170, 171 f.
Tieck, Ludwig   11, 57, 59, 86, 87, 158, 160, 163–165, 171 f., 240
Tigerstedt, Eugene Napoleon   192, 194
Till, Dietmar   29
Tilliette, Xavier   143
Tilly, Michael   182
Toczko, Rafał   213
Toit, Andrie du   43
Turk, Horst   170
Turner, John Evan   107
Twesten, August   51, 214
Tytler, Alexander Fraser   34

Ubersfeld, Anne   173
Ueding, Gert   28 f., 32
Unger, Johann Friedrich   102

Valla, Lorenzo   185
Varwig, Freyr Roland   61
Venuti, Lawrence   1, 17–22, 87, 117
Vermeer, Hans J.   63, 75, 98, 167, 209

Vietta, Silvio   87
Virmond, Wolfgang   2, 24, 26–31
Voß, Johann Heinrich   57 f., 84, 158, 191, 199

Wackenroder, Wilhelm Heinrich   86 f.
Wagner, Falk   237
Walker, Heike   21
Wallace, William   145
Wanning, Berbeli   77, 87
Watts, Cedri   171
Weber, Max   132
Wegner, Paul D.   181
Węgrzecki, Adam   145
Weinscheimer, Joel   15
Wertheimer, Jürgen   168
Weyel, Brigit   106
Wharey, James Blanton   111
Wieck, Fred D.   207
Wieland, Christoph Martin   29, 57, 166, 169, 218, 219
Wieland, Wolfgang   57, 166, 194, 219
Wiemann, Volker   205
Wiggin, Bethany   20
Wilamowitz-Moellendorff, Ulrich von   188, 199
Willich, Henrietta von   13
Wilson, A. Leslie   1
Wirth, Uwe   180, 191
Wittekind, Folkart   103
Witwicki, Władysław   201, 206 f.
Wojcik, Jan   2
Wolf, Friedrich August   195, 219
Wolff, Christian   8, 234
Woodruff, Paul   201, 204, 206 f., 209 f.
Wooten, Cecil W.   43
Woroniecka, Grażyna   5
Wuthenow, Ralph-Rainer   133, 164 f., 171, 188, 216, 235
Wysłouch, Seweryna   87

Zander, Horst   167
Zarychta, Paweł   11, 28, 86
Zdunkiewicz-Jedynak, Dorota   68
Zieliński, Edward Iwo   211
Zima, Peter V.   90
Ziomek, Jerzy   48
Zovko, Jure   77 f., 84, 90–92
Zwolski, Edward   201, 204
Zybura, Marek   160, 163
Życiński, Józef   231

www.ingramcontent.com/pod-product-compliance
Lightning Source LLC
Chambersburg PA
CBHW080048190426
43201CB00036B/2291